Eclipse of the Self

Eclipse of the Self

The Development
of Heidegger's

Self

Concept of Authenticity

Michael E. Zimmerman

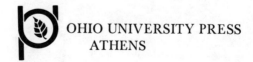
OHIO UNIVERSITY PRESS
ATHENS

Library of Congress Cataloging-in-Publication Data
Zimmerman, Michael E.   1946-
    Eclipse of the self.

    Bibliography: p.
    Includes index.
    ISBN 0-8214-0601-9 (pbk)
    ISBN 0-8214-0570-5 (cloth)
    1. Heidegger, Martin, 1889-1976.
2. Authenticity (Philosophy) 3. Self (Philosophy)
I. Title.
B3279.H499Z55   110   80-19042

To my Father, for resoluteness.
To my Mother, for releasement.

We receive many gifts, of many kinds. But the highest and really most lasting gift given to us is always our essential nature, with which we are gifted in such a way that we are what we are only through it. That is why we owe thanks for this endowment, first and unceasingly.

Martin Heidegger
(WHD, 94/142)

Contents

Acknowledgments ix

List of Abbreviations xiv

Preface to the Second Edition xix

Introduction xxiii

Preface to the Fourth Printing xxxv

Chapter One: Towards the Early Concept of Authenticity 1
   I.   **Religious Experience and the Struggle for
       Self-Understanding** 3
   II. **Phenomenology, Being, and Truth** 20
   III. **The Critique of Traditional Conceptions of Selfhood** 24
   IV. *Being and Time* **as Self-Analysis** 31

Chapter Two: The Inauthentic Everyday Self 43
   I.   **Everydayness, Inauthenticity, and Egoism** 44
   II. **Disclosedness, Care, and Falling** 53

Chapter Three: Authenticity as Resolute Being-towards-Death 69
   I.   **Anticipatory Resoluteness as Authentic Selfhood** 70
   II. **Death and Authenticity in Plato, the Myth of the Hero,
       and Nietzsche** 81
       A. *Plato on Socrates* 82
       B. *The Myth of the Hero and Authentic Being-
          towards-Death* 84
       C. *Nietzsche's Overman and Heidegger's Authentic
          Self* 89

Chapter Four: Temporality and Selfhood 100
  I.   Selfhood, Temporality, and Care 102
  II. Historicality, Repetition, and Authentic Temporality 119

Chapter Five: The Moment of Vision and World-Historical
Heroism 133
  I.   Kairos as the Augenblick 135
  II. Schelling, Authentic Temporality, and the Hero
     Chosen for Revelation..................................149
  III. Authentic Temporality and Nietzsche's "Eternal Return
     of the Same" 155

Chapter Six: National Socialism, Voluntarism,
and Authenticity...169
  I.   Authenticity, Historicality, and National Socialism.........170
  II. An Introduction to Metaphysics as an Interpretation of
     World-Historical Heroism 180
  III. Heidegger's Decision in 1933............................191

Chapter Seven: Inauthenticity, Technology, and Subjectivism 198
  I.   Nihilism, Inauthenticity, and the History of Being 200
  II. Technik and the Desolation of Modern Man 218

Chapter Eight: The Mature Concept of Authenticity 229
  I.   Ereignis, Mankind, and Language.......................231
  II. Releasement as the Mature Concept of Resoluteness 243
  III. Zen, Releasement, and the Limitations of
     Heidegger's Way 255

Appendix: Authenticity in Light of Heidegger's Gesamtausgabe.....277

Notes..301

Bibliography 325

Index..339

Acknowledgments

After writing this book, I finally realize how frustrating it is for an author to try to acknowledge the colleagues and friends who have been helpful in so many different ways. My acknowledgements are only a token offering toward repayments of debts which are truly incalculable. Two men in particular had a decisive influence on this work. The first is Professor Edward G. Ballard, my philosophical mentor, who gave so much of his time and energy in the attempt to teach me how to write and think philosophically. His life and work embody many of the themes which the present book tries to explain. Like many of his other students, I can thank him best by trying to pass on to others some of the gifts which he so generously bestowed on me. The second is Professor Thomas J. Sheehan, who personally encouraged the present work and gave philosophical direction to it. The reader will discover soon enough how much I have learned about Heidegger from this exceptional scholar. Time and again, his essays opened up doors for me when I was unable to find my way. Professor Charles M. Sherover was also of great assistance to me, both by explaining so well Heidegger's complex relation to Kant and by introducing me to the members of the Heidegger Conference in Waterloo, Ontario, in May, 1975. During subsequent meetings, members of this annual Conference offered helpful criticism of papers taken from early versions of this book. I would also like to thank Professor John D. Caputo, a kind friend, whose excellent analyses of Heidegger's thought are reflected in the pages which follow. The pioneering essays of my friend Professor Reiner Schürmann have also been most instructive to me. Had this book taken a somewhat different approach, I would have owed still more to his work, particularly on Heidegger's political philosophy. Professor Walter Eisenbeis unselfishly gave of his time in pointing out to me the importance of Heidegger's thinking for Rudolf Bultmann and Paul Tillich. Professor Andrew J. Reck, who provided advice about readying the manuscript for publication, was instrumental in helping to make possible my career as a professional philosopher. In a very important sense, this book would not have been possible without his confidence in my scholarly abilities. I am very grateful to him, as well as to the other members of my department, for having invited me to teach at Tulane University. My thanks also go to Professor Charles P. Bigger, whose stimulating lectures on the history of philosophy were largely responsible for leading me down the philosophical path as an undergraduate. During the three years it took me to complete this book, Patricia Elisar, director of Ohio University Press, encouraged me at every step. I thank her for all her help. Many of the positions adopted by this book were arrived at during long and animated conversations over the past several years with Dr. Edward Murphy, Donald McNabb, and Jerry Speir. Their patience and intelligence went a long way toward keeping me on a truer course. They know how much their friendship has meant to me, but I offer this word of thanks as a small testimony to their fine spirits. Professor Thomas J. Rice played an important role in the development of my thinking and character. He, too deserves my gratitude, as do Professor Barbara Ewell, who reminded me of things which needed to be remembered, and Souzen Deavers, who taught me something about being open.

Several friends, responding to a plea which took them far beyond the call of duty, did a remarkable job of bringing some order into the chaos of the manuscript at various stages of its growth. In particular, Professor Teresa Toulouse spent many hours in finding ways to heal my sometimes tormented prose. Her inspiring friendship was invaluable to me when I was preparing the manuscript for the publisher. Professors Martha Sullivan and Frank Jaster, along with Jerry Speir, also made valiant efforts to improve the quality of my writing. I would like to thank Dr. Michel Haar for his helpful comments on the text and for his encouraging remarks about my approach to Heidegger's thought. At Ohio University Press, Shari Schartman and Helen Gawthrop took painstaking efforts to correct many of my oversights and errors. Their intelligent criticisms were most welcome. The managing editor, Holly Panich, deserves my thanks for steering this bulky piece of work toward its final destination. I would like to emphasize, however, that any remaining mistakes and shortcomings are my responsibility. The reader can only be grateful that these people managed to improve the text as much as they did! I encourage the reader to respond critically to my views about Heidegger's thinking. So much remains to be learned. It is perhaps appropriate here to point out that much of what I learned during writing this book was made possible by three consecutive summer grants (1976, 1977, 1978) provided by the Committee on Graduate Research of Tulane University.

I would like to mention the following people who have offered such marvelous support and friendship during the past several years and who have thereby become part of this book: Professor Anne Andersen, Susan Alexander, Lois Conrad, Robert Dardenne, Professor Bernard Dauenhauer, John Foote, Professor John D. Glenn, Dr. David Goldblatt, Brenda Hillyer, Professor Francis Lawrence, Professor Eric Mack, The Rev. Ambrose V. McInnes, Professor Louise N. Roberts, Professor John Sallis, Professor George Sessions, Professor Thomas Spaccarelli, Professor Jacques Taminiaux, all my fine students (particularly from my course on the philosophy of self), and of course my brothers and sisters: Harry, Jr., Katherine, Barbara, Eric, John Patrick, Philip, and Robert. With great love and respect, I dedicate this book to my parents, Harry and Evelyn, who gave me the greatest of gifts: life and love.

We find spiritual guides when we are in need of them. Or should I say that they find us? The writings of Martin Heidegger, whom I never had the good fortune to meet in person, have played a unique and decisive role in my life. What can I say by way of thanks to one who has helped me so much on the long journey home?

Acknowledgements for Permission to Quote
from Copyrighted Material

I would like to thank Harper & Row, Publishers, Inc., for permission to quote from the following:

POETRY, LANGUAGE, THOUGHT by Martin Heidegger, translated by Albert Hofstadter. Copyright 1971 by Martin Heidegger.

ON THE WAY TO LANGUAGE by Martin Heidegger, translated by Peter D. Hertz. Copyright 1971 in English translation by Harper & Row, Publishers, Inc.

DISCOURSE ON THINKING by Martin Heidegger, translated by John M. Anderson and E. Hans Freund. Copyright 1966 in the English translation by Harper & Row, Publishers, Inc.

EARLY GREEK THINKING by Martin Heidegger, translated by David Farrell Krell and Frank A. Capuzzi. Copyright 1975 in the English translation by Harper & Row, Publishers, Inc.

THE END OF PHILOSOPHY by Martin Heidegger, translated by Joan Stambaugh. Copyright 1973 in the English translation by Harper & Row, Publishers, Inc.

BASIC WRITINGS by Martin Heidegger, edited and translated by David Farrell Krell. Copyright 1977 in the English translation by Harper & Row, Publishers, Inc.

ON TIME AND BEING by Martin Heidegger, translated by Joan Stambaugh. Copyright 1972 by Harper & Row, Publishers, Inc.

THE QUESTION CONCERNING TECHNOLOGY: AND OTHER ESSAYS by Martin Heidegger, translated by William Lovitt. Copyright 1977 in the English translation by Harper & Row, Publishers, Inc.

NIETZSCHE, Volumes I and II, by Martin Heidegger. Because David Farrell Krell's translation of this work was not available when I was writing this book, Harper & Row, Publishers, Inc., owners of the English translation rights, granted me special permission to use my own translation.

Acknowledgments

I would also like to thank the following publishers for permission to quote from their copyrighted material:

Basil Blackwell Publisher: BEING AND TIME, by Martin Heidegger, translated by John Macquarrie and Edward Robinson, 1962.

Vittorio Klostermann Verlag: DIE GRUNDPROBLEME DER PHÄNOMEN-OLOGIE; LOGIK: DIE FRAGE NACH DER WAHRHEIT; PHÄNOMENOL-OGISCHE INTERPRETATION VON KANTS KRITIK DER REINEN VERNUNFT, by Martin Heidegger.

Yale University Press: AN INTRODUCTION TO METAPHYSICS, by Martin Heidegger, translated by Ralph Mannheim.

University of California Press: PHILOSOPHICAL HERMENEUTICS, by Hans-Georg Gadamer, translated by David E. Linge.

Parts of Chapter Five are taken from my article "Heidegger and Nietzsche on Authentic Time," CULTURAL HERMENEUTICS, IV, no. 3 (1977), pp. 239-264. Reprinted by permission of D. Reidel Publishing Company.

Other parts of Chapter Five originally appeared as my article "A Comparison of Nietzsche's Overman and Heidegger's Authentic Self," THE SOUTHERN JOURNAL OF PHILOSOPHY. Reprinted with permission.

List of Abbreviations Used in This Study.

References to the works of Heidegger will use the following abbreviations. All references will include a cross-reference to the English translation, where such exists. Thus US, 159/57 indicates that I am quoting p. 159 of the German edition of Heidegger's *Unterwegs zur Sprache* listed below, a translation of which is found on p. 57 of the English translation listed beneath it. By consulting these translations, the reader will see for himself where I have adopted the translation entirely, adapted it, or even translated it rather differently. This method of abbreviating is modelled on the one used by John D. Caputo in *The Mystical Element in Heidegger's Thought* (Athens: Ohio University Press, 1978).

AR   "Antrittsrede," *Jahresheft der Heidelberger Akademie der Wissenschaften* (Winter, 1957-58), pp. 20-21.
    "Heidelberg Inaugural Address," translated by Hans Seigfried, *Man and World*, (February, 1970), pp. 4-5.

AED   *Aus der Erfahrung des Denkens*. 2. Auflage. Pfullingen: Günther Neske, 1965.
    "The Thinker as Poet," in Martin Heidegger, *Poetry, Language, Thought*, translated by Albert Hofstadter. New York: Harper & Row, 1971, pp. 1-14.

ALM   "Aus der Letzten Marburger Vorlesung," in *Zeit und Geschichte: Dankesgabe an Rudolf Bultmann zum 80. Geburtstag*, edited by Erich Dinkler, Tübingen: J.C.B. Mohr, 1964, pp. 491-507.
    "From the Last Marburg Lecture Course," translated by John Macquarrie in *The Future of Our Religious Past*, edited by James M. Robinson. New York: Harper & Row, 1971, pp. 312-332.

D   "Dank," a poem from Heidegger's "Gedachtes" in *René Char*, edited by Dominque Fourcade. Paris: L'Herne, 1971, pp. 169-187.

EHD   *Erläuterungen zu Hölderlins Dichtung*. 2. Auflage. Frankfurt am Main: Vittorio Klostermann, 1951.
  pp. 7-30   "Rememberance of the Poet," translated by Douglas Scott in *Existence and Being*, edited by Werner Brock. Chicago: Henry Regnery Co., 1949, pp. 243-269.

xiv

pp. 31-46   "Hölderlin and the Essence of Poetry," translated by Douglas Scott in *Existence and Being*, pp. 270-291.

EM   *Einführung in die Metaphysik*. 2. Auflage. Tübingen: Max Niemeyer, 1957.

An Introduction to Metaphysics, translated by Ralph Mannheim. Garden City, New York: Doubleday Anchor Books, 1961.

FS   *Frühe Schriften*. Frankfurt am Main: Vittorio Klostermann, 1972.

FW   *Der Feldweg*. 3. Auflage. Frankfurt am Main: Vittorio Klostermann, 1962.

"The Pathway," translated by Thomas F. O'Meara. *Listening*, II (Spring, 1967), pp. 88-91.

G   *Gelassenheit*. 2. Auflage. Pfullingen: Günther Neske, 1960.

Discourse on Thinking, translated by John M. Anderson and E. Hans Freund. New York: Harper & Row, 1966.

GP   *Die Grundprobleme der Phänomenologie*. Frankfurt am Main: Vittorio Klostermann, 1976.

GD   "Grundsätze des Denkens," *Jahrbuch für Psychologie und Psychotherapie*, VI (1958), pp. 33-41.

"Principles of Thinking," in Martin Heidegger, *The Piety of Thinking*, translated and edited by James G. Hart and John C. Maraldo (Bloomington: Indiana University Press, 1976).

HH   *Hebel: Der Hausfreund*. Pfullingen: Günther Neske, 1958.

H   *Heraklit*, with Eugen Fink. Frankfurt am Main: Vittorio Klostermann, 1970.

Hw   *Holzwege*. 5. Auflage. Frankfurt am Main: Vittorio Klostermann, 1972.

pp. 7-68   "The Origin of the Work of Art," in *Poetry, Language, Thought*, pp. 15-87.

pp. 69-104   "The Age of the World Picture," in Martin Heidegger, *The Question Concerning Technology*, translated by William Lovitt. New York: Harper & Row, 1977, pp. 115-154.

pp. 105-192   *Hegel's Concept of Experience*. New York: Harper & Row, 1970.

pp. 193-247   "The Word of Nietzsche: 'God is Dead'," in *The Question Concerning Technology*, pp. 53-112.

pp. 248-295   "What Are Poets For?" in *Poetry, Language, Thought*, pp. 91-142.

pp. 296-343   "The Anaximander Fragment," in Martin Heidegger, *Early Greek Thinking*, translated by David Farrell Krell and Frank Capuzzi. New York: Harper & Row, 1975, pp. 13-58.

ID   *Identity and Difference*, translated by Joan Stambaugh. New York: Harper & Row, 1969. The German text, *Identität und Differenz*, appears in the Appendix.

KPM   *Kant und das Problem der Metaphysik.* 2. Auflage. Frankfurt am Main: Vittorio Klostermann, 1951.
       Kant and the Problem of Metaphysics, translated by James S. Churchill. Bloomington: Indiana University Press, 1968.

LR   "Letter to Father Richardson," dated April, 1962, serving as a Preface to William J. Richardson's work, *Heidegger: Through Phenomenology to Thought.* The Hague: Martinus Nijhoff, 1967. The German original faces the English translation.

L   *Logik: Die Frage nach der Wahrheit.* Frankfurt am Main: Vittorio Klostermann, 1976.

NI, NII *Nietzsche.* Zwei Bände. 2. Auflage. Pfullingen: Günther Neske, 1961.
NII
  pp. 399-*The End of Philosophy,* translated by Joan Stambaugh. New York:
   490   Harper & Row, 1973, pp. 1-83.

PIK   *Phänomenologische Interpretation von Kants Kritik der reinen Vernunft.* Frankfurt am Main: Vittorio Klostermann, 1977.

PT   *Phänomenologie und Theologie.* Frankfurt am Main: Vittorio Klostermann, 1970.
  pp. 13- "Phenomenology and Theology," in *The Piety of Thinking,* pp. 5-21.
   33
  pp. 37- "The Theological Discussion of 'The Problem of a Non-Objectifying
   46   Thinking and Speaking in Today's Theology'—Some Pointers to Its Major Aspects," in *The Piety of Thinking,* pp. 22-31.

SA   *Schellings Abhandlung über das Wesen der Menschlichen Freiheit* (1809). Tübingen: Max Niemeyer, 1971.

SG   *Der Satz vom Grund.* 4. Auflage. Pfullingen: Günther Neske, 1971.
  pp. 191-"The Principle of Ground," translated by Keith Hoeller. *Man and
   211   World,* VII (August, 1974), pp. 207-222.

Sp   "Nur noch ein Gott kann uns retten." *Spiegel*-Gespräch mit Martin Heidegger am 23 September, 1966. *Der Spiegel* (Hamburg), Nr. 26, May 31, 1976, pp. 193-219.
       "Only a God can save us: *Der Spiegel's* interview with Martin Heidegger," translated by Maria P. Alter and John D. Caputo. *Philosophy Today,* XX (Winter, 1976), pp. 267-284.

SZ   *Sein und Zeit.* 11. Auflage. Tübingen: Max Niemeyer, 1963.
       Being and Time, translated by John Macquarrie and Edward Robinson. New York: Harper & Row, 1962.

TK   *Die Technik und die Kehre.* Pfullingen: Günther Neske, 1962.
  pp. 1-36"The Question Concerning Technology," in *The Question Concerning Technology.* pp. 3-35.
  pp. 37- "The Turning," in *The Question Concerning Technology,* pp. 36-
   47   49.

US   *Unterwegs zur Sprache.* 3. Auflage. Pfullingen: Günther Neske, 1965.

pp. 9–33   "Language," in *Poetry, Language, Thought*, pp. 189–210.

pp. 35–   *On the Way to Language*, translated by Peter D. Hertz. New York:
ff.   Harper & Row, 1971.

VA, I   *Vorträge und Aufsätze*. 3. Auflage, Pfullingen: Günther Neske, 1967.
VA, II
VA, III

VA, I   "The Question Concerning Technology," in *The Question Concerning*
pp. 5–   *Technology*, pp. 3–35.
36

pp. 37–   "Science and Reflection," in *The Question Concerning Technology*,
62   pp. 155–182.

pp. 63–   "Overcoming Metaphysics," in *The End of Philosophy*, pp. 84–110.
91

pp. 93–   "Who Is Nietzsche's Zarathustra?", translated by Bernd Magnus. *The*
118   *Review of Metaphysics*, XX (March, 1967), pp. 411–431.

VA, II

pp. 19–   "Building Dwelling Thinking," in *Poetry, Language, Thought*,
36   pp. 143–162.

pp. 37–   "The Thing," in *Poetry, Language, Thought*, pp. 163–186.
59

pp. 61–   ". . . Poetically Man Dwells . . .", in *Poetry, Language, Thought*,
78   pp. 211–229.

VA, III

pp. 3–26   "Logos (Heraclitus, Fragment B 50)," in *Early Greek Thinking*,
           pp. 59–78.

pp. 27–   "Moira (Parmenides VIII, 34–41)," in *Early Greek Thinking*, pp. 79–
52   102.

pp. 53–   "Aletheia (Heraclitus, Fragment B 16), in *Early Greek Thinking*,
78   pp. 102–123.

WBW   "Warum bleiben wir in der Provinz?" *Der Alemanne*, March 7, 1934,
           pp. 216–218.

           "Why Do I Stay in the Provinces?" translated by Thomas J. Sheehan.
           Listening, 12 (Fall, 1977), pp. 122–125.

WHD   *Was Heisst Denken?* Tubingen: Max Niemeyer, 1954.

           What Is Called Thinking?, trans. by Fred D. Wieck and J. Glenn Gray.
           New York: Harper & Row, 1972.

WG   *Vom Wesen des Grundes*, appearing in a bilingual edition as *The Es-
           sence of Reasons*, trans. by Terrence Malick. Evanston: Northwestern
           University Press, 1969.

WGM   *Wegmarken*. Frankfurt am Main: Vittorio Klostermann, 1967.

pp. 1–20   "What Is Metaphysics?", trans. by David Farrell Krell, *Basic Writings*,
           ed. by David Farrell Krell. New York: Harper & Row, 1977, pp. 95–112.

pp. 73–   "On the Essence of Truth," trans. by John Sallis, *Basic Writings*,
98   pp. 117–141.

pp. 99–
108

"Postscript to 'What Is Metaphysics?'," trans. by R.F.C. Hull and Alan Crick, *Existence and Being*, pp. 349–361.

pp. 109–
144

"Plato's Doctrine of Truth," trans. by John Barlow, *Philosophy in the Twentieth Century*, Vol. III, *Contemporary European Thought*, ed. by William Barrett and Henry D. Aiken. New York: Harper & Row, 1971, pp. 173–191.

pp. 145–
194

"Letter on Humanism," trans. by Frank A. Capuzzi, with J. Glenn Gray and David Farrell Krell, *Basic Writings*, pp. 189–242.

pp. 195–
212

"The Way Back into the Ground of Metaphysics," trans. by Walter Kaufmann in his *Existentialism from Dostoevsky to Sartre* (Cleveland: The World Publishing Company, 1956), pp. 207–221.

pp. 273–
308

"Kant's Thesis about Being," trans. by Ted E. Klein and William E. Pohl, *The Southwestern Journal of Philosophy*, IV, 3 (Fall, 1973), pp. 7–33.

pp. 309–
373

"On the Being and Conception of *Physis* in Aristotle's Physics B, 1", trans. by Thomas J. Sheehan, *Man and World*, IX, 3 (April, 1976), pp. 219–270.

ZS

Zur Sache des Denkens. Tübingen: Max Niemeyer, 1969.

On Time and Being, trans. by Joan Stambaugh. New York: Harper & Row, 1972.

ZSF

Zur Seinsfrage, appearing in a bilingual edition as *The Question of Being*, trans. by Jean T. Wilde and William Kluback, New Haven: College and University Press, 1958.

Preface to the Second Edition

When I wrote the present book, only a few volumes of Heidegger's *Gesamtausgabe* (collected works) had appeared. Since then, however, many volumes have been published, including several lecture courses from the 1920s, which was a crucial period in the development of Heidegger's thought. These volumes seem to confirm an important aspect of my thesis about the development of Heidegger's concept of authenticity: namely, that this concept originally included a voluntaristic strain that would later disappear in the notion of authenticity as releasement (*Gelassenheit*). In this third edition of *Eclipse of the Self*, the publishers have graciously permitted me to add an Appendix in which I rework some aspects of my thesis in light of this new material from the *Gesamtausgabe*.

In the Appendix, I also take the opportunity to answer indirectly those critics who suggest that by discussing Heidegger's historical-geographical roots, and by introducing the possibility that his own life-experience may have had something to do with developments in his thinking, I have tended to "psychologize" that thinking. Such critics contend that a psychologistic approach lends itself to interpreting Heidegger as an "existentialist," thereby elevating the human factor above the ontological factor in a way that Heidegger himself refused to do. While I agree with the concern of such critics, I also believe that at times they talk as if Heidegger's work had not been written by a concrete, individual human being.

I maintain that a thinker's historical life-context *is* important for understanding some aspects of the development of his thought. Basic hermeneutical principles of the kind employed by Heidegger indicate that certain possibilities of thinking are foreclosed to people born in an era not yet prepared for those possibilities. A medieval thinker, for example, could not have posed the question of the meaning of Being in the fashion that Heidegger did. According to Heidegger, medieval philosophers were dominated by the metaphysics of presence, which led them to define Being as the permanently present Supreme Entity that creates all other entities. It had not yet been granted to medieval philosophers to think of Being in Heidegger's way as the self-concealing presencing (*Anwesen*) through which entities are revealed as such. A culture's understanding of Being and the self-understanding made possible thereby, are closely related and are essentially *historical* in character.

The present book agrees that a person's understanding of Being and his/her self-understanding is largely determined by the historical era in which he or she is born and raised, but personal, familial, geographical, and political factors also help to characterize the way in which an individual takes on the ontological understanding of his or her era. Such factors may become even more important in the case of an essential *thinker*, who does not simply adopt the ontological understanding of the age, but who instead lets himself or herself be appropriated for a new way of understanding Being. Had Heidegger been born in a different time and place, under different personal and historical circumstances, he would not have been able to write what he did. He was born not in the fifth or fifteenth century, but in the late nineteenth; he was raised not in France or Norway, but in southern Germany; he was brought up not as a liberal Protestant or agnostic, but as a strict Roman Catholic; he was not lazy or indifferent, but energetic and passionately concerned about Being and human existence. While knowledge of such factors about Heidegger would not have allowed one of his contemporaries to predict that he would have ended up talking about Being in such an extraordinary manner, we can make use of such information retrospectively as a way of helping ourselves to see how essential thinking passes through the prism of a thinker's life.

Despite Heidegger's occasional claim that biography is irrelevant for understanding a thinker, some of his own essays—such as "The Pathway" and "Why Do We Remain in the Province?"—are plainly autobiographical and attempt to show the way in which his own personal-historical-geographical context was intricately interwoven with the course of his thinking. To use the vocabulary of *Being and Time*: he took seriously the importance of the "existentiell" dimension of thinking. This does not mean that *die Sache*, the real "matter" of thinking, is somehow invented by a thinker, or that a thinker's discussion of *die Sache* can simply be deduced on the basis of his or her psychological disposition, tastes, relationship with parents, and the like. If Heidegger is right, a thinker is in effect appropriated by *die Sache* to be the clearing through which the play of presencing-absencing can announce itself. What interested Heidegger, especially in the 1920s and 1930s, but throughout his career as well, was certainly *die Sache*, but also the *process* required for a thinker to be open for *die Sache*. As I indicate in the early chapters, Heidegger's depiction of this process is related to the decision-process so important to the Christian conversion experience. He always wondered how finite human Dasein can be become cleared for a new disclosure of the Being of beings.

In the Appendix, I have included a remarkable account of one of Heidegger's personal experience that—according to his close friend, Medard Boss—was apparently decisive in his move toward the notion of *Gelassenheit* and *Ereignis*. Do such "experiences" really have any role to play in essential thinking? Does the discussion of them within an account of Heidegger's thinking "psychologize" that thinking? Does it reduce his thinking to the level of anthropology-psychology in a manner that undermines or ignores the overriding ontological insights that transcend the merely human? Or instead, does it help to illuminate the way in which the interplay of presencing-absencing happens through finite, historical, personal human existence? Is there a way of talking about the "self" that takes account of the role played by human Dasein in the history of Being, without lapsing into a naive psychologism that reduces Being to a human project? Each reader must answer these questions in his or her own way, but I urge every reader to take seriously the fact that throughout the 1920s Heidegger emphasized that philosophy is an activity demanding the life-commitment of the individual philosopher. The difficult thing is to specify, in a way consistent with Heidegger's ontological concerns, the "who" doing the philosophizing.

In the Appendix, I also point out that in his lecture-course from 1928 Heidegger was already seeking a way of talking about authenticity in a non-voluntaristic manner. Although it would take some years before he found the proper vocabulary, the fact that he was looking for it underlines what I contended in the first edition: that there is no radical "turn" in Heidegger's thought, but instead a ripening or developing of themes that were present from the beginning. One of the ideas that underwent such a ripening was that of authenticity, originally described as "resoluteness" and later described as "releasement."

I would like to thank those people whose critical comments about and reviews of the first edition of this book have been helpful in deepening my understanding of Heidegger's thought. Fully to address and to take into account their critical suggestions would require a revision that would go well beyond the addition of an appendix, but would not change the essential direction of the book. Hence, except for some minor typographical corrections I leave the original text intact and use the Appendix to amplify this text in light of Heidegger's *Gesamtausgabe*. Since this Appendix was written, more of Heidegger's lecture courses have been published, but in my view they do not contain anything that is in conflict with the interpretation of authenticity offered in the present book. Reading these lecture-courses has reconfirmed my conviction that Heidegger was a needed thinker in our challenging time.

New Orleans
June, 1985

Introduction

As an adolescent, I learned several epigrammatic sayings so obviously true that they hardly seemed worth preserving as I grew older. One was from the Bible: "Ye shall know the truth, and the truth shall set ye free." In my intellectual games, I would occasionally use these sayings. Because I was interested in protecting myself from the truth, however, the sayings never affected me. In college, where I became skilled at using philosophical terms, I assumed I was pursuing the truth about myself and the world. In fact, by depending on theories to explain things, I was able to postpone confrontation with the truth. These sayings and theories revealed their proper depth only when I was called on to make decisions which altered my self-understanding. After one such decision, when I had experienced how truth could free me from self-imposed bondage, the real meaning of the Biblical epigram manifested itself through me. I say "through" instead of "to" in order to emphasize that the insight did not stand apart from me as a mere concept. It broke in upon me and transformed me. For the first time, I understood the difference between easily acquired intellectual comprehension and hard-won insight. The latter is far more threatening because it involves change. In that moment, I was re-integrated with the world. No longer was I an isolated ego amidst a collection of objects. For a time, I was open to myself and to the world. Everything seemed to be renewed and filled with possibilities. This kind of experience, which happens to all of us, enabled me to understand more profoundly what Martin Heidegger has said about the relation between authentic human existence and Being. This deeper understanding has, in turn, helped me to become more open. As Heidegger used to say, the text speaks only to those who are ready to hear it. We can judge the adequacy of his theory of authenticity only because we can compare it with our own experience.

The topic of this essay is the development of Heidegger's concept of authentic human existence. This concept unites in a unique way two of the major strands of Western philosophy: the theoretical-ontological and the practical-dramatic. The former maintains that philosophy is ontology: the theoretical understanding of Being. The latter holds that philosophy is the quest for self-understanding which results in a dramatic change in one's existence. According to Heidegger, this change allows us to become more fully what we already are: beings who understand what it means for things *to be*. If we exist in a way true to our own Being, we *experience* the Being of things far more profoundly than we do by manipulating *concepts* about Being. Presupposition-laden theories about Being often prevent the philosopher from experiencing the truth directly. Without such experiential insight, however, his work remains second-hand. The true philosopher knows that wisdom comes only when one takes risks and endures suffering.

In *Being and Time* Heidegger explained that human existence constitutes the openness where beings can be revealed. For Heidegger, for something "to be" means for it to be revealed, uncovered, made manifest. Being refers not to a thing but to the *event* of being manifest. Without the openness which occurs only through human beings, other beings would persist but they would not be disclosed. Humans exist as this openness in an inauthentic or an authentic way. To be inauthentic means to objectify oneself as a continuing ego-subject, thereby concealing the fact that one is really openness or emptiness. To be authentic means resolving to accept the openness which, paradoxically, one already is. One can be open to other people and to possibilities only when freed from the distortions of egoism. Authenticity means to be most appropriately what one already is.

Although there is some danger in applying the notion of "development" to a thinker's work, Heidegger himself provides some justification for this approach when he talks about the "turn" *(Kehre)* in his thinking. (LR, xvi; WGM, 159/207-208) In some sense, all of his philosophical work involves a turning-back or returning to beginnings, to what is primordial but forgotten.[1] Yet he mentions two particular "turnings" (understood here as "changes") in his thinking. In his "Letter on Humanism" (1946), he says that his earlier essay "On the Essence of Truth" (1930) reflects such a change. (WGM, 159/207-208) The latter essay tries to find a way beyond the residual subjectivism of *Being and Time* by claiming that truth (unconcealment) possesses human existence, and not the other way around.[2] This attempt to move away from the humanism and subjectivism characteristic of transcendental philosophy was not wholly decisive, however. Heidegger had still not adequately dealt with the fact that voluntarism, too, is a kind of subjectivism. For several years he continued to maintain that courageous resoluteness is a necessary element in any new disclosure of Being. In his "Letter to Father Richardson" (1962), he alludes to another change which occurred in his thinking around 1936 (LR, xiv), the period in which he was developing the notion of *Ereignis*. (ZS, 46/43) For the present study, this change is important. It was only then that he found the vocabulary to say that authenticity is not so much self-possessedness *(Eigentlichkeit)* as "being-appropriated" *(ver-eignet)* by the disclosive event of which we are always a part. For the purposes of this essay, Heidegger's "early" thinking is found in work done before about 1936; his "later" thinking is found in work done thereafter. I offer the usual reservations about making such chronological distinctions in the work of an author. Indeed, it will become clear in the course of this essay that there are remnants of voluntarism in Heidegger's work after 1936, and that there are important efforts to overcome subjectivism in work done long before that. I take seriously his admonition to Father Richardson not to understand his thinking after 1936 as something wholly different from the thinking which had gone on before. The turn in Heidegger's thinking was not an abrupt about-face but, instead, a kind of ripening in which certain impediments fell away so that the flower of his thinking could bloom. One of the major impediments was his early overemphasis on the role of will in authenticity.

Heidegger's thinking moves in the "hermeneutic circle." In *Being and Time*, for example, he begins to analyze human existence at the level of everyday life. From here he penetrates deeper to the Being of Dasein (human existence), and finally arrives at the temporality which unifies Dasein's Being. As he attains each new level, the analyses preceding it are re-cast in light of the insight provided by it. This widening and deepening of ideas is characteristic of Heidegger's treatment of the theme of authenticity not only in *Being and Time* but throughout his writings. By reading *Being and Time*, one gains an understanding of authenticity which provides insight into Heidegger's later version of this concept. In turn, the later version helps to clarify obscure matters in *Being and Time*. In the present essay, the hermeneutical circle is also at work. What I have to say in the first chapters will be clarified by what comes later, just as what I say in the beginning helps to anticipate my discussions in the final chapters. An analysis of authenticity is a fruitful way of gaining access to many of Heidegger's important philosophical themes, and these will be introduced here whenever they help to illuminate the concept of authenticity.

In Chapter One Heidegger's effort to formulate the idea of human existence as Dasein is considered. First, I show that from the beginning he was torn between religious-theological issues on the one hand and philosophical-speculative issues on the other. He was drawn to the work of such thinkers as Kierkegaard, Dilthey, Nietzsche, and Rickert because they attempted to give philosophical expression to spiritual themes which were important to him. His distinction between authenticity and inauthenticity stems from his "de-mythologizing" analysis of the Christian distinction between faithfulness and sinfulness. Next, I consider Husserl's influence on the formation of Heidegger's idea that "to be" (Being) means to be manifest, and that truth means unconcealment. Then I discuss how the concept of Dasein explains the ontological conditions for selfhood ignored by the traditional concepts of self as substance, subject, and self-consciousness. Finally, a preliminary treatment of *Being and Time* demonstrates that the dramatic theme of authenticity plays a crucial role in the analysis of Dasein.

Chapter Two is an analysis of *Being and Time*'s claim that by concealing his finitude, the inauthentic individual is able to understand himself as an eternal thing (ego). The inauthentic individual seeks security by attempting to manipulate the world. Although the egoist thinks that he is fully individuated, the fact is that his goals, opinions, and desires are largely determined by prevailing social customs and expectations. The egoism of inauthenticity corresponds to the Christian idea of sinfulness as depicted by Rudolf Bultmann, with whom Heidegger worked closely in the 1920s. Heidegger and Bultmann agreed that the opposite of inauthenticity and sinfulness is openness; they disagreed on how such openness can be gained. As a young man, Heidegger stressed the need for courage and will; Bultmann stressed the need for grace.

Heidegger's account of authenticity as anticipatory resoluteness is explored in Chapter Three. The authentic individual heeds the call of conscience when it summons him to be what he already is: temporal (finite) openness. By resolving to accept his mortality, the individual stops the egoistical self-objectification which had prevented him from being open for his possibilities. Heidegger later minimized the voluntaristic overtones present in this conception of authenticity. To fill out the abstract account of authenticity in *Being and Time* and to demonstrate how much it resembles traditional descriptions of authenticity, I conclude with three examples of the idea of authentic Being-towards-death: Plato's characterization of Socrates; the universal myth of the hero; and Nietzsche's conception of the Overman.

While Chapters Two and Three deal largely with the practical-dramatic aspects of human existence, Chapter Four initially focuses on the theoretical-ontological aspects: how mankind's temporal openness makes possible any understanding of Being. Here, too, the issue of authenticity is inextricably involved. Considerably influenced by Kant's first *Critique*, Heidegger asserts in *Being and Time* that beings can be revealed only within the horizons of human temporality. An individual can be this temporality authentically or inauthentically. If he chooses inauthenticity, his openness is marred by egoism; hence, beings appear to him merely as objects for domination. Because the egoist conceals his mortality and pursues security, his life becomes fragmented into separate episodes. If he chooses authenticity, however, he resolutely affirms his finitude; hence, he becomes open to his own limited possibilities. His life becomes unified because his temporality circles into itself in an intrinsically satisfying way. His future (freedom) is revealed as the unfolding of his past (necessity, fate). I conclude by treating Heidegger's ultimately unsatisfying attempt to describe the relation between the authentic temporality of an individual and the authentic "historicality" of a people.

In Chapter Five I show how a significant change in Heidegger's thinking resulted in part from his deepening understanding of the relation between the authentic individual and his people. First, I consider the origin of the notion of authentic temporality (the "moment-of-vision") in the New Testament idea of the "time of fulfill-ment" (*kairos*). After a discussion of the moment-of-vision as depicted by Tillich, Jaspers, Kierkegaard, and Schelling, I turn to Heidegger's 1937 lectures in which he suggests that the moment-of-vision resembles Nietzsche's "eternal return of the same." As Heidegger's thinking ripened, he interpreted authentic temporality less from the perspective of the resolute individual and more as an historical event happening through the poet, thinker, or artist destined to receive a new revela-tion of Being. The authentic self is the vessel to be emptied so that Being can manifest itself in a way which changes history. While the reader could identify himself to some extent with the authentic self described in *Being and Time,* it becomes more difficult to do so with the heroic figure described in some of Heidegger's later works. The hero must struggle to remain open for the revelation which will happen through him; he cannot, however, *will* it to happen. Authenticity happens to him; he does not choose it. The revelation granted to him, moreover, is not for him, or even for humanity, but is an episode in the "history of Being."

In Chapter Six I contend that Heidegger began to minimize the voluntaristic aspect of authenticity partly because he recognized the *hubris* he displayed in supposing that—by his own resoluteness—he could influence the direction of National Socialism, which he sup-ported in 1933-34. After 1936 his writings contain less of the violent talk which permeated *An Introduction to Metaphysics,* lectures pre-sented in 1935. Eventually he conluded that authenticity requires the release from will and from a thinking which perpetually objectifies. His lectures on Nietzsche's idea of the Will to Power (1936-1944) helped to reveal the problem of voluntarism and led him to a deeper understanding of resoluteness as "releasement."

Heidegger's mature concept of inauthenticity, one which reflects his decreasing emphasis on individual will in achieving authenticity, is the topic of Chapter Seven. Instead of saying that individuals choose inauthenticity in order to conceal their mortality, Heidegger now says that people are inauthentic because they live in a world where authenticity has become nearly impossible. Inauthenticity has become a destiny, not something elected. In the modern industrial world where everything is understood to be a commodity, individuals treat themselves and others as objects. Heidegger maintains that Western civilization has developed in this way because Being has concealed itself from us. As Being has become hidden, we have been led to forget that we are the openness *for* the Being (manifestness) of beings. Western man now understands himself as the self-willed Subject who regards everything as an object for economic exploitation. Western society is egoism on a planetary scale. The same traits which belong to the inauthentic self described in *Being and Time* are also discernible in Western man as self-certain Subject. This subjectivistic age cannot be ended by human effort but requires a change in our destiny. In *Being and Time,* Heidegger was guided by the Greek view that the human individual is partially self-perfecting. Later, he returned to the Christian notion that humanity cannot redeem itself but requires divine intervention. He sought to de-mythologize this religious conception by explaining intervention (destiny) in ontological-historical terms, not in terms of a personalistic-eschatological conception of God. In his talk of how Being "conceals itself" and thereby governs human history, Heidegger seems to have developed a mythology of his own.

In Chapter Eight I discuss the mature concept of authenticity in light of the idea of *Ereignis.* This idea, which is in certain respects synonymous with "Being," has at least three senses. First, it means much the same as Heraclitus' *Logos:* the dynamic interplay of concealment and appearance, absence and presence, which constitutes the cosmos. Second, *Ereignis* refers to the fact that mankind is destined to understand this dynamic play and the beings which take part in it. Mankind is appropriated (*ver-eignet*) by *Ereignis* so *Ereignis* can manifest itself. Third, *Ereignis* refers to the authenticity (*Eigentlichkeit*) of those thinkers and poets appropriated by *Ereignis* to remind their fellow men of their cosmic obligation: to let the cosmos display itself. Although Heidegger concluded that authenticity cannot be willed but must be granted, it would be mistaken to say that steadfastness and courage play no role in his mature conception of authenticity. Indeed, in his discussions of the valiant hero who struggles mightily to hold himself open for his fated revelation, Heidegger sometimes reverts to his earlier voluntaristic vocabulary. In general, however, the voluntarism of the earlier view of authenticity changed to the will to renounce willing. It is important to see that the major residues of voluntarism belong to discussions of world-historical heroism in the service of the "history of Being." The idea that Western man plays a crucial role in the history of Being implies that Heidegger was always affected by Hegel's claim that man has a "special" relation to the universe. Such a claim is anthropocentric and subjectivistic. It is not surprising, then, that overtones of voluntarism and humanism are found in Heidegger's analyses of the world-founding thinker or poet. In his famous essay on releasement, we find few voluntaristic terms, little talk of world-historical heroism, and limited references to the history of Being. In this essay, the notion of releasement bears remarkable resemblance to the notion of "enlightenment" in Zen Buddhism. In this context, *Ereignis* can be understood as analogous to the *Tao*. Taoism is a kind of "naturalism" which does not agree with those who elevate human history to a special place within the cosmos. When Heidegger says that man is most himself when he acts spontaneously or naturally ("like the rose"), he shows his sympathy for a non-historical, non-subjectivistic understanding of the "happening" called *Ereignis* or Being, *Tao* or *Logos*. The authentic person, then, is one who is in tune with this happening; released from the artificiality of egoism, he is open for the natural "way" of things. With regard to the subtle interplay between resoluteness and releasement, the question arises: whose will is it that wills an end to our will? Each of us is called on to answer this question.

I contend that Heidegger's concept of authenticity changed as the result of insight he gained during his own life. Some of his followers would object that this contention runs the risk of psychologizing his works, undermining their validity by interpreting them as "emotive" or "personal" statements. One of Heidegger's major claims, however, is that a change in one's understanding of Being presupposes a change in one's existence. His concept of authentic human Being changed because he himself changed. The probable motive behind the desire to separate Heidegger's thinking from his life is to protect that thinking from defilement by his involvement with National Socialism. Just as many people have committed the genetic fallacy of saying that Nietzsche's works are irrational because he went insane, others have committed the same fallacy by calling Heidegger's work immoral because, for a time, he supported Hitler. This conclusion is understandable, since Heidegger did use his philosophical vocabulary to support Hitler and some of his political aims; but it is invalid. In arguing against this conclusion, however, I do insist that Heidegger's use of his own philosophical concepts (including that of authenticity) cannot be ignored in a study of the development of those concepts. Heidegger himself insisted that a thinker must be understood in light of his historical context. This context must include the thinker's own activities. A thinker hopes to express what he has learned in his own life. It is true that the change in Heidegger's conception of authenticity, from resoluteness to releasement, occurred because the concept itself demanded the change. It is also true that Heidegger himself had to change in order to understand this demand. Philosophical theory cannot be divorced from the practice of human life. My biographical treatment of Heidegger will be based on his own remarks about his development as well as deduced from changes in his concept of authenticity.

The title of this essay, *Eclipse of the Self,* should be understood in two ways. First, it refers to Heidegger's radical critique of the Western understanding of the self as ego-subject. Authentic existence occurs only when the self (as ego) is eclipsed by the manifestation of one's finitude. Only when the self-serving ego weakens can one become truly open to one's possibilities. Second, as his thinking developed, Heidegger grew to regard the entire issue of "selfhood" as intrinsically colored by subjectivistic thinking. His interest in the question of selfhood was gradually eclipsed in developing his notions of the "history of Being" and *Ereignis.* The theme of authentic existence, however, was vitally important in his thinking to the very end. One of his concerns was to explain such existence in non-subjectivistic, non-anthropocentric terms. In his effort to find such an explanation, he pushed against, and sometimes beyond, the limits of Western thinking. As an older man, seeking to give voice to the experience of authenticity, he returned to the phenomenon which had so inspired him as a young man: the Word, *Logos*, language. The brightness of the Word eclipses the distortions of the self. Self and world, subject and object, emerge only in the clearing opened by the inspiring, illuminating Word.

A NOTE ON TERMINOLOGY.

Although this essay is not an introduction to Heidegger's thinking, I hope that it proves accessible to the non-expert. To that end, I have attempted so far as is possible to clarify or eliminate much of the terminology that so often obscures Heidegger's points. Thus, some preliminary clarification of key words is in order. His most important term is the word "Being."

Being is a translation of the German *Sein,* a substantive form of the infinitive *sein,* meaning "to be." Our word Being is a gerund which lacks the fully active sense of the infinitive, to be. Hence, when we hear the word Being we often think of something which *is,* a "being" (*Seiende*). Heidegger stresses, however, that Being does not mean any particular being, or even the totality of beings. Being ("to be") means for a being to be manifest or revealed. Being refers, therefore, to a happening or an event. We must hear the infinitive "to be" whenever we read the word Being in translations of Heidegger. To call attention to the active sense of the term *Sein* and to call to mind the relation between *Sein* and human existence, I often use the term "to be" in place of "Being." For example, instead of saying "Heidegger tried to understand Being," I might say "Heidegger tried to understand what it means to be." Such phrasing is intended to have a dual meaning. Heidegger wanted to discover both what it means (or how it is possible) for beings to be, *and* what it means to be human. That Being, as such, and human Being are inextricably related can be easily demonstrated. There is a difference between how a dog experiences its food and the way a person experiences his. If hungry, both dog and man devour their food. Unlike the dog, however, the man is presumably aware both that he himself *is* eating and that there *is* food *being* eaten. Each of us already has some vague understanding of Being; we are acquainted with what it means to be. To be means to be manifest. To be human means to be the openness where that manifesting can occur.

Heidegger also distinguishes between the ontological (*ontologisch*) and the ontical (*ontisch*). Ontological matters concern Being; ontical matters concern the structures and relations of beings. Scientific investigations, for example, are ontical concerns since they examine the structures of various kinds of beings. Philosophy deals with the Being of entire regions of beings (e.g., Nature, history, human existence) and is therefore an ontological concern.

Heidegger distinguishes further between existential (*existenzial*) and existentiell (*existenziell*), terms derived from the word "existence" (*Existenz*). Human beings exist, while other beings merely are: our being differs from that of natural objects. The term "categories" applies to the ontological structures of natural beings, while the term "existentialia" (*Existenzialen*) applies to the ontological structure of human beings. Existential matters concern the a priori, ontological features of human Dasein. Existentiell matters concern particular acts, decision, or modes of behavior which are made possible by the existential features of Dasein's Being. To show that human Dasein can exist either authentically or inauthentically is an existential task. To claim that a person becomes authentic by believing in the Christian God, or by becoming a socialist, is an existentiell matter. Existential matters interest the philosopher who wants to understand the universal features of human Being. Existentiell matters concern every person, each of whom must decide how he (or she) is going to exist. It is an existentiell decision for someone to study the existential structures of humanity or to read a book about them. As these terms overlap, it is at times difficult to separate existential from existentiell concerns.

To refer to human existence, Heidegger uses the term "Dasein," which in ordinary German means the reality or existence of a thing. The word is a composite of "*Da-*," meaning "here," and "*-sein*," meaning "to be." Literally, Dasein means "to be here," and more figuratively, in Heidegger's terms, it means to be the clearing in which beings can be manifest. Because there is no satisfactory translation for Dasein, I follow the usual practice of leaving it untranslated. For the most part, I also leave untranslated the term *"Augenblick,"* whose literal meaning is "blink of an eye" or "instant," but whose meaning for us will be "moment-of-vision." In leaving untranslated the crucial term *"Ereignis,"* I follow Heidegger's claim that the term is no more translatable than the Greek *"Logos"* or the Chinese *"Tao."* The customary translation of *"Eigentlichkeit"* as "authenticity" is retained but only in light of the following reservations. The German word *eigen* means "own" in the sense of "my own" or what is proper to me. Hence, a literal reading of *Eigentlichkeit* might be "ownedness," while a translation true to Heidegger's early conception of authenticity might be "self-possessedness."[3] Neither translation makes for smooth English. There are at least two problems with using the term authenticity, however. First, it has ethical and moral overtones which are not so evident in *Eigentlichkeit.* For Heidegger, morality is an existentiell matter; authenticity is an existential matter. Hence, one's behavior might be morally correct, even though one might be existing inauthentically. One might exist authentically, moreover, while engaging in actions deemed immoral. It has long been debated whether Heidegger can legitimately separate authenticity from morality. I deal with this issue in Chapter Six. The second problem with the term authenticity is that it lacks the sense of self-ownership clearly present in *Eigentlichkeit.* Although at times we use the word authenticity to describe the way a person really *is,* more often we use it to refer to what is genuine, true, and real as opposed to the counterfeit or fake. The word authenticity does not carry with it the sense of self-possessedness so crucial to Heidegger's early version of "authentic" existence.

As we shall see in the course of this essay, Heidegger's use and interpretation of language is provocative. He reminds us that words can become worn-out, losing the revelatory power they once possessed. Learning Heidegger's vocabularly, the reader attempts to apply it to himself and his world. His words are an appeal to us. His complicated style insures that this appeal cannot be easily popularized, but this essay will serve its purpose if it helps make Heidegger's insights more accessible.

Preface to the Fourth Printing

Two years after the second edition of this book appeared in 1985, I learned that Heidegger's involvement with National Socialism was both more enduring and more related to his own philosophy than I previously believed. Were it feasible to write a new version of *Eclipse of the Self*, I would need to take these findings into account. Nevertheless, my new version would retain a positive evaluation of many aspects of his concept of authenticity. The views of such a remarkable thinker cannot be reduced to the ideological reflex of a reactionary movement.

Heidegger's idea that human existence constitutes the temporal-historical-linguistic "openness" in which things may manifest themselves; his contention that death-anxiety constricts that openness and thus allows things to be manifest only as objects for our purposes; his analysis of the disclosive phenomenon of nothingness; his treatment of the interplay between presencing and absencing, being and time; his critical examination of subject-object dualism; his critique of the technological domination of nature; his call for "releasement" (*Gelassenheit*) from the Will to Power; his notion that we are authentic when we "let things be"; his idea that humans must begin to "dwell" appropriately on earth—all of these are central to his concept of authenticity and retain their validity, despite the political problems in his thinking which need to be addressed.

I am grateful to Duane Schneider and the staff of Ohio University Press for their assistance in reprinting this book.

Munich
February, 1992

CHAPTER ONE

Towards the Early Concept
of Authenticity

IN POSING the philosophically fundamental question of the "sense" or unity of Being, Heidegger had an answer in mind which arose from his passionate interest in the nature of human Being. He claimed that "to be" (Being) means for something to be revealed or manifest. But beings cannot be manifest without a clearing or opening in which their self-manifesting can occur. Human existence is said to constitute the temporal-historical clearing in which beings can be revealed. Even as a graduate student, Heidegger believed that there was an intimate relation between the categories of Being and the a priori structures of the transcendental subject. Later on, he was to suggest that the categories of Being are unified in terms of the temporal dimensions of human Dasein. For years before he published *Being and Time,* however, he was to complicate the problem of the relation between Being and temporality by insisting that we can choose to be this temporality in an authentic or inauthentic way. This chapter outlines how the young Heidegger's interest in both practical-dramatic and theoretical-ontological concerns led him to the concept of Dasein in *Being and Time.*

Part One explains that Heidegger came to philosophy by way of theology, although he was always intrigued by speculative issues. As a devout Catholic, deeply concerned about the issues of salvation and damnation, he was convinced that the struggle to decide in favor of the truth was crucial to human life. Hence, for him, any

1

philosophy which paid insufficient attention to the dramatic aspect of spiritual life was misguided. Although he left his theological studies to pursue philosophy, he tried to find philosophical expression for many of the religious themes which remained important to him. In his dissertation, he attacked the prevalent psychologism which failed to recognize the autonomy of logical truths and moral values. And in his *Habilitationsschrift,* he suggested that the problem of the categories could only be solved in light of a radically new understanding of the "living" spirit in all its historical concreteness. Finally, he based his distinction between authenticity and inauthenticity partly on his interpretation of the ontological presuppositions of the New Testament distinction between faithfulness and sinfulness.

Part Two shows that Heidegger's study of Husserl's sixth "logical investigation" helped lead him to the conclusions that truth means unconcealment, and that "to be" means to be manifest or revealed. Part Three describes his criticisms of the three prevailing interpretations of selfhood—substance, subject, and self-consciousness—which fail to take account of: (1) the Being of the self: (2) the dramatic nature of selfhood; and (3) the self's relation to Being as such. The concept of human Dasein explains the nature of the self by taking cognizance of the ontological and dramatic elements ignored by the philosophical tradition. Part Four shows that *Being and Time,* the work in which Heidegger tried to synthesize his dramatic and ontological interests, is a self-analysis in at least two senses: it both examines the conditions necessary for the possibility of being a self and requires the reader to apply the analysis to himself. Only by personally opening up in this way can he verify the results of the analysis of selfhood. An analysis of the "concept" of Dasein is fruitful only if the individual reader becomes open to the truth about himself *as* Dasein. Hence, while the *content* of *Being and Time* is apparently devoted to theoretical issues, the very *form* of the book requires the reader to undergo dramatic change if he is to understand that content adequately. Heidegger's existential analysis makes an existentiell demand on its readers. Finally, a brief sketch of the structure of the argument in *Being and Time* clears the way for the three following chapters, which consider the book's treatment of the relation among ontology, authenticity, and inauthenticity.

PART ONE: **Religious Experience and the Struggle for Self-Understanding.**

Martin Heidegger (1889-1976) was born in Messkirch, a little town in Swabia.[1] Although he undertook voyages of the spirit, he never strayed far from his native region of the Black Forest. He described his life and thinking as a "way" or "journey" which had no final destination. He was always "underway." As a child he dreamed of the far-off places where his hand-carved toy boats would carry him. But "Those trips of play still knew nothing of wanderings when all shores stay distant." (FW, 3/89) Although attached to the rugged countryside of his youth, Heidegger also felt homesick for a place he had never known, but for which, he tells us, his spirit longed. From the beginning, he felt drawn along a path with few signposts. He remarks that as a young man he would grapple with philosophical works which were often over his head. When frustrated by a difficult idea, he would strike out along the pathway which led out of town, through the meadows, and into the woods. They were filled with majestic trees that bore silent witness to the changing seasons of his own life. The trees seemed to fathom quite naturally what poets and thinkers struggled desperately to say with words: to be oneself authentically requires that one both reach to the heavens and down into the earth. Heidegger appreciated the harmonious interrelation of Nature and man in his rural province. While city people hurry after recognition and wealth, the peasants patiently till the soil and hew the wood in tune with the cycles of the natural world.[2] Although he recognized the limitations of peasant life, he was convinced that rootedness is essential for authentic existence. He claimed that Western humanity will remain alienated and homesick for as long as it fails to become rooted once again in its own historical sources. In his long life as a teacher and scholar, Heidegger grew famous for his patient digging into the depths of Western thinking.[3] He was at times stubborn and even arrogant, traits which led him to trouble as well as to insight.

Although small in stature, Heidegger had a powerful presence. Near the end of his life, he gave permission for publication of personal photographs, some of which portray him as a child and young man.[4] The camera captured some of the intensity of the dark eyes remembered so vividly by those who knew him. These eyes were also said to shine with humor, but the photographs do not reveal much levity. One gets a sense of great purposiveness and resolve. Recalling their early times together, Karl Jaspers observes:

> [Heidegger's] obvious philosophical enthusiasm made an impression on me. He had validated his philosophical calling in the manner of those men who, in making great decisions, are prepared to gamble and sacrifice in their choice of a path through life. Among his contemporaries in the philosophical guild, it was Heidegger alone whom I found compelling. And that still remains true today.[5]

Since Heidegger's philosophical erudition was made possible by prodigious quantities of hard work, as well as by his native genius, he demanded much of himself and expected much of others. He thus tended to be a critic both of mediocre thinking and of the mannered life-style of rootless burghers. Disdaining artificial social conventions which impeded the expression of life and thought, he spurned fashionable clothes for a modified regional costume. His direct behavior often caused a stir. On one occasion his department chairman at the University of Marburg, the dignified Nicolai Hartmann, came upon him giving skiing instructions in the hallway to some of his students.[6] An interest in skiing seems particularly appropriate for a man who stressed the importance of decisions made while one is open to the demands of the moment.

Outside of the events surrounding his infamous involvement with National Socialism, Heidegger's life was relatively uneventful. Like many other Germans of his generation, he served for a time in the army during World War I. He also married and had children, one of whom was captured by the Russians during World War II. He enjoyed good wine and long walks in the Black Forest and, of course, was totally immersed in his work. He died an old man. What C.G. Jung

remarked about himself in his autobiography holds true for Heidegger as well: the important events in his life were internal, not external.[7] His journey took him far beyond the familiar boundaries of
the spirit. It is little wonder that he found the steady, unchanging
life of the peasants so reassuring. He continued to associate with
them long after he had become a famous philosopher. His spiritual
travels were first guided by Catholicism; his father was sexton of
his home-town church. And although he seemed to leave the Church
far behind in the course of his wanderings, he nevertheless asked a
priest to make some remarks over his grave.[8]

At fourteen, Heidegger left home to attend the Gymnasium at
Constance and three years later went to the Gymnasium at Freiburg-
im-Breisgau. There, between 1906 and 1909, he studied German and
Latin and—like so' many other German philosophers before him—
developed a fascination for Greek literature, thinking, and culture.
In 1907, Dr. Konrad Gröber presented the fifteen-year old Heidegger
with a copy of Franz Brentano's *On the Manifold Sense of Being
According to Aristotle*. This book, along with Carl Braig's *On Being:
Outline of Ontology*, helped set Heidegger on a path from which he
never strayed. (US, 92-93/7) As he much later remarked:

> The quest for the unity in the multiplicity of Being, then only ob-
> scurely, unsteadily, and helplessly stirring within me remained,
> through many upsets, wanderings, and perplexities, the ceaseless
> impetus for the treatise *Being and Time*, which appeared two decades
> later. (AR, 21/4)

In 1909 Heidegger enrolled at the University of Freiburg as a
theology student and became a novice in the Jesuit order. He comments:

> At that time, I was particularly agitated over the question of the
> relation between the word of Holy Scripture and theological-
> speculative thinking.... Without this theological background I
> should never have come upon the path of thinking. But origin al-
> ways meets us from the future. (US, 96/9-10)

This passage makes clear that religious issues not only gave rise to
Heidegger's thinking, but helped guide that thinking in unexpected

ways. The last sentence is particularly provocative. Heidegger's interpretation of dynamic human existence is analogous to Aristotle's
notion of the growth of living beings. Organisms are "dynamic" because they contain within themselves the possibility for their own
development. They circle back upon themselves for nourishment as
well as direction for growth.[9] Human existence also unfolds as a
kind of spiral which continually brings us back to our origins. One of
Heidegger's favorite phrases was "Become what you are!" (Pindar).
To say that "origin always meets us from the future" suggests, of
course, that the lasting importance of Heidegger's early religious
interests became more evident to him as his thinking developed.

The young Heidegger was torn between philosophy and his Catholic
Christianity. Even as a theology student, he was particularly attracted
by the theoretical and speculative issues, not merely by the religious
and doctrinal ones. While still a seminarian, his faith began to be affected by his readings:

> What the exciting years between 1910 and 1914 meant for me can-
> not be adequately expressed; I can only indicate it by a selective
> enumeration: the second significantly enlarged edition of Nietzsche's
> The Will to Power, the works of Kierkegaard and Dostoevsky in
> translation, the awakening interest in Hegel and Schelling, Rilke's
> works and Trakl's poems, Dilthey's "Collected Writings"! (AR, 21/4)

Studying such authors broadened the world-view of the small-town
seminarian. Partly as the result of the discovery of these new intellectual vistas, Heidegger left his theological studies and the seminary
in order to pursue mathematics, science, and philosophy at Freiburg
in 1911. During his years as a graduate student, however, he apparently remained a practicing Catholic. In a letter to Paul Natorp in 1916,
Edmund Husserl said that "It is certain that [Heidegger] has con-
fessional ties, because he stands, so to speak, under the protection
of our 'Catholic historian,' my colleague Finke."[10] In a later letter,
Husserl claimed that around 1916, Heidegger underwent a "radical"
change in his religious beliefs.[11] His study of Kierkegaard, Luther,
and Augustine, among others, helped him to move from Catholicism
to Protestantism, which is one reason he was able to work so closely
with Rudolf Bultmann a few years later.[12] Gradually, Heidegger

seems to have lost his faith altogether, although he never ceased to be concerned with issues arising from religion and theology.

While studying philosophy at Freiburg, Heidegger became familiar with the current issues in logic and epistemology, particularly as delimited by his teacher, Heinrich Rickert, a leading neo-Kantian. Rickert was concerned with establishing a place for value (the "ought") in the face of the scientific materialism and positivism which wanted to reduce reality to physical events or "facts." He denied the universal applicability of the methods of natural science *(Naturwissenschaft)* and tried to found a rigorous science of culture *(Kulturwissenschaft)*. Rickert criticized psychologism because it tried to explain logical truths in terms of physiological happenings in particular human minds. Heidegger's dissertation (1914), *The Doctrine of Judgment in Psychologism* (FS, 1-129), owes much to themes developed by his mentor. The young doctoral candidate asserts the need to establish a "pure logic" (FS, 6), one which would distinguish adequately between unchanging logical truths on the one hand and changeable mental or physiological events on the other. As a form of empiricism, pyschologism could only admit two realms of reality: the physical and the psychical, the latter being understood as mental processes founded in the cerebral cortex. Hence, psychologism could not adequately account for logical and mathematical truths which are valid *(gilt)* independently of the particular thought-processes which an individual happens to go through in arriving at those truths. Psychologism *"does not know logical 'actuality' [Wirklichkeit] in general."* (FS, 103. Emphasis in original.) In concluding that valid judgments "hold" *(gilt)* but do not have material existence (FS, 112), Heidegger reflects Rickert's notion of "validity" *(Geltung)*, which postulates that logical and mathematical truths have a different ontological status than do material objects or physiologically-grounded mental happenings.

Rickert's attraction for the young Heidegger is not hard to understand. As a philosophically inclined but devout Christian, Heidegger would have been drawn to a thinker who opposed the reductionistic materialism so prevalent at the turn of the century. Rickert's interest in value and culture appealed to this student, so passionately concerned about the meaning of human life. While a graduate student,

Heidegger was groping for a way to give secular-philosophical expression to themes which Holy Scripture had first given voice for him. Rickert's distinction among the realms of the "is," the "ought," and the "valid" was evidently an attempt to explain the categorical structure of Being, a topic which had fascinated Heidegger long before he began his formal philosophical education. Rickert also introduced his pupil to the transcendental-critical idealism which was to guide his thinking for several years thereafter. Heidegger was struck by the notion that there is a relation between the categories of "reality" (the realm of objects which can possibly be experienced) and the transcendental categories of the human subject.

In 1916, not long before he was drafted into the army, Heidegger completed his *Habilitationsschrift, The Doctrine of Categories and Meaning of Duns Scotus.* (FS, 131-353)[13] Although he once again acknowledges his debt to Rickert, as he had done so unreservedly in his dissertation, here he tries to stake out his own "standpoint" in a "fully free fashion." (FS, 133) Although of some intrinsic interest, the details of his analysis of Scotus' concept of the categories are less important for our study than his concluding chapter *(Schluss)* in which he sketches out the work remaining to be done in order to gain a complete understanding of the nature of the categories. Given his interest in spiritual-religious affairs on the one hand and ontology on the other, it is not surprising to hear him say that we need to comprehend the "living spirit" *(lebendiger Geist)* and to give logic a proper metaphysical foundation if we are ever to solve the problem of the categories. (FS, 347-348) In his *Habilitationsschrift,* he makes use of Rickert's work as well as Husserl's, and admits that only a transcendental-philosophical approach can possibily bring the looked for results. But in describing how one might go about placing Scotus' notion of the categories *"within the problem of judgment and subject"* (FS, 343. Emphasis in original), or in giving Scotus the "sharp concept of the subject" which he lacked (FS, 343), Heidegger distinguishes himself from the neo-Kantians. In bypassing the question of whether validity *(Geltung)* refers to a peculiar "Being" or an "Ought," he claims that validity can only "be comprehended by means of deeper lying groups of problems which are included in the concept of living spirit and unquestionably are closely connected with the problem of value." (FS, 347) By restricting their analysis of the subject to that of the theoretical knower, the neo-Kantians had made a "fundamental and fateful error." (FS, 348)

> The epistemological subject does not explain the metaphysically most significant sense of spirit, not to mention its full content. But only through being situated in this sense does the problem of the categories receive its authentically deep dimension and enrichment. *The living spirit is as such essentially historical spirit in the widest sense of the word.* The true world-view is far removed from the merely punctual existence of a theory detached from life.... History and its cultural-philosophical-teleological interpretation must become a sense-determining element for the problem of the categories. (FS, 349-350)

The religiously-minded Heidegger, set aflame by the works of Kierkegaard and Nietzsche, proposed a new understanding of the "subject" or self, one which would have to take account of the breadth and concreteness of real life. Already we can see Heidegger pointing toward the idea of human existence he was later to call "Dasein." That his interest in developing an adequate conception of spirit or self sprang from his *personal* desire to exist in a truthful way, can be discerned in the following passage:

> The store of philosophical thought is more than a scientific subject-matter with which one occupies himself from personal preference and from the will to advance and share in the formation of culture. Philosophy lives in a tension with the living personality, draws content and the claim to value from its [the personality's] depth and fullness of life. For the most part, there lies at the basis of every philosophical conception a personal position of the philosopher in question. Nietzsche, in his unyieldingly harsh way of thinking and his plastic capacity for representing, has produced the well-known formula for this determination of all philosophy by the subject: "The drive, which philosophizes." (FS, 137)

Heidegger hoped that a radically new understanding of the human subject in its concrete historical nature, combined with an ontological inquiry set free from an outmoded epistemological bias, would lead to the solution of the problem which had puzzled Brentano: the problem of the "unity" of the categories. In emphasizing that the new conception of the subject would have to express the *historical* character of human *Geist*, Heidegger was following not only Rickert's effort to develop *Kulturwissenshaft*, but more importantly Wilhelm Dilthey's earlier effort to found *Geisteswissenschaft*, "science of [human] spirit." Dilthey believed that cultural truths and values are not eternal but historical creations of particular groups of people who respond in different ways to their own historical situation. For Dilthey, human life involves continual self-interpretation from within a specific and limited historical context. We are always in the process of redefining ourselves in light of fresh insights which reveal the limitations of our previous self-understanding. The real "subject," then, is not the worldless and abstract ego which lives outside of time and change, but the concrete, historically situated, living human being who is always engaged in trying to give meaning to his own life. No final understanding of self or culture is possible because individuals and their cultures are constantly, if slowly, changing. The methods of the natural sciences cannot be used to study the phenomena of cultural history, because cultures (like individuals) are unique and particular, while natural science is suitable primarily for what is universal and repeatable. Many people in the late nineteenth century had accepted the view that Nature is a totality of material objects which can be understood and controlled by the rational subject. Hence, they tended to regard the self one-dimensionally, as a purely rational being quite aloof from the objects it manipulates. Such a conception of the self is well-suited for the ideal of research in the natural sciences, which demands that the researcher be as free as possible from distortions caused by personal or "subjective" factors. Because experiments must be repeatable by other subjects, there is no room for individual quirks in the laboratory.[14] According to Dilthey, however, the student of culture must use the method of *Verstehen*, i.e., he must project himself imaginatively into the historical life of the culture in question if he hopes to learn anything essential about it. Dilthey used the term "hermeneutics" to describe this sympathetic understanding of cultural history. Hermeneutics was originally defined as the method for interpreting Holy Scripture in light of its social and historical context.[15] Dilthey expanded the scope of hermeneutics by saying that all cultural and personal life is an interpretative process. The student of culture can understand its essentially historical nature only because he is able to see the historical nature of his own life. In *Being and Time*, Heidegger incorporated many of Dilthey's insights. There he tells us that "The researches of Dilthey were...pioneering work; but today's generation has not yet made them its own. In the following analysis the issue is solely one of furthering their adoption." (SZ, 377/429) We can see the influence of Dilthey's distinction between *Geisteswissenschaft* and *Naturwissenschaft* in *Being and Time's* distinction between the Being of historical human Dasein and the Being of nature.

Yet Heidegger did more than adopt Dilthey's work. He transformed it by applying its historical-hermeneutical methodology to ontology. He interpreted the Being of the being, man, who exists *as* self-interpretation. Moreover, Heidegger's ontology provided what Dilthey's *Geisteswissenschaft* had always lacked: an ontologically adequate explanation of why cultures differ from one another. According to Heidegger, they differ because they understand the Being of beings in different ways. Dilthey's historicism enabled Heidegger to interpret Kant's notion of the categories of the human understanding in a dynamic-historical manner. Although Hegel had done something similar a century earlier, Heidegger followed Dilthey and Nietzsche in denying the validity of Hegel's attempt to reconstruct Christian eschatology in the form of the self-directing drive of Spirit toward Absolute Consciousness. For Heidegger, history *(Geschichte)* is not pre-ordained by a transcendent God, nor is it the working-out of the hidden plan of the Hegelian Idea, but is an ontological happening *(Geschehen)* conditioned by the way in which human Dasein responds to destiny *(Geschick)*. As we will see later on, however, Heidegger had still not arrived at a fully satisfactory rendering of this concept of history even in *Being and Time*.

Kierkegaard was at least as important a figure to the young Heidegger as Dilthey and Nietzsche. Jaspers informs us that he and Heidegger shared a "passion" for the writings of the famous Dane.[16] In his valuable study, *Existence and Freedom*, Calvin O. Schrag argues that "an existential ontology was already implicit in Kierkegaard's writings, later to reach its most systematic expression in the philosophy of Heidegger."[17] Heidegger's ontology of human existence includes the following themes, all of which are supposedly found in Kierkegaard's writings: decision, freedom, destiny, resoluteness, the ecstatic concept of temporality, distinction between authenticity and inauthenticity, the importance of the individual person, rejection of abstract thinking, critique of mass culture, the concept of "existence" *(Existenz)*, and so on. In a more recent work, George J. Stack makes a similar claim and concludes that Heidegger was unfair to Kierkegaard. Although Heidegger makes only three footnote references to Kierkegaard in *Being and Time*, Stack asserts that "he ought to have made at least a hundred."[18] Taken together, the books by Schrag and Stack suggest that *Being and Time* is just a formalization of what the Danish thinker had understood decades earlier. It is true that Heidegger did not acknowledge the extent of his debt to Kierkegaard, whom he regarded as an edifying writer and not a real thinker; that is, one who grapples with the question of the sense of Being. Heidegger often seemed to regard himself as superior to his philosophical predecessors. He claimed that he was the first to understand what a previous thinker, such as Kant or Nietzsche, had been trying to say but had failed to grasp. Despite his rough treatment of his forebears, however, Heidegger was devoted to the history of philosophy. The supreme compliment one thinker can pay to another is to engage him in a serious dialogue. Heidegger did this with thinkers from Anaximander to Nietzsche.

Thus, Heidegger borrowed much from Kierkegaard, but it would be a mistake to say that his thinking is totally derived from the Danish writer. Every thinker owes much to those who have gone before, but great thinkers add to the tradition. While Heidegger employed many of the concepts developed by Kierkegaard, he did so in light of his own unique insight: that we are the absence in which beings can be present. Schrag comes close to the mark when he says that Heidegger tried to reconcile Dilthey's historicism, Kierkegaard's existentialism, and Husserl's phenomenology.[19] Tracing the influences of a thinker is a tricky business, however. We know, for example, that one of Heidegger's concerns while at Freiburg in the early 1920s was to demonstrate the existential relevance of the existentiell themes found in the New Testament. In particular, the idea of faithfulness came to be seen as an ontico-religious exemplification of the ontological possibility of authenticity. Stack informs us that "It was Kierkegaard, and not (as is commonly supposed) Heidegger who first applied Christian notions (e.g., conscience and guilt) to states of being of man that have a purely existential significance and are not necessarily related to a religious mode of existence."[20] Although this is true, it is possible that Heidegger's interest in a non-mythological, non-theological interpretation of the New Testament may have also been provoked by Dilthey and Graf Paul Yorck. With regard to the idea of "Christianity without Christ," Yorck wrote to Dilthey in 1892 that "Dogmatics was an attempt to formulate an ontology of the higher historic life."[21] Dilthey replied:

> All dogmas need to be translated so as to bring out their universal validity for all human life. They are cramped by their connection with the situation of the past in which they arose. Once they have been freed from this limitation they become...the consciousness of the supra-sensual and supra-intelligible nature of historicity pure and simple.... Once [the principal Christian dogmas] are reinterpreted as statements of universal validity they express the highest living form of all history. They thus lose their rigid and exclusive reference to the person of Jesus, which deliberately excludes all other references.[22]

While teaching at Freiburg, Heidegger followed the hermeneutical avenue opened up by Kierkegaard and Dilthey in a course called "Introduction to the Phenomenology of Religion" (1920-21), which focused on St. Paul's letters to the Galatians and Thessalonians. As Professors Pöggeler and Sheehan have indicated, Heidegger claims that Paul's letter offers an insightful account—couched in terms of the religious conceptions of the time—of the new experience of temporality involved when one abandons security and leads a faithful life.[23] Paul's descriptions are not existential, but existentiell, i.e., he does not provide us with an account of the ontological conditions necessary for the possibility of redemption, but instead simply asserts—on the basis of faith—that to be saved means accepting Christ as one's redeemer. Heidegger formalized ontologically the temporal understanding of human existence presupposed by Paul's conception of faithful existence. According to Professor Sheehan, in these lectures Heidegger was already moving toward the concept of human temporality elaborated in *Being and Time*.[24] He focused particularly on Paul's usage of the verb *genesthai* (to have become), as well as on the verbs *mnaomai* (I remember) and *eido* (I know). For Paul, the man of faith has a totally new self-understanding because he experiences the presence of God here and now. Only for that reason can he let go of the desire for security which at one time concealed God from him. Experientially, this radically new mode of existence involves sensing that one has recovered or remembered what one already is. Redemption means waking up from the sleep of selfishness, *recalling* what one already somehow knew: that my life is not my own, but Christ lives through me. Awaiting the *parousia* ("second coming of Christ") does not mean expecting an event in the future, but holding oneself open for the divine presence which has always already been with us. As Sheehan explains, on the basis of Paul's revolutionary understanding of human temporality, Heidegger developed his crucial concept of *Gewesenheit* ("alreadiness") in *Being and Time*.[25] As we will see in more detail later, for Heidegger the past is nothing dead and gone but the living matrix which is constantly defining our future possibilities. When we exist authentically, we recognize that our past is our future, that we are now and will be who we already have been. Authenticity means self-recollection and self-discovery, though within the framework of Christianity such a new way of life comes as a gift, not as an achievement.

Heidegger's lectures on the New Testament were also the proving grounds for his notion of factical life experience. As opposed to the abstract epistemological subject, he wanted to posit the fully human self who is essentially historical and self-concerned. In his lectures on "Augustine and Neo-Platonism," Heidegger agreed with Luther's assertion that the real theologian does not understand God theoretically but by identifying with the pain and suffering of Christ. Pöggeler tells us:

> Heidegger even elaborates the Pauline theme of pneumatic-mystical *charismas* (cf. 2 Cor. 12:2-10) and the theme of the thorn in the

flesh, on which Kierkegaard so painstakingly elaborates. Heidegger makes it clear how (by abandoning visions and apocalypses) the orientation toward the facticity of life consists in the renouncing of having received a special grace and in taking upon oneself one's own weaknesses. Thus, primitive Christian religiosity was rooted in the factical experience of life, indeed, *is* this experience of life.... It lives not only "in" time—it "lives" time itself. By means of this explication of early Christian religious experience, the young Heidegger gains those important insights which lead to his basic concept of "facticity" (later, factical "ek-sistence").[26]

An adequate philosophical conception of the human self must take into account the emotional, artistic, and religious aspects of life, as well as the rational and deliberative aspects. Human life is intrinsically finite and historical. Heidegger knew that just as the existing individual gains self-understanding only through a painful struggle to accept the truth about human finitude, so, too, the philosopher can gain philosophical understanding about human existence only through the struggle to understand *his own existence.* No profound philosophical comprehension of what it means to be human is possible for the person who has not examined his own practical experience of trying to be human.

In these same lectures, Heidegger criticized Augustine's idea that the soul finds rest in the "fruit of God." This concept, which stems from the neo-Platonic notion that contemplation is the chief mode of access to God, diverts attention from the necessity of the continuing struggle to be faithful. The idea of peaceful beholding suggests that faith is an intellectual achievement, but Heidegger argued that faith is a matter of the whole person, not just the intellect, and must be re-confirmed every day. Heidegger recognized that Augustine also had an active notion of faith; yet he believed that Augustine was partly responsible for the shift in religion from lived experience to detached contemplation. He helped give birth to *theory* about God (theology) and helped spur the decline of the *experience* of God (religion). Because Heidegger, like Luther and Kierkegaard, regarded personal decision as essential to faith, he did not appreciate a theology which replaced decision with rational reflection. The wedding of Christianity with philosophy led to the demise of the former—God was reduced to the status of the primal ground of reality. As Heidegger noted years later, "a man can neither fall to his knees in awe nor can he play music and dance before this God." (ID, 140/72)

Heidegger extended his critique of theology *mutatis mutandi* to metaphysics, which also tended to ignored the concreteness of life. As Pöggeler says, metaphysics

> thinks Being as Being-constantly present-at-hand and thereby cannot satisfy the temporality of the execution of factical life. Metaphysical thinking since its earliest beginning was oriented by seeing. Thus, for example, even for Augustine Being means Being-present-before-the-eyes and thereby Being-present-at-hand or constant presence *[Anwesen]*.[27]

The Western understanding of Being is conditioned by an over-emphasis on vision, which is oriented toward permanently present objects (e.g., Plato's "forms"). Western philosophy long overlooked the fact that the idea of Being as permanent "presence" *(eidos, essence, An-wesen)* is intrinsically connected with temporality, since presence (the present) is a mode of temporality. Because human existence is fundamentally temporal, Dasein holds open the "clearing" in which beings can be manifest in past, present, and future. Heidegger's preferred mode of "sensing" was hearing instead of seeing. Seeing is restricted to what is immediately present, while in listening we can recall what was and anticipate what will be, while also being attentive to the present. Hence, listening is more appropriate to our temporal existence.

In 1922 Heidegger went to teach at the University of Marburg, where he remained for six years. During this time, in which he worked closely with Bultmann, he wrote *Being and Time*. Bultmann and Heidegger attended each other's seminars.[28] Heidegger helped Bultmann develop his method of "de-mythologizing" scripture, while Bultmann helped confirm Heidegger's idea that much of the New Testament exhibits profound insight into the nature of human existence. As Bultmann observed in the late 1940s:

> Above all, Heidegger's existentialist analysis of the ontological structure of [Dasein] would seem to be no more than a secularized

philosophical version of the New Testament view of human life....
Some critics have objected that I am borrowing Heidegger's categories and forcing them upon the New Testament. I am afraid that
this only shows that they are blinding their eyes to the real problem
which is that the philosophers are saying the same thing as the New
Testament and saying it quite independently.[29]

Of course, Bultmann's own interpretation of the New Testament is
guided in part by Heidegger's analysis of Dasein, so it is not surprising
that he views Heidegger as saying much the same as the New Testament! If Karl Barth is correct in his estimation that "There is one thing,
and only one thing which [Bultmann] does not get from Heidegger,
and that is his description of the transition [to redemption] as an
act of God,"[30] then a consideration of Bultmann's interpretation of
the New Testament would provide considerable insight into Heidegger's thinking. In later chapters, I shall call on Bultmann's thinking
in this way. Here I want only to note that Heidegger's distinction
between authenticity and inauthenticity corresponds to Bultmann's
distinction between faithfulness and sinfulness. Both inauthenticity
and sinfulness spring from an attempt to gain security in the face of
death by interpreting oneself as a permanent, self-created ego. To
become authentic or faithful, the individual must undergo a dramatic change in self-understanding. Christ and grace are mediating elements necessary for redemption from sinfulness according to Christianity, but no such divine elements figure in Heidegger's concept of
the change from inauthenticity to authenticity. For one thing, authenticity is an ontological possibility of which faithfulness is, supposedly, an example within the ontical realm of religious experience.
For another thing, although Heidegger based much of his interpretation of human existence on the New Testament, he also appealed
to the Greek ideal of human self-perfectibility (cf. Aristotle) to
explain how an individual can choose to become who he is without
the aid of grace.[31]

In his 1928 lecture, "Phenomenology and Theology," dedicated
to Bultmann, Heidegger differentiates sharply between philosophy
and theology. Theology is said to be a positive, ontical science which
studies a kind of being: faith. Ontology, on the other hand, deals
not with anything which is, but with Being as such. Faith, which

theology illuminates, involves a kind of rebirth in which the believer takes part in the event of the crucifixion by placing his "entire Dasein as Christian, i.e., one bound to the cross—before God." (PT, 19/10) As opposed to philosophy, which arrives at understanding by way of reason, faith "understands itself only in believing. The believer never knows anything about his specific [faithful] existence on the basis of a theoretical confirmation of his inner experiences." (PT, 19/10) The task for theology is to explain concrete Christian experience, not to express universally valid statements about religious experience in general, for this would be philosophy of religion.

Although philosophy can be of no benefit to faith and even hinders it, philosophy can help the positive science of theology. When a person is re-born through faith, for example, his previous non-Christian existence is transformed *(aufgehoben).* In its interpretation of this transformation, theology must appeal to some philosophical interpretation of the Being of man. Philosophy helps theology answer the question, What kind of beings are we that we can be transformed by faith? Particular characteristics of pre-Christian existence, e.g., sinfulness, can be clarified by analysis of the Being of Dasein.

> Thus the more primordially and appropriately the basic constitution of Dasein is brought to light in terms of genuine ontology, e.g., the more the concept of guilt is grasped in its origin, the more clearly can it function as a guide for the theological explication of sin. (PT, 30/19)

But philosophy cannot define sin, the understanding of which emerges only within the realm of faithful existence. Sin itself is not a philosophical issue, although the conditions necessary for the possibility of sin are philosophical issues. *"Therefore ontology functions only as a corrective to the ontic, and in particular pre-Christian, contents of basic theological concepts."* (PT, 30/19) Reversing the medieval relation between philosophy and theology, Heidegger implies that philosophy exercises a kind of "negative rule" over theology and, indeed, over ethics as well. Philosophy can say when theology or ethics have made ontologically inappropriate assumptions about human existence. Theology's interest in philosophy must be restricted to how philosophy can free theology for the task of disclosing the origins of theological concepts.

Heidegger also insists that philosophy is self-justifying; it does not need to perform this corrective role for theology (or ethics) in order to be a legitimate undertaking. For philosophy is "the free questioning of purely self-reliant *[auf sich gestellten]* Dasein." (PT, 31/20) Faith, hardly an activity of self-reliant human existence, is the "mortal enemy" of philosophy. Hence, the concept of a "Christian philosophy" is an absolute contradiction. Heidegger's rather unkind attitude toward Kierkegaard may become more understandable when we consider that Heidegger regarded the Dane's writings as an unacceptable mixture of philosophy and theology and/or ethics. Heidegger relegated Kierkegaard to the status of an "edifying" thinker in much the same way as Hegel might have done.

It was clear to the young Heidegger that human life is a process of growth, change, and becoming. The dynamic character of our existence means that we are constantly confronted with decisions. Human freedom is exhibited in the fact that we can choose to commit ourselves to one thing and to abstain from another. Human finitude is manifested by the fact that we cannot choose to do, or be, everything. Our lives are circumscribed by limitations. Changes in self-understanding come about through the conflict between freedom and necessity, possibility and fate. During his years at Marburg, Heidegger was convinced that to be a self in an authentic way meant to elect those specific possibilities which are uniquely one's own. Authenticity requires that one be just who one already is: finite transcendence or concrete Being-in-the-world. Heidegger's early concept of authenticity emphasized the importance of *willing* to take responsibility for one's own finite existence. Such willing is always an element in a new disclosure or understanding of what it means to be human. To be authentic means to understand Being in a way free from the concealments and ambiguities of inauthenticity. The dramatic theme of authenticity is directly connected with the theoretical interpretation of Being. Phenomenology taught Heidegger that Being means to be manifest, truth means unconcealment, and human existence is the clearing in which beings are manifest (true). Let us consider for a moment Heidegger's encounter with phenomenology.

PART TWO: Phenomenology, Being, and Truth.

When Husserl arrived at Freiburg in 1916, Heidegger was just beginning his post-graduate academic career. Husserl's opinion of Heidegger warmed as he observed the younger man's excellence in the
classroom.[32] Eventually Husserl came to expect Heidegger to become
the leading figure in phenomenology, much as Freud looked upon
Jung as his successor in psychoanalysis. But just as Jung turned out
to be far too original a thinker to remain within the intellectual
realm established by Freud, so, too, Heidegger used phenomenology
as it suited his interest in ontology, an area Husserl considered to be
subsidiary to phenomenology.[33] Their relationship deteriorated in
the 1920s; finally, an open break occurred. Husserl felt betrayed
by Heidegger, while Heidegger felt he was remaining true to the
slogan of phenomenology: "To the things themselves!" For Heidegger, these "things" or "matters" *(Sache)* were human existence
and the sense of Being. It would require another essay to detail
the relation between Husserl's phenomenology and Heidegger's,
and another essay would be needed to treat their personal relationship. Perhaps it is enough to say that in his relation to Husserl,
Heidegger revealed some of his tendency to belittle other philosophers:
a tendency we have already encountered in his treatment of Kierkegaard. Jaspers notes that while in private Heidegger would speak
"with contempt" of Husserl, in public he dedicated *Being and Time*
to him.[34]

Heidegger asserted his independence from phenomenological
"scholasticism" by declaring in 1927 that he was not interested in
talking about the "theory" of phenomenology but "in being able
to do it." (GP, 1) Phenomenology is *"the method of scientific
philosophy in general [wissenschaftlichen Philosophie überhaupt]."*
(GP, 3) Phenomenology has only one major "object" to investigate: the unifying structure ("sense") of Being. Heidegger summarizes the phenomenological-ontological task as follows:

> The horizon from which something like Being in general becomes
> understandable is time. We interpret Being from time *(tempus).*

The interpretation is a temporal one. The fundamental problematic of ontology, as the determination of the sense of Being from time, is that of temporality *[Temporalität]*. (GP, 22)

In *Being and Time* we are told that human existence holds open the temporal horizons necessary for beings to be manifest. Temporality reveals or "un-conceals" beings. Unconcealment or revelation is the primordial meaning of truth *(a-letheia)*. Heidegger was led to this conception of truth by his study of "categorial intuition" in the sixth chapter of Husserl's *Logical Investigation.* Husserl distinguishes between "meaning intentions," intentional acts which mean some object, and "fulfilling intentions," acts in which the object presents itself so as to fulfill the meaning intention. For example, if my meaning-intention is a friend of mine, the corresponding fulfilling-intention would be the actual presence of the friend when I meet him.[35] Fulfilling intentions involve some sort of intuition. Husserl insists that there must be fulfilling intentions for such "categorial" meanings as "is," "if," "and," "nothing," "relation," and "identity."

> If we are asked what it means to say that categorically structured meanings find fulfillment, confirm themselves in perception, we can but reply: it means only that they relate to the object itself in its categorial structure. The object with these categorial forms is not merely referred to..., but is set before our very eyes in just these forms. In other words, it is not merely thought of, but intuited or perceived.[36]

According to Heidegger, the idea of categorial intuition rivals Aristotle's account of the categories of Being.

> What occurs for the phenomenology of the acts of consciousness as the self-manifestation of phenomena is thought more originally by Aristotle and in all Greek thinking and existence as *aletheia*, as the unconcealedness of what is present, its being revealed, its showing itself. That which phenomenological investigations rediscovered as the supreme attitude of thought proves to be the fundamental trait of Greek thinking, if not indeed of philosophy as such. (ZS, 87/79)

In all my intentional acts, there is some simple "givenness" of categorial structures which I somehow intuit. When I perceive a table, for example, it is manifest that a sensuous object *is* before me and that this object is *identical* with itself. Truth does not lie in the verbal judgment, for a judgment presupposes the *givenness* of the state of affairs about which the judgment is made. A fulfilling-intention (my seeing the table before me) provides intuitive fulfillment for a meaning-intention prior to any explicit judgment (e.g., "This table is brown."). Truth, therefore, is the state of affairs in which there is an agreement between what is meant and what is given. (L, 107-109) In categorial intuition, there is an agreement between my meaning intention of the Being of beings and the intuitive fulfillment of the meaning intention when Being gives or manifests itself to me. For Husserl, this is the primordial form of truth presupposed by every particular true judgment. But Heidegger went beyond even this fundamental *"adequatio"* to say that the essence of truth is the un-concealment which lets Being give or manifest itself; that is, the un-concealment which lets beings present themselves as beings. This un-concealment occurs within the horizons of temporality opened up by human existence. Heidegger's notion that human temporality is the dynamic-historical clearing for the disclosure of Being arose from his synthesis of the Greek insight (mediated by Husserl's phenomenology) that truth means un-concealment and Kant's conception of time (as mediated by Paul's revolutionary understanding of human temporality and Dilthey's radical historicism).

The notion that Being reveals or gives itself to us is supported by Heidegger's belief that the analysis of Being should not begin with vague theories about Being but with our experience of things in everyday life. We always have some vague understanding of the Being of the things we deal with. I can use the typewriter because I have already understood it to be a writing instrument. Because we are usually unaware that what things *are* is "given" to us, we conclude that Being is simply a philosophical "concept." Common sense, however, never notices anything puzzling about everyday life. Philosophers, on the other hand, are "constantly aroused by and immediately sensitive to the completely enigmatic character of

what, for sound common sense, is without question and self ex-
planatory." (L, 23-24)

Not only common sense, but metaphysics, too, is oblivious to the
fact that Being gives itself for understanding. Metaphysics has concentrated on studying Being as the ultimate ground or structure of
beings *(ousia, physis, actus purus,* Will, Will to Power, etc.) but has
failed to ask how this primal ground is, itself, accessible for understanding. By Being, metaphysicians mean "beingness" *(Seiendheit),*
or the "reality of the real,"while by Being, Heidegger means "to be
manifest." Hence, he tries to do the "metaphysics of metaphysics,"
or to point out that unconcealment is the necessary condition for
the metaphysical study of the reality of the real.

> Being is given *[es gibt Sein]* only insofar as disclosedness *[Erschlos-
> senheit]* i.e., truth, is. But truth is only if a being exists which opens
> up, which discloses, indeed such that disclosing belongs to the mode
> of Being of this being. We ourselves are such a being. Dasein itself
> exists in the truth.... Being is given only if truth, i.e., if Dasein,
> exists.... (GP, 24-25)

For common sense, it is outrageous to say that Being "is" only
so long as Dasein exists, for this seems to make "reality" dependent
on humanity. Yet Heidegger is no subjective idealist. The totality
of natural beings persists whether or not Dasein exists. (GP, 313)
Without Dasein, however, these beings would not be manifest: all
would be dark, hidden, unknown. Human existence lets the intelli-
gibility of what *is* be revealed. Only in his later writings did Heidegger explain adequately the importance of language *(Logos)* for the
revelation of what is.

Heidegger concurred with the idea that Being is given, but he disagreed with Husserl's view of how this givenness takes place. Heidegger felt that Husserl's emphasis on intentionality led to the conclusion
that the categories are "constituted" by the ego-subject or transcendental ego. Overemphasis on consciousness and ego-subject were
signs that Husserl remained with the Cartesians. Heidegger, however,
tried to develop a non-egological interpretation of selfhood. More
primordial than the judging ego is the temporality (nothingness,
openness, transcendence, clearing, disclosedness) in whose horizons

beings (*including* the ego) can be manifest. If this temporality generates itself in an authentic way, one's understanding of Being undergoes a radical transformation. Authenticity is essentially bound up with an authentic comprehension of Being in general and of one's own Being in particular. In the course of developing this idea of self-hood, Heidegger had to criticize three traditional conceptions of the self: (1) as substance; (2) as subject; (3) as self-consciousness.

PART THREE: The Critique of Traditional Conceptions of Selfhood.

According to Heidegger, many ideas about the self are based on the inadequate Latin translation of the Greek *"ousia"* as *"substantia"* (substance). To be a substance supposedly means to stand under, support, or unify a group of qualities. The self is often interpreted as the substantial core which gives identity to the manifold experiences of a human life. This view of self as substance can also be extracted from neo-Platonism, which holds that the self is the eternal soul placed in the body at birth. The "self" is thus the unchanging inner reality of the person. Heidegger rejected the interpretation of *ousia* as substance and replaced it with the idea that *ousia* means the dynamic absence which lets a living being manifest its appearances. To regard the self as a substantial core wrongfully objectifies human existence, which is never fixed but always open for change. And to talk about the immortality of the soul is a matter for faith not philosophy. Knowledge about human existence is limited to what we can experience in *this* life. As we shall see, Heidegger's conception of the temporal "basis" for selfhood owes much to his re-interpretation of Aristotle's conceptions of *ousia* and *dynamis.*

The concept of substance eventually led to the idea of the "subject." The word "subject" is derived from the Latin *"sub"* and *"iaceo,"* which, taken together in "subject," means "thrown under." Much like the term "substance," subject came to mean that which supports or unifies the predicates of natural beings. In the Middle Ages, the term could designate any individual being; but Descartes used the word preeminently to designate the human self. The self-certain

Cartesian subject became the the "substance" (underlying ground) for natural "objects," understood as all non-subjective (non-thinking) beings. For modern man an object is said *to be* only if it can be represented or explained by the human subject. Heidegger tried to interpret human existence in a way which would undermine Cartesian dualism, but his lectures from the 1920s demonstrate that his thinking was still conditioned by the prevailing subjectivism. In the course of defending his idea of Dasein, for example, he maintained that "Philosophy must perhaps start from the 'subject' and return to the 'subject' with its final question, but nevertheless ought not to pose its questions in a one-sidedly subjectivistic way." (GP, 220) Even if subjectivistic language crept into his lectures, Heidegger recognized the major shortcoming of dualism: it cannot explain how the thinking subject can get outside of itself and over to the known object. Modern philosophy posits a gap between subject and object because it has failed to notice that a temporal clearing (transcendence) is needed for subject and object to present themselves in the first place. Metaphysics forgets about Being (manifestness) and focuses on the relations among and structures of beings, for example, subjects and objects. How the idea of temporal transcendence avoids dualism can be seen in Heidegger's critique of Husserl's concept of intentionality.

The concept of intentionality, which claims that all consciousness is consciousness *of* something, maintains the distinction between subject and object. "Husserl refers constantly to this distinction, and precisely in the form in which Descartes expressed it: *res cogitans—res extensa.*" (GP, 176) Heidegger asserted that intentional consciousness, far from being absolute, presupposes temporal transcendence.

> The intentional structure of modes of behavior is not something which is immanent in the so-called subject and then has need of transcendence, but the intentional constitution of the modes of behavior of Dasein is precisely the ontological condition of any transcendence. Transcendence, transcending, belongs to the essence of the being which (upon its ground) exists as intentional, i.e., which exists in the mode of dwelling *[Sichaufhaltens]* alongside of the present-at-hand. Intentionality is the *ratio cognoscendi* of transcendence. The latter is the *ratio essendi* of intentionality in its various modes. (GP, 91; cf. also 223-224, 230-239)

For ego-consciousness to intend an object, e.g., to notice that a car is passing me, the ego and the object must first be revealed. Husserl adopted the Cartesian standpoint that consciousness is prior to the Being of the objects intended by consciousness. Heidegger, however, insisted that an adequate understanding of the nature of consciousness is impossible without insight into the Being of consciousness.

Heidegger used a similar argument against Max Scheler's discussion of selfhood. In *Being and Time*, Heidegger concedes that Scheler had already recognized that the self or person cannot be defined as a thing, object, or substance, since the person is essentially different from any kind of thing. Scheler talked of the person as the "unity of lived experience *[Er-lebens]*," and as the performer of intentional acts bound together by the unity of a meaning. (SZ, 48/73) Heidegger asks: "What, however, is the ontological meaning of 'performance'? How is the kind of Being which belongs to a person to be ascertained ontologically in a positive way?" (SZ, 48/73) Although influenced by Scheler and Dilthey's "philosophy of life" *(Lebensphilosophie)*, Heidegger believed that these thinkers went astray by failing to consider the Being of life in general and of human life in particular. He concluded that we can be aware of ourselves as living subjects only because we are the temporal transcendence in which subjects and objects can be revealed. (GP, 230) In 1929 he remarked:

> If we choose the term 'subject' for the being which all of us are and by which we understand Dasein, then transcendence can be said to denote the essence of the subject or the basic structure of subjectivity.... To be a subject means to be a being in and as transcending.... (WG, 36/37)

As transcendence, we are not ego-subjects locked within the "sphere of immanence." Instead, we are always in the world. If one studies human existence by reading philosophy texts, one might be led to all sorts of abstract conclusions. If one examines human existence directly, however, one can avoid many of them. Everyday life is always open to beings in the world. When engrossed in reading the morning paper or when driving down the street, I usually do not perceive myself as an isolated subject. In fact, I often forget myself and simply become an element in the activity which engages me. I can, of course, disengage myself from the activity and note that *I* am doing something. When this happens, as it does with some frequency, my openness to the world is impeded: my ego gets in the way. Subjective philosophy mistakenly makes this reflective ego-consciousness the fundamental human trait. In so doing, philosophy overlooks man's *worldly* character. Human beings are inescapably involved with worldly affairs. As Being-in-the-world "Dasein *has always stepped out from itself, ex-sistere,* it *is* always *in* a world. Thus, there is never something like a subjective inner sphere." (GP, 241-242) Some critics claim that Heidegger ignores the phenomenon of the human body, but, in fact, he presupposes that bodily experience is as "worldly" as my seeing a bird on a fence. Experiences which are normally regarded as "inner" or "subjective" are entirely wordly; they are part of *my* worldly experience. Even my experience of myself as a conscious subject is a worldly experience, for I cannot escape the world: I *am* always in the world of my experience. The world is not a collection of objects outside of me, and my self is not a bundle of ideas and feelings inside of me. The world is the interrelated set of relationships which give form and content to my experience.

> Understanding of the world, as understanding of Dasein, is self-understanding. Self and world belong together in one being, Dasein. Self and world are not two beings, as subject and object, also not as I and you, but self and world are—in the unity of the structure of Being-in-the-world—the fundamental determination of Dasein itself. (GP, 422)

Dasein is embodied openness to what is. A feeling is manifest to me just as much as is a friend. Although a feeling is different from a friend, both are manifest insofar as there is some temporal openness in which that manifesting can occur. A gnawing pain manifests itself in my stomach; as I open the refrigerator door, a turkey leg manifests itself. Seeing the turkey leg is not more "objective" than feeling the pain in my stomach. Of course, a turkey leg is not like a pain in any ontical way, but ontologically both turkey leg and pain are revealed through me.

As worldly beings we are not only open to things immediately present to us, we are also open to past and future. Temporal transcendence is historical; hence, we are always out ahead of ourselves, anticipating and planning. Although the body is always located in a particular time and place, human Dasein is not identical with its body considered as a physical object. Our openness to things is not restricted to the present moment. We can transcend the given understanding of what it means to be and gain a new understanding. Human freedom is the temporal transcendence which allows us to be open to our own possibilities for growth and development. Freedom presupposes awareness and understanding. Dasein exists as the "ontological difference" between Being and beings; that is, we are not only beings, but we understand what it means to be. We are aware of the difference between the manifestness (Being) of beings and the beings which are manifest. We pass beyond or transcend beings to their Being. In advance of any particular encounter with a being, we understand the fundamental ways in which a being may present itself. Only because we "step out from ourselves" or "ek-sist" as temporal transcendence can we become aware of ourselves. "In surpassing [*Übersteig*], Dasein first attains to the being that is; what it attains to is its 'self'. Transcendence constitutes selfhood." (WG, 38/39) The true Self is not the self-conscious ego-subject, but temporal transcendence.

Having considered Heidegger's critique of the ideas of self as substance and as subject, we are now prepared to examine his critique of the idea of self as self-consciousness. This idea, an elaboration of the subjectivistic view of the self, was developed most rigorously in German idealism. Hegel, who made the *cogito* into a fundamental philosophical principle, defined the self in terms of self-consciousness. To be a genuine self means to have an adequate concept of oneself. According to Heidegger, however:

> the determination of the subject as self-consciousness says nothing about the mode of Being of the I. Even the most extreme dialectic of self-consciousness, as it gets constructed in various forms by Fichte, Schelling, and Hegel, is unable to solve the problem of the existence of Dasein, because (the problem) is not posed. (GP, 218)

Caught up in their theoretical constructions, the idealists failed to turn to the phenomenon itself—everyday worldly existence. Fichte, in particular, claimed that the self is consciousness or transcendental subjectivity, and spoke of the self as "positing" itself or even as creating itself. For Hegel, the self constructs itself in the dialectic which ends in total self-consciousness. The "self" becomes identical with the rational totality of Absolute Spirit. Overemphasis on the reflective capacity of the self arises from the supposition that ego-consciousness is the most fundamental element in human existence. Once this self-awareness detaches itself from its everyday Being-in-the-world, self-awareness can make itself absolute; indeed, self becomes the rational basis for all reality. Unlike Hegel, Heidegger adhered to Kant's assertion that human understanding is essentially *finite*. "I stress 'human,' because we must ween ourselves in philosophy from confusing ourselves with dear God, as is a principle for Hegel." (L, 267)

Heidegger also criticized the depiction of the self as the unified awareness which can accompany its representations with the "I think." Husserl spoke of the "ego-pole" as the center from which "I-acts" stream out to constitute intentional relations. (GP, 225) Heidegger had no doubt that humans are self-conscious, but he refuses to make such self-consciousness the ground for selfhood. Moreover, he regarded the "ego-pole" as a needless construction. I am not a self simply because I reflect on myself.

> The self is there for Dasein itself without reflection and without inner perception, before all reflection. Reflection in the sense of turning-back is only a mode of self-grasping, but not the mode of primary self-disclosing. (GP, 226)

To be a self means to be finite transcendence: Being-in-the-world. My self is not primarily revealed when I engage in theoretical self-reflection; it is revealed when reflected in the worldly beings with which I concern myself. Thus Dasein *finds itself* primarily and constantly *in the things* of the world in which it exists. "Each is that which he pursues and takes care of *[betreibt und besorgt]*" (GP, 226) My "self" is always my openness and involvement with beings in the world. "There is no need of a specific observing and spying on the I in order to have the self; in immediate, passionate, being-delivered over to the world itself the particular self of Dasein appears again." (GP, 227)

Often a person does not become self-aware until adolescence. Although they are not fully self-conscious, children do make judgments about good and evil, they do speak a language, and they make and do things. If such activities are those we associate with being a self, then each of us acts as a self before he becomes aware that he is a self. Worldly experience is possible only because we exist as temporal transcendence. I come to know myself not so much by abstract self-reflection as by taking on roles in the various social groups into which I am born. I learn about what it means to be human from the very activity of being human. But to be a human always means to be with other people. My parents, friends, associates, books, magazines, television, radio, and advertising—all of these offer me ways to understand who I am. For the most part, unfortunately, the self-interpretation offered to us by Others is misguided. We understand ourselves all too often, not as openness, but as things—egos in need of gratification and security. This inauthentic self-understanding arises because we are unable to bear the truth about what it means to be human—that we are finite and mortal Being-in-the-world. In the face of our mortality, we interpret ourselves as enduring substances. We become so lost in our worldly affairs that we never have time to wonder how it is that our experience is possible in the first place. As inauthentic, I fling myself into whatever possibility presents itself, for I have no sense of limitations. As authentic I disclose and accept my finitude and devote myself to my own possibilities. I let myself be the finite openness which I already am. I can take care of my bodily needs, concern myself with daily affairs, and make the attempt to let myself be who I am. Heidegger claims that I can be concerned in these ways because I *am* "care" *(Sorge)*. To be human is to be concerned both about worldly affairs and about my own existence. Self-consciousness arises only because we can be concerned about ourselves. Professor Schrag points out that "Kierkegaard describes the self as related to itself in the consciousness of an infinite passion. Heidegger describes Dasein as that being who is concerned for his Being, and who, in this concern, relates himself to his Being."[37] While Heidegger believed Kierkegaard's description of the self as self-conscious self-relatedness was overly laden with Hegelian overtones, he appropriated the Dane's idea that the human being is a self-concerned and finite individual. To this idea he added the insight that we can be self-concerned only because we are temporal transcendence.

From phenomenology, Heidegger learned that truth means unconcealment and that "to be" means to be revealed. Hence, he caught a glimpse of the inner link between Being and truth. In trying to understand how beings are revealed for human understanding, he recognized the inadequacy of prevailing accounts of the "relation" between subject and object. The conception of Dasein in *Being and Time* stems from Heidegger's attempt to exhibit the hidden relation among selfhood, Being, and truth. The sense of Being, that unity of the ways in which beings can be manifest, is intrinsically bound with the sense of the temporal Being of human Dasein. Again, to be a self is to be the temporal openness or truth in which beings can be revealed. To be a self in the most suitable way is to be wholly open to those possibilities which are uniquely one's own. The published portion of *Being and Time* is largely an account of what it means to be a self. Let us now examine this bold attempt at self-analysis.

PART FOUR: *Being and Time* as Self-Analysis.

Heidegger began work on *Being and Time* in the early 1920s, and he had to rush it to print in 1927 in order to satisfy the minister of education in Berlin. The minister had refused to allow Heidegger to replace Nicolai Hartmann at Marburg because Heidegger had not published enough. Although the manuscript of *Being and Time* was at first rejected as "insufficient," the minister eventually gave his approval. On the basis of this book, as well as on the basis of his growing fame as a lecturer, Heidegger was invited in 1928 by the

University of Freiburg to fill the chair of philosophy vacated by the retirement of Husserl.[38]

Being and Time altered the philosophical landscape in Europe. It is difficult for us to comprehend the shock waves it sent through the philosophical "establishment." In the course of an article very critical of Heidegger's political actions, Jürgen Habermas called it "the most significant philosophical event since Hegel's *Phenomenology*."[39] Although the book opened up new ways of thinking which simply bypassed many of the favored philosophical conundrums, it was unfinished. The published portion consists of only two-thirds of the first half of the projected version. In 1954 Heidegger reflected on the pressures to publish and concluded that "The fundamental flaw of the book *Being and Time* is perhaps that I ventured forth too far and too early." (US, 93/7) He tried to express ideas which could not be expressed in the vocabulary in which he had been trained. At the end of *Being and Time*, he acknowledges that he took a risk in writing the book: "One must seek a *way* of casting light on the fundamental question of ontology, and this is the way one must *go*. Whether this is the *only* way or even the right one at all, can be decided only *after one has gone along it*." (SZ, 437/487)

At first, few took seriously Heidegger's claim that his book sought to answer the question of the sense of Being, for the published portion is devoted almost entirely to the analysis of the sense of *human* Being. Small wonder that Husserl viewed it as a work of philosophical anthropology and others regarded it as an elaboration of Kierkegaard's "existentialism."[40] Thomas J. Sheehan reminds us that Heidegger contributed to the confusion about the book's purpose by shortening the crucial phrase "the question of the sense of Being" to "The question of Being" *(die Seinsfrage)*.[41] This helped give the impression that *Being and Time* was a metaphysical treatise. In fact, the book aimed more to demonstrate the conditions necessary for the possibility of metaphysics. To inquire into the "sense" of Being is to ask about the source of the unity which governs the various ways beings can be revealed. The sense of Being is determined by self-generating temporality. Temporality opens up the horizons in which beings can manifest themselves in various ways. Since we, ourselves, exist as temporality, the inquiry into the sense of Being must begin with an inquiry into the sense of *human* Being. *Being and Time* is a "self-analysis" not only because it investigates the conditions necessary for the possibility of being a self, but also because the reader is investigating himself, not some alien object.[42] The reader is investigating the existential-ontological features of human Dasein of which he is an example.

Dasein is characterized by two fundamental traits. First, the essence of Dasein is its existence. Things merely *are*; we are said to *exist* because we hold open the temporal horizons in which beings can be manifest. As temporal existence we are always in the process of becoming; we are always an issue to be decided. It has been pointed out on many occasions that Heidegger probably took the idea of "existence" from Kierkegaard, but he used the idea in ways which the Dane did not. The second trait of Dasein is called "mineness" *(Jemeinigkeit)*; human existence is always personalized. Like Kierkegaard, Heidegger insisted that there is no abstract, universal ego; each human life is a project which must be taken over by a particular human being. The idea of existence represents Heidegger's *ontological* interest: beings can be manifest only insofar as we exist. The idea of mineness represents his *dramatic* interest: we can choose to be this temporal-historical openness in an authentic or inauthentic way. The concept of human Dasein unites the ontological and dramatic elements intrinsic to all human life.

One can read about Dasein as if one were reading an account of the ontology of a natural object. This approach lets the reader distance himself from the text and forces it to conform to his own need for security. He makes the text conform to his sense of what a philosophical analysis is supposed to be. To approach *Being and Time* in this way may bring the reader some measure of conceptual understanding; it may permit him to enrich his philosophical vocabulary; it may even promote his career. *But it will bring him no change.* Learning means venturing to let things show themselves in new ways. Making such a venture with respect to human existence means putting one's present way of life on the line. The effort to disclose the truth requires courage to face the possibility of error. It is most difficult to accept that one has been wrong, especially if that error has involved concealment of the truth.

> The courage for error does not only mean courage to bear it, but much more: courage to admit it, i.e., this courage is for the inner freeing of the genuine self for being able to hear and learn, the courage for analytical dialogue *[Auseinandersetzung]*.
>
> *Not only in the field of scientific research, but in every possible kind of human existence, the individual is always only what he demands of himself, or can demand.* (L, 18)

To read *Being and Time* appropriately requires that the reader struggle to understand himself and, thus, to *exist* appropriately. This struggle leads one to undertake a voyage which may lead to a dramatic change in self-understanding. Because the book demands that the reader undergo for himself the self-disclosure traced in its pages, *Being and Time* resembles other philosophical works such as Descartes' *Meditations*, Spinoza's *Ethics*, and Plato's *Dialogues*. All these works are designed to provoke a change in their readers. *Being and Time* traced for readers in the early twentieth century what Hegel's *Phenomeonology* traced for readers in the early nineteenth century: an outline of the path to self-discovery. It is true that *Being and Time* never says that the reader should choose to be authentic. To have said this would have meant the end of existential describing and the beginning of existentiell prescribing. Surely it is a careless reader, however, who fails to notice the exhortative dimension in this book.

Like Nietzsche's *Thus Spoke Zarathustra, Being and Time* is a book "for all and none." It is for all because it describes the ontological structure of human existence; it was for none since few of its readers were prepared to understand it, especially in light of its forbidding complexity and its novel concepts. Perhaps Heidegger wrote in this way to demonstrate to his skeptical colleagues that dramatic themes such as authentic Being-towards-death were compatible with "rigorous" philosophy. What he said in 1925 about the reception of Kant's first *Critique* is applicable to the reception of *Being and Time* in 1927:

> Contemporaries stood completely helpless before the work. It was far beyond all current philosophical literature through the rank of its questioning, the rigor of the formulation of its concepts, the

novelty of its language, and the extensive design of its problematic. (PIK, 9)

Kant's thinking significantly affected *Being and Time*. His notion of "transcendental knowledge" is analogous to Heidegger's notion of "pre-ontological understanding of Being." Just as for Kant an object can be experienced and known only if it is organized according to the categories of the human understanding, so, too, for Heidegger a being can manifest itself for understanding only within the temporal horizons opened up in Dasein's transcendence. Heidegger claims that Kant's first *Critique* already suggested that the modes of time determine the categories of the understanding. Kant, however, restricted his analysis to the self as scientific knower, as the ego capable of accompanying all its representations with the "I think." Heidegger surpassed Kant by adding the concept of world, the question of the sense of Being, the notion that existence is essentially historical, and the idea that beings manifest themselves according to how the individual chooses to be temporal transcendence.

Heidegger's phenomenological analysis of Dasein involves three stages: reduction, destruction, and construction. Reduction brings attention back from investigating particular beings "to the understanding of the Being of beings." (GP, 29) The analysis of Dasein is ontological, not anthropological. Destruction is the necessary dismantling of traditional concepts which block access to Dasein's Being. Construction is a form of interpretation made possible by our understanding *(Verstehen)*.

> In interpretation, understanding does not become something different. It becomes itself. Such interpretation is grounded existentially in understanding; the latter does not arise from the former. Nor is interpretation the acquiring of information about what is understood; it is rather the working-out of possibilities projected in understanding. (SZ, 148/188-189)

Every time I do anything, I am "working out possibilities projected in understanding." To say that understanding "projects" possibilities means that it reveals the Being of beings. For example, understanding reveals that a doorknob, a car, and a telephone all *are* handy *(zuhanden)* as tools or instruments. Using the telephone presupposes that I have already projected it upon—understood it in terms of—its Being as a tool. Thus "interpretation must already have understood what is to be interpreted." (SZ, 152/194) We interpret things in everyday life long before we learn how to interpret things theoretically. Phenomenology is a unique kind of interpretation because its primary "object" is not a being, but Being. The problem is that

> Being is not as accessible as beings; we do not simply find it before us, but it must—as will be shown—presently be brought into view in a free project *[Entwurf]*. This projecting of the pre-given being on its Being and its structure we characterize as *phenomenological construction.* (GP, 29-30)

Being, the real "phenomenon" of phenomenology, conceals itself so that beings can be revealed. For example, for a being *to be* a tool means for it to manifest itself as useful or handy. I know a hammer *is* a tool when I use it to pound home a nail. But when hammering away, I don't notice the manifestness (Being) of the hammer. My attention is turned away from handiness (Being) and toward the task I am involved with. Only when the tool breaks down or functions awry (as when I smash my thumb with the hammer) do I notice that the tool *was* something handy but now *is* something useless (or the cause of pain!). Although the Being of the tool has to be manifest if I am to use the tool as a tool, the Being of the tool is also concealed. I simply do not notice that the tool (or anything else) is manifest.

The foregoing discussion of the Being of the tool is an interpretation or construction which describes *how* a particular kind of being *is* (present, manifest). I already know what tools are; I have used them. By interpreting them *theoretically*, I make explicit the anticipatory ("pre-ontological") understanding which enables me to interpret (use) them *practically*. We disclose the Being of a thing theoretically by examining its traits and deciding how to describe the way in which it and its traits appear. The traits we examine are chosen according to some more or less well-defined pre-ontological understanding of what the thing is. Without this anticipatory understanding, the being could not be present as an object for interpretation. To construct an interpretation is to engage in the hermeneutical enterprise of revealing in ever greater depth the understanding which we always bring with us in advance. Since understanding allows beings to be manifest, clarification of understanding allows them to be revealed more and more adequately. The words of the interpretation provide a kind of invisible frame in which the thing can be unveiled. We are all familiar with how a timely explanation can suddenly allow things to appear in a new way. In such an event, we do not notice the words which make this revelation possible; we notice what is revealed. Words are primordial "phenomena." Words let beings be revealed precisely because the words conceal themselves in pointing to the beings. When we speak clumsily, or when words "get in the way," our attention is drawn to the words themselves— so no revealing takes place. Degraded language conceals as much or more as it reveals. The language of the poet or thinker unveils beings in a new way. With the idea that language is the self-concealing realm in which beings can be manifest, Heidegger anticipates his later characterization of language as the "house of Being."

It is particularly difficult to interpret our own Being, since we are not like other beings. To repeat: we exist as the temporal-historical "clearing" *(Lichtung)* in which beings (including ourselves) can be manifest.

> When we talk in an ontically figurative way of the *lumen naturale* in man, we have in mind nothing other than the existential-onto-logical structure of this entity [being] that it *is* in such a way as to be its "there." To say that it is "illuminated" *["erleuchtet"]* means that...it is cleared *[gelichtet]* in itself, not through any other entity [being], but in such a way that it *is* itself the clearing. (SZ, 133/ 171)

This passage can give the impression that Dasein understands things by casting a kind of mental light on them. The phenomenological notion of the "intending ray" of conscious is influenced by what has been called "light metaphysics." According to Heidegger, however, transcendence is ontologically prior to intentionality. For there to be an intending ray or an object to be intended, there must be a "clearing" in which these phenomena can manifest themselves. Heidegger was later to insist that by "clearing" he meant not "lighting" but "lightening," in the sense of making less heavy, clearing away, making room. Only when there is such a clearing can light (illumination) and darkness be experienced. This clearing is not a thing, but no-thingness: the absence needed for beings to be present.

To interpret Dasein's Being, the interpretor must inquire into the conditions necessary for the possibility of interpreting. To be human means to interpret self and world. The analysis of Dasein is, therefore, the interpretation of interpretation, or the hermeneutics of hermeneutics.[43] Just as we have an anticipatory understanding of what things are, we also understand who *we* are. Analysis of Dasein increases this self-understanding. Although this enterprise involves a kind of circle, it is not a vicious one. The right way to enter the circle is by a leap, "so that even at the start of the analysis of Dasein we make sure that we have a full view of Dasein's circular Being." (SZ, 315/363) Later, we shall see that our circular Being is connected with our temporality.

To say that we must leap into the hermeneutical circle reminds us that *Being and Time* is only the formal expression of a journey we ourselves must make. If we do not try to deepen our own self-understanding, Heidegger's words will not reveal much. Any effort at self-interpretation is risky because we might discover that some cherished belief is groundless or outmoded. *Being and Time* is, in part, Heidegger's expression of what he understood about human existence at that point in his life. Just as I gradually learn to understand myself in light of my own experience instead of in terms of parental expectations, so, too, Heidegger's work demonstrates that man has learned to understand himself more directly instead of in terms of traditional philosophic or religious views. To become free from traditional prejudices means "to ground philosophy from itself, insofar as it is a work of the freedom of man." (GP, 16) Because human freedom is limited, however, Heidegger's analysis of Dasein necessarily involves presuppositions. Instead of presupposing that man is a thinking ego, Heidegger presupposes that man is openness for Being and that thinking is just one way in which to be open. More fundamental than theoretical reflection is everyday life. His analysis of everyday life requires certain pre-suppositions which he calls fore-having, fore-sight, and fore-conception. Taken together, these presuppositions constitute the hermeneutical situation of the analysis of Dasein.

The fore-having of Dasein-analysis is the everyday life which each of us leads prior to any reflection about who we are. Precisely because everday life is so "common," most philosophers—burdened with ideas about what human beings *should* be—have paid little attention to it. According to Heidegger, however, everyday life is essential to human Dasein. The thinking so esteemed by philosophers always takes place in the context of everday life. To guide his interpretation of the phenomenon of everyday life, Heidegger adopts the fore-sight of the idea of "existence," an idea derived from his own self-understanding as it was mediated by thinkers such as Aristotle, Luther, Kierkegaard, and Nietzsche. That he has high hopes for his analysis of human Dasein can be seen when he asks whether his interpretation will be the first one to let Dasein "put itself into words," so that each Dasein may decide whether the analysis is adequate. (SZ, 314-315/362)

Finally, Heidegger posits a fore-conception based on the other two elements of the hermeneutical situation. This fore-conception, "Being-in-the-world" *(In-der-welt-sein),* provides a way of conceiving what fore-having and fore-sight bring into view. The fore-conception aims to interpret everyday existence without resorting to the dualistic notions that plague modern philosophy. John Sallis has summarized Heidegger's hermeneutical situation:

> Heidegger's project is then a projection from the fore-having based upon the pre-ontological understanding of Being as manifest in the horizon of everydayness. From this fore-having arises the fore-sight provided by the idea of existence, and from the latter arises, in turn, the fore-conception of the Being of Dasein as Being-in-the-world. Together these three items provide the essential moments of the interpretative projection, the articulation of which constitutes the existential analytic of Dasein.[44]

This hermeneutical situation is valid only for Division One of *Being and Time.* Division One is a "preparatory analysis" of Dasein's inauthentic everydayness. Division One explains that Dasein opens up a world in which things, Others, and Dasein itself can be revealed as beings with which Dasein can be concerned. But this world-disclosure is usually accomplished according to an average interpretation of things, Others, and self. Dasein has an intrinsic tendency to conceal its own finitude and the Being of other beings. Division One of *Being and Time* concludes that the Being of Dasein is care, whose structural elements are existence, facticity, and falling. Division Two of that book is structured according to a new hermeneutical situation designed to reveal the temporality which is the sense of Dasein's Being as care. The fore-having of this new hermeneutical situation is care; the fore-sight is not just existence but *authentic* existence; and the fore-conception is temporality as the horizon of Being. In Division Two we learn that the account of inauthentic everydayness does not reveal Dasein in its unity and wholeness; that is, in its authenticity. We are then told that Dasein can become authentic only by accepting its finitude, only by resolutely accepting its Being-towards death. As resolute, Dasein lets itself be temporal transcendence in the most appropriate way. Temporality turns out to be the sense of Dasein's Being because the three dimensions of temporality (future, past, present) unify and make possible the three moments of care (existence, facticity, falling). Division Two also suggests that temporality is the sense of Being as such since temporality constitutes the hidden horizons in which beings can manifest themselves in various ways. The following three chapters describe how inauthenticity, authenticity, and temporality are depicted in *Being and Time*.

A major theme of *Being and Time* is that a genuine understanding of Being is possible only if the individual chooses to accept his finitude. For the most part, we conceal that we exist as the disclosedness (truth) which lets beings be manifest. To be this disclosedness authentically requires a courageous struggle. An adequate theoretical understanding of what it means to be human must be rooted in a dramatic change in the self-understanding of the theoretician. Heidegger makes this point in a passage which discusses the relation between Being and Dasein's temporal disclosedness:

> If, however, 'there is' Being only insofar as truth 'is', and if the understanding of Being varies according to the kind of truth, then

truth which is primordial and authentic must guarantee the understanding of the Being of Dasein and of Being in general. (SZ, 316/364)

Being and Time uses voluntaristic language to describe Dasein's resolve to disclose its own mortality. At times Heidegger seems to say that if Dasein wills courageously enough, the truth will be revealed. But he also says that a change in self-understanding only occurs when our temporality generates itself in a new way. Such a change in temporality cannot be willed by any individual. The possibility for such a change announces itself unexpectedly in the mood of *Angst*. To be resolute means to let this change happen even though in that moment we become aware of the certainty of our death. To be irresolute (inauthentic) means to prevent the change from happening by fleeing into worldly distractions. In his later writings, Heidegger concluded that the conception of resoluteness in *Being and Time* contained voluntaristic elements which are incompatible with his mature concept of authenticity as releasement *(Gelassenheit)*.

In this chapter, I have explained that Heidegger united the ontological-theoretical theme with the dramatic-practical theme in the concept of Dasein. From his theological background and from readings in Kierkegaard, Nietzsche, Dilthey, and others, he concluded that authentic human existence means beings passionately involved in deciding *how* to be human. From phenomenology and Greek philosophy, he discovered that "to be" (Being) means to be revealed, and that "truth" means unconcealment. Kant's doctrine of temporality suggested to Heidegger that human temporality constitutes the openness (truth, disclosedness) in which beings can be revealed. This conception of the self as temporal openness stands in contrast to the traditional views of self as substance, subject, or self-consciousness. He argued that these views were either instances of self-objectification (self as substantial core), subjectivistic dualism (self as ego-subject), or one-sided subjectivism (self as self-consciousness). There are at least two reasons for his criticism of the concept of self as subject.

First, the idea of the worldless subject overlooks the fact that we are always *in* the world. As Dasein, we are the temporal "here"

(Da-) in which beings can be manifest *("-sein")*. We can interpret ourselves as subjects only because we hold open the temporal horizon in which such interpreting can occur. Second, the ego-subject appears to be abstract and emotionless—a mere shadow of a living person. Like Kierkegaard, Heidegger wanted to abandon philosophical abstractions and to express the nature of lived human existence. Although his major interest was the question of the sense of Being, the dramatic theme of authenticity is intrinsically connected with the ontological theme. We understand Being in one way when inauthentic, in another when authentic. Choosing authenticity is so difficult because it requires us to confront our mortality. In everyday life, we forget about our mortality. When that mortality threatens to manifest itself to us, we are inclined to flee into inauthenticity. Only by affirming and accepting mortality, however, do we become most fully what we are. The following chapter examines the relation between inauthenticity and everydayness.

CHAPTER TWO

The Inauthentic, Everyday Self

FOLLOWING THE phenomenological principle of returning "to the things themselves," *Being and Time* begins to analyze human existence at the level of everday life. The analysis orients itself around two questions which will be treated in the two parts of this chapter. The first question is: "who" inhabits the everyday world? The second question is: what kind of disclosedness belongs to everyday existence? An obvious answer to the first question is that I (ego) inhabit the everyday world. Heidegger claims, however, that interpreting oneself as an ego is a kind of self-objectification which conceals the fact that we are really finite openness. The everyday self is egoistical. Because we understand ourselves as separate objects in need of gratification and security, we tend to manipulate people and things. When this everyday egoism is intensified, we become inauthentic. When it is alleviated, we become authentic. Both inauthenticity and authenticity are modifications of the egoism or self-objectification which always characterizes our existence.

In answer to the second question, Heidegger says that inauthentic, everyday disclosedness reveals things at the superficial level of gossip, entertainment, and diversion. He uses the word "falling" to refer to our inescapable tendency to conceal the truth about ourselves and the world. Falling makes possible the egoism of everydayness. To illuminate the meaning of falling and inauthenticity, I draw a parallel between Bultmann's theological concept of sinfulness and Heidegger's ontological concept of falling. The analysis of inauthentic, everyday falling demonstrates that we usually disclose things egoistically and, hence, deficiently. Because even an inauthentic disclosure of something is a way of being *concerned* with it, however, Heidegger concludes that the Being of human Dasein is "care" *(Sorge)*. To care for something inauthentically would be to manipulate it for selfish purposes. To care for something authentically would be to let it manifest itself in its own way. Care includes three structural elements: existence, facticity, and falling. In concluding the chapter, I describe the complex structural parallel between these three elements and the three major elements of disclosedness: understanding, state-of-mind, and the "degree of Being-in-the-untruth."

PART ONE: Everydayness, Inauthenticity, and Egoism.

Upon a first reading, *Being and Time*'s discussion of everydayness strikes a familiar chord, especially for those familiar with descriptions of the inauthentic life of mass man in modern industrial society. Everydayness is supposedly just another word for inauthenticity. Inauthentic people live in accordance with the dictates of mass media, advertising, and consumerism. Authentic people, however, refuse to conform: they lead lives of their own choosing. Although these statements express Heidegger's meaning correctly in some respects, they distort it in others. To understand him correctly we must begin by distinguishing between everydayness and inauthenticity. Unfortunately, in *Being and Time* and in lectures read around the time that book was written, Heidegger himself does not always distinguish adequately between these two phenomena. It is not surprising, therefore, that his readers are often misled.

Everydayness refers to our usual tendency to conceal things, to regard them superficially, often accepting what "everyone" (*das Man,* "they") says about them. This tendency toward concealment is intrinsic to us; it cannot be escaped. Sometimes we become dominated by this drive to conceal; in these cases we become inauthentic. While in everyday life we have simply forgotten that we are really finite openness, in the mode of inauthenticity we desperately try to conceal the fact of our openness. Inauthenticity is flight from the revelation of our mortal freedom. Authenticity is resolute acceptance of that freedom. Heidegger remarks that

> *Authentic-Being-one's-Self* does not rest upon an exceptional condition of the subject, a condition that has been detached from the "they"; *it is rather an existentiell modification of the "they"—of the "they" as an essential existentiale.* (SZ, 130/168)

In this passage, I take the "they" to refer to everydayness which can be modified authentically or inauthentically. On the previous page, however, Heidegger says that

> The Self of everyday Dasein is the *they-self*, which we distinguigh from the *authentic Self*—that is, from the Self which has been taken hold of in its own way.... As they-self, the particular Dasein has been *dispersed* into the "they," and must first find itself. (SZ, 129/167)

Here, the "they" evidently refers to inauthenticity. Hence, everydayness and inauthenticity appear to be the same. Yet, later in *Being and Time*, we read that *"authentic* existence is not something which floats above falling everydayness; existentially, it is only a modified way in which such everydayness is seized upon." (SZ, 179/224) Still later we learn that "inauthenticity is based upon the possibility of authenticity." (SZ, 259/303) Taken together, these two passages say that authenticity is a modification of everydayness, and that inauthenticity is a modification of authenticity. If inauthenticity and everydayness were identical, authenticity would both be a modification of everydayness *and* that which makes everydayness possible. This, however, is impossible. I agree with Professor Rosales when he remarks that "Not only inauthentic existence is everyday. Everydayness is a structure of all existing; but in inauthenticity, it achieves total domination."[1] When Heidegger says that Dasein exists authentically, inauthentically, or else is "modally undifferentiated" (SZ, 53, 232/78, 275-276), he seems to mean that everydayness is the undifferentiated (average) kind of existence which can be modified inauthentically or authentically. Sometimes he emphasizes that everydayness is the horizon for both authenticity and inauthenticity: "This undifferentiated character of Dasein's everydayness is *not nothing*, but a positive phenomenal characteristic of this entity [being]. Out of this kind of Being—and back into it again—is all existing, such as it is." (SZ, 43/69) Heidegger reaffirms this view in his *Logik* lectures from 1925-26:

> For the most part, and this is important, Dasein holds itself neither in the mode of authenticity nor in that of an utter lostness, but in a remarkable indifference which again is not nothing but something positive: the averageness of Dasein, which we characterize as every-dayness and which is particularly hard to grasp categorically in its structure and its sense of Being. (L, 229-230)

In a lecture read about a year later, however, Heidegger seems to identify everydayness with inauthenticity.

> We understand ourselves in an everyday way...not authentically [*nicht eigentlich*] in the strict sense of the word, not steadfastly from the most proper [*eigensten*] and uttermost possibilities of our own [*eigenen*] existence, but inauthentically [*uneigentlich*]. We understand ourselves, to be sure, but such that we do not have ourselves for our own [*aber so, wie wir uns nicht zu eigen*], as we have lost ourselves in the everydayness of existing into things and men. Not authentically means: so that we are at bottom not *able* to be our-selves for our own. Yet this Being-lost has no negatively evaluated meaning but means something positive, something which belongs to Dasein itself. The average self-understanding of Dasein takes the self as in-authentic. This in-authentic self-understanding of Dasein signifies totally and absolutely not an impure self-understanding. Just the opposite: this everyday self-having with factically existing, passionate dealings with things can be very pure indeed, whereas all extravagant burrowing into the soul can be in the highest degree impure, or even eccentric and pathological. (GP, 228)

Despite these inconsistencies, I am convinced that we can make sense of *Being and Time* only if we see that inauthenticity involves a deliberate choice to conceal the truth, while everydayness is to a large extent unavoidable and necessary. Even though we are essentially openness, this openness tends to close itself off. Heidegger calls this dynamic tendency toward concealment "falling." Since falling is essential to our existence, the authentic individual must accept that his authenticity is intrinsically limited. It is impossible for a human being to become completely open and empty. We are mortals, not gods. Our everyday egoism is tenacious. Keeping in mind the distinction between inauthenticity and everydayness, let us consider in more detail why the concept of everydayness is best understood as egoism.

Being and Time's analysis of Dasein as Being-in-the-world begins by asking: "who" is the self in everyday life? The obvious answer is "I." Heidegger qualifies this answer by saying:

> Perhaps when Dasein addresses itself in the way which is closest to itself, it always says "I am this entity [being]," and in the long run says this loudest when it is 'not' this entity [being]. Dasein is in each case mine, and this is its constitution; but what if this should be the very reason why, proximally and for the most part, Dasein *is not itself*? (SZ, 115-116/151)

When I am "closest to myself," or authentic, I resolve to be the finite openness which I already am. Here, "I" refers to that openness. When I am inauthentic, however, I try not to be open. Here, "I" refers to something solid and closed: the ego. Inauthenticity is an intensification of everyday egoism; authenticity is a diminution of it. In the passage cited above, Heidegger suggests that the fact that I can choose how to exist is the reason why, for the most part, I am not myself. By "myself" here, he means myself as authentic openness. For the most part I am this openness only in a deficient, average, everyday way. This average way is egoism. The two major aspects of egoism, self-objectification and selfishness, are manifestations of the two fundamental features of Dasein, existence and mineness. In everyday existence, I understand myself as an object or thing (ego). I am able to understand myself in this deficient way because my existence is mine to understand as I choose. For the most part, I simply understand myself in the way acceptable to my culture.

It is natural for us to objectify ourselves since we live in a world of objects. Theories about the self as soul, substance, or subject make the same mistake we often do in everyday life: they interpret the human being with inappropriate categories. Heidegger admits that our bodies share properties with objects, but he insists that our

existence differs from the Being of objects. We are embodied openness or emptiness. By understanding ourselves as objects, even as
conscious ones (subjects), we conceal the truth about ourselves.
This tendency toward self-concealment, which Heidegger calls
"falling" *(Fallen)*, is intrinsic to us.

The egoism or self-objectification of everyday life necessarily
arises because of our tendency toward concealment. My *decision*
for authenticity or inauthenticity is always an alteration of this
abiding egoism. For the most part, I understand myself according
to the expectations of the "they," *(das Man)*:

> We take pleasure and enjoy ourselves as *they* take pleasure; we read,
> see, and judge about literature and art as *they* see and judge; like-
> wise, we shrink back from the 'great mass' as *they* shrink back; we
> find 'shocking' what *they* find shocking. The "they," which is no-
> thing definite, and which all are, though not as the sum, prescribes
> the kind of Being of everydayness. (SZ, 126-127/164)

The "they" is nothing definite since it differs somewhat for each
person. Each of us, having become oblivious to the fact that we are
mortal and free, lets himself be guided by the judgments and attitudes of others. Each of us, moreover, is the "they" insofar as we
glibly pass along ideas and opinions which we have not really made
our own. The "they" has only as much power as I give to it. It is
not a group of people but a way in which individuals *exist*. We can
be so affected by others because we are always more or less open to
them. We inhabit overlapping worlds. The philosophical issue of
whether there are "other minds" besides mine is a psuedo-problem.
The real problem is learning to differentiate ourselves from others.
We resist the process of individuation, however, because it demands
that we accept our freedom and mortality. It is far less threatening
to drift along with "everyone" else. In so drifting, however, we do
not think of ourselves as members of some vast herd: we think of
ourselves as individuals. How is it possible that we think ourselves
to be free and individuated while we usually conform to social
roles and expectations?

To answer this question, we need to examine briefly the origin of
the everyday notion of "individuality" or "selfhood." Because we

have such a strong craving for gratification and security, we easily assume that the real "self" is the rational ego which shows us ways to manipulate the world in gratifying ways. Our parents and friends help teach us to think and act in these ways, so we assume that such behavior is consistent with being a person. We are also taught, however, that we should not be selfish or use other people for our own ends. In the contemporary world, however, in which the ideals of acquisitiveness and self-gratification have become political ideologies,[2] the ideal of selflessness is regarded as somewhat naive. The everyday view that happiness lies in gratification of desires, of course, is not peculiar to modern Western society. Plato was aware of the same attitude in Athens when he asserted that a life led in the service of desire is a life of slavery. Desire is insatiable; it demands more and more. Aristotle, too, pointed out that the best human life cannot be based on *having* things, whether they be food and sex, or fame and wealth, but on *being* fully human. It is unwise to let one's well-being depend on things which can be taken away. The highest form of life is *theoria*, in which the person exercises his specifically human capacity of being aware of the structures of reality. Heidegger agrees with Arisotle that we are truest to our existence when we are open to the world. He also maintains that our essential openness is more fundamental than the desires which manifest themselves in that openness. The real "I" is this temporal openness, not the manipulative ego which serves our cravings.

Because the ego's role is to provide security from pain and death, it cannot admit its mortality. We usually avoid talking about death because we prefer to think of ourselves as enduring objects. We want our egos to become stronger and more solid so that we can more effectively conceal our emptiness. Unfortunately, however, only in letting ourselves acknowledge and become this emptiness can we love ourselves and Others. Our efforts to love in everyday life are usually tinged with paranoia because we feel threatened by the Other. Our natural tendency to regard ourselves as objects is reinforced by our aversion to our mortality and by the fact that others treat us and themselves as objects. The more solid our egos become, the more isolated and separate we feel from the world. We see things primarily through the perspective of whether they are potentially threatening or gratifying. This everyday egoism, which when intensified becomes inauthenticity, is an unavoidable characteristic of human life. It is the source of tremendous suffering. As we shall see later on, the Bible describes the origin of this egoism as the "original sin" of Adam and Eve. The harder we try to compel others and events to meet our expectations or gratify our desires, the more we suffer. Yet we are taught that being an individual means being able to get what we want.

Erich Fromm has argued persuasively that my ideal of "individuality," along with most of my attitudes, feelings, and even desires, are learned from Others. Fromm points out that I easily attach the word "my" to judgments and values which appeal to me, in part because they are expressed by people whom I admire and from whom I would like to get recognition.[3] By learning to think and act in ways appealing to my peers, I gain security and identity: I am one of "them." Because I have the intrinsic motivation to choose to be myself in the most appropriate way, however, I find that I am not content to be just a carbon-copy of the others. Since genuine individuation requires that I confront and accept my mortal openness, I find it easier to be a "unique individual" by giving my own "flair" to the ideas which I have taken from the Others. The process of individuation involves peeling off the opaque layers of ego which act as a screen between my openness and Others. This process leads to anxiety, however, since there is "nothing" (openness) at the bottom of all those layers. The everyday self is something like an onion—each has many layers—but the everyday self both wants and doesn't want to be peeled.

We all know that our egos protect us from the truth about ourselves and prevent us from being open to the stressful situations of everyday life. When someone begins to peel off some of our protective layers, we become defensive. We become critical of the Other, or project hostile characteristics on him. We withdraw, become sullen, build fences, run away. A primary but very subtle form of such defensiveness takes the form of talking to ourselves. Very often we assume that this voice is the expression of the "real me." In fact, however, the voice belongs to the ego. The ego chatters on to reassure itself that the situation is in control and to assure that it remains in control. By constantly talking to ourselves, we retreat into the bulwark of our interior "reality," while the "external" world remains threatening and separate. In conversation, for example, we can become so engrossed in figuring out what we want to say next, that we miss what our partner is saying.

Everyday egoism can lead to a Faustian drive to power. For the most part, however, we are unaware of our egoism. We fail to recognize how much we manipulate others. We take it for granted that our way of looking at things, our needs and opinions, are the most important things in the world. We think that we understand ourselves and the world pretty well. In fact, however, we try to ignore or repress things which threaten our usual self-understanding. We cooperate in this effective, and often subtle, form of concealment. In everyday life

> Every kind of priority gets noiselessly suppressed. Overnight, everything that is primordial gets glossed over as something that has long been well-known. Everything gained by a struggle becomes just something to be manipulated. Every secret loses its force. (SZ, 127/165)

Because we are necessarily inclined to self-concealment and self-objectification, egoism cannot be done away with by "more advanced stages of human culture." (SZ, 176/220) In fact, so-called advanced cultures have elevated the art of self-deception to its highest level as "mass culture," criticized so well by Kierkegaard in *The Present Age*.[4] Advertising, mass media, and consumerism lead to what Todd Gitlin has called the "society of the spectacle."

> The spectacle is the continuously produced and therefore continuously evolving psuedo-reality, predominantly visual, which each individual encounters, inhabits and accepts as public and official *reality*, thereby denying as much as is possible, the daily private reality of exploitation, pain, suffering and inauthenticity he or she experiences.[5]

In *Being and Time* Heidegger presumes that mass culture, the contemporary form of everydayness, is made possible and sustained by individuals who choose to exist in the way promoted by it. According to a social critic such as Marx, mass culture is a product of late capitalism designed to keep peoples' minds off the real source of their unhappiness: an exploitative economic system. Supposedly, people are driven to egoism because they live in a competitive society which treats everything and everyone as an object or commodity. Social critics have often accused Heidegger of "mystifying" the truth by saying that egoism and alienation result from lack of individual courage, or from "original sin" (falling). In his later writings, he no longer said that inauthenticity happens because people have the tendency to conceal the truth about their mortality and freedom. Instead, he said it is our destiny to inhabit a world where everything appears to be an object for economic exploitation. In a world dominated by exchange-relations, it becomes very difficult for individuals to be "authentic."

Everydayness, then, is the egoism whose two main traits are self-objectification and selfishness. Egoism is unavoidable. Because I tend to conceal my Being, I tend to interpret myself as a thing. I encourage this tendency because I find it difficult to accept my finitude and shoulder the responsibility of freedom. In seeking security and gratification, I often regard people and things as objects to be manipulated. This selfishness is the ordinary way in which I try to make myself "mine." Inauthenticity intensifies everyday egoism; authenticity alleviates it. Authenticity is "always accomplished as a clearing-away of concealments and obscurities, as a breaking up of the disguises with which Dasein bars its own way." (SZ, 129/167) The term "egoism," which Heidegger does not use, has moral connotations he would not want associated with his analysis of everydayness. That analysis has ontological, not ethical, motives. He could hardly deny, however, that self-ignorance and selfishness have long been regarded as the cause of moral evil. *Being and Time* discloses the existential conditions necessary for the possibility of evil.

The answer to Heidegger's first question, "who" is in the everyday world, is the everyday egoist who discloses the world much like everyone else: as a world of objects to be manipulated to gain pleasure and avoid pain and death. This answer leads to the second question about how this everyday disclosedness is possible.

PART TWO: Disclosedness, Care, and Falling.

Chapter Five of *Being and Time*, titled "Being-in as such," claims to analyze the nature of Dasein's *everyday* disclosedness. In my view, however, it analyzes Dasein's *inauthentic* disclosedness. The analysis of disclosedness reveals the same confusion about the relation between everydayness and inauthenticity that we have already mentioned. The chapter is divided into two parts, the first of which Heidegger calls "A. The existential constitution of the 'there'," the second he calls "B. The everyday Being of the 'there,' and the falling of Dasein." His methodology in this chapter differs from that used in earlier analyses; for example, the analysis of the "worldhood of the 'world.'" There he began with a consideration of the activity of the cobbler in his shop (world) and drew out the structures of worldhood which manifested themselves in that everyday world. Here, in Section A, he begins with a description of the three major aspects of disclosedness: understanding *(Verstehen)*, state-of-mind *(Befindlichkeit)*, and discourse *(Rede)*. In Section B he then tries to show how these a priori structures can be discovered at work in what he calls "everyday" disclosedness. We expect, of course, to find discussions of understanding, state-of-mind, and discourse in their "average" or everyday mode. Instead, we find discussions of "idle talk" *(Gerede)*, "curiosity" *(Neugier)*, and "ambiguity" *(Zweideutigkeit)*. I discuss the relation between these phenomena and the structures of disclosedness later on. In reading Section B, I find that Heidegger is speaking not about average disclosedness but about *inauthentic* disclosedness. The self-destructive egoism which he describes, building up to a crescendo in his remarkable description of the "falling of Dasein," is clearly not an average, undifferentiated phenomena but an intensification and modification of everyday egoism.

His analysis of disclosedness intends to explain the conditions necessary for the possibility of existing in a world, not the conditions necessary for a worldless subject to know an external object. Theoretical knowing is only a specialized version of something more fundamental—our everyday understanding of the world. Understanding the world means knowing how to get around in it. In everyday life there is no gap between mind and body, theory and practice. Knowing how to drive means being able to take my car downtown. Everyday life is always purposive; we find ourselves in a world of possibilities, some threatening, others appealing. The world appears to be either for us or against us because we are only open to it through the narrow perspective of egoism. There is a danger, of course, in speaking as if the world were something separate from, or facing, us. Such talk is essentially dualistic. In fact, we *are* the world in the sense of the openness or clearing in which beings can manifest themselves. As I understand my world, so I understand myself. If I see it as a group of objects, I see myself as another object. The more I understand myself as finite openness, the less I understand things and Others merely as objects for me to manipulate. Heidegger maintains that my worldly understanding is always colored by a mood. I do not behold the world as a set of pure possibilities or as a external object; instead, I always understand the world according to a particular state-of-mind *(Befindlichkeit)* which lets it matter to me in one way or another. Moods and states-of-mind are not merely psychological "projections" on independently subsisting external objects. Instead, moods are an essential aspect of the openness in which beings can manifest themselves. Different moods let beings be revealed in different ways. No single mood can let beings appear in all their possibilities. When I am in love, things really do seem to *be* different than when I am angry or bored. Even a "detached" mood, such as the one which supposedly prevails in scientific research, is still a mood. When Heidegger says that we should become "masters" of our moods (SZ, 136/175), he admits that he speaks somewhat voluntaristically. Yet he adds that moods are ontologically prior to any willing or knowing. Mastering a mood means replacing it with another one. Such talk of mastery over moods, however, does not accord well with what Heidegger has to say about the distinctive mood of *Angst. Angst* discloses my mortality and nothingness; *Angst* reveals the uselessness of anything in the world for overcoming my own death. Inauthenticity refers to the attempt to "master" this mood by replacing it with the mood of fear, which is always directed at something in the world. Authenticity means letting *Angst* prevail with all its disclosive power. Extrapolating from this, we might say that we should seek not so much to master our moods as to acknowledge and accept them. Instead of yearning for a "happier" mood when disheartened, perhaps it would be more appropriate just to experience the sadness and to see how our experience of the Being of beings is affected thereby. If authenticity means being open for what *is*, then as authentic I must be open for the moods which are constantly coming upon me.

The third element of disclosedness, along with understanding and state-of-mind, is "discourse" *(Rede)*. When he wrote *Being and Time*, Heidegger had not yet developed an adequate interpretation of the nature of language. He spent much of the latter part of his life attempting to "hear" what language says to and through us. In the limited and provisional discussion of language in *Being and Time*, Heidegger uses the word "discourse" in a way analogous to his interpretation of the *"-logos"* of "phenomenology." *Logos* refers to the capacity to let something show itself. Human beings are embodiments of *Logos*. Hence, we are able to let beings show themselves through language. Because language is usually so shallow and worn-out, beings can only present themselves in limited ways, e.g., as objects for exploitation or as items for idle chatter *(Gerede)*. Heidegger's views on language were deeply affected by his early theological concerns. According to Holy Scripture, the Word speaks with healing and transforming efficacy for him who has ears to hear. According to *Being and Time*, the silent word of conscience summons us to authenticity, calls on us to understand ourselves in an ontologically appropriate way. But we can only hear this call if we are ready for it.

After he discusses the three primary elements of disclosedness in Section A of Chapter Five of *Being and Time*, Heidegger considers what he calls "everyday" disclosedness in Section B. Everyday disclosedness, which as described seems to be inauthentic, is characterized by idle talk, curiosity, and ambiguity. There is not an exact correspondence between these three phenomena and the three elements of disclosedness (understanding, state-of-mind, discourse). Idle talk apparently includes both understanding and state-of-mind. Curiosity is the kind of "sight" which guides inauthentic understanding. And ambiguity can be regarded as the degree of concealment operative in inauthentic disclosedness.

In his analysis of idle talk, Heidegger asserts that the true function of language is to let beings "be appropriated in a primordial manner." (SZ, 168/212) When not devoted to this task, language degenerates into gossip, rumor, and empty reflection. "Idle talk is the possibility of understanding everything without previously making the thing one's own. If this were done, idle talk would founder; and it already guards against such a danger." (SZ, 169/213) Idle talk is a primary instrument of self-deception. Although he wavers between describing the everyday and the inauthentic mode of idle talk, Heidegger makes clear that it is a fundamental aspect of disclosedness.

> This everyday way in which things have been interpreted is one into which Dasein has grown in the first instance, *with never a possibility of extrication*. In it, out of it, and against it, all genuine understanding, interpreting, and communicating, all re-discovering and appropriating anew, are performed. *In no case* is a Dasein, untouched and unseduced by this way in which things have been interpreted, set before the open country of a 'world-in-itself' so that it just beholds what it encounters. (SZ, 169/213—emphasis mine)

Idle talk is the everyday way of speaking and communicating which tends to look at things superficially and from the ego's narrow viewpoint. At times, Heidegger speaks as if idle talk is a *deliberate* way of concealing the truth. Such idle talk, however, would be an intensification of the everyday kind and would thus be inauthentic. For the most part, we cannot help but talk in a shallow manner. We necessarily incline away from the truth.

Curiosity is a perversion of the circumspection *(Umsicht)* directing our everyday dealings with things. When we are at work, our attention is absorbed by the tasks at hand. We may approach them without fresh vision, but we manage to keep ourselves more or less occupied with them. Our everyday activity is usually not affected by the intense desire for distraction and novelty which Heidegger calls curiosity. When the mood of *Angst* or anxiety strikes us, however, we often became very restless. The activities which usually keep our minds off the truth about our mortal freedom suddenly are no longer able to do so. As the revelation of our finitude presses closer, we have the choice of facing it or fleeing from it. If we flee, we choose to deny the truth and, hence, to be inauthentic. Restlessness is the manifestation of our anxiety. To ease our anxiety, we take flight into distraction and entertainment. We gorge ourselves with "experiences," using them as narcotics to dull the painful truth. In everyday life, this curiosity is moderated by the routines which in themselves conceal the truth.

Heidegger uses the word "ambiguity" to describe the way in which idle talk and curiosity conceal the truth. Idle talk in particular may be understood as analogous to ideology. A political ideology, which recommends that we organize society according to certain principles, offers a description of reality which both reveals and conceals that reality. If an ideology were simply and obviously a lie, people would not pay much attention to it. Ideologies are most effective if they contain some element of truth. Idle talk is the ideology of everydayness and inauthenticity. Mass media advertising is a clear example of such idle talk, but we make frequent use of it in our own conversations. The things we say are to some extent true, but what is important is how much is left *concealed*. Moreover, in the interest of maintaining our security about the way things are, we tend to trivialize ideas or incidents which ask us to think about things differently. "Idle talk and curiosity take care in their ambiguity to ensure that what is genuinely and newly created is out of date as soon as it emerges before the public." (SZ, 174/218) Ambiguity particularly affects our relations with Others. While pretending, or even trying, to be open to them, we are more often manipulative and egoistical.

> Everyone keeps his eye on the other first and next, watching how he will comport himself and what he will say in reply. Being-with-one-another in the "they" is by no means an indifferent side-by-side-ness in which everything has been settled, but rather an intent, ambiguous watching of one another, a secret and reciprocal listening-in. Under the mask of "for-one-another," an "against-one-another" is in play. (SZ, 175/219)

It seems to me that this passage describes inauthentic rather than everyday relations with one another, although there is no clear-cut demarcation between these two. Everyday life can move in and out of inauthenticity quite rapidly.

Idle talk, curiosity, and ambiguity result from falling, our intrinsic tendency toward concealment. "Falling reveals an *essential* ontological structure of Dasein itself. Far from determining its nocturnal side, it constitutes all Dasein's days in their everydayness." (SZ, 179/224) It is not easy to accept that we are constantly deceiving ourselves, repressing the truth, denying our own feelings. Although this self-deception is unavoidable, its power can be decreased. When we let the truth about ourselves be revealed, we experience a kind of release. The self-deceptive, egoistic life is burdensome. As authentic, we resolve to accept the fact that we are necessarily mortal and open (free). "Only where the most primordial necessity is binding, only there is the highest freedom possible." (PIK, 38) Because we are by nature ambiguous, however, the moment of authenticity does not last for long. The insight it offers, moreover, is always limited. Decisions made in light of the moment of truth can go astray, "for authentic understanding, no less than that which is inauthentic, *can* be either genuine or not genuine." (SZ, 146/186)

Before completing consideration of *Being and Time*'s account of falling, it will be helpful to examine its similarities to the Christian doctrine of sinfulness, particularly as expounded by Rudolf Bultmann. The word "falling" has obvious theological overtones, but Heidegger uses the term ontologically. He points out, however, that falling refers to the ontological condition necessary for the possibility of "original sin."

> Our existential-ontological interpretation makes no ontical assertion about the "corruption of human Nature," not because the necessary evidence is lacking [!], but because the problematic of this interpretation is *prior* to any assertion of corruption or incorruption. Falling is conceived ontologically as a kind of motion. Ontically, we have not decided whether man is "drunk with sin" .... But insofar as any faith or "world view" makes any such assertions, and if it asserts anything about Dasein as Being-in-the-world, it must come back to the existential structures which we have set forth, providing that its assertions are to make a claim to *conceptual* understanding. (SZ, 180/224)

Bultmann, who discussed these issues at length with Heidegger in the 1920s, offers an account of sinfulness which is clearly affected by Heidegger's ontological concept of falling. In an essay from 1932 Bultmann says that Paul does not view man as a conscious subject or a thinking ego. Human striving transcends the limited sphere of the subject or ego-consciousness.[6] Paul talks as if man wills under the domination of either "flesh" or "Spirit." Human existence is always at war with itself. The individual is concerned about his authenticity but "constantly fails to find it."[7] Life is uncanny because if we *will* to be authentic, we fail. We fail because, in trying to become authentic through our own efforts, we forget that we are not self-created, but creatures of God. Self-will is the root of all sin.

> Sin is man's wanting to dispose of his own existence, to raise claims for himself, to be like God. Inasmuch, then, as this "sin" brings "death," it becomes evident (1) that the man who wants to be himself loses himself; instead of the "I," "sin" becomes the subject...; and (2) that being a self nevertheless belongs to man, for in losing himself he dies...; but also that his self is not realized when he himself tries to lay hold of it by disposing of his existence, but only when he surrenders himself to the claim of God and exists from him. This would be "life" from him; then he would exist in his *authenticity*. It is precisely through his willing to be himself that man fails to find the authenticity he wills to achieve; and thus is the deceit of sin....[8]

In another essay written four years later, Bultmann interprets sin as *superbia*, man's will "to be himself by himself and for himself."[9] Bultmann asserts that as a creature, I am dependent on my Creator, God. Selfish action is guided by the mistaken notion that I am self-grounding. If my existence is a gift from God, I should exist in a way most appropriate to His intentions and in so doing give thanks for the gift of life. This submissive spirit is voiced by Jesus while He agonized in the Garden of Gethsemane: "My Father, if it be possible, let this cup pass from me; nevertheless, not as I will, but as thou wilt."[10] Just as Jesus bore his cross, so, too, the believing Christian must bear the sorrows of life. To avoid the suffering required to re-main true to one's convictions is to fall back into egoism:

> Were I to try to dispose of the gift of life as something I myself, by myself and for myself, had under my power, then I would break the bond of love and the love of the other would become a reproach to me. It is a universal human experience that no one wants to be indebt-ed to the other for his existence, but rather endeavours to seclude himself in the illusion that he exists by himself and for himself.[11]

It is for good reason that the greatest sin has long been regarded as pride.

Bultmann's talk about self-will is similar to Heidegger's idea that we fall into worldly activities because we think we can gain security on our own. Inauthentic acts result from the desire to be authen-tic. If we think we are truest to ourselves when we are swollen up with self importance, however, we are sadly mistaken. As inauthentic (Heidegger), we become dominated by our tendency toward conceal-ment. As sinful (Bultmann), we become dominated by the power of the flesh. As John's Gospel says, "men loved darkness rather than light."[12] In 1928 Bultmann remarked that

> When a man *commits himself to his fallenness*, he surrenders his authentic possibility.... Man is at all times called to decision, to risk himself. The world rejects such decision—and in the rejection it has already made the decision and has cut off its existence as a potentiality-to-be.[13]

As *authentic* we accept the summons of conscience to become as open as possible to the world. This opening-up always wants to hap-pen in us but cannot happen unless we agree to it. We must somehow cooperate in the process. When thus opened, we are freed from the burden of trying to do what others expect and free to undertake our own possibilities. As *faithful* we give ourselves up to God by accep-ting Jesus Christ as our saviour. This acceptance frees us from anxiety, guilt, and self-will and thus opens for us a new way of life. Instead of being nailed to the past, we are free for the future. Instead of being isolated egos, we are united with God and His Creation. By accepting our dependence on God, we receive a new mode of self-understanding: "when a man turns to the Lord the veil [over his mind] is removed."[14] The idea that redemption means turning away from ambition, selfishness, and greed is found throughout the New Testament, especially in those parables which tell us that "he who humbles himself will be exalted."[15] In Luke's Gospel we read: "If any man would come after me, let him deny himself and take up his cross daily and follow me. For whoever would save his life will lose it; and whoever loses his life for my sake, will save it."[16] Bultmann assures us that such acceptance is not easy, since

> to choose God means to let the world go and to let one's security go with it. There is nothing enticing about that! On the contrary, that demands a "hard saying," a "stumbling block" which terrifies because it is the end of man.... But just that end is *life*; to win back one's self as possibility, once again to be in the potentiality of being and to have a future.[17]

Despite the parallelism in their conceptions, however, Heidegger and Bultmann had different tasks. Heidegger's analysis of human existence is existential-ontological, not existentiell-ontical. In *Being and Time* he never specifies what existentiell (personal, specific) decisions are appropriate for an individual. Some people have concluded that he means, therefore, that one should "resolve on nothingness," i.e., become a nihilist; but they are wrong. He insists that the resolute individual is always open to a particular group of possibilities: his own. As authentic, the individual resolves to become open to these possibilities and thus to do what is necessary. Unlike the philosopher Heidegger, the theologian Bultmann is interested in leading people to make a choice for God. Although he uses philosophical insights to demythologize the New Testament, his aim is to make it a more powerful instrument for converting modern people. His interpretation of human existence is thus existentiell, not existential. Instead of being concerned to show the conditions necessary for the possibility of being Christian, he wants to show why one *should* be a Christian.

Although Heidegger's task was ontological, not theological, he was hardly disinterested in the effect of his words on his readers and listeners. He talked in a way which, even if only indirectly, summoned people to face the truth. In 1933-1934, of course, he abandoned any pretext of separating existential from existentiell concerns when he used his philosophical vocabulary in support of National Socialism. We do not have to resort to such an extreme example, however, to recognize that there is an exhortative (existentiell) dimension in Heidegger's approach to philosophy. Hans-Georg Gadamer, a student of Heidegger's in the 1920s, reports that his teacher's

> severe style of lecturing and the pointedness of his invective made it appear simply incredible when Heidegger described the world of the "they" and "idle chatter" with bitter acrimony and then added, "this is intended without any negative meaning." The existential seriousness that characterized Heidegger in his lectures seemed to suggest that the rejection of inauthenticity and the embracing of authenticity was the meaning of his doctrine. Against his will, then, he became a kind of philosopher of existence.[18]

With this comparison between Bultmann and Heidegger in mind, let us now return to our treatment of the falling in *Being and Time*. Heidegger claims that falling is a dynamic activity, not a static condition. His description of the movement of falling reminds us of a soul being dragged into the whirlpool of hell. The movement of falling is tempting, tranquillizing, alienating, self-entangling, and turbulent. Clearly, the kind of falling under discussion here is not average and everyday, but intense and inauthentic. We can be tempted by worldly affairs only because our "Being-in-the-world is in itself *tempting [versucherisch]*." (SZ, 177/221) We have an intrinsic tendency, to get involved in things which lead us away from what we should be doing. Not the Devil, but man's own Being is the source of his evil ways, i.e., his inauthentic behavior. Although lost in idle talk and curiosity, the ego often assumes that it is "leading and sustaining a genuine 'life'... for which everything is 'in the best of order' and all doors are open." (SZ, 177/222) I can be *tranquillized* by my self-deception until *Angst* arises to make me restless again. This restlessness spurs us to take the turbulent plunge *(Absturz)* into inauthenticity. Cast adrift on a stormy sea, we are driven from one episode to the next, hoping against hope that the next thing will provide security and peace. We become alienated from ourselves, treating ourselves as hard-driving machines designed to dominate the world, or becoming withdrawn into the realm of fantasy, delusion, and self-pity.

In authentic falling, we give in to the "throw" which always characterizes our existence. Analysis of the phenomenon of falling reveals

> that the thrownness which can obtrude itself upon Dasein in its state-of-mind has the character of throwing and of movement. Thrownness is neither a 'fact that is finished' nor a fact that is settled. Dasein's facticity is such that *as long as* it is what it is, Dasein remains in the throw, and is sucked into the turbulence of the "they's" inauthenticity. (SZ, 179/223)

For the most part, we forget about our mortal freedom by losing ourselves in the possibilities offered by the "they." When we are thus moving with the stream (the everyday interpretation of self and world), we are not even aware that we are moving away from ourselves. Although suffering from the problems brought on by everyday egoism, we think that basically everything is alright. If the mood of *Angst* breaks in on us, we deseprately look for rapids or white-water in the stream to absorb our attention. We are also able, however, to become aware that we are constantly moving away from the truth about ourselves. Even if we resolve to gain a footing in the stream-bed in order to become open to possibilities, however, we are inevitably pulled downstream again. With steadfast effort, we are not swept along so far or fast to self-deception. But there is never a point in human life when we have "achieved" the "state" of authenticity. Resoluteness must be repeated again and again.

In his interpretation of falling, Heidegger was influenced by Pascal, who anticipated Kierkegaard's philosophical interpretation of religious motifs. In his *Pensées*, Pascal spoke often of the desire of men "to be diverted from thinking of what they are."[19] He went on to say that men "have a secret instinct driving them to seek external diversion and occupation, and this is the result of their constant sense of wretchedness."[20] Heidegger used the term "falling" to express this secret "instinct," which involves both the tendency to interpret ourselves as immortal substances and the concomitant eagerness to be distracted by the things which surround us. According to Pascal, we are envious of the man who is king because he has an entire retinue devoted to the task of keeping him distracted and unaware of himself.[21] Although man is a creature filled with darkness, a weak reed, he is also a "thinking reed"; his nobility lies in the fact that he is aware of his own mortality.[22] In trying to conceal that fact, he acts basely. Pascal insisted, of course, that a man's anguish cannot be ended by his own efforts: only God's grace can liberate him from his blindness and attachment to things. On this issue, Heidegger parted company with Pascal.

On the basis of his analysis of Dasein's disclosedness, Heidegger defines Dasein as "Being-in-the-world which is falling and disclosed, thrown and projecting, and for which its ownmost potentiality-for-Being *[Seinkönnen]* is an issue, both in its Being alongside the 'world' and its Being-with Others." (SZ, 181/225) This definition, which is said to describe Dasein in its "average everydayness," supports my contention that everydayness differs from inauthenticity. A definition based on Dasein in its inauthenticity would have had to lay much more stress on the flight from truth. On the basis of this definition of everyday Dasein, Heidegger derives the three structural elements of care, Dasein's Being. This derivation is guided by his consideration of how the mood of *Angst* discloses that Being.

As already explained, *Angst* is the mood which causes us to flee into the intensified egoism of inauthentic everydayness. *Angst*, unlike fear, is not anxiety about some thing or other, but about "nothing": about our openness, emptiness, no-thingness. We become anxious because we are convinced that our security rests on solidity. If the ego is nothing solid, however, but merely a fabrication designed to conceal the truth, then we are without security. In the face of death, moreover, our schemes for securing a place for ourselves in the world are utterly useless. When we die, we leave the world altogether. It is extremely difficult to accept these harsh, but profound, truths. If we accept them, however, our lives undergo a significant change. We learn to be more open to our own possibilities and to the possibilities of Others. We learn that we feel most ourselves when we are taking care of things, nurturing our friends, and being open to our own needs. We also see that in everyday life, and even as inauthentic, we are also concerned about things, but primarily from our narrow, egoistical point of view. If we let the mood of *Angst* disclose our mortality, we discover that we are really not egos but care. The Being of Dasein is care: in being open for things, we care for them.

Care includes three elements: existence, facticity, and falling. In existing, I am usually out ahead of myself planning and preparing. As factical, I am thrown into a particular situation and endowed with limited possibilities. As falling, I am usually concealing the truth by becoming absorbed in worldly affairs. To each of these three elements of care there corresponds a dimension of temporality: future (existence), past (facticity), and present (falling). These temporal dimensions constitute my openness to beings. The future dimension opens up my possibilities so I can be concerned about how I shall become. The past dimension opens up my fate so I can take care that it unfolds appropriately. The present dimension lets beings be present so I can care for and use them. Temporality automatically structures my openness into a three-dimensional temporal realm in which I can be "care-ful." The three elements of my Being (care) are unified because the temporal dimensions which makes them possible are intrinsically self-unifying. Because temporality unifies care, it can be called the "sense" (unity) of care. Heidegger alludes to the temporal character of care when he defines it as "ahead-of-itself-Being-already-in-(the-world) as Being-alongside (entities encountered within-the-world)." (SZ, 192/237)

The word "Dasein" itself reflects the fact that our temporal disclosedness and care are intimately related. Dasein's Being (the "*-sein*" of "Dasein") is care. To be human means to be concerned about oneself and other beings. Caring takes place in the "here" (the "*Da-*" of "Dasein") opened up by temporal disclosedness. The more open or authentic I am, the more able I am to care for myself and Others. The stronger my care becomes, the more open I am to myself and Others. The reciprocity between care and disclosedness can be made clear by considering their structural elements. We recall that care is constituted by existence, facticity, and falling, while disclosedness includes understanding, state-of-mind, and discourse. Existence corresponds to understanding. I can exist, that is, I can act on my possibilities only because I understand them. Facticity corresponds to state-of-mind. Moods disclose my limitations and let things matter in determinate ways. Given this parallelism, it is interesting to learn that falling does *not* correspond to discourse. Heidegger does not note this discrepancy. I contend that the parallel between care and disclosedness can be completed by making falling the third element of disclosedness as well as of care. Discourse must be regarded as dependent on understanding and state-of-mind. Although *Being and Time* says that discourse is "equiprimordial" with understanding (projection) and state-of-mind (thrownness), it is in fact included in the latter two. W. F. von Herrmann notes that "The equiprimordiality of discourse with state-of-mind and understanding rests on the fact that thrown projection is in itself a signifying discourse."[23] Further:

> Discourse is indeed a fundamental existentiale; it articulates worldly Being-disclosed. It is always, however, already included in projection and thrownness.... Although thrownness, project, and discourse are equiprimordial, nevertheless, project and thrownness are more fundamental, because they characterize the fundamental structural articulation of human Being, within which the discoursing *[Reden]* of discourse *[Rede]* is first possible. But even so, project and thrownness are not what makes discourse possible; discourse is always given along with them.[24]

My contention that falling is the third element of disclosedness can be supported by examining the structures of inauthentic disclosedness. We recall that inauthentic disclosedness is composed of idle talk, curiosity, and ambiguity. Idle talk, we recall further, is the inauthentic mode of state-of-mind and understanding as well as of discourse. Curiosity refers to the frantic "sight" which guides inauthentic understanding. Ambiguity refers to the intense degree of concealment at work in inauthentic disclosedness. All disclosedness, which we might call "Being-in-the-truth," involves concealment, which we might call "Being-in-the-untruth." Falling, the third element of *care*, makes possible the intrinsic tendency toward concealment at work in all *disclosedness*. Because even authentic disclosedness involves concealment, it, too, is necessarily ambiguous to some extent. Falling, therefore, makes possible the Being-in-the-untruth (concealment) which characterizes all Being-in-the-truth (disclosedness). Falling is the dynamic tendency which seems to work against the other elements of care and disclosedness. With regard to care, falling leads me to neglect my possibilities (future) and fate (past) by letting me become too absorbed in everyday worldly affairs. With regard to disclosedness, falling tends to conceal what understanding and state-of-mind reveal. Falling and Being-in-the-untruth, therefore are on different "planes" than their structural counterparts. In the following diagram, which compares the elements of care and disclosedness, I show this difference by indenting the descriptions of falling and Being-in-the-untruth.

Disclosedness
1) *Understanding*
2) *State-of-Mind*
   (*Discourse*—included in the above two elements)
3) *Degree of Being-in-the-untruth*
   a) *Intense:* Here not only does concealment predominate, but Dasein conceals this concealment from itself. Intense self-concealment characterizes *inauthentic* disclosedness.
   b) *Less intense:* Here concealment predominates, but is not aggravated by the flight from *Angst* as it is in inauthenticity. This average degree of ambiguity characterizes *everyday* disclosedness.
   c) *Alleviated:* Here concealment remains, but Dasein is now aware of its tendency toward self-concealment. By accepting its finitude, Dasein struggles against the tendency toward concealment. The increased openess which results characterizes *authentic* disclosedness.

Care
1) *Existence*
2) *Facticity*
3) *Falling* (tendency toward concealment)
   a) *Intense:* Here Dasein is wholly absorbed in distractions designed to conceal its finitude. This condition is called *inauthenticity*.
   b) *Less intense:* Here Dasein is caught up in everyday affairs but is not in full flight from the truth about itself. This condition is called *everydayness*.
   c) *Alleviated:* Here Dasein is not so absorbed in the world that it forgets to care about itself and other beings as appropriately as possible. This condition is called *authenticity*.

In this chapter, we have seen that self-objectification and selfishness are major features of the self in everyday life.²⁵ Our intrinsic tendency toward concealment inevitably leads us to regard ourselves as ego-objects and to regard everything else from the standpoint of our narrow self-interest. Everyday egoism is the fundamental mode of existing. This egoism can be intensified (inauthenticty) or alleviated (authenticity), but never eliminated. As inauthentic, we flee into distractions to repress the revelation of our mortality and freedom. Even this reaction, however, shows that we necessarily *care* for ourselves, even if only deficiently. We can care for ourselves authentically by resolving to be the finite openness which we already are. In the following chapter, we learn more about authenticity as resolute Being-towards-death.

CHAPTER THREE

Authenticity as Resolute
Being-towards-Death

IN *Being and Time*, Heidegger wanted to prove that there is a direct relation between authentic existence and an authentic understanding of Being. Although influenced by Kierkegaard's idea of authenticity as resoluteness, he wanted to do more than repeat the Danish writer's existentiell analysis of human life. Because his major interest was in the question of the sense of Being, he sought to disclose the ontological-existential conditions necessary for the ontical-existentiell experience of a change in one's understanding of Being. In Part One of this chapter, I analyze the concept of anticipatory resoluteness as authentic Being-towards-death. In the next chapter, I explain how resolute anticipation of one's death means becoming more appropriately the temporality one already is. This change in temporality alters one's understanding of Being. Part Two of this chapter provides concrete examples to complement the abstract discussion of authentic Being-towards-death in *Being and Time*. Complete insight into authentic Being-towards-death, however, can follow only from an individual's own experience. Compared to such direct insight, all explanations are second-hand. I call on Plato's account of Socrates, the myth of the hero, and Nietzsche's idea of the Overman to show how the Western tradition supports the view that authenticity is resolute Being-towards-death. Heidegger's ontological concerns led him to conclude that previous interpretations of authenticity grasped implicitly what he wanted to make explicit: to understand authenti-

69

cally what it means to be requires that one resolve to be human authentically.

PART ONE: Anticipatory Resoluteness as Authentic Selfhood.

Heidegger's own existentiell interests sometimes color his existential analysis in *Being and Time*. Those people who suggest that his writings are free of personal interests suppose that he was super-human. In fact, he was a man whose own prejudices could not be totally suspended when he analyzed a phenomenon like authentic Being-towards-death. Some of his ideals are inevitably mirrored in his writings. He was part of the generation which viewed World War I as the culmination of the spiritual decline which had reduced Europeans to a "herd" of producers and consumers. Like many Germans, he was shaken by the slaughter of European youth between 1914 and 1918. He was determined, moreover, to help prevent Germany from sliding back into the conditions which had led to war, defeat, and humiliation. Although his political activism only began in 1933, he was already convinced in the 1920s that philosophy could demonstrate (if only indirectly) that his generation faced an inevitable *decision* about how to live in the modern world. His talk of authentic Being-towards-death appealed to those who had been changed by their experience in the trenches. Gadamer reports that in the Heidegger of the 1920s there was

> an existential passion, an emanation of intellectual concentration, that made everything which preceded it seem feeble.... One could actually recall the romantic furioso of Van Gogh, whose letters appeared at that time and made a deep impression on the young Heidegger. And in fact, those letters gave representative expression to the life-feeling of the epoch. Just as might have been the case in fifth-century Athens when the young, under the banner of the new sophistic and Socratic dialectic, vanquished all conventional forms of authority, law, and custom with radical new questions, so too the radicalism of Heidegger's inquiry produced in the German universities an intoxicating effect that left all moderation behind.[1]

Current conditions are no longer what they were in the 1920s, so *Being and Time* does not speak to its readers as it once did. Although historical contexts change, the problem of existing authentically does not. If approached in a way true to the text and to oneself, *Being and Time* retains its vigor for each generation. It is a mistake to say that historical factors so conditioned *Being and Time* that it is now only of interest to historians of philosophy. Such an attitude tries to defuse the threat the book poses to the reader's comfortable self-understanding.

Division One of *Being and Time* explains that as care, we are always concerned about deciding who we are becoming and are thus always "ahead of ourselves." As "potentiality-for-Being" *(Seinkönnen)*, we are never complete but always in the process of becoming. If I am always becoming, however, will any attempt at self-understanding be complete? Heidegger says that self-understanding is possible because we can exist in a way which unifies our past, present, and future. He calls this self-gathering the "anticipation" *(Vorlaufen)* of one's death. Anticipation is an existential-ontological possibility requiring verification. "Resoluteness" is the existentiell-ontical verification that anticipation of one's death is possible. Authentic existence is resolute anticipation of one's own death. With this conception, Heidegger sided with those who wanted to re-establish the values of individuality, courage, and candor in a culture which seemed to worship conformity, cowardice, and mendacity.

In *Being and Time* Heidegger informs us that he arrives at the idea of anticipatory resoluteness by assessing Division One's analysis of Dasein's Being. Three criteria measure the adequacy of ontological analysis: first, the hermeneutical situation must *conform* to the phenomenon being investigated; second, the *whole* of the phenomenon must be brought into the fore-having, or scope, of the investigation; third, the interpretation must exhibit the *unity* of the phenomenon. The *second* criterion (wholeness or totality) is satisfied by the claim that Dasein can anticipate its death. The *third* criterion is satisfied by the idea of resoluteness, which verifies the possibility of anticipating one's own death. The resolute individual gains unity by trying to become who he is fated to be. His future becomes intelligible in terms of of his past, and his past makes sense in terms of his future. He thus becomes temporality in the most profound way possible. Once Heidegger demonstrates that human existence is essentially temporal, he must re-structure the hermeneutical situation to conform to this insight, thus satisfying the *first* criterion of ontological analysis. (SZ, 235-267/279-311) Division Two of *Being and Time* shows that Dasein can exist as a totality (authentic Being-towards-death), that resoluteness verifies this possibility, and that the unity of the resolute individual is made possible by the unity of authentic temporality. While Division One analyzed Dasein in terms of average everydayness, Division Two analyzes Dasein in terms of the *temporality* which makes "everydayness" possible.

Heidegger begins by noting that as temporal beings we are radically finite. We not only die; we *know* that we will die. We understand our own mortality, even though we try to conceal it. Awareness of mortality makes our existence an issue for us. If we did not know we were mortal, we would not be so anxious about what might happen to us. Not only are we mortal, but we are also free. We can choose to act according to our own possibilities or according to the "they." This freedom is possible because we understand what it means to be. We usually understand ourselves as ego-subjects and act as if our possibilities were the same as everyone else's. Heidegger claims, however, that there is one possibility which is uniquely my own: my death. Disclosure of my mortality can therefore serve to *individuate* me.

As long as I conceal my mortality, I can go along with the "they" because, supposedly, there is plenty of time to be "myself" later. *Angst*, however, reveals that I will die, and no one can remove this fate from me. Idle talk about death makes it seem to belong to everyone else but me. By making all contemplation of mortality seem to be a sign of weakness, moreover, idle talk takes away the possibility for courage in the face of my death. Death cannot be evaded, however; it strips me of my relations to Others. No one can die for me. I cannot know in advance how I am going to die, but I can anticipate my death as a necessary event. If I reveal and accept this necessity, I recognize that there are certain possibilities which are uniquely my own. Disclosure of my finitude makes me aware that I have neglected these possibilities in favor of those promoted by the "they." Anticipating my death frees me to be myself:

> When, by anticipation, one becomes free *for* one's own death, one is liberated from one's lostness in those possibilities which may accidentally thrust themselves upon one; and one is liberated in such a way that for the first time one can authentically understand and choose among the factical possibilities lying ahead of that possibility which is not to be outstripped. Anticipation discloses to existence that its uttermost possibility lies in giving itself up, and thus it shatters all one's tenaciousness to whatever existence one has reached. (SZ, 264/309)

Anticipating my death destroys my egoistical attachment to unexamined ways of living. Revelation of my finitude severs constricting bonds to the past and frees me for the future. If I accept that death is always possible, the complacency of egoism disappears. Since I am here only for a brief time, there is no better moment than the present for choosing my own limited possibilities. Too often, I assume that my "moment of truth" lies off in the future. This romantic conception denies the intrinsic importance of the present and excuses the slackness of my existence.

Heidegger admits that the notion of authentic Being-toward-death is apparently a "fantastic exaction" of Dasein and says that

> we must investigate whether to *any* extent and in any way Dasein *gives testimony*, from its ownmost potentiality-for-Being, as to a possible *authenticity* of its existence, so that it not only makes known that in an existentiell manner such authenticity is possible, but *demands* this of itself. (SZ, 267/311)

So far, he has only claimed that since Dasein is potentiality-for-Being which understands itself, it has the possibility of anticipating its own death. He must now demonstrate that this existential-ontological possibility is existentially-ontically realizable. The "call of conscience" *(Ruf des Gewissens)* provides the necessary testimony to show that anticipation of death can occur.

Heidegger's concept of conscience is ontological, not theological or ethical. Some religions claim that conscience is the voice of God warning us against sinning. Heidegger asserts, however, that this is only one particular (existentiell) way of interpreting the universal (existential) phenomenon of being summoned away from our usual way of doing things. The philosopher cannot decide for the religious person whether, in fact, God speaks in conscience, but he can show that such speaking could not occur unless we were ontologically structured to be able to hear it. Often what we assume to be the voice of conscience turns out to be what Freud called the "super-ego," the punishing voice which leads us to avoid doing things deemed "bad" by our parents. Even if I manage to loosen the grip of the super-ego, however, I sometimes turn to other authorities (religious or moral) who promise to act as my conscience and guide me in the "right" direction. Kant said that acting in accordance with an external authority is heteronomy. Autonomy, however, means acting in accordance with one's own authority. There are times when we are called on to do things which go against our customary moral code, but which are really appropriate to the situation and true to ourselves. It is also possible to have a "clean" conscience while failing to be true to ourselves—if we understand conscience to mean the dictates of external moral authority.

For Heidegger, religious and moral views of conscience are specific ways of expressing the fact that our very Being (care) summons itself to function in its most appropriate way. Conscience is an element in the authentic disclosure of one's mortality. This disclosure cannot be willed by an individual. The call of conscience

> is precisely something which *we ourselves* have neither planned nor prepared for nor voluntarily performed, nor have we ever done so. 'It' calls, against our expectations and even against our will. On the other hand, the call undoubtedly does not come from someone else who is with me in the world. The call comes *from* me and yet *from* beyond me and over me. (SZ, 275/320)

The call seems alien to me because it is not the voice of the ego. Indeed, it is no voice at all but a silent call. The chattering of the ego must be stilled if we are to hear such a call. While religious traditions explain the alien character of the call by saying it is the voice of God, Heidegger explains it by saying it is the voice of our

Being—the Being which we usually conceal. The phenomenon of con-science testifies that human existence has the power of self-correction. In Aristotelean terms, human beings have their own *telos* and move towards its full manifestation. Our *telos* is to become open to our possibilities: existence yearns to be truthful. To be fully open, however, requires disclosure of our mortality. This disclosure is hard to bear; hence, existence also inclines to be untruthful. Con-science is the sign that our temporal openness is dissatisfied with functioning deficiently. Because conscience calls without warning, we must be vigilant for it. We must continually *want* to be summoned if we are to heed the summons when it unexpectedly comes.

Conscience calls us back to ourselves by revealing that we are essentially "guilty," a term whose German stem is *Schuld*, meaning "lack." Moral indebtedness is possible only because we are in debt ontologically; that is, because our very Being is characterized by finitude, negation, and limitation. Our Being is guilty (lacking) not only because we are not self-grounding, but because our choices are limited. To choose one thing means not choosing everything else. In this "nullity" lies freedom, which "*is* only in the choice of one possibility—that is, in tolerating one's not having chosen the others and one's not being able to choose them." (SZ, 285/331) By disclosing our finitude, conscience calls on us to decide in favor of our own possibilities and to abandon our delusions about a dead past and an impossible future.

Conscience is the discourse which belongs to the authentic mode of self-disclosedness. The silent call of conscience is the highest form of communication. In wanting to be called by conscience, an individual must relinquish the numerous self-interpretations offered by the "they" and accept himself as finite openness which is an issue for itself. To hear the call, he must not engage in intensive "inner dialogue," since this is often just a sophisticated way of re-pressing the summons to authenticity. Acceptance of oneself as finite existence is the understanding which, along with the dis-course of conscience, constitutes authentic disclosedness. The third element of authentic disclosedness is the state-of-mind of *Angst*. *Angst* is the mood which lets an individual be directly affected and touched by his own mortality, which he usually keeps at a distance as a concept. "This distinctive and authentic disclosedness, which is attested in Dasein itself by its conscience—*this reticent self-projection upon one's ownmost Being-guilty, in which one is ready for Angst*— we call *'resoluteness'*." (SZ, 296-297/343) Resoluteness *(Entschlossenheit)* is authentic disclosedness *(Erschlossenheit)*. Because all existence tends toward concealment, even authentic disclosedness is never completely transparent. "Even resolutions remain dependent upon the 'they' and its world." (SZ, 298/345-346) Resoluteness is a decisive disclosure of my own specific possibilities; it is not a theoretical picture of what I am "in general." Heidegger emphasizes that *"resolution is precisely the disclosive projection and determination of what is factically possible at the time."* (SZ, 298/345) As resolute, I am open for my own particular possibilities.

Debate has been aroused concerning the meaning Heidegger assigns to the word "resoluteness." It usually means decisiveness but derives from the verb *"schliessen,"* meaning to latch, shutter, or lock. *Entschliessen*, then, literally means to un-shutter or un-lock. Resolute Dasein is freed from its former bondage to the "they" because it has chosen to disclose *(erschliessen)* its own finite existence. In English the term "resolution" can refer to the quality of an optical image. An image with good "resolution" is clear and well-defined. *Being and Time* stresses the clarity and determination necessary for disclosing one's mortality. The voluntaristic or willful strain in resoluteness appears in the idea of "wanting-to-have-a-conscience" *(Gewissenhabenwollen).* Such voluntarism is characteristic of the subjectivism which Heidegger hoped to transcend. Nine years after the appearance of *Being and Time*, he interpreted resoluteness in a way which minimized its voluntarism:

> Knowing that remains a willing, and willing that remains a knowing, is the existing human being's entrance to and compliance with the unconcealment of Being. The resoluteness intended in *Being and Time* is not the deliberate action of a subject, but the opening up of human being, out of its captivity in that which is, to the openness of Being. However, in existence, man does not proceed from some inside to some outside; rather, the nature of *Existenz* is out-standing standing-within the essential sunderance of the clearing of beings. Neither in the creation mentioned nor in the willing mentioned now

do we think of the performance or act of a subject striving toward
himself as his self-set goal. (Hw, 55/67)

Heidegger's self-interpretations must be taken with a grain of
salt. We must let his texts speak for themselves. In the 1920s, he
regarded courageous will as a necessary condition for the disclosure
of Being, including one's own Being. He did suggest, however, that
since Being manifests *itself*, human action is not a sufficient condition
for its disclosure. These two somewhat conflicting themes are found
throughout Heidegger's writings and lectures during the 1920s. In
1928, for example, Heidegger claimed that in philosophy and science

> the struggle *[Kampf]* is directed solely to the being itself and for
> the sole purpose of tearing it away from its hiddennness and pre-
> cisely in that way to assist it into its own *[ihm zu seinem Recht
> verhelfen]*, that is, to let it be the being which it is in itself. (PIK, 26)

Philosophy is the struggle to let things be what they are. Because of
the demands it makes concerning self-understanding, however,
philosophy is not for everyone. Most people avoid it.

> One can [avoid] it precisely because philosophy is a matter of the
> highest personal *freedom*. One can avoid philosophy, and every-
> thing remains as it was. But one can also freely seize on it as the
> most radical necessity of human existence; certainly only if the
> individual existence itself understands itself—but that always means:
> has resolved to understand itself. (PIK, 39)

The young Heidegger was insistent: revelation of the Being of beings
requires a struggle on the part of the one through whom the revelation is to occur. It is not difficult to imagine how easily this struggle
to "let things be" can become the will to impose oneself upon them.

Heidegger's conception of resoluteness owes much to Kierkegaard,
but the latter thinker did not share the former's ontological interest.
For Heidegger, authenticity is always examined in connection with
the problem of the authentic revelation of Being. He acknowledges
his debt to Kierkegaard but also distinguishes his thinking from that
of his predecessor when he says:

In the nineteenth century, S∮ren Kierkegaard explicitly seized upon the problem of existence as an existentiell problem, and thought it through in a penetrating fashion. But the existential problematic was so alien to him that, as regards his ontology, he remained completely dominated by Hegel and by ancient philosophy as Hegel saw it. Thus, there is more to be learned philosophically from his 'edifying' writings than from his theoretical ones—with the exception of his treatise on the concept of *Angst*. (SZ, 235/494)[2]

A thorough comparison of Kierkegaard and Heidegger on resoluteness can be found elsewhere.[3] Here I only want to mention the following points. For Kierkegaard, the human subject is authentic only when infinitely concerned about its own subjectivity; the highest task of human life is to become a subject in the most appropriate way.[4] Accomplishing this task requires the commitment to our own particular possibilities. Being fully human means deciding to be oneself. More important than any particular moral choice is choosing to will in the first place. Only in choosing to will to be ethical can one discern good and evil as choices.[5] The aesthete, described in *Either/Or*, is desperate because he refuses to make such a choice; he is morally neutral. Proud and defiant, he seeks fulfillment in the astounding and sensual.[6] But, paradoxically, in chasing after infinite possibilities, he loses himself as a particular individual. The truly daring adventure is the quiet but demanding effort to become oneself.[7] This effort begins only if the individual accepts that he is in despair—in flight from himself. Only in courageous resoluteness, however, can he see the absolute importance of choosing himself.[8] To choose himself absolutely requires that he acknowledge his own guilt, finitude, and limitations.[9] In choosing to be his own subjectivity, he gives up the longing for security. He begins to understand that only objects are complete; human beings are always in the process of becoming. Resoluteness does not end his uncertainty and ambiguity, but lets him accept that all spiritual life is necessarily ambiguous. In resoluteness, or in wanting to have a conscience, the individual acknowledges that his primary responsibility is to be himself.[10] When he flees from this responsibility, he becomes a self-hating coward. Being true to oneself requires endurance, patience, courage, steadfastness, will, and striving. The "reward" is nothing other than being the finite subjectivity one already is. "The truly extraordinary man is the truly ordinary man."[11] According to Kierkegaard, most of us do not want to be ourselves; we want to be something else.

The similarities between Kierkegaard's "ethical individual" and Heidegger's "authentic self" should be evident. The differences stem from the fact that Kierkegaard is critical of philosophy, while Heidegger wants to revitalize it. Kierkegaard claimed that philosophy had degenerated into the abstract thinking of Hegel, who seemed to overlook the importance of the individual person. Philosophy had become abstract reflection, but the life of reflection is desperate. Genuine life is always concrete and demands that one shoulder particular responsibilities. For Heidegger, although philosophy must be rooted in concrete human existence, its task is—above all—to make possible the authentic disclosure of Being. Authenticity is, of course, important in itself, but for the philosopher authenticity is a crucial element in the event of the revelation of Being. The revelation of Being, as such, only happens in conjunction with the authentic revelation of an individual's *own* Being.

It is debatable whether Heidegger's analysis of resoluteness really demonstrates that authentic Being-towards-death (anticipation) is realizable.[12] We may ask whether his conclusions about the self satisfy the criteria of ontological analysis. As we recall, one such criterion was wholeness. *Does* resolute anticipation of death allow Dasein to get all of its Being before itself? There is no sure way of answering this question. Each must answer it as best he can. It is possible, however, that Heidegger had too much faith in his interpretative method, especially when applied to human existence.

The analysis of authenticity in *Being and Time* becomes particularly difficult to understand when it comes to the relationship between resoluteness and anticipation. As resolute, Dasein discloses its own Being-guilty (finitude) and recognizes this guilt as essential. To disclose that guilt is permanent and essential requires that Dasein disclose itself as guilty right to the very end:

Existentially, however, Dasein's "Being-at-an-end" implies Being-*towards*-the end. As *Being-towards-the-end which understands—*

> that is to say, as anticipation of death—resoluteness becomes authentically what it can be. Resoluteness....*harbors in itself authentic Being-towards-death, as the possible existentiell modality of its own authenticity.* (SZ, 305/353)

As resolute, Dasein discloses its ontological finitude (guilt). But for such resoluteness to be fully authentic, Dasein must disclose itself in terms of its most unique and individuating possibility: Being-towards-death. Anticipation of death reveals the mortality at the heart of ontological guilt. Resoluteness, the disclosure of Dasein's own finitude, becomes fully authentic when it anticipates Dasein's death. In anticipatory resoluteness, Dasein gathers itself into a unified whole. Dasein becomes fully resolute only because it anticipates its own end. The existential possibility of anticipating my death, however, requires the existentiell act of resolving to actualize it. Let me explain this in less Heideggerean language.

Any time I make a specific resolution, for example, to marry someone, I choose to actualize certain possibilities and to let others go. Resoluteness presupposes some recognition that I am limited. The more steadfast I am in my resolve, the more I understand my finitude. The practice of resolving leads to deeper individuation. Becoming more aware of my mortality, I become more aware of my individuality. Anticipating death is possible for me because I always have some self-understanding. My theoretical knowledge about my mortality becomes concrete, however, only when I make a specific life-decision: when I choose to go this way, not that way. Decision makes me more aware of my mortality, and awareness of my mortality makes me more resolved to be who I am: a mortal being trying to be who he already is.

Anticipatory resoluteness is not "a way of escape, fabricated for the 'overcoming of death'," but lets me take over my life for the first time. Heidegger goes on to say that

> anticipation reveals to Dasein its lostness in the they-self and brings it face to face with the possibility of being itself, primarily unsupported by concernful solicitude, but of being itself, rather, in an impassioned *freedom towards death*—a freedom which has been released from the illusions of the "they".... (SZ, 266/311—entire passage emphasized in original with additional emphasis on "freedom towards death")

Although he usually avoids emotional phrasing in *Being and Time*, Heidegger's existentiell interest sometimes overcomes his existential reserve, as in the passage just cited and later when he asserts that in authenticity there lies "*an unshakeable joy*," the joy of shattering the grip of the "they" and of accepting one's own possibilities. (SZ, 310, 358—emphasis mine) Self-understanding is not gained by detached and rational self-reflection, but by the violent struggle for releasement to oneself. As Gadamer reminds us:

> In certain ways, the concept of self-understanding is an heirloom of transcendental idealism and has been propagated in our own time as such an idealism by Husserl. It was only through Heidegger's work that this concept acquired its real historicity, and with this change it became capable of supporting the theological concern for formulating the self-understanding of faith. It is not, therefore, as a sovereign self-mediation of self-consciousness but rather as the *experience* of oneself that what happens to one and (from the theological standpoint) what takes place in the challenge of the Christian proclamation, can remove the false claims of gnostic self-certainty from the self-understanding of faith.[13]

Like Kierkegaard, Heidegger was inspired by the experience of religious conversion. The latter, however, wanted to disclose the existential structures underlying *all* the various ways in which people become open to the truth about themselves. This existential motive, of course, means that his analysis of authenticity was bound to be abstract, not to mention complex. I have rounded out Heidegger's abstract discussion by describing Kierkegaard's understanding of resoluteness, guilt, and decision. In the next part of this chapter, I provide more concreteness by appealing to Plato, Jung, and Nietzsche, all of whom claim that there is an intrinsic connection between accepting one's death and being authentic.

PART TWO: **Death and Authenticity in Plato, the Myth of the Hero, and Nietzsche.**

By examining certain themes in Plato, the myth of the hero, and Nietzsche, I show that there are precedents to Heidegger's notion

that authenticity requires accepting one's mortality, and to his idea
that a dramatic change in self-understanding accompanies a change
in one's understanding of Being. Heidegger worked out explicitly
what the Western tradition knew implicitly. I have chosen Plato,
because he begins the tradition of Western philosophy, and Nietzsche,
because he ends it. And I have chosen the myth of the hero, as interpreted by Jung, Neumann, and Campbell, because Heidegger's
notion of authenticity owes so much to the traditional idea of the
hero.

A.   *Plato on Socrates*

It is fitting to begin with Socrates, the founder of Western philosophy, whom Heidegger considered to be "the purest thinker of the
West, since he wrote nothing down and thereby kept alive the matter
of thinking." (WHD, 52/17) Socrates said that we ought to seek
not merely to live, but to live well. Living well, however, requires
self-knowledge which can only be gained by a struggle. He was well
aware of the human tendency to wallow in self-ignorance which
pretends to be absolute knowledge. He experienced an "inner voice"
which warned him when he was about to do something out of line
with the demands of truth. Plato depicts Socrates as the antagonist
of idle chatter and curiosity. *The Apology, Crito,* and *Phaedo* all
express the fact that accepting death is crucial for leading the good
life. In *The Apology*, Socrates exemplified what he helped to establish as the highest principle of the West: to choose to die rather
than to conceal the truth. He thereby demonstrated that dying well
is part of what it means to live well. In *Phaedo*, when he was talking
about philosophy as the practice of dying, Socrates referred to the
necessity of preparing the soul for the after-life. But *Phaedo* represents more than an attempt by Socrates to "prove" that life goes on
after death. He failed in that attempt. After all, his friends wept
bitterly at the end because they were convinced that he was gone
forever. They wept for themselves, of course, as well as for their
dying friend. While Socrates had confronted his own death throughout his life so that he could die gracefully, his friends still had to
discover how to accept their own mortality. In *Phaedo*, we find the
following discussion:

Cebes laughed. Suppose we are afraid Socrates, he said, and try to convince us [that the soul is immortal]. Or rather don't suppose that it is we that are afraid. Probably even in us there is a little boy who has these childish terrors. Try to persuade him not to be afraid of death as though it were a bogy.

What you should do, said Socrates, is to say a magic spell over him every day until you have charmed his fears away.

But, Socrates, said Simmias, where shall we find a magician who understands these spells now that you... are leaving us?

Greece is a large country, Cebes, he replied, which must have good men in it, and there are many foreign races, too. You must ransack all of them in your search for this magician, without sparing money or trouble, because you could not spend money more opportunely on any other object. And you must search also by your own united efforts, because it is probable that you would not easily find anyone better suited for the task.

We will see to that, said Cebes. But let us return to the point where we left off, if you have no objection.

Of course not. Why should I?[14]

Interpreted in terms of our discussion to this point, the quoted passage can be understood in the following way. The "little boy" afraid of death is the ego, so attached to worldly affairs and pleasures that it supposes are of the highest value. When Cebes asks for Socrates to persuade the little boy not to be afraid, Socrates does not comply because no one can take over for another person the task of facing his own mortality. Socrates says that a magic spell must be said over the little boy until his fear of death has been charmed away. Until now, Cebes and his friends have depended on Socrates to provide the spell by his own magic, hence allowing themselves to postpone their own "self-charming." To charm themselves, Socrates' friends must halt the idle chatter which conceals their mortality. When asked where they might find a magician to replace him, Socrates suggests that in the end they themselves are best suited for the task. When he points this out to them, Cebes adds quickly, "We will see to that," and then asks Socrates to carry on his "charming" activity as before. Another time will be better for Cebes to learn how to accept his mortality. When Socrates is asked whether he minds going on with his talk, he replies: "Why should I [mind]?" The "I" should he stressed here, because he does not mind discussing his *own* mortality. The point is that Cebes should mind turning the discussion over to Socrates, since so much remains for Cebes to do for himself.

Socrates never really proves that the soul lives on after the body dies. Although we cannot be sure that there is life after death, however, this does not mean that living in a way true to ourselves is merely a gamble. Living well is not only a means to a happy after-life, but— perhaps more importantly—is an end in itself. For Socrates, the essence of man is the knowing soul, not the decaying body. Clinging to the body and its many needs leads one away from the highest kind of life; that of the soul mingling with the eternal Forms. For Heidegger, the authentic life lies in letting go of the ego and becoming as open as possible for the manifestness of beings. Socrates, of course, does seem to understand the soul as an eternal being. In this respect, he differs from Heidegger, who considers human existence to be intrinsically finite. Yet it is possible that Plato's version of Socrates in *Phaedo* characterizes him as more other-worldly than he actually was. The outcome of the ancient dispute about the accuracy of Plato's depiction of Socrates is not crucial for my claim that there are important similarities between Plato's account of how one lives well and Heidegger's account of authentic Being-towards-death. Both conclude that only by accepting our limitations can we be true to ourselves.

B.   *The Myth of the Hero and Authentic Being-towards-Death.*

Many German philosophers have introduced elements of the myth of the hero into their works. Perhaps the best example is Hegel; his *Phenomenology of the Spirit* is a cosmic saga whose hero is Absolute Spirit. Heidegger was well aware of the importance of myth in the development of human culture,[15] so it is not surprising that his notion of authentic Being-towards-death shares many themes with the universally recounted myth of the hero. The myth of the hero, which takes countless forms in various human cultures, usually has two interrelated goals. First, it relates the struggle of the individual to become enlightened—open to and accepting of his role in the cosmic scheme. Carl Jung, Erich Neumann, and Joseph Campbell claim that the life-risking episodes depicted in heroic myths are external projections of psychological battles taking place within the individual. These psychologists further claim that such individual battles are universal. Each of us is confronted with similar "dragons" to slay in the process of becoming individuated. Hero myths have a similar structure because they are symbolic expressions of an archetypal pattern found in the "collective unconscious." Jung asserted that the conscious ego is but an island floating atop the dark sea of the unconscious. Only by learning about the dynamics of this unconscious aspect of the self can an individual become an integrated personality. Although individual egos appear to differ from each other, the fundamental structures of the unconscious are the same for all of us. This underlying similarity of all people is why we repond so similarly to fairy tales, myths, and works of art. All of these symbols help us to gain insight into the workings of the unconscious which cannot be understood directly by the rational ego. By meditating on an archetypal symbol such as the hero's struggle for freedom, an individual can gain insight into his own struggle.

The second aim of the myth of the hero is to remind its listeners that they are part of an ancient tradition which, according to Jung, is based on the founding hero's insight into the demands of the collective unconscious. The myth of the hero is only a surrogate for the emergence of a genuine hero at a particular historical juncture. The hero's task is to share his insight with and, thus, re-unite his people, who have fallen into confusion after having lost sight of the truths which previously united them. A good example of this kind of heroism is Moses' communication of the Ten Commandments to his idolatrous people. This event revitalized the community by introducing a new covenant. In heeding the summons of the hero, people once again perceive the spirit at work in their culture and can eliminate those traditions which are inimicable to that spirit. Christ was such a hero. He reminded his people that obedience to theocratic law was no substitute for the two primary laws: love God with your whole heart, and love your neighbor as yourself. The hero's summons is effective only insofar as he reminds people of their finitude. Erik Erikson remarks that great men "save others not so much from their sins..., but from the fantastic effort *not* to see the most obvious of all facts: that life is bounded by non-life."[16]

A typical myth of the hero, therefore, summons an individual and gives him guidance in his adventure of individuation. The myth also reminds him that successful completion of his adventure will mean revitalizing the values of his community. True individuation transcends egoism. Although most of *Being and Time* interprets individuation from the standpoint of authentic Being-towards-death, a late chapter on "historicality" shows that individuation always takes place within an historical community. The fate of an authentic individual is always bound up with the destiny of his people. Heidegger says:

> The authentic repetition of a possibility of existence that has been—
> *the possibility that Dasein may choose its hero*—is grounded exis-
> tentially in anticipatory resoluteness; for it is in resoluteness that
> one first chooses the choice which makes one free for the struggle
> of loyally following in the footsteps of that which can be repeated.
> (SZ, 385/437—emphasis mine)

Moreover, "In repetition, fateful destiny can be disclosed explicitly as bound up with the heritage which has come down to us." (SZ, 386/438) Repetition is not a mechanical repeating of a past event, but an appropriating of the living tradition in a way commensurate with changed historical circumstances.

Heidegger's notion that individual authenticity involves repetition of traditional possibilities is analogous to the claim of Jung and Neumann that genuine individuation involves repetition of the primordial patterns of the collective unconscious. These depth psychologists, along with philosophers such as Ernst Cassirer, stress the role of the archetypal symbol in mediating between the individual and her heritage. Each person is heroic if he breathes life back into his culture's symbols. World-historical heroes give *new* symbolic expression to the collective unconscious. For Heidegger, Hölderlin was such a hero. It is doubtful that Heidegger would have ever subscribed to the idea of the collective unconscious, since the terminology itself suggests a kind of subjectivism. Yet he was sympathetic to the suggestion that all important human deeds involve revitalizing one's tradition.

As he remarked in 1966: "I know that everything essential and great originated from the fact that man had a home and was rooted in tradition." (Sp, 209/277) Traditions are not "inventions" of individual subjects, but—according to Heidegger—result from the unexpected revelations made through poets and thinkers. Modern man is alienated because he denies the validity of tradition and tries to live according to rational-technical projects designed to increase the "standard of living." These themes are returned to in later chapters.

In *The Hero with a Thousand Faces*, Joseph Campbell describes the three stages in the history of every mythical hero: (1) the call to adventure; (2) the quest for the treasure (insight); (3) the return. In the first stage, the unsuspecting hero is summoned away from his everyday routine by a strange voice, often represented by an old and wizened figure. The summoned individual starts being heroic when he heeds the call. His parents and friends plead with him to remain with them instead of embarking on an apparently foolhardy and dangerous venture. After he takes his leave, he finds himself faced with the task of performing a series of difficult deeds in order to gain the treasure of insight, often represented as a magnificent physical object (the Holy Grail), or divine-like human being (the Beautiful Virgin). His suffering and temptations correspond to those of the individual who, finding it painful to gain insight into himself, is thus tempted to delay the journey to self-discovery. In some myths, the hero as an individual personality or ego is slain. When he comes back to life, he is transformed. His head may be replaced by a shining orb, which signifies the radiance of self-understanding. One is reminded here of Plato's myth of the cave, in which the truth-seeker is blinded by the brilliance of the sun (the "good") after he emerges from the darkness of the cave. The story of Christ's death and resurrection, of course, is also pertinent here.

The destruction of the hero's old self symbolizes his encounter with death, which reveals to him the relative insignificance of his life in the face of the eternal cosmos. The death of his ego does not mean that the hero gives up on life, however. Instead, because he is freed from egoism and opened up to his finitude, he can turn to his own possibilities for the first time. He can now accept the fact that he is not his own creator, that life is a mysterious gift to be cultivated, and that striving to avoid change is detrimental to the aim of life. Life demands that one be both a witness to and participant in the ever-changing cosmic play. Acceptance of mortality and suffering frees one to assume one's proper role in the Divine Comedy. In connection with Gandhi's heroism, Erikson says that "out of the acceptance of nothingness emerges what can be the most central and inclusive, timeless and actual, conscious and active position in the human universe."[17] Existing in a way appropriate to the gift of life means giving thanks for it. Thanksgiving occurs when one accepts one's fate. We are in awe of heroic deeds because we have an inkling of what they exact of those who carry them out. As Campbell tells us:

> Where the moralist would be filled with indignation and the tragic poet with pity and terror, mythology breaks the whole of life into a vast, horrendous Divine Comedy. Its Olympian laughter is not escapist in the least, but hard, with the hardness of life itself—which, we may take it, is the hardness of God, the Creator. Mythology, in this respect, makes the tragic attitude seem somewhat hysterical, and the merely moral judgment shortsighted. Yet the hardness is balanced by an assurance that all we see is but the reflex of a power that endures, untouched by the pain. Thus the tales are both pitiless and terrorless—suffused with the joy of a transcendent anonymity regarding itself in all of the self-centered, battling egos that are born and die in time.[18]

The third and final stage of the hero's development is his return home to everyday life after winning the treasure of insight. Heidegger's version of this "return" holds that authentic existence does not "float above" everydayness but always arises within it. For Plato, too, the seeker of truth must return to the darkened cave. Because his eyes are accustomed to the light on the surface, he is blinded on his return to the affairs of everyday life. Because he acts in accordance with a deeper vision of things, he may be scorned by his fellow men who resent his reminders that there is a dimension of life which they are concealing. Socrates was killed because he refused to quit reminding his countrymen of their self-ignorance. Buddhism also emphasizes that the enlightened man returns to the market place in order to help alleviate the suffering of those still enslaved to greed, hate, and delusion. The gift of insight carries with it the obligation to pass it along. Sometimes the myth of the hero suggests that the treasure of insight is won once and for all. In actual human life, however, the treasure must be won again and again. Insight does not remain forever, but must be renewed.

The analogy of the myth of the hero to the account of authentic existence in *Being and Time* should be evident. First, there is the summons to adventure, a summons which corresponds with the call of conscience. Second, both hero and authentic self must struggle to accept the summons, even though it means losing the comfortable self-understanding that relieves them of responsibility for their lives. If the struggle to accept the truth about mortality and freedom is successful, the hero and the authentic self experience the joy accompanying emancipation from attachment to worldly things. Now free for death, they are unified and endowed with the resolve needed to act in accordance with the exigencies of finite existence. For Heidegger, the hero's "moment of truth" is the only experience of eternity possible for finite human beings. Finally, both hero and authentic self must return to everyday life. Although everything remains the same, it has nevertheless also changed. The authentic self knows that his life is no longer in the service of self-promotion, but in the service of revealing the truth to all who are prepared to receive it. Many of these themes are also present in Nietzsche's account of the trials facing the individual who wants to "overcome" himself in order to become a creator. Let us now consider the parallels between Nietzsche's concept of the Overman and Heidegger's concept of the authentic self.

C. *Nietzsche's Overman and Heidegger's Authentic Self.*

While Aristotle, Kant, and Husserl were influential in the development of the ontological theme in Heidegger's early writings, Kierkegaard and Nietzsche were particularly important in the development of the dramatic theme. The latter two emphasized the importance of decision and will in becoming fully human. As Calvin Schrag points out, "Choice always involves an act of will. The crucial determinant in decision is not the deliberation, important as it may be, but what Kierkegaard calls the 'baptism of the will'."[19] The greater one's resoluteness, the more unified is one's self. Nietzsche, too, stresses the importance of will for living the great human life. The following discussion should demonstrate that Nietzsche's voluntarism had a profound influence on Heidegger's early concept of authenticity as resolute Being-towards-death.

Nietzsche's doctrine of the Overman can be summarized in this way: The Overman is the transformed human being who enhances his own Will to Power by a self-creating which involves the founding of new values, a founding which demands the overcoming of pity through a confrontation with, and an affirmation of, human finitude. For Nietzsche, Being means the Will to Power. Unlike his predecessor, Schopenhauer, who claimed that the primary motive of life is the Will to Survival, Nietzsche asserted that the primary motive is the Will to Power. Since in Nietzsche's view there is no after-life, the goal for man becomes the enhancement of the power of living individuals, not the cultivation of the "immortal" soul. A significant value is one which enhances life by increasing power or the feeling of power. Nietzsche wanted to replace eroded European values with a new standard which would promote the development of great examples of the human species: the Overmen.

An essential presupposition for the appearance of the Overman is that man (or at least certain men) can develop himself by creating his own standards for life. Nietzsche usually talks as if the vast majority of people simply lack the capacity to change. Here he seems to differ from Heidegger, who claims that human Dasein is fundamentally authentic but falls inevitably into everydayness. The idea of the Overman as self-creator arises from Nietzsche's belief that art is the highest expression of the Will to Power. In creative activity, man opens himself up in the spirit of pure enjoyment to new perspectives from which to view himself and his world. This "perspectivism" is given voice in Nietzsche's claim that "Truth is the kind of error without which a certain species of life could not live. The value for *life* is ultimately decisive."[20] Truth is a value (evaluation) whose importance lies in the fact that it preserves life. Nietzsche claims, however, that art enhances life even more than truth, since art offers new perspectives, while truth clings to existing standards.[21] Because art enhances life, life-decisions should be based on aesthetic considerations: the great life is analogous to a great work of art.

Nietzsche was aware of the obstacles lying in the path of the creator. These obstacles are not only external ones, placed before him by the "herd" that fears and resents creative individualism, but also internal ones, placed before him by himself. We are our own worst enemies.[22] To avoid self-perversion, the individual must struggle against self-deception. In striving to remain open to the truth, however, even the strongest can succumb to self-pity.

Pity, the major obstacle on the road to self-overcoming, is an insidious emotion which, under the guise of kindness, weakens the person being pitied and makes him the slave or debtor to the one who pities.[23] According to Nietzsche, contemporary political ideals (socialism, democracy, communism) are expressions of the herd's desire for "happiness," defined as a life without effort or risk. These political theories are the secular offspring of ideas about God and heaven developed long ago by those who were tired of life and took pity on themselves by inventing the idea of a heavenly reward for earthly suffering. The reward was admission into the "real" world of eternal, unchanging heaven (Being) and departure from the "unreal" world of temporal, finite human life (Becoming). Nietzsche regarded all of this as the expression of self-pity, which is really no more than a kind of self-hatred. By postulating an eternal world beyond this one, man took revenge on his earthly life by denying its worth. Overcoming pity, then, means overcoming self-hatred and acknowledging that life *is* suffering and death, as well as joy and triumph. In affirming finitude, the creative individual must also affirm that "God is dead," that the Christian-Platonic table of values which denigrated life is now "devalued."

In his metaphor of play, Nietzsche demonstrates the joy of the affirmation of life. The creator is like a child at play, willing to create new values because creative activity brings aesthetic pleasure. "A man's maturity—consists in having found again the seriousness one had as a child at play."[24] To become like a child again is to achieve the innocent capacity for free play, in which one can surpass the outmoded values which hem in his life. The child is serious in his play for he is caught up in the activity of making a world. The creative individual must be as open to new possibilities as a child. Nietzsche even suggests that the universe itself is akin to a child at play. It, too, lacks a final goal, but simply happens because it happens. The Overman must be willing to establish values in the face of the realization that the whole cosmos is without ultimate "meaning."

Creating new values involves great responsibility, for "Whoever must be a creator always annihilates."[25]

> But have you ever asked yourself sufficiently how much the erection of every ideal on earth has cost? How much reality has had to be misunderstood and slandered, how many lies have had to be sanctified, how many consciences destroyed, how much "God" sacrificed every time? If a temple is to be erected a temple must be destroyed: that is the law—let anyone who can show me a case in which it is not fulfilled.[26]

Even the creative individual, one on his way to becoming an Overman, shrinks back from his creativity because it brings pain and destruction. Eventually, however, he must accept responsibility for his deeds. Responsibility is distinct from guilt, a form of self-pity. By punishing oneself with guilt, one seeks to alleviate responsibility for one's actions.[27] The herd tries to produce obedience to prevailing standards by inculcating guilt and self-pity in everyone. As long as values are accepted uncritically, the illusion can remain that they are absolute and eternal. Nietzsche, of course, holds that all values are relative and historical. There can be no eternally-valid standards in a universe without ultimate meaning. The creative individual takes responsibility for his creations even in the face of this lack of cosmic purpose.

For Nietzsche, a thought even more terrible than that of the ultimate purposelessness of the cosmos is the thought of the "eternal return of the same." Besides overcoming self-pity, the greatest task for the Overman is to will that *this* life, with all its pettiness, suffering, and death, should return an infinite number of times *just as it is*. To confront death, finitude, and their eternal return demands that one overcome the nausea and self-pity which they inspire. Such overcoming demands courage and will:

Courage also slays dizziness at the edge of abysses; and where does
man not stand at the edge of abysses? Is not seeing always seeing
abysses?

Courage is the best slayer: courage slays even pity. But pity is the
deepest abyss: as deeply as man sees into life, he also sees into
suffering.

Courage, however, is the best slayer—courage which attacks: which
slays even death itself, for it says, "Was *that* life? Well then!
Once more!"

In such words, however, there is much playing and brass. He that has
ears to hear, let him hear![28]

The Overman, then, is the courageous human being who overcomes leveling restrictions of the old values and constructs a noble,
powerful, and aesthetically pleasing way of life from his limited
possibilities. The Overman is an ideal against which to measure one's
own attempts at self-overcoming. Any person who tries to shape
himself is on his way to being an Overman. Nietzsche recognized,
however, that human beings are "human, all-too-human." No human
life is perfect. Accepting this fact is part of the test for the creative,
yea-saying individual.

Like the Overman, the authentic self depicted in *Being and Time*
affirms joyfully its limited possibilities. Dasein individualizes itself
by disclosing its mortality. "In anticipation, Dasein guards itself
against falling back behind itself, or behind the potentiality-for-
Being which it has understood. It guards itself against 'becoming too
old for its victories' (Nietzsche)." (SZ, 264/308) The fact that this
reference to Nietzsche is one of the few made to any person in *Being
and Time*'s discussion of authenticity demonstrates the importance
of Nietzsche for Heidegger's concept of authenticity. The idea that
Dasein can become "too old for its victories" seems to refer to our
tendency to give up the struggle for authenticity and to fall back
into the comfortable life defined by the "they."

The "they" is similar to, but not identical with, Nietzsche's concept of the herd.[29] Both the "they" and the herd refer to man's
tendency to conceal his finitude by conforming to social norms. For
Heidegger, however, the "they" is not a collection but a particular
way to exist (egoism) chosen by an individual. The herd refers to
the masses, whereas the "they" is the way of existing which makes

something like the masses possible. The "they" is an existential-ontological term, therefore, while the herd is an existentiell-ontical term. For Nietzsche, the vast majority of people do not even have the possibility of living a life which is true to itself. For Heidegger, however, each of us chooses to be authentic or inauthentic, because

> inauthenticity is based on the possibility of authenticity. Inauthenticity characterizes a kind of Being into which Dasein can divert itself and has for the most part always diverted itself; but Dasein does not necessarily and constantly have to divert itself into this kind of Being. Because Dasein exists, it determines its own character as the kind of entity [being] it is, and it does so in every case in terms of a possibility which it itself is and which it understands. (SZ, 259/303-304)

For both Heidegger and Nietzsche, pity is man's most serious enemy. Both suggest that life is usually a charade in which disturbing aspects of existence are hidden beneath a surface of distractions. We take pity on ourselves by refusing to face the truth and by avoiding crucial decisions. We pity Others by playing along with their self-deceptions and by avoiding appropriate acts because they might bring discomfort to Others (as well as to ourselves!). Nietzsche distinguishes between pity and compassion. When compassionate, we act so as to promote the strength of the Other; we want him to become independent. Compassion is free of the egoism and paternalism which inspires pity. When we pity, we are motivated either because the Other's condition causes *us* pain or because we want to make ourselves appear superior. In compassionate acts, we must be willing to endure the pain caused by the sight of the Other in his struggle for independence. Acts of pity may alleviate some of the symptoms of the Other's plight, but do not root out the disease itself.

Being and Time includes a brief discussion which seems to distinguish between pity and compassion. (SZ, 122/158-159) Heidegger distinguishes two extreme ways for Dasein to relate to Others. On the one hand, I can "leap in" for the Other and take over responsibility for him. In so doing, I make him dependent on me. What seems to be an act of kindness (pity) turns out to be a way of contributing to the un-ownedness (inauthenticity) of the Other. It does no good, for example, to cover up for a friend's alcoholism. I may want to protect him (and possibly myself) from embarrassment or losing his job. But what are these things in the face of his self-destructive drinking? Real love (compassion) might involve letting him fail for the moment, so that he has to start taking responsibility for himself. In acting in a solicitous way toward the other, Heidegger says that I "leap ahead" of the other to let him take over his own possibilities. In leaping-ahead, I try to act so that the Other can gain some confidence in himself. For such deeds to be successful, they usually have to be performed anonymously. By informing someone that I have helped him, I turn an act of compassion into one of pity. The desire to take credit for helping another is a sign of egoism.

With regard to the general idea of the creative or authentic individual, Heidegger and Nietzsche seem to agree that the individual must affirm his own finitude. Both claim that most human beings either lack the resolve (Heidegger) or the capacity (Nietzsche) for such a confrontation and live instead by clinging to comfortable routines. Although Heidegger does not say so explicitly, he seems to agree with Nietzsche that the greatest impediment to individuation is self-pity. Both agree that the creative-authentic individual opens himself to his own limited possibilities. And both suggest that those individuals often turn out to be cultural heroes who renew the tradition by freeing it from the crust of routine.

There are, of course, differences between their views. Richard L. Howey has noted that Heidegger's major interest is not so much in authenticity or even humanity, but the *Dasein* in humanity. Nietzsche, however, is interested in the fate of man as a species. Nietzsche's focus is anthropological, while Heidegger's is ontological.[30] Heidegger claims that Nietzsche is unaware of the question of the sense of Being and brings the subjectivistic tradition to its high point by reducing Being to the Will to Power. Nietzsche is oblivious to the fact that a person can establish a new value or power-perspective only because he exists as the temporal openness in which such evaluating can occur. While Nietzsche denied all transcendence and made man the center of all things (as supreme evaluator and law-giver), Heidegger claims that Being is utterly transcendent. In *Being and Time*, however, Heidegger seems to share some of Nietzsche's "humanism." In speaking of how authentic Dasein projects itself on its own possibilities, Heidegger tends to interpret authenticity in a romantic way: the self-willed individual struggling mightily to break free from conventional values so he can achieve his own possibilities. Heidegger also seems to interpret the collective deeds of an historical group *(das Volk)* as the drive to actualize possibilities which have been buried by neglect. In his later writing, he placed the initiative for historical change in the "destiny of Being," instead of in the hands of the resolute individual or people. This shift of emphasis away from humanity and toward Being corresponds to the change in his attitude toward will. Although *Being and Time* knows something of the importance of letting-be, it also stresses the importance of resolute striving.

His divided attitude toward the will is reflected in his ambivalent interpretation of Nietzsche's thinking.[31] At first, he seemed to appropriate many of Nietzsche's ideas about will as courageous struggling. He admired the idea of the Will to Power. When it became clearer to him that voluntarism is a form of subjectivism, he interpreted Nietzsche as the culminating figure in the history of subjectivism-nihilism. Heidegger also saw, however, that one does not have to interpret the Will to Power in a subjectivistic, voluntaristic way. Instead, one can interpret the highest form of Will as the Will to acceptance or forgiveness: the Will to let things be. I discuss this view of Nietzsche's Will to Power in Chapter Five.

In concluding this chapter, I want to consider the following question: if human beings are so victimized by self-pity and self-concealment, what can possibility motivate a person to face the truth? Ernst Tugendhat suggests that when we fall into the everyday way of understanding self and world, we do so by holding on to particular "truths" (perspectives, values, attitudes) which give meaning to everyday life. In clinging to such prevailing truths, we conceal the fact that to affirm a particular truth presupposes that we are open to choice and truth in the first place. Because we do not like to confront our mortality, however, we are inclined not to reveal the fact that we are finite openness: primordial truth. Instead, we prefer to posit particular truths as absolute.

Every [worldly] interest...is always already penetrated by interest in the untruth, because the disclosing Dasein is directed to hold as correct the horizon of understanding of its interest. In general, to be able to hold itself to an interest, it must avoid the question about truth. The interest in the untruth lies at the ground of all other interest....[32]

This interest in the "untruth"—that is, the partial truths or perspectives needed to give meaning to everyday life—springs from the ego's desire for permanence and security. Although we are naturally inclined to become dispersed in everyday activities, we do not have to give in to this inclination. We only gain a sense of individuality, moreover, in the endeavour to *be* the openness (truth) which we already are. As Tugendhat says:

Now while the tendency toward supression [of the truth]—since it cannot be a goal of the Self, but is motivated by the manifold needs of life—remains as it were splintered apart from itself in this very manifoldness, the possible will to truth about Being itself, however—since it is determined by no other interest besides the demand for truth itself—is unified in principle. In the possibility of self-responsibility, therefore, the unity of the Self gets constituted for the first time.[33]

The motivation for facing the truth is not ethical or religious, according to Heidegger, but ontological. We *want* to be truthful, although we find it hard to do so. The *telos* of our Being (care) is to be open, but this *telos* is intrinsically self-perverting. It is not difficult to see how this ontological interpretation of authenticity can be used to de-mythologize the experience of religious "conversion." A person who has undergone such an experience feels that he is a changed man. Endowed with a more truthful self-understanding, he regards his former self as a stranger. If he has been raised as a Christian, he might conclude that his conversion is the result of an act of God: the gift of Christ's redeeming grace. Heidegger might suggest that this conversion be understood as the self-corrective act of the person's own careful Being. With this suggestion, he offers to the post-Christian world a non-theological way of understanding the undeniable experience of conversion or authenticity.

There are, of course, echoes of the Christian idea of grace in the notion that conscience breaks in upon us to summon us to a more truthful existence. *Being and Time* explains that those who are *willing* to be open for the revelatory call of conscience are those who *will* to be self-possessed and unified—authentic. But the voluntarism present in this view is tempered by the claim that an individual cannot will for the call of conscience (the event of revelation) to occur. Authenticity (redemption, conversion) requires "good works": vigilant wanting-to-have a conscience. Vigilance alone, however, does not itself produce insight and self-transformation. Wanting-to-have-a-conscience, then, also seems to be akin to "faith." The resolute person faithfully holds himself open for the moment of truth, although he cannot know when it will come.

Christian theology has long been divided over the role of human will and works in receiving divine grace. As a Jesuit seminarian and student of theology, Heidegger was well-versed in this ancient controversy which came to a head during the time of the Reformation. Luther and Calvin emphasized that, according to their interpretations of St. Paul and St. Augustine, grace is a gift from an inscrutable God. Human works and prayers are of no help in securing redemption; one is either "elect" or not. The Catholic Church, of course, had long maintained that one could gain merit by making use of the sacraments. Yet during the Reformation, a group known as the Jansenists (later condemned as heretical) arose within the Church to reject the doctrine of the efficacy of good works. Pascal took the side of the Jansenists and engaged in a brilliant but acrimonious debate against the Jesuits, who defended the more established view.[34] Heidegger, Jesuit-trained but greatly influenced by Pascal, seemed to support the view that human will can be of help in correcting human existence. There is no discussion of anything like grace in *Being and Time*, however, unless grace be considered "conscience." Heidegger's analysis of human existence drew on ancient Greek thinkers, as well as New Testament writers. Aristotle, in particular, convinced him that man is endowed with some measure of self-perfectibility. Yet the voluntaristic language of *Being and Time* can obscure Heidegger's claim that no one can simply will to be authentic. For authenticity means authentic temporality, and human beings cannot control the way in which temporality generates itself through them.

In this chapter, I have outlined the disclosive event of authenticity as anticipatory resoluteness. I have also explained that authentic Being-towards-death is a traditional way of understanding the process of individuation. What makes Heidegger's effort philosophically important is neither the idea of authenticity as Being-towards-death nor his description of it (which is surpassed in great literature, drama, and myth), but his claim that authentic Being-towards-death involves a change in the temporal openness which lets beings *be* in a new way. A profound understanding of Being is impossible for the individual who has not undergone a transformation of his own temporality. Put in another way: beings cannot be manifest as they are in themselves unless egoism dissolves into openness. In subsequent chapters, I explain the relation among authenticity, authentic temporality, and authentic understanding of Being.

CHAPTER FOUR

Temporality and Selfhood

IN THE previous chapter, I showed that one must anticipate one's own death in order to have a genuine understanding of Being. Anticipatory resoluteness makes possible authentic human disclosedness or openness. In the present chapter, I explain that this openness is best interpreted as temporality, and that a change in temporality is a necessary condition for the possibility of choosing authenticity. I also demonstrate that the unity of the self is made possible by the self-unifying activity of temporality. In authentic existence, one's past, present, and future are brought together in a kind of spiral: future illuminates past, and past guides the future. Before we begin, some observations on Heidegger's methodology are in order.

We see the importance of concrete experience for grounding Dasein-analysis in Heidegger's transcendental-hermeneutical method. As a *transcendental* analysis, *Being and Time* argues that the three-dimensional structure of temporality makes possible our understanding of Being. Heidegger employs concrete examples, such as our ability to use tools, to explain how temporality lets beings manifest themselves to us. As a *hermeneutical* analysis, *Being and Time* begins within the context of everyday life. Interpretation of the ontological conditions necessary for everyday life reveals that care is the Being of Dasein. The "hermeneutical circle" always circles back to its starting point, but from a more-inclusive perspective. Once temporality has been shown to be the "sense" of Dasein's Being (SZ, 327/375), the earlier analysis of everydayness must be repeated in light of the new hermeneutical situation. The new interpretation of Dasein is structured according to the leading idea of temporality. Heidegger concretizes the theoretical discussion of temporality when he explains how it makes everyday life possible. Each of us has some understanding of everyday life; only for this reason can we assess the adequacy of Heidegger's analysis of human existence. He says "Unless we have an existentiell understanding, all analysis of existentiality will remain groundless." (SZ, 312/360) Recalling that in *Being and Time* Dasein is analyzing its own Being, Heidegger asks: "can ontological interpretation do anything else than base itself on *ontical possibilities*—ways [modes] of potentiality-for-Being—and project these possibilities upon *their ontological possibility*?" (SZ, 312/360) We saw earlier how Heidegger depicts resoluteness as the ontical-existentiell verification of the ontological-existential possibility of anticipation of death. Time and again, he emphasizes that all authentic disclosedness is the disclosure of particular possibilities. The adequacy of *Being and Time*'s analysis of authentic selfhood cannot be assessed merely theoretically. Each reader must measure that analysis in terms of his own life-experience. Admittedly, however, Heidegger did not provide an adequate description of the existentiell dimension of authenticity. His account of the experience of authentic and inauthentic temporality remains too abstract. In the next chapter, I attempt to make his account more concrete through a discussion of the New Testament idea of *kairos* and by reference to his lectures on Nietzsche and Schelling.

The first part of this chapter explains how selfhood is rooted in care. The unifying sense of care is the three-dimensional temporality which makes possible any understanding of Being. Temporality generates horizons or dimensions, each of which makes it possible for a different mode of Being to manifest itself. Everday dealings with tools, for example, are possible because tools are revealed *as* tools within the horizon of "presence." Heidegger interprets Kant's transcendental schematism to show that the horizons of temporality determine the categories of the understanding, which for Heidegger are analogous to the various modes of Being. He concludes that subjectivity and rationality are grounded in temporality. More fundamental than the rational ego-subject is the temporality which makes possible the experience of the subject. The human self *is* this self-unifying temporality. The second part of this chapter reveals that the "connectedness" of the self is made possible because Dasein exists as temporal-historical transcendence which "stretches itself out" between birth and death. When Dasein exists as self-circling temporal openness, the historical moments of the self are united in an intrinsically satisfying way. Although Heidegger tried to undermine the substantial-subjective interpretation of the self, his idea of authenticity as resolute self-possessedness retains elements of the voluntaristic-subjectivistic view of the self. By beginning his ontological study with the analysis of the Being of humanity, and by orienting himself from within the transcendental philosophical tradition which he yet wanted to overcome, he inevitably interpreted human existence in a somewhat subjectivistic way. Later I explain how he gradually minimized that subjectivism as he continued to develop his concept of authentic temporality.

PART ONE: Selfhood, Temporality, and Care.

It will be helpful to distinguish some of the different meanings of the term "self" which come into play in Heidegger's analysis of selfhood. First, self refers to the everyday "I," which is a kind of objectification of our existence. Second, self refers to the authentic way of existing as anticipatory resoluteness. Both these modes of selfhood are ways of Being-in-the-world. We exist in the world because we understand what it means to be. Our understanding of Being is possible because we exist as the temporal openness which lets beings (including human beings) be manifest. In an important sense, then, the real "self" is this temporality which makes possible all experience, whether it be everyday, inauthentic, or authentic. It is quite difficult, however, to understand the relation between my own experience of myself and the temporality which makes this experience possible. Explaining this relation is a major task for *Being and Time*.

Heidegger makes it clear that selfhood is rooted in temporality, the sense of Dasein's Being:

When fully conceived, the care structure includes the phenomenon of selfhood. This phenomenon is clarified by interpreting the meaning [sense] of care; and it is as care that Dasein's totality of Being has been defined. (SZ, 323/370)

Three-dimensional temporality is the unifying sense for the three-fold Being of Dasein as care. Hence, temporality makes possible the unity of the human being. More fundamental than the personal ego is the temporality which "generates itself" *(sich zeitigt)*. "Temporality generates itself, and indeed it generates possible ways of itself. These make possible the multiplicity of Dasein's mode of Being, and especially the basic possibility of authentic or inauthentic existence." (SZ, 328/377) As Heidegger said in 1929: *"More primordial than man is the finitude of Dasein in him."* (KP, 207/237) In the following passage, he hammers home the following interconnected themes: the subject is not a self-grounding substance; the self is a way of existing which is always found in a worldly context; this context is constituted by temporal disclosedness—the sense of Dasein's Being; the inauthentic self lacks genuine "standing" because it flees from the truth; the authentic self is integrated and unified because it resolves to disclose itself as, and to become in the most appropriate way, the temporality which it already is.

If the ontological constitution of the self is not to be traced back either to an "I"–substance or to a "subject," but if on the contrary, the everyday fugitive way in which we keep on saying "I" must be understood in terms of our *authentic* potentiality-for-Being, then *the proposition that the self is the basis of care and constantly present at hand is one that still does not follow.* [My emphasis.] Self-hood is to be discerned existentially only in one's potentiality-for-Being-one's-self, that is to say, in the authenticity of Dasein's Being *as care*. In terms of care, the *constancy of the self*, as the supposed persistence of the *subjectum*, gets clarified. But the phenomenon of this authentic potentiality-for-Being also opens up our eyes for *the constancy of the self* in the sense of its having achieved some sort of position. *The constancy of the self*, in the double sense of steadiness and steadfastness, is the *authentic* counter-possibility of the non-self-constancy *[Unselbst-standigkeit]* which is characteristic of irresolute falling. Existentially, *"self-constancy"* signifies nothing other than anticipatory resoluteness. The ontological structure of such resoluteness reveals the existentiality of the self's selfhood. (SZ, 322/369)

The inauthentic self is "inconstant" because its experience is a collection of fragmented moments. Because we like to believe that there is something uniting these moments, we often speak of the self as if it were a substance underlying the "predicates" of experience. Heidegger, of course, rejects this substantial view of the self. He explains that we usually experience ourselves in a fragmented way because our temporal openness reveals things primarily as objects. If I understand Being to mean "objectivity," it is hard for me to avoid thinking of myself as an object, too: an ego. Objects are things to be manipulated for the benefit of the ego. This narrow, selfish way of understanding things results from my everyday experience of time as an endless stream of "now-moments."

The ordinary understanding of time as a series of "nows" is rooted in Aristotle's definition of time as the measure of motion. We think that the more precisely we measure motion (using atomic clocks, for example) the deeper our grasp of time. In fact, however, measuring the "nows" involved in motion is possible only because we ourselves exist as a kind of movement: the temporal transcendence which is always opening up the horizons of past, present, and future. To notice a continuous motion and to count the "nows" involved in it, I must be able to say with respect to the moving object: *now* it is here, *formerly* it was back there, and *later* it will be over there. For Aristotle, to say that things are "in time" means that their movement is countable. The movement of things is countable (able to be "timed") because it is "surrounded" by the temporal movement (transcendence) of the soul which opens up the "earlier" and "later" in which counting the "nows" becomes intelligible. As Kant says, time does not belong to things *in* time but is the "wherein of their ordering." Heidegger remarks in his 1927 lectures:

> Through the interpretation of "Being in time" we see that time as the all-encompassing, as that wherein natural processes are, is nevertheless more objective than all objects. On the other hand, we also see that it is only if the soul *[Seele]* is. It [time] is more objective than any object and at the same time subjective, i.e., it is only when subjects are. (GP, 359)

The philosophical tradition often neglected the temporal movement of the soul and focused on the idea of time as an independently existing, infinite series of moments which are accurately measured by the clock. Once time is understood as a stream which flows on independently of the subject, things can be understood to be only insofar as they are in that stream. The transcendent movement of the soul is concealed in favor of the motion of physical bodies. Even Aristotle failed to see that his own notion of Being as *ousia* (which Heidegger interprets as "constant presence": *An-wesen*) was essentially determined by the pre-eminence of the temporal dimension of the present. Just as the history of philosophy obscures the connection between temporality and the understanding of what it means to be, so the individual understands himself merely as one object (ego) among others and experiences time as the series of nows in which all these objects (including himself) are found (GP, 384-385).

The existential temporality (transcendence) which makes possible any understanding of Being can be revealed by a brief analysis of the temporal dimensions underlying the three elements of care: existence, facticity, and falling. As existence, Dasein is always out ahead of itself, engaged in planning and projecting itself on future possibilities. As facticity, Dasein's possibilities are determined by its limited historical circumstances. I act toward the future in terms of what I have been and still am. Finally, as falling, Dasein is dependent on and absorbed in the world. Essential to the future is *coming-toward* those possibilities which are already set up in terms of my past. Essential to the past is *coming-back* to what I already am. Essential to the present is *dwelling-alongside* the beings with which I am concerned. The "directionality" of the terms coming-toward, coming-back, and dwelling-alongside suggests that as temporal transcendence Dasein is always *outside* of itself and directed toward its worldly possibility. Because Dasein exists *as* temporal openness, there is no such thing as an "inner" self which is removed from worldly existence. Heidegger calls the dimensions of temporality "ecstases," the root meaning of which is to "stand out" or to be "outside of." As ecstatic, Dasein stretches itself out towards the future in terms of the still determinative past. This ecstatic self-stretching is the temporal transcendence which constitutes the clearing in which beings can be manifest.

Heidegger hoped that the problem of the unity of Being could be solved in terms of the self-unifying temporal ecstases, each of which allows a different mode of Being to manifest itself for understanding.

Although he never quite succeeded in this attempt, he took important steps in that direction. He demonstrated that to understand a thing means that I understand what it *is*. I can use this typewriter because I understand it *to be* "handy"; it presents itself to me *as* an instrument. Heidegger asked how this prior understanding of the Being of beings is possible. He answered in the following way: just as beings are understood in terms of their Being, so, too, Being itself is understood in terms of (or is "projected on") something: "There is no need of extensive evidence to make clear how we are immediately involved in a fundamental problem of Plato, in the attempt to pass beyond Being to the light from which and in which, it itself comes into the light of understanding." (GP, 400) Plato's myth of the sun says in images what Heidegger seeks to express conceptually: "The understanding of Being already moves itself in a general, light-giving, illuminating horizon." (GP, 402) Each of the ecstases of temporality opens up such an illuminating horizon in accordance with a specific "schema." Heidegger's debt to Kant is obvious in the idea that the various temporal schemata determine the particular ways in which Being can manifest itself for understanding. Because temporality unifies and makes understandable the various modes of Being, temporality is the "sense" (unity) of Being. Heidegger's talk about temporality as providing a light-giving horizon for Being is misleading. Ecstatic temporality opens up a clearing or absence in which beings can present themselves in various ways. To say that Dasein is transcendence, that Dasein is the "ontological difference" between Being and beings, that Dasein is ecstatic temporality—to say all this means that human *Dasein* opens itself up so that beings can *be* (manifest, present, revealed). The Being of beings can "give" itself for understanding only insofar as human existence holds open a clearing in which that giving can occur. Far from being a lighting or shining, temporality is the *absence* of light which enables beings to shine forth.

In his first book on Kant, Heidegger credited him with laying the groundwork necessary for re-opening the question of the sense of Being. But Heidegger also added that Kant, in the second edition of the first *Critique,* recoiled from the startling discovery he made in the first edition, viz., that temporality is the source not only of pure intuition but of the pure categories of the understanding as well. Kant could not accept the implications of his analysis, which suggested that the rational categories of the knowing subject are determined by the schematizing activity of the transcendental imagination, the heart of temporality. For such a conclusion implies that the subject is grounded in what is non-subjective, and rationality is rooted in the non-rational. Heidegger went on to claim that since the categories are not functions of the ego-subject, we can dispense with the idea of a thing-in-itself which is purportedly hidden behind the representations produced by the subject when it applies the pure categories of the understanding to the manifold of sense-data. There is no thing-in-itself because "to be" *means* to appear, to be manifest, to be present in accordance with determinate temporal ecstases. The pure categories are not the products of reason, but are the particular ways that temporality opens up horizons in which Being can manifest itself in its various modes. Further consideration of how Being manifests or gives itself will provide us with insight into the relation among temporality, selfhood, and Being. First, however, we must consider Kant's concept of the "schematism" of the understanding in his first *Critique*.

Kant tried to explain how objective experience is possible, how there can be objects about which I can make valid judgments. To be able to make such an empirical judgment as "this typewriter is noisy," I must be able to be affected by the keys hitting the roller and paper. Of course, animals are also affected by sensations and to that extent are receptive beings, but animals cannot make judgments about their sense experience in the same way we can. Our minds are active as well as receptive. The pure categories of the understanding determine in advance the way in which a given sensation is *taken.* There are never any raw sensations, but only sensations which belong to some object or other. Anything not subsumed under the pure categories cannot be manifest as an object and thus cannot be part of my experience. Experience is always the experience of an object. Put in Heidegger's terms: in advance of any particular sensation I have an understanding of the Being of the beings which offers sensations to me. This anticipatory understanding of Being (analogous to Kant's pure categories of understanding) is possible because the horizons of temporality permit beings to be (manifest) only in certain ways. Hence, temporality is *receptive* because it lets the Being of beings give itself, but also *active* in that it determines a priori the manner in which this giving can occur. Were I endowed only with *sense* intuition, I could be affected by the sensations produced by things. But because of my temporal transcendence, I am endowed with *categorial* or *ontological* intuition as well. Hence, when I see the frying pan I am looking for, I not only have the sensation of "black-round-handled" but I also have the intuition of the Being of the frying pan. The pan reveals itself as a tool for use. Hence I can say to myself "There it is!" when I have found it. Temporality is *receptive* insofar as it lets beings be manifest; that is, insofar as it lets the Being of beings "give" itself. Temporality is *active* insofar as it holds open the horizons in which this giving can occur. Temporality can be receptive and active because it "affects" itself. Let us consider for a moment the self-affective character of temporality.

To be affected does not only mean to be affected by sensations. Kant claims that "space and time...must always affect the concept" of our representation of objects. (*Kritik*, A77, B102) "Concept" here must be understood in an active sense, as a "grasping together" (*be-greifen, con-cipere*). The "concept of our representation of objects" does not mean a theoretical idea about representation. It means instead the *activity* of "objectification"—the very activity whereby a given sensation is interpreted in terms of the pure categories of the understanding. This interpretation, unnoticed by the empirical ego, determines in advance that objects must be spatio-temporal substances with predicates and reciprocal causal relations. This a priori objectifying activity might be called the "pure self," in contrast to the "empirical self" making particular judgments (e.g., "This typewriter is noisy."). A priori objectifying activity lets sensations be manifest *as* objects about which an empirical judgment can be made. But how is it that time as pure intuition "affects" this objectifying activity?

> To affect *a priori* the act of objectification as such, i.e., the pure act of orientation toward...means: to bring up against it something on the order of an opposition, "It"—the pure act of objectification—being pure apperception, the ego itself. Time is implicated in the internal possibility of this act of objectification. As pure self-affection, it originally forms finite selfhood in such a way that the pure self can become self-consciousness. (KPM, 172/195)

The conditions necessary for the possibility of experience include not only given sensations which are interpreted or taken in determinate ways, but also the *awareness* that the object *is* an object (*Gegenstand*): something which stands over against the self. Such self-consciousness is not the product of the empirical ego reflecting on itself; self-reflection is itself only possible insofar as the temporality which I am can affect itself. Time as pure receptivity is also receptive of itself. I can be self-related (self-conscious) because temporality is self-related (self-affecting). Heidegger explains:

> As pure self-affection, time is not an active affection concerned with the concrete self; as pure, it forms the essence of all auto-solicitation. Therefore, if the power of being-solicited as a self belongs to the essense of the finite subject, time as pure self-affection forms the essential structure of subjectivity.
>
> Only on the basis of this selfhood can a finite being be what it must be: a being dependent on receptivity. (KPM, 172/194-195)

Objects can be given to us as objects, and the empirical ego can give itself to us as a subject (as the "I"), only because the "pure self" is a self-affective, self-receptive temporality which opens up the clearing in which subject can confront object. The empirical ego ("I") is as much an object of my experience as the table in front of me. Prior to the distinction between ego-subject and object is the temporal openness in which subject and object can be manifest.

Temporality also affects itself in the sense of determining the way in which it generates itself. If temporality is the "pure self", and if the pure self is the objectifying activity of which we have just spoken, then temporality affects itself as this pure objectifying activity by determining a priori the categories of this activity. This temporal determination of the pure categories of the understanding is what Kant meant by the schematism of the categories. In his first *Critique,* he distinguished between the pure intuition of space and time (receptive faculty) and the pure categories of the understanding (active faculty). In making this distinction, he found himself faced with the usual problem of dualism: how can the rational, non-intuitive categories be related to the pure intuition of time (space being considered subsidiary to time)? As receptive beings, we require an intuition which lets us be affected by sensations. Without such sensations, there would be no experience. As thinking (active) beings, we require pure categories which let us take what is given in a determinate (objective) way. Without such categories our sensations would not be organized; we would not be able to distinguish self from object. Kant resolved the dualism between the active (rational) and the receptive (intuitive) by suggesting that the pure categories are pure determinations of time. The categories are useless unless they are schematized through an intrinsic link to a particular mode of pure intuition—time. This schematizing, which is somehow accomplished by the activity of the transcendental imagination, can be clarified by an example.

Substance, a pure category of the understanding, is defined in terms of an aspect of time: to be a substance means enduringly to be present. In the act of objectification, schematizing activity produces a pure temporal image (the present—an aspect of time) for a pure concept (substance—that which endures through time). Schematism is the regulated production of a pure image for a pure concept. Just as an empirical concept requires an empirical image for an empirical judgment to occur ("This mouse is hungry"), so, too, a pure category requires a pure image for the act of objectification to occur. In the case of substance, the pure image of time is the dimension of the present. The image is pure because it is non-empirical and non-sensory. The pure image of time does not itself appear, but lets beings appear as substances. A non-appearing image which lets things appear is what Heidegger means by a pure "phenomenon." Hence, phenomenology is the analysis of the structure of non-appearance (temporal absence, openness, transcendence) which lets appearing (Being) take place. The schematized category of substance is a universal and necessary determination of the pure intuition of time which lets sensations be given as enduringly present objects. I can make the empirical judgment, "This mouse is hungry," because temporality opens up a horizon ("pure image") which lets me encounter an enduring substance with specific predicates. Note that the categories do not determine time; rather, *time determines the categories.* Indeed, categories are the specific ways in which time affects or generates itself. The rational categories are rooted in intuitive temporality. Heidegger claims that Kant was too much a part of the rationalist tradition to be able to accept the implications of this discovery. Hence he changed the doctrine of the schematism in the second edition of the *Critique.*

Let me summarize what has been said. Heidegger claims that a being can be manifest only because the temporal horizons offer a clearing in which that manifesting can occur. There are different modes of Being, or different ways in which beings can be manifest. Temporality generates the specific horizons which let this manifesting happen. The various modes of Being are unified because they are determined by the horizons of temporality. Without temporal horizons there would be neither subjects nor objects, since there would be no disclosedness or clearing ("world") in which subjects and objects could be manifest. The most fundamental sense of "self," therefore, is not the rational ego-subject but the self-unifying temporality which determines the categories of the subject and which enables the subject to be self-conscious. Temporality is always "personalized" insofar as it is embodied in a human being who is always concerned about himself. To be human is to care about self and world. Such caring can take place only because temporality lets me encounter myself as a being who is in the process of becoming.

In his first book on Kant, Heidegger points out that Kant uses the same basic predicates when speaking of time and the "I think" or ego-self. For example, Kant refers to the "abiding and unchanging 'I' (pure apperception....)" (*Kritik,* A123; KPM, 174/197). He also says that "The existence of what is transitory passes away in time but not time itself." (*Kritik,* A143, B183; KPM, 174/197) The similarity of predicates suggests that time and the "I think" are closely related. Heidegger proposes that the predicates "abiding" and "unchanging" refer not to the immortality of the soul, but are instead transcendental determinations "which signify that the ego is able to form an horizon of identity only insofar as *qua* ego it pro-poses to itself in advance something of the order of permanence and immutability." (KPM, 175/198) That is, the abiding nature of the self is grounded in the self-unifying activity of temporality. "The ego cannot be conceived as temporal, i.e., as intra-temporal, precisely because *the self* originally and in its innermost essence *is time itself.*" (KPM, 177/200-201) The self is the self-generating temporality which opens up the ecstases or horizons in which beings can manifest themselves in various ways.

Because temporality is self-affecting or inherently receptive, the being who *is* this temporality can be aware of beings and of itself as the
being without whom other beings could not be revealed. Heidegger
gives the name "transcendence" to the ecstatical-horizonal human
existence which opens up the temporal-historical world in which beings are manifest and in which human beings must decide how to be
human. In his excellent book. *Heidegger, Kant, and Time,* Charles M.
Sherover informs us that:

> This same transcendence Heidegger can now explicitly describe "as
> the essence of the finite self." It is this imaginative capacity to achieve
> transcendental modes of knowing that makes it possible for me to be
> having an integrated knowledge, a continuing achievement, that makes
> me aware of my own reality, of my own be-ing as the knower. Thus
> the 'essence of the self'—mine or yours—is no longer to be described
> merely in terms of 'subjectivity'. The 'subjectivity of the subject' is
> 'revealed' in the nature of transcendence, an act of be-ing which is
> present in any and every particular act. The self, *qua* knower, is not
> discovered as a 'thing' but as the dynamic demarcating and evoking
> of knowing to-be. In the ontic cognizing which our transcending per-
> mits, we are able to discover our own to-be, our own mode of act-ing,
> our own be-ing, which we name with the label 'self'. The self then is
> not so much a subject as it is an act-ing, a way of be-ing in, at least,
> a cognitive relationship to other be-ings and things.[1]

For Heidegger, the unity of experience and the unity of self are
grounded in the unity of temporality. The self is not subject or substance, but the self-unifying activity of three-dimensional temporality embodied as a being who must decide how to be. Professor Sherover seems to suggest something different when he says:

> The self, then, is not a thing but an activity; it is not *in time* precise-
> ly because it projects time; it is the source of temporality in its ex-
> periential field; it is the ground of time when it projects and main-
> tains itself as the relatively-abiding center of its experience under the
> form of time it 'offers' to the objects around it. It [the self] makes
> time possible.[2]

Sherover's suggestion that the self makes time possible tries to bring
Heidegger back within the framework of Kant's transcendental philo-

sophy. But in *Being and Time* and in his first book on Kant, Heidegger was trying to work his way *out* of the transcendental tradition even while using many of its concepts. For Heidegger, to say that the self makes time possible is a lapse into subjectivism. It is more proper to say that time makes the self possible.

F.W. von Herrmann in *Subjekt und Dasein* supports the contention that Heidegger wanted to surpass the transcendental-subjectivistic tradition by (1) showing that the self or subject is not self-grounding but arises within the disclosedness constituted by temporality, and (2) claiming that this disclosedness occurs *not* for the sake of man or subject but so that Being might display *itself.* Already *Being and Time* hints that the Being of man (as Dasein) is no longer to be considered from the standpoint of the self-directing subject ("humanism"), but from the *relation* of human Dasein (finite transcendence) to the Being of beings. Insofar as Dasein is the temporal-historical "here" in which beings can be manifest, Dasein holds open the ontological difference between Being and beings. According to von Herrmann, in *Being and Time* disclosedness refers both to man's self-illumination or self-understanding and to the self-illumination of Being as such. Human Dasein is thus in the service of the historical self-disclosure of the Being of beings. The historical changes in how we understand what it means to be are not explicable in terms of human decisions. History is determined by the "destiny of Being," which is neither organized, nor initiated, nor understood by human beings. Von Herrmann goes on to say that a non-subjectivistic understanding of Dasein requires that we distinguish between the temporality of *human Dasein* and the temporality of *Being.* Dasein's temporal disclosedness:

> is no subjective structure, because in the ecstases Dasein is opened up to itself only insofar as it is opened up also for the disclosedness of Being-in-general. The latter reaches out beyond the self-disclosedness of existence. In the disclosedness of Being as such, Dasein stands so little upon itself, that it stands there precisely in the disclosedness of Being-in-general, which it has not posited and into which it has not brought itself, but in which it always already finds itself placed with its ecstases. [Dasein] is not abandoned to itself merely in order to circle about in its own Being, but in order to hold open ecstatically (by temporalizing with its own Being) the temporal disclosedness of

Being-in-general. In the same way, the temporal disclosedness of Being-in-general is no subjective time posited by the subject, because this [disclosedness] *always already runs under the time of Dasein.* Only in the ecstatically held-open temporal disclosedness (executed in [Dasein's] temporality) of Being-in-general can the "subject" reach the "object." Only on the basis of the ecstatically-temporally held-open essential time of Being can Dasein form this subjective and objective time oriented to the now.[3]

Because he interprets the intention of *Being and Time* from the perspective gained by studying Heidegger's later writings, von Herrmann sometimes gives the impression that *Being and Time* already says everything found in the later works, but in a different vocabulary. Although there is much to be said for this point of view, I believe that in *Being and Time* Heidegger did not yet fully understand the relation between the temporality of Dasein as human existence (that is, as concerned Being-in-the-world) and the temporality of Dasein as the site for the historical disclosure of Being. He never adequately explained the nature of the relation between the historical *self-disclosure* of Being and the *experience* of the individual through whom this self-disclosure takes place. Without individuals who exist authentically; that is, without individuals who let temporality generate itself most appropriately, Being could not manifest itself in new ways. Von Herrmann's desire to show that Heidegger's early writings anticipate his later efforts to surpass subjectivism and humanism causes von Herrmann to play down Heidegger's enduring interest in the dramatic theme of authenticity.

Being and Time is devoted almost entirely to the analysis of the Being of Dasein, although this analysis was intended to provide the basis for an understanding of the sense of Being as such, not just of human Being. Dasein is a living being who is concerned about its life. Hence, we usually understand things in terms of our life-needs. Things usually appear to us as instruments or tools which can be used to gratify those needs. The question is: does our instrumental understanding of things arise from the fact that temporality lets beings show themselves as tools, or does it arise from our need to use things in order to overcome material scarcity? It does not seem to make much sense to say that beings would manifest themselves as tools except to a being (such as man) which *needs* tools in order to survive.

Karel Kosik, a Marxist thinker influenced by Heidegger, claims that we are temporal beings because we are laboring beings. We see things instrumentally because we must work to satisfy our needs, not because the "temporality of Being" reveals things to us as tools.

> The same act of mediation in which animality begets humanity and in which animal craving is transformed into humanized craving, into the craving for being craved, i.e., the craving for recognition, also forms the *three-dimensionality of human time:* only a being which transcends the nihilism of its animal craving in labor will in the act of harnessing its craving uncover a *future* as a dimension of its being. Through work, man controls time (whereas the beast is exclusively controlled by time), because the being that can resist immediate satiation of its craving and can 'actively' harness it forms a present as a function of the future, while making use of the past. In so doing it uncovers the three-dimensionality of time as a dimension of its own being.[4]

Kosik goes on to say that

> In the labor process, results of *past* labor are transformed while realizing intentions of the *future*. The three-dimensionality of human time as a constitutive dimension of man's being is anchored in labor as man's *objective doing*. The three-dimensionality of time and the temporality of man are based on objectification. *Without objectification there is no temporality.*[5]

Heidegger seems to say that without temporality there is no objectification. That is, we can turn things into objects only because temporality discloses things to us as "objectifiable." He also says, however, that our Being is care. And at one point in *Being and Time*, he even claims that care makes temporality possible. (SZ, 317-372/423) As finite beings who are concerned about ourselves, we must understand things instrumentally. If we could not see that the earth is "good for planting," we would starve. Heidegger, thus, would agree with Kosik that temporality is bound up with the ways in which we work on things to turn them into objects for consumption. Heidegger would add, however, that the instrumental temporality of everyday life is not the only kind of temporality. He resists those who want to say that the horizons of temporality are totally determined by the

material needs of life. Interpreting Heidegger's view of human existence as a version of Nietzsche's "perspectivism," Vaihinger's "philosophy of 'as if'," or one of the psychologisms popular at the turn of
the century has the merit of "naturalizing" his concept of selfhood.
If we assume that we are natural organisms, we can conclude that it
is "adaptive behavior" to treat things as tools and to plan for the future in light of past behavior. Heidegger does not want his thinking
to be regarded as *Lebensphilosophie,* however. In *Being and Time,* he
was trying to provide the ontological foundation necessary for any
"philosophy of life," but he was also trying to answer the question
of the sense of Being. Being as such transcends the needs of the human organism. Put in another way: beings can reveal themselves as
other than objects, tools, or instruments *for us.* It is true that *Being
and Time* only describes instrumental and objective ways of understanding Being: handiness (*Zuhandenheit*) and objectivity (*Vorhandenheit*). At this stage in his thinking, he may not yet have known
how to describe a nonobjective understanding of Being. Even the activity of tool-using, however, does not have to be regarded in a purely
subject-oriented manner. Michelangelo, for example, explained his
sculpting by saying that he only tried to release the form already
slumbering in the stone: he tried to let the marble slab be what it
could be. One can also till the soil without destroying its vitality; one
can let the earth be the source of life by planting seeds in it.

In the 1930s, Heidegger became more and more aware of the fact
that modern man treats everything as an object for human domination. Even in *Being and Time,* he was critical of the subjectivism
which reduces Being to "objectivity," or to a "mere vapor." He
wanted to demonstrate that Being transcends human control, that
beings manifest themselves to us, that we are not the lords of Nature.
As long as he tried to explain Being (manifestness) in terms of the
temporality of human existence, however, he found himself veering
toward subjectivism. Temporality too easily gets interpreted as a
property of man, when in fact man is a property of temporality. In
1940 he acknowledged this problem in his earlier thinking:

> The reason for this non-understanding [of the relation of Dasein to
> Being] lies first in the indestructible and self-strengthening habit of

the modern way of thinking: man gets thought as subject; all reflection on man gets understood as anthropology. On the other hand,
however, the reason for the non-understanding lies in the attempt
itself [that is, *Being and Time*], which derives from what went on
before, but which breaks itself free from it and as a result necessarily
and constantly still refers back to the path of what went on before,
and even calls on this for help in saying something wholly different.
Above all, however, this way ruptures in a decisive place. This rup-
ture is grounded in the fact that the way and attempt which has been
taken comes against its will into the danger of becoming anew only
a strengthening of subjectivity, and that it itself hinders the decisive
steps; that is, its adequate explanation in its essential power. (NII,
194-195)

The path from which he was trying to diverge was the transcendental thinking which holds that the structures of subjectivity determine the Being of beings. Although he wanted to show that the subject is conditioned by temporality, and that temporality is in the service of the self-manifesting of Being, he nevertheless approached these
issues through the analysis of human existence. *Being and Time* moves
toward this subjectivism because it spends so much time analyzing
selfhood, although in a manner which attempts to surpass Kant's
more restricted analysis of the "subjectivity of the subject." Although
Heidegger sought to ontologize the ontical insights of Kierkegaard
and Nietzsche, St. Paul and Bultmann, Dostoevsky and St. Augustine, Luther and Pascal, he did not manage to adequately separate
the existentiell questions of selfhood from the existential ones. Perhaps it is impossible to do so. In his later writings, Heidegger recognized that by beginning his analysis of Being with the analysis of
ontological conditions necessary for the possibility of concrete, personal human existence, he tied Being too closely to the ontical-existentiell features of humanity. In 1949 Heidegger said:

To be a self is admittedly one feature of the nature of that being
which exists; *but existence does not consist in being a self,* nor can
it be defined in such terms. We are faced with the fact that metaphysical thinking understands man's selfhood in terms of substance or—
and at bottom this amounts to the same thing—in terms of the subject. It is for this reason that the first way which leads away from
metaphysics to the ecstatical existential nature of man must lead

through the metaphysical conception of human selfhood (BT, sections 63-64). (WGM, 204/215)

Heidegger eventually abandoned the transcendental perspective because it tended to suggest that temporality is a projection of the subject designed to reveal those aspects of Being which are beneficial to the needs of the subject. He concluded that any merely naturalistic or subjectivistic account of the understanding of Being ends by reducing Being to a function of humanity; but Heidegger always insisted that Being is *transcendent:* beyond the control of man. As his thinking matured, Heidegger moved away from his earlier position which could be construed as a kind of humanism, an interpretation of history in terms of the needs, decisions, and actions of human beings. His essay "On the Essence of Truth" (1930) signals the end of his attempt to approach the question of the sense of Being from within the framework of a critical version of transcendental philosophy. In this essay he claims that Being (to be manifest) requires a nothingness (*das Nichts*) or absence in which this self-manifesting can occur. Human existence embodies this nothingness, temporality, finitude, or transcendence. Although *Being and Time* already includes many of these insights, the portion which would have dealt with the relation between time and Being was omitted because Heidegger had not adequately worked out the relation between human temporality and the temporality of Being. In the 1930s he changed his concept of truth (unconcealment) from that of the "disclosedness of Dasein" to the "truth of Being" itself. This shift corresponds to his gradual abandonment of the humanistic elements which color *Being and Time.* I return to these topics in later chapters.

So far I have explained that the unity of the self is made possible by self-unifying, self-generating temporality. As the self is unified not only for any particular moments, however, but over a "stretch of time," human life is essentially historical. Heidegger tried to answer the following question: Without resorting to the idea of a substantial core, how can we explain the connectedness or identity of the self through its lifetime? He claims that for the most part our lives are in fact *not* connected but disintegrated. The everyday self is without a genuine history. Only the individual who resolves to renew the possibilities inherent in his fate exists as a unified, self-possessed self.

PART TWO: Historicality, Repetition, and Authentic Temporality.

At the beginning of the chapter of *Being and Time* called "Temporality and Historicality," Heidegger remarks that the concept of Dasein as Being-towards-death seems to overlook the fact that Dasein is also *born*. A self is not only a unified awareness at each moment but is somehow historically connected from birth to death. Human temporality is always historical. (SZ, 382-383/434) How are we to explain the historical "connectedness" of the self? If we proceed on what Heidegger calls the "perverse assumption" that the self is a substance, we conclude that the self is an unchanging core moving along through the stream of life. (SZ, 117/153) This core supposedly unifies the self's experiences from birth to death. In rejecting this view, Heidegger adds that so much attention is paid to the problem of the connectedness of the self because in everyday life we are, in fact, disconnected and disintegrated. In order to become self-possessed, Dasein

> must first *pull itself together* [*zusammenholen*] from the *dispersion* and *disconnectedness* of the very things that have 'come to pass'; and because of this, it is only then that there at last arises from the horizon of the understanding which belongs to inauthentic historicality, the *question* of how one is to establish a 'connectedness' of Dasein if one does so in the sense of 'Experiences' of a subject—Experiences which are 'also' present-at-hand. The possibility that this horizon for the question should be the dominant one is grounded in the irresoluteness which goes to make up the essence of the Self's in-constancy. (SZ, 390/441-442)

With regard to the connectedness of the self, the real question is how Dasein *"loses itself in such a manner that it must, as it were, only subsequently pull itself together out of its dispersal, and think up for itself a unity in which that 'together' is embraced."* (SZ, 390/442) We lose ourselves in everyday distractions, because we interpret ourselves as gratification-needing ego. By concealing the truth about our mortal openness, we busy ourselves with worldly activities promoted by the "they." In everyday life, our routines and associates help conceal the fact that our lives lack meaning and unity. When *Angst* strikes, everyday routines lose their power to unify and conceal. When we flee into inauthenticity, we begin to fall apart. The only "connected-ness" left is the constancy of the flight from truth.

The disconnectedness of our inauthentic existence can be explained by the fact that we experience time under the domination of the ec-stasis of the present. Professor Schrag has observed that Kierkegaard uses the ecstatic conception of time in describing how the aesthete lives in "now-moments" without any connection to past or future.[6] Because he denies his finitude and interprets himself as eternal, the aesthete has no sense of his own *telos,* or self-development. Since for him there is no sense that he belongs to past or future, time becomes a series of now-moments which must be filled with pleasurable dis-tractions. Although thus bound to the present, he is not satisfied with what it offers. He cannot "be here now" because he wants all future possibilities to be actualized along with the present one.[7] There is never enough time for anything. He races through life think-ing that—as each minute ticks away—he is missing out on gratifica-tion. He experiences the past not as dynamic fate but as a collection of memories which can be entertaining when he is bored. Because he is constantly fleeing from the disclosure of his mortality through the mood of *Angst,* he refuses to let his temporality generate itself au-thentically. He elects to remain locked in his own ego.

Authentic temporality leads to a very different experience of one-self. The nature of authentic temporality can be discovered by exam-ining the structure of anticipatory resoluteness. Only by anticipating my own death, my most unique possibility, am I free to cultivate my other limited possibilities. Authentic temporality makes possible this future-oriented development of my possibilities. Although primarily oriented toward the future, authentic temporality also discloses the past, not as a collection of by-gone events, but as dynamic fate. In resolving to anticipate my death, I resolve to devote myself only to those possibilities which have always been my own. As authentic, I interpret my past in terms of my future: I am in the process of be-coming who I *already* am. Fate comes to meet me from my future possibilities; it does not lie in the dead past. Future circles back to past and past points ahead to future. Anticipatory resoluteness not only opens me to future (possibility) and past (necessity, fate), but also to the present. I become open in a new way to the beings and

Others of the world I presently inhabit. As authentic, I live everyday life in a transformed way.

The anticipation of death is a mere possibility unless it can be realized in a concrete life-situation. A resolute individual responds affirmatively to the disclosive overtures of his own conscience. In heeding the call of conscience, which reveals our utter finitude and guilt, he lets temporality generate itself in its authentic way. As James M. Demske says,

> there...appears a remarkable relation to reciprocity between temporality and authentic Being-unto-death. On the one hand, temporality is the ontological [sense] and the enabling ground of authentic Being-unto-death. Dasein can let itself come back to itself in its extreme possibility through [anticipation], come back upon its guilt resolutely, and respond to its situation authentically, only insofar as it exists in the roots of its Being as futural, having-been, and presencing. In other words, Dasein can exist as authentic Being-unto-death only insofar as its innermost ontological [sense] comprises the three aspects of futurity, past, and present. On the other hand, the ontic existentiell realization of authentic Being-unto-death produces the authenticity of Dasein's temporality. The illuminative power contained in [anticipatory] resoluteness brings Dasein to the awareness of its own deepest structure and this structure's ontological [sense] .[8]

Heidegger's account of authentic temporality explains what it means to exist historically in an authentic way. (SZ, 383/434) His understanding of history is influenced by Kierkegaard's Christian-eschatological interpretation of the Greek notion of fate. Professor Schrag claims that Kierkegaard favored the Christian anticipation of the future (possibility, freedom) as opposed to the Greek emphasis on the past (necessity, fate).[9] The Greeks' orientation toward the past led to their emphasis on recollection. In recalling the pre-existing decrees of fate, the Greek tragic hero resigned himself to the inexorable necessity of actuality. Kierkegaard believed that a person subverts his own *telos* by regarding the past as a burden. Human life involves the interplay between freedom and necessity, possibility and actuality. For Kierkegaard, Christian faith redeems the individual from the crippling weight of the past (guilt) and frees him for future growth. Hence, Kierkegaard transforms the Greek ideal of recollection (which is oriented toward the past) into the ideal of repetition (which is oriented toward the future). The ethical man "recollects forward" in the sense of recommitting himself to the possibilities he has recognized as his own.[10] His fate makes more sense only as he actualizes the possibilities it sets up for him.

Professor Stack claims that the idea of repetition is derived from Aristotle, who said that only practice brings to fruition the natural potential for virtue (*arete*).[11] Kierkegaard, who read Aristotle in light of his own "existential" concerns, insisted that becoming an integrated individual requires effort, recognition of life's limitations, and recommitment to one's chosen possibilities. Resolute repetition alone can end the aesthete's doubt, cynicism, and despair. The resolute individual, no longer experiencing time as a series of discrete now-moments, no longer feels that his life is splintered into a myriad of disconnected episodes. Now he experiences past, present, and future drawing together into the "moment-of-vision"—the *Augenblick*. Authenticity occurs when temporality generates itself as a spiral in which past is transformed by future in the resolve of the present. Heidegger remarks:

> Only an entity [being] which, in its Being, is essentially *futural* so that it is free for its death and can let itself be thrown back upon its factical "there" by shattering itself against death—that is to say, only an entity [being] which, as futural, is equiprimordially in the process of *having-been* [*Gewesenheit*] can, by handing down to itself the possibility it has inherited, take over its own thrownness and be in the *Augenblick* for 'its time'. Only authentic temporality which is at the same time finite, makes possible something like fate—that is to say, authentic historicality. (SZ, 385/437—entire passage emphasized in original.)

Professor Stack asserts flatly that Heidegger "wholly appropriates" Kierkegaard's category of repetition.[12] He argues further that from Kierkegaard's study of Aristotle Heidegger learned that human existence is essentially potentiality-for-Being, that choice and practice are necessary for human excellence, and that there is a specific movement (*kinesis*) to human life which can be called "existence." Stack does note some differences between the two thinkers in their concept of repetition. "For Heidegger, *Dasein* takes over its history through repetition, whereas for Kierkegaard, it is through repetition that man acquires a history for himself."[13] As an *ontological* thinker, Heidegger tried to explain the historical changes in Western man's understanding of Being. These changes are supposedly guided by the destiny of Being which an historical people must resolve to re-appropriate. In *Being and Time,* he first showed that an individual becomes authentic by repeating his fate (*Schicksal*), but then added that this fate is always tied up with the destiny (*Geschick*) of the individual's community. (SZ, 385-386/436) As a *religious* thinker, Kierkegaard regarded the individual's salvation as the matter of ultimate importance. He maintained that talk about the destiny of historical peoples ignored the demands of individual existence. Each individual, he believed, begins his own history when he resolves to commit himself to a few important possibilities. Resolute existence itself can be transformed by faith, in which eternity breaks into the finite. In religious experience there occurs the "time of fulfillment" (*kairos*), a concept which I consider in the following chapter.

When critics imply, however, that Heidegger borrowed everything important from previous thinkers such as Kierkegaard and Aristotle, they go too far. If everything in *Being and Time* had already been said, why did it cause such a stir? Clearly, Heidegger did something with the insight of his predecessors that they had not done themselves. He re-appropriated their thinking in light of what he was able to understand in the early twentieth-century. Heidegger learned much from Kierkegaard, but he did not have to depend on the Danish author to learn something about Aristotle. Heidegger studied Aristotle directly, as Thomas J. Sheehan has demonstrated in his excellent essay, "Getting to the Topic: On the New Edition of *Wegmarken*."[14] This essay, based on Heidegger's 1928 seminar "Phenomenological Exercises: Interpretation of Aristotle's *Physics II*," explains that Aristotle himself went beyond the usual Greek interpretation of Being as constant presence (*ousia*) and tried to explain the Being of moving, living things. Living beings are "a-telic" in the sense that they are always on their way to their *telos*. They are always in the process of manifesting their self-determined series of appearances. These stages can be present (manifest) only because of something else which is *not* manifest. *Dynamis* refers to the kind of Being in which something appears because something else does not appear.

> Precisely this "atelic" quality of a moving being is what allows it to remain in movement, for were the *dynamis* brought forward into the *telos* the being would be achieved and the movement would cease. This atelic presentness constitutes a unique interplay of presence and absence, for along with its limited presence, a moving being's non-presence or possibilizing absence *also becomes present* in a special way.[15]

Heidegger holds that the customary interpretation of *dynamis* as the "actualizing of a potency" is based on an inadequate Latin translation of Aristotle's Greek. Heidegger interprets *dynamis* as the way in which new aspects of a living being keep emerging into manifestness (unconcealment) from out of something which is itself not manifest. For example, the manifest aspects of a plant (leaves, stem, flowers) are dependent for nourishment and direction on the source of growth hidden within the plant itself. This hidden source cannot be seen with the eye, although it can be disclosed for the understanding when we inquire into how the visible manifestations of the plant are possible. The hidden source of growth is akin to what Heidegger calls a true "phenomenon": that which does not manifest itself but (like Kant's temporality) lets something else be manifest. A living being constantly spirals back in upon itself at the same time that it moves out from itself. It continually retrieves or repeats (*wiederholt*) its own *dynamis*. Professor Sheehan summarizes the idea of retrieval, so crucial for Heidegger's idea of selfhood as well as for his method of interpreting the history of philosophy, when he says:

> We may say that the plant constantly "goes back into" its *dynamis* (*Insichzuruckgehen*) as it comes forth into appearance. Or we may say that the plant again and again seeks (re-peats) and draws upon (retrieves) its *dynamis* in order to appear. In order to name this process of drawing upon *dynamis* for the sake of *energeia* while allowing *dynamis* to remain relatively absent, Heidegger comes up with "*Eignung*," "appropriation." *This is Heidegger's proper title for movement, and it is the basic model for the concept of Ereignis.*[16]

The concept of *Ereignis* becomes even more important for Heidegger's thinking after about 1936. In *Being and Time*, he described human Dasein as the temporal disclosedness needed for Being to manifest itself. Around 1930 he began to try to explain that Being (presencing, manifesting) somehow includes its own disclosedness, temporality, or nothingness. Human temporality now comes to be understood as a specific way in which this absence (temporality) is embodied. As long as he retained the idea of authenticity as human self-possessedness, as well as the elements of humanism which regard history as the actualization of the possibilities of an historical people, he could not complete the shift away from the subjectivism-voluntarism-humanism of his early ontology to the non-humanistic approach of his mature thinking.

The "movement" of authentic temporality bears a striking resemblance to the movement of a living being. Just as a living being "presents" itself, or grows, by spiraling in upon and out from its own internal *dynamis,* so, too, authentic existence is a spiral in which future is an unfolding of possibilities inherent in one's fate. Temporality is Dasein's *dynamis.* Authenticity means becoming this temporal dynamic in the most appropriate way. Authenticity or self-possessedness comes about through resoluteness, which "constitutes the *loyalty* of existence to its own Self." (SZ, 391/443) Note that it is not the "I" or ego which chooses itself; individual existence chooses to be what it already is. Put in another way: care chooses to care about itself. Who, then, *is* the "self" who chooses to be self-possessed? Further consideration of the analogy between authentic temporality and the *dynamis* of living beings will help suggest an answer to this puzzling question.

The expression "temporality generates itself" is a translation of the phrase "*Zeitlichkeit sich zeitigt,*" which can also be translated as "temporality ripens" or "temporality matures." A fruit is ripe when it has manifested all the stages pre-ordained by its *dynamis.* To say that temporality "ripens" suggests at least two things. First, temporality organizes itself according to its internal dynamic, just as the plant ripens in accordance with its *dynamis.* Second, temporality seems to develop during the course of a person's life. Inauthentic temporality may be "immature." Our temporality fails so often to ripen appropriately because temporal existence involves freedom. Unlike plants or animals, we are free to choose one way of living over another. As finite potentiality-for-Being, we are always in the process of becoming. I am most free when I bind myself to the possibilities defined by the heritage which I inescapably share with others. I am not a human being "in general," but a particular person in a particular historical community. If I let myself be the care that I am, I become concerned about my most proper possibilities. I let go of the tendency to manipulate my situation, and I accept my limitations.

Writing in 1934 in a regional periodical, *Der Alemanne*, Heidegger offers a revealing portrait of his personal understanding of the relation between heritage and the resolute individual. The title of the essay, "Why Do I Stay in the Provinces?", refers to his decision to turn down the offer of the chair of philosophy at the University of Berlin in order to remain at Freiburg. His most striking claim is that his philosophical work is intimately involved with the natural and human cycles of Swabia. He tells us that he is never a subject observing the landscape as an object; instead, he experiences

> its hourly changes, day and night, in the great comings and goings of the season. The gravity of the mountains, the hardness of their primeval rock, the slow and deliberate growth of the fir-trees, the brilliant, simple splendor of the meadows in bloom, the rush of the mountain brook in the long autumn night, the stern simplicity of the flatlands covered with snow—all of this moves and flows through and penetrates daily existence up there, and not in forced moments of "aesthetic" immersion or artificial empathy, but only when one's own existence stands in its work. It is the work alone that opens up space for the reality that is these mountains. The course of the work remains embedded in what happens in the region. (WBW, 216/122)

Much like the slow development of trees, the thinker develops by gathering together his own forces within the soil of philosophical tradition. He is transported into the rhythm of the work over which he does not exercise full control. This work "belongs right in the midst of the peasants' work." (WBW, 216/123) Just as the peasant farmer is aware of the presence of the earth he tills, so Heidegger is aware of the presence of the mountains when he tries to give expression to the experience of this presence. He sits and talks with the peasants about simple things, such as the weather or a neighbor's health, but mostly they remain silent. They are simply aware of their own presence to each other as neighbors. Heidegger makes clear how seriously he takes his peasant origins when he writes: "The inner relationship of my own work to the Black Forest and its people comes from a centuries-long and irreplaceable rootedness in the Alemannian-Swabian soil." (WBW, 217/123)

Such remarks about rootedness in the soil take on a changed meaning when we recall that Heidegger made them during the time of his involvement with National Socialism. His praise of the country life appealed to many Germans whose lives had been disrupted by the industrialization of the late nineteenth and early twentieth centuries. He was careful to distinguish himself, however, from those propagandists who "chatter about 'folk-character' and 'rootedness in the soil'". (WBW, 218/124) City-dwellers, we are informed, have a difficult time of understanding the solitude and depth of country life. The implication is plain that Heidegger's thinking, so interwoven with the rhythms of his ancestral region, has a more legitimate claim to being true to the rhythms of the German people. These rhythms are unlike the fast-paced tempo of life in mass-culture. Far more important than the praise of some fashionable newspaper, Heidegger remarks, is the death-bed inquiry made about him by an old friend, a peasant women. (WBW, 218/124) These same peasants also offered advice about some of his most crucial decisions. He asked a 75-year-old farmer, for example, what he thought about the offer made to Heidegger to go to Berlin: "Slowly he fixed the sure gaze of his clear eyes on mine, and keeping his mouth tightly shut, he thoughtfully put his faithful hand on my shoulder. Ever so slightly he shook his head. That meant: absolutely no!" (WBW, 218/124)

Heidegger's attachment to his homeland explains in part why he was critical of technological-industrial civilization: it uproots people from the earth to which they belong. People who claim that industrialization promises to liberate mankind from the drudgery of labor, such as Marx, would regard Heidegger's praise of the country life as reactionary and romantic. Marx spoke often about the "idiocy" caused by rural life. Although it is true that country people sometimes suffer from isolation and poverty, many have testified that they gain strength of spirit in the presence of their land. The fact that this possibility seems foreign to intellectuals raised in Manhattan or Paris in no way undermines the claims made by people raised on the soil. Already in the 1930s Heidegger was speaking in a way very congenial to contemporary ecological thinkers: both believe that human beings become healthy and whole only when they learn how to dwell within the natural world, not when they attempt to subjugate it. We are to take seriously Heidegger's interpretation of the ancient fable which claims that man is made from the Earth. (SZ, 196-200/241-243) We are earthly beings who care for ourselves. "Man's *perfectio*—his transformation into that which he can be in Being-free for his ownmost possibilities (projection)—is 'accomplished' by 'care'." (SZ, 199/243) Our ability to be open to ourselves and others is enhanced when we are in tune with the natural movements of the earth from which we spring. Plato suggested that we live most harmoniously when the circles of our minds are in tune with the spheres of the cosmos. Heidegger at times suggests that caring for ourselves in the right way means letting ourselves be cared for by the natural order. Hugh Prather echoes some of these themes when he says:

> We are forced to grow whether we want to or not, and for me that is a comforting fact. It evidences at least one aspect of the workings of the universe that could be compared to human love. In being made to look at my own mortality, I was in some way being cared for, because the result was that I gained respect for the common material of my life and began a more considerate use of the time I had left.[17]

What Heidegger means by care can perhaps best be understood as love. We often confuse genuine love with romantic infatuation, which is usually a form of egoism and lust. Genuine loving means being *open* to our possibilities and to those of others. Only when we are freed from self-hatred, greed, and delusion can we really love, for only then does egoism fade away. In Paul's first letter to the Corinthians, we find a wonderful existentiell expression of the existential idea of authentic care:

Love [*agape*] is patient and kind; love is not jealous or boastful; it is not arrogant or rude. Love does not insist on its own way; it is not irritable or resentful; it does not rejoice at wrong, but rejoices in the right. Love bears all things, believes all things, hopes all things, endures all things.

Love never ends; as for prophecies, they will pass away; as for tongues, they will cease; as for knowledge, it will pass away. For our knowledge is imperfect and our prophecy is imperfect; but when the perfect comes, the imperfect will pass away. When I was a child, I spoke like a child, I thought like a child, I reasoned like a child; when I became a man, I gave up childish ways. For now we see in a mirror dimly, but then face to face. Now I know in part; then I shall understand fully, even as I have been fully understood. So faith, hope, and love abide, these three; but the greatest of these is love.[18]

"Childish ways" might be those of the ego, while "adult ways" might be those of one who is open. To "see in a mirror dimly" might mean to obscure our openness in which things manifest themselves. To "see face to face" might mean to become fully open for what is. Christianity maintains that we cannot become open (or redeemed) without the intervention of divine grace to free us from our fallen ways. Although Heidegger was influenced by Paul, Augustine, and Luther, all of whom stressed the relative impotence of human will in gaining salvation, he placed considerable emphasis on the courage and will required to heed the summons of conscience. He is in accord with the Christian doctrine of grace insofar as he admits that we cannot initiate the call of conscience which announces that a change in our temporal openness is about to occur. But he makes no appeal to God. His concept of authenticity as resoluteness is evidently affected by Aristotle's notion that the human being is naturally capable of perfecting himself to some degree; by the ideals of autonomy and self-determination so important to Enlightenment thinkers such as Leibniz and Kant; and by the voluntarism of Nietzsche. The strain of subjectivism-voluntarism in his early notion of authenticity is tempered by the suggestion that authenticity is an *ontological*, not just a personal, event. In his later writings, Heidegger describes authenticity as something which happens *to* an individual. Authenticity is the moment when a new revelation of Being occurs. He came to see ever more clearly that the true "self" is not the self-willed individual but the temporality which belongs to Being. I am most myself when "I" disappear and become the openness needed for beings to be manifest.

Authentic temporality makes possible historically-decisive changes in how Western man understands Being. Already in *Being and Time* Heidegger suggests that "world-time" is more fundamental than individual temporality. *"World-time...is also 'more subjective' than any possible subject; for it is what first makes possible the Being of the factically existing Self—that Being which, as is now well understood, is the meaning [sense] of care."* (SZ, 419/472) At this point, he had not yet arrived at a clear understanding of how individuals "participate" in this world-time. Later on, he developed the notion that modern world-time discloses beings primarily as objects for exploitation by the human Subject. The fact that we all share in world-time means that we share a common destiny. Only by reappropriating our common heritage can we meet the challenge of that destiny. All resoluteness is inextricably bound up with the tradition into which one is born:

> The authentic existentiell understanding is so far from extricating itself from the way of interpreting Dasein which has come down to us, that in each case it is in terms of this interpretation, against it and yet again for it, that any possibility one has chosen is seized upon in one's resolution. (SZ, 383/435)

Heritage is often regarded as a set of old-fashioned ideas, attitudes, or values. Rarely do we see how our heritage is always at work setting up our future possibilities. Attempts to revitalize heritage often become businesses devoted to turning out marketable facsimiles of the era chosen for veneration. The leaders of mass-culture prey on the real sense of rootlessness by cultivating instant nostalgia for styles and customs of the previous decade. By accepting this ersatz heritage, an individual can avoid the resolve required to become rooted in his cultural traditions. In a passage manifesting his existentiell attitude toward inauthentic cultivation of tradition, Heidegger says:

> Once one has grasped the finitude of one's existence, it snatches one back from the endless multiplicity of possibilities which offer themselves as closest to one—those of comfortableness, shirking, and tak-

ing things lightly—and brings Dasein into the simplicity of its *fate*.
(SZ, 384/435)

Earlier we considered the parallels between the *dynamis* of a plant
and the authentic temporality of a human being. Another parallel
now presents itself. The healthy plant reaches toward the sky because
its roots go deep into the earth. A shallow-rooted plant is subject to
disease; it can easily be swept away by storms and floods. Heritage is
the soil of an individual and of his community. The deeper people
sink their roots into their heritage, the greater will be their own development as human beings. Heidegger regards creative transformation of tradition as the source of communal health: "If everything
'good' is a heritage, and the character of 'goodness' lies in making
authentic existence possible, then the handing down of a heritage
constitutes itself in resoluteness." (SZ, 383/435) Although Heidegger
prefaces this statement by "if," there is little doubt that he agrees
that goodness does involve the promotion of authenticity. Promoting
authenticity in my community means acknowledging that my fate is
bound up with a more inclusive historical destiny:

> Our fates have already been guided in advance, in our Being-with
> one another in the same world and in our resoluteness for definite
> possibilities. Only in communicating and in struggling does the power
> of destiny become free. Dasein's fateful destiny in and with its 'gen-
> eration' goes to make up the full authentic historizing of Dasein. (SZ,
> 384-385/436)

The authentic individual subordinates his personal aims to the
effort of his community to cultivate its heritage and thus to keep
itself healthy. Subordination does not mean blind following, since
one can best maintain those commitments made on the basis of genuine understanding. When Heidegger says that "Higher than actuality
stands *possibility*" (SZ, 38/63), he means that we are always free to
make a creative response to destiny—we are not merely victims of it.
We stand in a dialogue with a tradition. It not only inspires us: we
also inspire it! As authentic, we are the center of the dialogue between
necessity and freedom, actuality and possibility. As we struggle to
help bring forth what is highest in destiny, we are the place where it
is decided. The following chapter explores the role of the cultural

hero, who renews the dormant tradition in a dramatic and unsuspected manner. He reveals a set of possibilities which seem to be the necessary subsequent stage in the development of that tradition.

Some have asserted that Heidegger was naive to assume that his notion of interpretation as a tearing-away of concealments could be transferred to the sphere of politics. Yet this assumption is not surprising in a thinker for whom Nietzsche was so important. Like Nietzsche, Heidegger regarded self pity—"shirking, taking things lightly" —as the enemy of the highest possibilities of a community. Like the prophets of old, he believed that a way had to be made for truth. He who is called on to summon his people to a resolute reappropriation of their tradition must be prepared to take responsibility for suffering and sacrifice. Gandhi and Martin Luther King, Jr. were well aware that non-violent protest, designed to bring social justice by appealing to the conscience of the oppressor, must be *militant* to be effective. Individuals can on occasion transcend the limitations of their egoistical points of view and become the informed communal clearing in which their slumbering tradition can resume its proper development. All great socio-political movements, however, risk sacrificing to their high purposes people who do not *choose* to be sacrificed. I return to some of these themes in Chapter Six, which examines Heidegger's effort to bring about a change in German destiny in 1933-1934.

In this chapter, I have explained that the unity of our experience is made possible by the self-unifying activity of temporality. I have also shown that the self is fully integrated only when it resolves to retrieve its own possibilities. The possibilities of an individual are inextricably involved with the possibilities of his community. When our historical existence is authentic, our past is freed for the future by the resolve of the present. *Being and Time's* notion that authentic temporality is the *Augenblick* contains the seed of his mature conception of authenticity. In Heidegger's later writings, the authentic self does not clear itself, nor does it set out to achieve its own possibilities. Instead, the authentic self is cleared by the "destiny of Being," and becomes the communicative vessel required for a world-historical change in how beings manifest themselves. In chapters to come, I consider this subtle shift from individual and communal *human* authenticity to the "authenticity of Being" (*Ereignis*).

CHAPTER FIVE

The Moment of Vision and World-Historical Heroism

THE PREVIOUS chapters examined the concept of authenticity which Heidegger developed in the 1920s. Authenticity means self-possessed, temporal-historical Being-in-the-world, which is concerned about itself. In anticipatory resoluteness, an individual discloses his finitude and appropriates his own possibilities. These possibilities are bound up with the heritage in which he must root himself. Heritage, paradoxically, does not lie behind us; it stands before us as our future. To exist toward the future authentically means freeing heritage for a change commensurate with the demands of the present. Authentic existence means authentic temporality, the moment of vision (*Augenblick*) in which an individual's past, present, and future generate themselves in a great spiral. An individual's life acquires continuity and depth as he repeats his resolutions. In each *Augenblick*, he gains a more profound understanding of what it means "to be." Hence, authentic temporality is an ontological event, not merely a personal experience.

Being and Time's analysis of authenticity is so appealing because it deals in part with the universal problem of individuation. Although the book's major intention was to demonstrate the relation between human temporality and the event of Being (unconcealment), it was largely received as an existentialist manifesto favoring individual self-actualization. Heidegger's readers seized on the powerful dramatic theme of authenticity, to the neglect of the overriding ontological

theme. Dismayed by this reception of his work, he set out to emphasize his ontological concerns. For our study, it is important to note
that he did not abandon his interest in authenticity, but approached
this phenomenon from a different perspective. It might be more accurate to say that he assumed the perspective which was to have been
developed in the never-published second-half of *Being and Time.* In
that portion of the book, he intended to describe the important
changes in the "history of Being." In the 1930s he devoted himself
to understanding two aspects of this history. First, he tried to describe the subtle but crucial shifts in Western man's understanding of
Being. Second, he sought to explain *how* these changes have occurred.
His interpretation of man's relation to the history of Being resembles
Hegel's interpretation of man's relation to the history of Absolute
Spirit. Hegel claimed that the real "meaning" of history is not found
in human achievements (whether individual or collective), but in the
stages achieved by Absolute Spirit on its way toward total self-consciousness. New stages in this history are introduced by world-historical individuals who may think they are acting solely for personal reasons, but who are in fact fated to play roles in a drama whose importance transcends their individual interests. Heidegger, too, regarded
history, not as a human event, but as a cosmic one—the history of
the revelation of the Being of beings. By suggesting in places that
history involves the self-actualization of the possibilities of individuals or historical peoples, *Being and Time* concealed the transcendent
and historical nature of the event of Being. To correct this suggestion,
Heidegger later explained that authenticity is not a matter of personal
achievement or arbitrary choice, but is a matter of fate. Authentic
individuals are those chosen as sites for new, historically-decisive
revelations of Being. His mature version of authenticity minimized
voluntarism (the will to self-actualization) and anthropocentrism
(interpreting the understanding of Being as a human possession, instead of as a gift). Authenticity happens to an individual when he is
released from self-will so he can be open for what transcends him:
the Being of beings. At times, however, in discussing the authentic
world-historical individual, Heidegger still referred to the struggle
required to accept the role of being open for revelation. To the very
end, he continued to describe authenticity in terms of a radical alter-

ation of temporality. World-historical heroism occurs when an individual overcomes the egoism which threatens to prevent this crucial alteration from happening. The later version of authenticity, then, lacks much of the "existentialist" flavor which belongs to the voluntaristic version found in *Being and Time*. The topic of this chapter is the way Heidegger developed *Being and Time's* notion of the *Augenblick* as the way an individual is chosen to be cleared for a new manifestation of Being.

Part One of this chapter demonstrates that the idea of the *Augenblick* is similar to the New Testament concept of *kairos*, the "time of fulfillment." In *kairos*, eternity breaks in upon historical existence, the Word becomes flesh. Properly "de-mythologized," *kairos* means that an individual undergoes the change of temporality necessary for a new understanding of Being. Heidegger appropriated the theological idea of *kairos* for his own ontological purposes. Part Two considers Heidegger's 1936 lectures on Schelling, which—as part of his continuing meditation on the religious-theological understanding of authentic temporality—helped clarify for him the relation between the authentic individual and the historical change in the self-disclosure of Being. Part Three, which focuses on Heidegger's 1937 lectures on Nietzsche, describes the blossoming of the idea of the *Augenblick*, now understood as the moment in which a poet or thinker receives a new revelation of Being. Such a world-historical revelation is not achieved *by* an individual but happens *through* him. Authenticity (*Eigentlichkeit*) means being "appropriated" (*er-eignet*) by the "event of appropriation" (*Ereignis*). *Ereignis* will be treated in detail in later chapters.

PART ONE: *Kairos* as the *Augenblick.*

As I indicated earlier, theology and philosophy were closely related in the development of Heidegger's understanding of authenticity. His study of the New Testament provided him with an existentiell model for the existential analysis of human Dasein. He found that the New Testament interpretation of human temporality, which differs considerably from the Greco-modern interpretation, was in harmony with his idea that human existence constitutes the interplay between presence and absence. Heidegger regarded Kant as the only previous thinker to surmise that there is an intrinsic relation between Being (presence, manifestness) and time (absence), although even Kant did not work out this relation explicitly. Yet when Heidegger remarked that "So far as anything essential has been achieved in today's analyses which will take us beyond Aristotle and Kant, it pertains more to the way time is grasped and to our 'consciousness of time'"(SZ, 443/501), he was probably referring to Husserl's lectures on internal time consciousness, which Heidegger edited.[1] To criticize the conventional wisdom about time and Being, Heidegger first learned the tradition better than anyone else. Then, opposed to it, he developed an alternative conception of time from an equally respected, but different, tradition: the one represented by the New Testament. Only such a confrontation between these radically different traditions could make Being and time questionable again.[2]

The idea that the *Augenblick*—self-circling temporality—is the only experience of eternity possible for finite human beings stems from Heidegger's attempt to interpret in existential-ontological terms the New Testament's eschatological pronouncements, especially concerning the possibility of everlasting life. As part of the generation following Dilthey and Nietzsche, and as a theology student exposed to the views of the liberal theologians of the era, Heidegger was influenced by the attitude that belief in a literal life after death and in the Second Coming (*paraousia*) as an actual historical event were remnants of an other-worldliness whose time had passed. Freud's attitude toward religion is not unrepresentative of other intellectuals of his day. According to Freud, religious beliefs (including hope for life after death) are rooted in an infantilism and mass neurosis, the continuation of which leads to a sense of despair for anyone with a "friendly" attitude toward mankind.[3]

In Chapter One of this essay, we discussed briefly Heidegger's lectures on the phenomenology of religion (1920–21), in which he interpreted Paul's letters as expressing a revolutionary notion of time.[4] According to Paul, the sinful person is asleep to God, unaware of the presence of the Lord. As a result, he experiences the past as a dead weight (sin, guilt) and the future as threatening. In trying to live by and for himself, the sinful person fails to understand himself as a creature or child of God. When, through God's grace, a person is freed from his blindness, he suddenly recognizes that he has always been a child of God; that God has always been somehow present in his life; that his life has been unfolding in accordance with some hidden dynamic; that he is now and always has been who he is supposed to be. Heidegger uses the term *Gewesenheit* ("being-as-having-been," or "alreadiness") to give voice to this experience of the past as the ever-present, future-determining fate which draws us along. For Paul, of course, the sense of being drawn along into what one has always already been is precisely the presence of God in one's life. Clearly, though, God is not present in any ordinary way; He is not an object in time. Instead, God is present as absence, that is, as the temporality which clears the individual of selfishness which had led him to forget about the ever-present God. The truly Christian life means living *as* this temporality, letting this self-absencing presence be operative in everything one does. In the life of faith, one must be constantly vigilant, always resolving to keep oneself open for God's presence, instead of trying to manipulate the world so as to gain an illusory "security." Indeed, faithful life demands an end to all hope for security and demands that one take the leap of affirming that one has already been saved.

Heidegger set out to provide a phenomenological interpretation of *kairos,* the "time of fulfillment," in order to reveal its ontological-existential structure. In his analysis, which involves reduction, destruction, and construction, he first calls attention to the existential question: what are the conditions necessary for the possibility of an experience like the one described mythologically-existentielly in the New Testament as *kairos*? After this reduction (de-mythologizing), he tries to de-structure the traditional interpretation of eternity by showing it to be groundless. Finally, he constructs an interpretation which lets the phenomenon be revealed. The Western theological-philosophical tradition, which interpreted the New Testament in terms of the ordinary notion of time, failed to see that the time of fulfillment (*kairos*) does not necessarily refer to some "point" of time in the unspecified future, but can also mean the experience of eternity right here and now, if eternity is understood in terms of the self-circling temporality whose ontological possibility is described in *Being and Time*. Although Heidegger regarded belief in the afterlife strictly as a matter of faith (SZ, 247-248/292), he did point out that, philosophically, there are serious problems in understanding the meaning of eternal life if we regard eternity as an infinite stream of nows. Such a view of eternity and time is derived from an inauthentic experience of temporality. In a note in *Being and Time*, we read:

> The fact that the traditional concept of "eternity" as signifying the "standing now" (*nunc stans*), has been drawn from the ordinary way of understanding time and has been defined with an orientation towards the idea of 'constant' presence-at-hand, does not need to be discussed in detail. If God's eternity can be 'construed' philosophically, then it may be understood only as a more primordial temporality which is 'infinite'. (SZ, 427/499)[5]

The New Testament is filled with passages which warn that the *paraousia*, the return of the Lord, will happen at the right time and without any warning.[6] That the Lord will return "like a thief in the night" means that the Christian must be ever vigilant and prepared for His coming. Paul apparently believed that His return was imminent. In his letters we find descriptions of human life lived out on the edge, open to the abyss of death, and faithful to the Lord who promised eternal life to those who chose to be faithful. It has been suggested that Heidegger's existential concept of *Angst*, which was heavily influenced by Kierkgaard, is revealed existentielly in Paul's suffering, homesickness, danger, proximity, and watching in the dark night.[7] Despite his trials and tribulations, indeed because of them, Paul is filled with joy. By accepting the "thorn in the side," he took upon himself his own cross and gained the experience of eternity thereby. That Paul believed that there is a this-worldly experience of *kairos* or redemption, and that such an experience presupposes the resolute acceptance of one's dependence on God, can be gleaned from statements such as the following:

> Besides this you know what hour it is, how it is full time now for you to wake from sleep. For salvation is nearer to us now than when we first believed; the night is far gone, the day is at hand....[8]

Therefore, if any one is in Christ, he is a new creation, the old has passed away, behold, the new has come.[9]

Working together with him, then, we entreat you not to accept the grace of God in vain. For he says,
  "At the acceptable time, I have listened to you,
   and helped you on the day of salvation."
Behold, now is the acceptable time; behold, now is the day of salvation.[10]

Such statements suggest that redemption occurs, or eternity breaks into the finite, when one accepts the grace of God and chooses to have faith in Christ. Paul's claim that "The last enemy to be destroyed [by God] is death"[11] can be taken literally to mean that at some future point, God will resurrect the dead and judge their worthiness to spend eternity with Him. But it can also be taken to mean that acceptance of the Lord here and now brings an end to the perception of death as an enemy. In Heidegger's way of thinking, as long as a person flees from his own mortality, he leads an inauthentic life based on his conviction that he is a self-grounding, immortal ego. To accept one's mortality is to become what one already is: finite temporality which is concerned about itself. As if to oppose his conception of authenticity to literal interpretations of the idea of salvation as an "overcoming" of death (in which human finitude is concealed!), Heidegger says:

Anticipatory resoluteness is not a way of escape, fabricated for the 'overcoming' of death; it is rather that understanding which follows the call of conscience and which frees for death the *power* over Dasein's existence and of basically dispersing all fugitive self-concealments. (SZ, 310/357)

Heidegger also speaks of how anticipation of death allows Dasein to be itself as an "impassioned *freedom towards death*." (SZ, 266/311) Evidently, there is not much room within this existential concept of authentic Being-towards-death for an existentiell concept permitting an individual to de-fuse *Angst* by believing he will not really die after all but will be saved from death by divine intervention. Real faith, however, acknowledges the abyss of death and in so doing shatters the egoism which often misuses religion in order to conceal death.

According to Heidegger, when a person is redeemed, he is emancipated from the egoism which stems from self-hatred and self-ignorance. Interpreted in light of Heidegger's existential analytic, Paul's letters can be read to say that one is re-born into eternal life right here and now, when one accepts Christ as saviour. Being re-born means waking up, gaining an entirely new self-understanding, and living in accordance with the fact that the return of the Lord has already happened and has been happening for all time. In spiritual re-birth, the individual feels as if his life has been bestowed upon him a second time. He now receives graciously and thankfully what he always already had been given: the presence of God as his very life. The future, which he had once both feared and hoped for, is now experienced as the present fulfillment of the living spirit he has always been.

Heidegger's analysis of the New Testament concept of *kairos* was mediated by his study of Kierkegaard. As a Christian theologian and an ethical thinker, Kierkegaard was concerned with understanding the ontological structure of human life in order to provide illumination for the individual life-task of becoming fully human in the act of faith. He attempted to understand the life, death, and resurrection of Jesus Christ, not as an event in the historical past, but as a present reality in the life of each individual. The expression "Christ has come, Christ has died, Christ will come again" includes the three dimensions of temporality as well as the notions of repetition and anticipation necessary for authentic temporality.[12] Calvin Schrag points out that in the "moment of vision" as understood by Kierkegaard, there occurs both the integration of the self *and* the breaking-in of the eternal into the finite existence of the self. Self-integration arises from the repetition of one's chosen possibility; the ethical man, for example, resolves to deepen his commitment to his wife. The eternal breaks into the finite, however, only when this resolute repetition is deepened in the leap of faith.[13] Kierkegaard's analyses of Job and Abraham describe the authentic temporality which characterize the acts of repetition made in light of faith. Schrag explains this very well when he says:

> Through faith Abraham miraculously receives Isaac, and by constantly repeating his faith he receives him again, after having "lost" him in the intended act of sacrifice. Abraham is contrasted with the trag-

ic hero, who, incapable of repetition, merely renounces in an act of resignation....He could have...thus fulfilled the role of a tragic hero who succumbs to fate or the necessity of the past. But Abraham willed repetition through an act of faith.[14]

Kierkegaard, critical of the conception of eternity as an infinity of instants, tried to comprehend the ecstatic moment in which an individual feels the presence of the eternal within his own finite existence. He interpreted eternity as "a qualification of existence which transfigures the temporality of the self in a moment of decision."[15] The crucial decision involves resolving to repeat the life of Christ, i.e., resolving to shoulder the burden of one's own cross. Yet precisely in this resolution, the weight of the cross (the burden of guilt and sin) is alleviated. The desperate life of the egoistical person arises from his failure to see that he is not self-creating and self-sustaining. The egoist resents his finitude and thus tries to dominate the world to gain compensation. He is freed from this compulsive life, however, when he recognizes that his life is not his own but a gift for which thanksgiving is appropriate. Giving thanks for life would mean to accept and affirm its limitations and pain. Such acceptance, however, is possible only because the redeemed person lives from out of a new mode of temporality in which he experiences himself as always becoming who he already is. This spiritual unfolding, in which the future is revealed as the present fulfillment of what has always been, is understood as the continual re-birth of Christ in the soul. There is a tendency, of course, for faith to become weak and thus for the experience of eternity to fade. Hence, it is crucial for the Christian to practice repetition of his commitment to faith; he must want to become who he already is; he must somehow anticipate the presence of God within his own finite life. In Kierkegaard's notion of repetition we can discern a model for Heidegger's idea of "retrieving" (wiederholen). For Kierkegaard, retrieving the past or resolving to repeat it means letting the power within operate as it has always been doing, but now without the obstacle of self-will or egoism. In authentic temporality we see that each moment is the necessary realization or fulfillment of what we have always been and will always be. The experience of eternity is a self-circling, self-unfolding spiral. God announces his eternal nature when he utters "I Am who Am." We become most like God when we let ourselves become who we already are: finite love or openness. The perversity of life lies in our denial of the enduring presence of love.

Heidegger regarded Kierkegaard's analysis of temporality and authenticity as brilliant but limited to the existentiell-ontical realm. The life of the resolute, faithful Christian is only one way to appropriate one's heritage, to become authentic, to be who one already is. Heidegger wanted to describe the ontological-existential conditions necessary for *any* possible moment of vision or resolute anticipation of death. His aim was not existentiell-religious, as was Kierkegaard's, but existential-ontological: he sought to answer the question of the sense of Being by analyzing the sense of *human* Being. Any particular resolve is possible only because human beings always have some self-understanding. In the resolve of faith, an individual no longer understands himself as a self-willed ego but as a child of God who must obey His commands in order to be most fully the individual he was created to be and already is. There is no guarantee, however, that this choice is the most appropriate one. That is why an act of faith, or any other instance of resoluteness, involves a risk. Kierkegaard, Paul, Augustine, Pascal, Luther, and Heidegger are all part of the ancient tradition which speaks of the danger and difficulty inherent in the life of faith or authenticity.

Heidegger's evaluation of Kierkegaard's conception of authentic temporality is summarized in the following note from *Being and Time:*

S. Kierkegaard is probably the one who has seen the *existentiell* phenomenon of the moment of vision with the most penetration; but this does not signify that he has been correspondingly successful in interpreting it existentially. He clings to the ordinary conception of time, and defines the "moment of vision" with the help of "now" and "eternity." When Kierkegaard speaks of 'temporality', what he has in mind is man's 'Being in time'. Time as within-time-ness knows only the "now"; it never knows a moment of vision. If, however, such a moment gets experienced in an existentiell manner, then a more primordial temporality has been presupposed, although existentially it has not been made explicit. (SZ, 338/497)

Heidegger suggests that Kierkegaard probably experienced a moment of vision (*Augenblick*) which could not be interpreted existentially without a Heideggerian understanding of the relation of time and Being. Kierkegaard was still too much a part of the metaphysical tradition represented by Hegel, Kierkegaard's great enemy, but also his great teacher. Kierkegaard reacted against Hegel's "essentialism" with his own "existentialism," but this inversion did not free Kierkegaard from the limitations of the metaphysical interpretation of time as instants and Being as constant presence. Yet Kierkegaard had insight into the relation of the change of human temporality to the alteration in self-understanding. Because he was a Christian theologian, however, Kierkegaard did not undertake an independent philosophical investigation of the conditions necessary for the possibility of Christian faith. His approach to the problem of what it means to be human was always a blend of the existentiell and the existential, with more emphasis on the former. Heidegger, on the other hand, emphasized the existential in his analysis of human Being. That Kierkegaard and Heidegger differed in this can be seen immediately by comparing *Either/Or* with *Being and Time*.

The question is, however, whether Heidegger's interpretation of Kierkegaard's understanding of time and eternity is really fair to the Danish thinker to whom he owes so much. At times Heidegger seems to make Kierkegaard more of a subjectivistic thinker than he actually was, particularly with regard to the question of the relation between temporality and eternity. At one point in *Being and Time,* Heidegger refers to Karl Jaspers' *Psychologie der Weltanschauungen* for confirmation of Kierkegaard's idea that the "lived moment" reveals more than the conclusions produced by rational calculation. Jaspers says:

> To see the life of man, one must see how he lives in the moment [*Augenblick*]. The moment is the single reality, the reality in general in spiritual life. The lived moment is that which is final, the warm-blooded, the immediate, the living, the vital [*leibhaftig*] present, the totality of the real, that alone which is concrete. Instead of losing the present itself in past and future, man finds *Existenz* and the absolute only in the moment of vision. Past and future are dark, uncertain abysses, they are endless time, whereas the moment can be the cancelling of time, the presence of eternity.[16]

Yet Kierkegaard, like Heidegger, did not want to "cancel" past and future. He wanted to show how they can be united in the *Augenblick;* he wanted to display the presence of the eternal within the temporal. Nevertheless, Kierkegaard's religious orientation did allow him to conceive of eternity as in some sense beyond time. Heidegger, however, regarded authentic temporality as the origin of the experience of eternity: eternity *is* authentic temporality. Taking heed from Nietzsche, Heidegger turned his eyes earthward and away from the ideal of eternity as unchanged reality (heaven), an idea which continued to affect Kierkegaard's thinking in certain respects, although not nearly so much as Heidegger would have us believe. Heidegger's hestitation to accord full recognition to the importance of Kierkegaard's thinking may arise in part from Heidegger's desire to put distance between himself and his own theological background. As his thinking developed and his own self-understanding grew, however, he became ever more aware of the decisive influence of these theological origins.

Bultmann's theology reflects the influence of Heidegger's interpretation of *kairos.* In 1928, Bultmann claimed that the flight into worldliness (egoism, sinfulness) is a rejection of one's own dynamic potentiality-to-be; that is, a rejection of the openness to the future, the sign of redemption. Bultmann says that "the world is always already the past. All that the world has is unreal and a lie; it has already passed away, since it remains with the old and never leads into the future. The world lies dead."[17] Sinful existence is living death, for in it an individual tries to conceal the source of the vitality for human life: readiness for growth, or readiness to become who we already are. Bultmann agreed with Heidegger that redemption involves acceptance of finitude. Only such an acceptance can destroy the power of the ego and allow the individual to be open to change. As a Christian theologian, however, Bultmann held that it is impossible for purely secular man to achieve such acceptance and redemption on his own. Philosophy can reveal the difficult truth about life: freedom for the future requires resoluteness in the face of death. But only *grace* makes such resolute faith possible. "Indeed, faith is identical with readiness for dread, for faith knows that God encounters us at the very point where the human prospect is nothingness, and only at that point."[18]

According to Bultmann, Heidegger cannot really explain how it is that an individual can accept his own finitude. Only the intervention of divine grace can give man the strength required to shoulder the burden of life, Bultmann insists.

Yet Bultmann seems to have a *this*-worldly concept of redemption. Right after he points out that faith (through grace) gives readiness for openness to the finite future, he refers to Paul's famous remarks:

> "Death is swallowed up in victory."
> "O death, where is thy victory?"
> "O death, where is thy sting?"
> The sting of death is sin, and the power of sin is the law.[19]

To say that the *sting* of death is sin is analogous to saying that *Angst* causes us to strive mightily (and vainly) to protect the ego. The egoistical life growing from this struggle is the real torment of death. Once the faithful individual has accepted suffering and death, his past is no longer something at which to gnash his teeth because it cannot be changed, and his future is no longer to be feared because it cannot be controlled. Instead, the redeemed individual is suffused by joy, for he is released from the egoistical desire to control everything. He is free to let things be in the most appropriate way. When one can say "To all that has been Thanks! To all that will be, Yes!" he shares John's claim that in the Lord, "it is always Yes." The event of redemption requires no "visions." It transforms one's everyday life. Luke says of Christ:

> Being asked by the Pharisees when the kingdom of God was coming, he answered them, "The kingdom of God is not coming with signs to be observed; nor will they say, 'Lo, here it is! or 'There!' for behold, the kingdom of God is in the midst of you."[20]

Passages such as this inspired Heidegger's attempt to offer a new understanding of redemption to a world in which "God is dead."

While at Marburg in the 1920s, Heidegger was also a colleague of Paul Tillich, another Protestant theologian influenced by his "existentialist" thinking. At least as early as 1926, Tillich had developed an interpretation of *kairos* which agrees in many ways with Heidegger's. For example, we read in his essay, *"Kairos* II: Ideas for the Spiritual Situation of the Present":

> *Kairos* means fulfilled time, the concrete historical moment of vision [*Augenblick*], and in the prophetic sense "time of fulfillment" [*"Zeit-enfülle"*], the breaking-in of the eternal into time. *Kairos* is thus not the "instant" [*Augenblick*] filled up in the same way, not the chang-ing fragment of the stream of time, but it is time insofar as there is fulfilled in it the utterly meaningful, insofar as time is fate. To con-sider time as *kairos* means to consider it in the sense of an inescap-able decision, an unavoidable responsibility, and means to consider it in the spirit of the prophets.[21]

In *kairos,* the individual is freed from the egoism which conceals his own possibilities. This unannounced transformation of existence brings with it a demand: Decide! Because of his emphasis on decision, Tillich's interpretation of *kairos* is close to that of Heidegger and Kierkegaard:

> To stand in Nature, to take upon oneself the unavoidable actuality and not to flee from it, either into the world of ideal forms or into the related world of the supernatural, but to decide oneself in the actuality itself, that is the fundamental activity of Protestantism. Here the subject has no possibility of an absolute position. [The sub-ject] cannot move from out of the sphere of decision. On every side of its essence, [the subject] stands in the "between" [*Zwiespalt*]. Fate and freedom reach into the act of knowledge and make it an historical act: *kairos* determines *logos.*[22]

For both Tillich and Heidegger, there is no absolute standpoint for thinking or action; man is essentially *historical.* Although man strives to become wholly self-grounding, especially in pursuit of the rational ideal, he can never do so because he is *thrown* into existence. Wisdom is not to be identified with knowledge achieved by supposedly objec-tive, rational calculation. Only the personal struggle, made within the limitations of one's own historical setting, leads to insight.

Heidegger and Tillich were not the only ones who, in the early part of the twentieth century, emphasized that instrumental rationality was unable to provide adequate answers for ultimate life-decisions. Instrumental rationality, rooted in Cartesian subjectivism, regards

Nature as an object to be known and controlled by man and for man. From this perspective, man regards himself as the Lord of Nature, the infinite consumer and producer who can transform at will the natural world as well as the human world. Although man thus raises himself to a god-like position, at the same time he sinks to the level of a mere commodity—the most important raw material in the gigantic processes of production and consumption characteristic of industrial society. The notion that *"kairos* determines *logos,"* or that insight gained in the decisive moment of vision is more significant than conclusions arrived at by impersonal calculation, was a recurrent theme for many Germans who were dissatisfied with the liberal rationality which reduced the individual to a cog in the technological-industrial-bureaucratic apparatus. Many were taken by the idea that the logic of history is determined by fateful insights which are unpredictable and thus inaccessible to rational inquiry. They supposed that answers could be found in the depths of the soul that the surface-level intellect could not conceive. Tillich appeals to this powerful but non-rational dimensional of the self when he claims that Nietzsche

> thinks continuously in *kairos.* He knows himself in the hour of fate, in the greatest midday, the beginning of the Overman; he knows that man cannot think everything at every time and even less in every place of society. He knows that *Geist* is blood and that only what is written with blood is worthy to be read and learned. Thus is the decision-character of truth brought clearly to expression.[23]

To hear Tillich speaking like this in the 1920s is instructive. It suggests the spiritually charged conditions of life in Germany at the time. And it may help us to understand more sympathetically Heidegger's decision to side with a political movement which promised to bring Germany back to its spiritual roots.

Heidegger continued to regard the Christian experience of authentic temporality as significant long after the so-called turn in his thinking. In 1941, for example, in notes added to his 1936 lectures on Schelling, Heidegger claims that there are four stages which must be traversed in the interpretation of temporality. First, the preconceptual notion of time as days and years. Second, the Greek understanding of time as what can be dated and numbered, and the modern

understanding of time as a parameter wherein points and their conditions can be measured. Third, "The question about time with respect to the Christian experience of the 'temporally' delimited journey of the individual human soul on earth. 'Temporality'—'Eternity'."
(SA, 229) Finally, "Time as the fore-name of the projective sphere of
the truth of Being. 'Time' as the ecstatic in-between (time-space), not
the wherein of beings, but the clearing [*Lichtung*] of Being itself."
(SA, 229) Analysis of the Christian experience of temporality showed
Heidegger: (1) that there is a radically different interpretation of temporality which can be used to criticize the prevailing interpretation
of time as an independent continuum of nows; (2) that temporality
can best be understood as the dynamic in-gathering of past and future
in the *Augenblick* in which past gets appropriated in terms of the
future; (3) that destiny can come to fruition in the appropriate way
only if the human being accepts his finitude and cultivates those historically limited possibilities which make an authentic community
possible; (4) that in the transfiguration of the self from ego (inauthentic temporality) to openness for the future (authentic temporality),
Being presents itself in a new way for understanding; (5) that history
is therefore the history of different manifestations of Being; and (6)
that changes in history occur when individuals are fated to be the site
for a new revelation of Being.

Although Heidegger's appropriation of the idea of *kairos* was fruitful for his interest in time and Being, his analysis involves certain dan-
gers. Karl Lehmann wonders whether it is really possible to take *kairos*
out of its religious setting and to broaden or formalize it. Are not
such existentiell experiences as *kairos* too intertwined with their concrete situation to be used in Heidegger's fashion?[24] We are also warned
against the possibility of reducing *kairos* to something subjective.
Lehmann says that the *philosophical* interpretation of *kairos* fails to
regard it as the summons of God and hence as an absolute command;
instead it suspends this issue by inquiring into the conditions necessary for the possibility of something like a divine summons. Caution
must be exercised, Lehmann continues, not to reduce or level the
otherness intrinsic to the breaking-in experienced in *kairos*. The
possibility of a kind of humanism or subjectivism can be found in
regarding *kairos,* the New Testament idea for the intervention of

divine power into finite life, as a name for *my* futurity.[25] Heidegger tries to avoid such subjectivism by claiming that the call of conscience lies outside the power of will, that one is *summoned* to be open to one's possibilities, and that these possibilities are found in an historical context which always involves others. Yet because Heidegger's ontological-existential analysis of authentic temporality *necessarily* omits any appeal to divine grace, he must call on the resoluteness of the individual as the response necessary to let temporality transform itself into its authentic mode. Resoluteness, however, includes an element of will which Heidegger later tries to exclude from his concept of authenticity as releasement. It always remained difficult for Heidegger to describe the relation between the *truth revealed* in the moment of vision and the *experience of the individual* who is called on to be the site for such a revelation.

In this part of the chapter, we have seen how Heidegger appropriates the existentiell-theological conception of *kairos* for his own existential-philosophical purposes. Already we have learned that the *Augenblick* breaks in upon the individual, although the individual must resolve to accept what it reveals. In the next part of the chapter, I offer a preliminary account of how Heidegger moves toward his mature conception of authenticity. This movement is partly mediated, appropriately enough, by Heidegger's study of Schelling, the philosopher-theologian whose philosophical path always kept returning to the religious themes from which it originated. Heidegger interprets Schelling's lectures on human freedom to mean that the authentic self is destined to be the place where there occurs a new revelation of what it means to be.

PART TWO: **Schelling, Authentic Temporality, and the Hero Chosen for Revelation.**

In his 1936 lectures on Schelling's essay, *On the Essence of Human Freedom,* Heidegger demonstrates the inner connection between the overcoming of egoism and the event of authentic temporality. In Schelling, whom Heidegger regarded as the most profound German idealist, we find many of the themes Heidegger discusses during his years at Marburg. In these lectures, and in the Nietzsche-lectures the following year (1937), Heidegger elaborated on the notion that in the *Augenblick* the world-historical poet or thinker receives the revelation which eventually alters the prevailing understanding of Being. He sees the *Augenblick* as a more rare event than he did ten years earlier when his thinking was still influenced by Kierkegaard's existentialism. To discover how Heidegger connects overcoming egoism, authentic temporality, and heroism, we need to understand his analysis of Schelling's essay.

Because Schelling was a kind of pantheist, he held that it was necessary to understand the nature of God before we can comprehend the nature of His creatures. Creatures *are* God in the sense of being aspects of Him. God is a process of self-manifestation: a dynamic, self-unifying activity of becoming. There are two primordial elements of God: existence and ground (*Grund*). The existence of God is the inner essence from which God as Word (light, universality, order) arises. The ground is the eternal yearning for darkness and self-concealment. *Geist* or Spirit is the dynamic union of these two counter-moving aspects of God. Love is the power which draws the ground and existence of God into their eternally-becoming union. The more God as ground yearns for self-concealment, the more God as existence strives to illuminate and manifest Himself as Word. God's majesty lies in the power of Love to unite into one process these two countervailing elements. The idea that God manifests Himself in different ways in different stages of his development runs counter to the notion that God is eternally the same, eternally present, eternally contemporaneous (*gleich-zeitig*), with past and future somehow eliminated. But Heidegger asserts:

> The primordial con-temporaneity rests in the fact that being-past and being-future maintain themselves and, equiprimordially with being-present, shove up against each other as the essential fullness of time. And this shove of *authentic temporality,* this moment of vision, "is" the essence of eternity, but not the mere stayed-put and staying-put present, the *nunc stans.* Eternity lets itself be thought truly, i.e., poetically, only if we conceive it as the most primordial temporality, but never according to the manner of healthy human

understanding which says: eternity, that is the opposite of temporality.... (SA, 136)

God, the eternal process of self-determining self-manifestation, the
eternally circling unity of past and future, creates mankind as the
image wherein God can perceive His own essential nature. As God's
image, man is also composed of existence and ground. Yet, as finite,
man is unlike God. Existence and ground are *separable* in man. Here-
in lies the possibility of evil, and paradoxically, the essence of human
freedom. In God the yearning of the ground for self-concealment is
always countered by and unified with the striving of existence (God's
essense) toward universality (the Word); in man the yearning of the
ground can split apart from the will to universality, order, and community; that is, the *particular* will can set itself up against the whole.
(SA, 171) When the individual ego strives to make itself universal and
absolute, it overturns the proper relation of ground and existence.
The source of evil is the self-ishness which strikes against the structure of Being (*Seyn:* God). Evil is ontological perversion, a way of
being a self outside the proper and essential law. Self-will can raise
itself over the universal will at times, and in this elevation a kind of
spiritual unification does occur. But such a unity is in direct opposition to the divine Will, and, hence, opposed to the primordial unity
of Being. (SA, 174-175) Although God is the inseparable unity of
ground and existence, the essence of God is existence: universal self-
illumination, *Logos.* This self-manifesting can occur only in the context of the counter-pull of the ground, the yearning is self concealment. But because the counter-pulling essense is intrinsic to God,
self-manifesting essence always prevails. The ground never manages
to set itself up as independent of the process of God's self-illumination. In opposing himself in his own particularity—unintelligibility,
non-rationality, ground—to universal lawful Word, man overturns the
very order of Being itself and thereby does evil. Illness is an example
of the overturning of the proper relation between the particular
(ground) and the universal (existence). When illness occurs, some
particular aspect of the organism sets itself up against the unified
whole and dominates it in a way which proves destructive to the
whole. (SA, 172-173)

Man is the separable combination of ground and existence, of darkness and light, of good and evil; the "deepest abyss" of Being and at the same time the "highest heaven." (SA, 163) Evil is nothing in and for itself, but always a possible way for man to be. Evil arises from particular human decisions. (SA, 177) Yet if man is essentially *both* good and evil, how can he choose one or the other? Man has no arbitrary freedom for such a decision. Instead, he can choose to become evil only because he already *inclines* to be evil in the first place. When the yearning of the ground takes over, it takes the form of self-assertive egoism, the source of all particular evil acts. One person can sin against another only if he has chosen to make himself absolute and universal, thus perverting the harmony of the individual with the cosmic order. Evil results from an ontologically perverted self.

The absolute brightness and universality of God, however, is a constant threat to the particular, self-absolutizing will. The individual experiences this threat as the possible eradication of his yearning for self-elevation and self-assertion. Heroic deeds are heroic because they involve the struggle to achieve the universal without perverting it through egoism. Such a struggle involves life-*Angst*.

> Life-*Angst* is a metaphysical necessity and has nothing to do with the petty troubles of the timidity and faint-heartedness of individuals. Life-*Angst* is the presupposition of human greatness; because such greatness is nothing absolute, it needs presuppositions. What could a hero be, who could not let himself unfold precisely into the deepest life-*Angst?* Either only a mere comedian, or a sham strong man and ruffian. (SA, 183)

The hero recognizes that the key to human freedom lies in submission to internal necessity. To be free means to understand oneself by letting oneself become what one has been fated to be from all eternity. There is no arbitrary, free-floating freedom; nor is there a blind, mechanical compulsion which catches us in an exorable causal chain. The human self can be free only when it recognizes that what is most possible within the self is also what is still determinative for the self—fate. In choosing this internal necessity, the self decides for temporality and finitude.

Where temporality is authentically present [*west*], in the *Augenblick*, where alreadiness [*Gewesenheit*] and future shove together in the present, where for man his whole essence lights up as his own, there man experiences that he must already always have been who is he is, as who has determined himself to this....

To this deepest point of the highest expanse of self-knowing in the decisiveness of the highest essence, to this point only a few arrive and they only seldom. (SA, 187)

In accepting the death which will eliminate his particular ego but which—as the sign of temporality and finitude—is also a necessary aspect of God's process of self manifestation, the heroic individual does not succumb to the yearning for particularity and self-concealment. The resolute self (hero) surmounts the egoism which usually prevents the self from assuming its proper role: to be an element in the process of God's self-manifestation. Resoluteness involves the subordination of the ego (yearning of the ground for self-concealment) to existence (love-motivated striving of existence toward self-revelation). As resolute, the self affirms its fateful role as part of the cosmic scheme which unfolds historically. The authentic self is the locus chosen for the *Augenblick* in which there is revealed a new understanding of Being. The experience of authentic temporality is rare and powerful because in that moment the individual has accepted the fateful summons to be the image and mirror of God.[26]

In Schelling's notion that God is the harmonizing struggle between the striving for manifestness and the yearning for concealment, we can discern similarities to Heidegger's notion that Being means self-manifesting presence which presupposes the constantly-hiding absence (truth, temporality). Without the emptiness of finitude or nothingness, there would occur no manifesting: beings would not "be." This absence necessary for presencing (Being) conceals itself so well that, beginning with Plato, metaphysics forgot about the intrinsic relation between Being and nothingness (temporality, finitude) and concentrated instead on interpreting Being as the "ultimate foundation" of reality. The whole mystery of the fact that we are *given* to understand beings in different ways at different times becomes neglected. Genuine ontology gradually degenerated into epistemology in the modern era. Even Schelling's thinking eventually went astray, according to

Heidegger, because he tried to unify ground and existence, concealment and manifestness, time and Being in terms of metaphysical categories which were inadequate for this radical insight. It was Schelling,
nevertheless, who brought Western thinking beyond the limits established by Hegel. Hegel culminated the metaphysical-subjectivistic
tradition which obscures the relation between time and Being, un-
concealment and presencing.

Heidegger's conception of the relation between Dasein and Being
resembles Schelling's conception of the relation between man and
God. According to Schelling, man is the "image" of God not only
because there is a structural similarity between the two (both involve
the struggle between ground and existence, darkness and light) but
also because in man the nature of God can be displayed, manifested,
"imaged." According to Heidegger, Dasein analogously exists as the
"image" of Being. First, there is a structural similarity between the
two; to be means to become unhidden or manifest, while Dasein
means to be the unconcealment where manifestness can happen. Second, through Dasein, Being itself, the event of manifestness/uncon-
cealment, can be revealed. Human existence is not so much an end in
itself as it is the opening through which the miracle of manifestness
(Being) can manifest itself. As we shall see later in more detail, Heidegger postulates three ways in which to talk about the event of
manifesting/unconcealing.

First, in the natural world beings manifest themselves in their stages
of development. A leaf on a tree which earlier *was not,* now *is.* It
sustains its presence over against the nothingness into which it must
inevitably lapse once again. This nothingness is the abyss (*Ab-grund*)
from which all beings spring into presence. Because they affect each
other and are essentially interrelated, all beings manifest themselves
to each other in some measure. *Second,* beings manifest themselves
in a more profound way for human beings, since we are *aware* that
beings are present or manifest. We understand what it means to be.
Through language, human beings can let themselves and other beings
be revealed *as* beings; that is, beings which have managed to gain and
sustain presence in the face of the all-pervading finitude. *Third,* a human being can be struck by the fact that beings are manifest, and
that he himself is *aware* that they are manifest. To be open to beings

makes everyday life possible; to be open to the essential structures of beings makes metaphysics possible; to be open to the event of Being as such makes *thinking* possible. Being open to the event of Being means being aware, not of any being, but of the non-appearing absence which lets beings be manifest. One can be aware of such absence only because one is absence (temporal transcendence). Historical changes in the way in which humanity understands Being occur because world-historical individuals are fated to become the openness through which such changes can be manifest. An epoch is conditioned by the language used by the thinker or poet to reveal what has been revealed through and to him. The thinker's words are not his personal creation, since he is the spokesman for a happening of which he is only a part. The thinker's words call his people back to their heritage, thus permitting them to understand in the most appropriate way what it means to be. From such a re-appropriation of heritage, the authenticity of a people is made possible. We shall return to these topics in the next three chapters.

In the final part of this chapter, I explore how Heidegger's 1937 lectures on Nietzsche use the idea of the *Augenblick* to point toward a non-voluntaristic conception of authenticity. The creative individual (Nietzsche's Overman) does not will in the sense of seeking to dominate or destroy something. He wills instead to let himself be what he already is from all eternity. He wills to let beings be what they are. In the *Augenblick* there occurs the moment of self-acceptance, the love of fate (*amor fati*), the "yes!" to the eternal return of the same. The highest will, thus, takes the form of the deepest submission.

PART THREE: **Authentic Temporality and Nietzsche's "Eternal Return of the Same."**

In his lectures "The Eternal Return of the Same," presented at Freiburg in 1937, Heidegger continued to work out his conception of the *Augenblick* and of authenticity; this time by showing that the *Augenblick* is the key to understanding Nietzsche's concepts of the eternal return, *amor fati*, will, and creativity. Heidegger's interpretation of Nietzsche is not an attempt to repeat what Nietzsche had already said. Such an effort would be scholarship; a task which Heidegger left to historians of philosophy. Instead, he engages in a creative dialogue with Nietzsche, not simply to twist his thinking so that it becomes "Heideggerean," but in order to arrive at insight. He thinks along with Nietzsche by reading him as he could not have understood himself. Heidegger says that only those who really understand a thinker are up to the task of changing what he said. (NII, 400) His interpretations of the history of philosophy resemble the self-unifying circle of authentic historicality, because he determines what already is (the philosophical tradition) by what will be (novel interpretations). He tries to draw out the hidden possibilities slumbering within the words of great thinkers. This procedure is kept from being arbitrary because Heidegger himself is guided by the question of the truth of Being. He approaches the writings of others to learn what they can tell him about what it means to be. Heidegger's lectures on Nietzsche make it difficult to tell when Heidegger is speaking for Nietzsche or for himself. What is important, however, is the issue (*die Sache*), which is no one's property.[27]

Nietzsche was so important to Heidegger because in his writings the subjectivism of Western metaphysics was taken to its furthest possible point, and, perhaps, even beyond it. Nietzsche's idea of the Will to Power is the ultimate expression of the metaphysical thinking which ends in the current disclosure of all beings as raw materials to be used by humanity in its quest for more power. Yet Nietzsche also united two sources of the Western tradition—Parmenides and Heraclitus—in a way which suggests an alternative to the pervasive subjectivism. (NI, 463-470) For Parmenides, Being means permanent presence; for Heraclitus, Being means becoming. In Nietzsche's idea of creating, these two leading ideas are joined, for creating demands both permanence and change. Creation is the highest instance of the Will to Power: the will to imprint Being (permanent presence) on Becoming. This Will to Power does not have to be taken as the effort to impose one's arbitrary whims upon mute material. Instead, creative activity can be seen as the attempt to retrieve what already is in order to bring forth something new. Genuine creating (and willing) involves *letting something be* what it can be. The Will to Power is the concrete expression of the Eternal Return of the Same: to will is to say "yes" to what has been and "yes" to what will be. To care for what is means to love fate. To love fate means to accept one's finite possibilities. To care requires that one be emptied of the egoism which seeks to manipulate things for the ego's purposes. Love of fate requires the end of resentment against finitude, the end to longing for an unchanging world, the end to clinging and grasping.

Heidegger's own thinking can be understood as an effort to help give birth to the possibilities he discerned in Nietzsche's thinking. By caring for Nietzsche's thinking, Heidegger sought to draw from it what was hidden within it. Given Heidegger's interest in temporality, it is not surprising to learn that he regards the idea of the eternal return as Nietzsche's fundamental doctrine. (NI, 256) This idea is not his personal thought, but instead an event of appropriation (*Ereignis*) in the history of Being. (NI, 264) Heidegger claims that the idea of the eternal return is the most difficult of all thoughts, because it demands the affirmation of the tragic nature of life—its suffering, evil, and death. For Nietzsche, tragedy is the fundamental character of the whole of being. (NI, 278-279) Tragedy is a kind of metaphysical art, insofar as it creates not only objects but also new ways of disclosing the Beings of beings. In tragedy lies the inner connection of the fearful and the beautiful. The tragic hero can say "yes" to life in the face of its pain and suffering. Nietzsche's Zarathustra is the tragic hero who, through the affirmation of the eternal return of things *just as they are,* says "yes" to life in the face of its uttermost "no." (NI, 280-281) Such yea-saying to mortality and finitude resembles the anticipatory resoluteness described in *Being and Time.* The acceptance and disclosure of life's finitude leads to a transformation of the temporality which is essential for life.

In "On the Vision and the Riddle," Zarathustra tries to understand the significance of a doorway which leads, on the one hand, into the eternity of the past and, on the other, into the eternity of the future. Past and future come together at the doorway itself, which is titled *"Augenblick."* Here it becomes clear that the puzzle of the eternal return involves the relation between time and eternity. The ordinary time of the "herd" becomes transfigured for the creator when he confronts his mortality and becomes fully individuated. Individuation, however, leads to loneliness. "In loneliness, precisely what is most severe and most dangerous are set free to our task and to ourselves...." (NI, 300) Loneliness is a terrible experience for a member of the herd who seeks to unburden himself of his responsibility for choosing how to live. For the creative individual, however, such loneliness becomes the highest form of life. He creates, in part, to enhance his life, which is hemmed in by the decadent values nourishing the herd.

With the erosion of the Platonic-Christian table of values which governed the medieval world, a new purpose for living had to be discovered. Unfortunately, in Nietzsche's view, this new meaning did not turn out to be one which would enhance human life by developing the creative capacities of great individuals. Instead, the new meaning of life became "happiness" for the herd. Nationalism, imperialism, liberalism, industrialism, and socialism arose in response to nihilism, the void resulting from the collapse of the old values. Nietzsche prophesized that these new "isms" would lead to mass movements and world wars. His idea of the eternal return offers a new meaning for life which both counters the loss of weight of the old values, as well as offering an alternative to the "isms" of the herd. Nietzsche claimed meaning arises in the affirmation of life as in ever-circling, ever-returning play of necessity. In this highest affirmation, an individual learns love of fate—amor fati.

Heidegger insists that Nietzsche's concept of the new life does not offer guidance in "practical ways of living," but "is a new way to stand in the midst of the whole of being, a new kind of truth, and thus a change of being." (NI, 337) A person will not arrive at this new life if he tries merely to conform to a program deduced from an interpretation of Nietzsche's writings. Just as Christ warned that salvation was possible only through the experience of faith, not through obedience to laws, so too Nietzsche warned that new life is possible only for those who experience the Augenblick, the authentic temporality which leads to a new understanding of Being. Those who misunderstand this point easily turn Nietzsche's writings into a fashionable commodity. In the 1930s, of course, National Socialist "thinkers" ripped Nietzsche's words out of context to use them for their own racist-ideological purposes. Heidegger's lectures deliberately oppose the National Socialist exploitation of Nietzsche's thinking.

Those few who can remain open to the vision of the eternal return are called on to convey their insight to others. This new understanding of the meaning of life can have the effect of changing history. "In history, words are often more powerful than affairs and deeds." (NI, 450) The idea that human life is an element in a magnificent, violent, and intrinsically purposeless cosmic play provides Western humanity with a new self-understanding as an alternative to the ideal of industrial "progress." The "progress" mentality is the secularization of the Platonic-Christian striving to attain a reality beyond the here and now. The goal has now become greater material gratification instead of the heavenly reward. If the universe is itself without a goal, and if man recognizes that he must somehow align himself with the workings of the universe, he will begin to regard his own activity as a kind of play. The purpose of human life will not be unending progress toward some unspecified material goal, but will be to encourage or promote great individuals: the Overman. The play of life will be an end in itself. The resentment which leads the herd to stifle individuality will give way to love for the ones who strive to become what they can be. All this requires, of course, that humanity affirm the finitude of life and will that this life (just as it is) return an infinite number of times as part of the endless cosmic play.

Heidegger informs us that the terrifying image from "On the Vision and the Riddle," which depicts the shepherd choking on the snake in his mouth, refers to Zarathustra himself choking on the thought of nihilism, the heaviest of thoughts which threaten to bring him down. Nietzsche, too, choked on this thought. Zarathustra realizes that he cannot tear the snake out of the shepherd's throat any more than nihilism can be destroyed from the outside, "by socialism [and here we must understand National Socialism, as well as Marxist Socialism] progress, reason." These only cause nihilism to bite all the harder. (NI, 442) Zarathustra thus calls to the shepherd to bite off the head of the snake. The bite corresponds to the thought of the eternal return, in which lies the overcoming of nihilism.

> Before the bite is carried out, the *Augenblick* is also not thought:
> for the bite is the answer to the question of what the doorway it-

self, the *Augenblick*, is. That is the decision in which history up until now as the history of Nihilism gets set to a positive dialogue *[Auseinandersetzung]*. (NI, 445)

To think eternity demands: to think the *Augenblick*, i.e., to set oneself in the *Augenblick* of Being-oneself *[Selbstseins]*. (NI, 447)

The eternal return of the same only gets thought when it gets thought in a nihilistic way and in an Augenblick-like way. In such thinking, however, the thinker moves himself back into the ring of the eternal return of the same, but so that he co-achieves and co-decides that ring. (NI, 447).

Hence, the *Augenblick*, in which the eternal return manifests itself, is a kind of vision of eternity. Zarathustra discloses the circle of necessity precisely by existing within the circular-like *Augenblick*. The *Augenblick* is the symbol for the eternal return, the necessity in chaos, the inexorability of fate. In the *Augenblick* Zarathustra can say "yes" to necessity, just as the authentic self (in *Being and Time*) can say "yes" to fate. The *Augenblick* discloses that past and future are bound together in a repeatable, ever-spiraling unity. The liberating acceptance of fate occurs only in the context of *Angst*. Only such a mood cuts through the delusions which lead an individual to act as if he were above fate. Paradoxically, affirming what once seemed most dreadful (mortality, suffering, risk) gives rise to joy. By accepting the finitude of life, one takes the sting out of death. Anxiety increases in a manner directly proportional to the tenacity with which the ego clings to life. That person is free who is passionately involved in giving birth to his own possibilities and to those of others, but who is also prepared to let go of his projects at any moment. Nietzsche's great test for those on their way to being Overmen was whether they could affirm that all of life returns again and again just as it was, is now, and ever will be.

Nietzsche's most vivid image of the eternal return is the doorway of eternity depicting the connection between finitude and eternity.

This is the most difficult and most authentic aspect of the doctrine of the eternal return, that eternity *is* in the *Augenblick*, that the *Augenblick* is not the fleeting now, not the moment shooting by for a view, but the thrusting-together of future and past. (NI, 312)

As *Augenblick*, we determine that time in which future and past meet head-on, in which they—in a decisive manner—get empowered and executed by man himself, since man stands in the place of this hitting-together, indeed *is* this place himself. The temporality of the time of eternity, which is demanded to be thought in the eternal return of the same, is the temporality in which above all—and so far as we know—man stands alone, since he—resolved to the future, empowering what has been—shapes and bears the present. (NI, 356-357)

In these passages we hear strong echoes of Heidegger's notion that human existence constitutes the temporal clearing in which beings can be manifest. Moreover, we are also reminded that when human existence is authentic, temporality is experienced as the self-spiraling unity of past and future—the *Augenblick*. The *Augenblick* discloses the past as the tradition which stands before us as future possibilities. To retrieve the tradition and to set it free for its hidden possibilities requires violence against the previous appropriations of tradition. In doing such violence, the creative individual risks violence to himself as well. According to both Heidegger and Nietzsche, fundamental changes in history are the result of epoch-founding revelations which occur through heroic individuals. The great thinker, poet, artist, or statesmen is the storm center for the clash of past and future. He alone is granted the vision necessary to understand what must be said and done in order to love fate by following it.

In commenting on a passage from one of Nietzsche's unpublished writings, Heidegger remarks that the event of insight called the *Augenblick*

has its time and hour; it is "for mankind the hour of midday." We know what this word means for Nietzsche: the moment of the shortest shadows, where forenoon and afternoon, past and future, blend into one. This blending-point is the *Augenblick* of the highest unity of all times *[Zeitlichen]* in the greatest clarity of the brightest light: this is the *Augenblick* of eternity. The hour of midday is the hour when human Dasein in each case gets clarified in its highest height and in its strongest will. With the word "midday," there is determined for the *Ereignis* of the thought of the eternal return its own time-point within the eternal return of the same, a time-point which misses no hour for it means the point in the whole of being

> which is time itself as the temporality of the *Augenblick*. The inner-
> most, but also most hidden relation of the eternal return of the same
> (as the fundamental character of the whole of being) to time lights
> up therewith. (NI, 402)

This passage suggests that the *Augenblick* itself represents the eternal return, insofar as the *Augenblick* includes both past and future in the self-circling moment characteristic of the eternal return. According to Nietzsche's theory, the eternal return is a necessary thought which has occurred before and which will occur again. In the brightness of the *Augenblick*, the authentic individual resolves to affirm life in the face of the necessary end of life. Even more, he must will that this life return again and again just as it is. Only then does he over-come the meaninglessness of empty serial time, since only then has he willed to align himself with cosmic destiny. To love fate is to take care that the good which *can* be, *will* be.

Heidegger is aware of objections to the doctrine of the eternal return. One major objection is: If we are bound up in the chain of *necessary* recurrence, what sense does it make to talk of "will," "resolve," and "affirmation"? Does not the efficacy of the will presuppose *freedom*, not necessity? Heidegger replies by saying that the categories of free-will and determinism belong to a mechanistic metaphysics which is grounded in the inauthentic experience of time as a continuum. Human beings are never absolutely free, any more than they are ever merely cogs in a machine running independently of them. The romantic ideal of freedom stakes the self-assertive ego against the cosmos. Genuine freedom, however, involves releasement from egoism and attunement to the possibilities which one can help bring to fruition. These possibilities are not *created* by the individual. He *discovers* them in his fateful situation. The highest form of willing is the will to let things grow, change, prosper, and develop. Willing is circular in that the will wills into the future but into the past as well, since the future is always the tradition to be appropriated anew. Willing to become part of the great wheel of necessity is not capitulation to the dead past but openness to the living future, which always alters the tradition from which it springs. Because we are finite human beings, we can never be sure that our wills are in accord with the highest possibilities, with destiny, or with tradition. All great attempts involve risk. To attempt to avoid such risk, however, usually means to go against fate, and this invites destruction; or conversely to try to rise above it, and this denies one's humanity. Heidegger notes pointedly that each of us must decide for or against the notion of the eternal return, and thus must choose whether or not to step into a new kind of temporal existence. To understand the concept of the *Augenblick* requires that one take his place *within* it, i.e., that one *experience* it, just as it is necessary for the reader to *become* authentic in order to fully comprehend the concept of authentic existence in *Being and Time*.

At one point in his lecture, Heidegger attempts to explain to his students what the idea of the *Augenblick* can mean for them, especially since he has been talking all along about the rarity of the *Augenblick* as an event of world-historical significance. Here he tries, as he did in *Being and Time*, to show the existentiell importance of his conception of authentic existence as the *Augenblick*. He notes that an individual cannot look back into the eternal past to discover what has been for him, but he may be able to discover what *was* by seeing what *will be*.

> What then already was, and what will come back when it comes back? Answer: that which will be in the nearest *Augenblick*. If in cowardice and ignorance you let Dasein slip away with all its consequences, then this will come back, and it will be that which already was. And if you, from the closest *Augenblick* and thus from every one, form a highest one and from it take hold of and take note of its results, than this *Augenblick* will come again, and that will have been what already was: "Eternity holds." But this will be decided in your *Augenblicken* and only there decided, and from that which you *will* and can will from yourself. (NI, 398—emphasis mine.)

It is escapism to regard oneself as a mere cog in a chain of events, helpless to act in a way appropriate to the situation.

> In this failure to reckon ourselves [as part of the situation] we no longer consider that we (as temporal, self-responsible selves) are responsible to the future in will and that the temporality of human-being is what first and alone determines how man stands in the ring of being. (NI, 399)

Here Heidegger emphasizes how authentic temporality as the *Augenblick* differs from the conception of time as a stream of moments flowing from future into past, as well as from the conception of causality as a series of past influences which wholly determine the future. In authentic temporality, past and future are somehow right here and now in the present. How we project ourselves into the future determines our past as heritage. Human freedom makes it possible to change our temporal existence. Instead of being enslaved to the past (fate) like the tragic hero, or escaping into the future like the romantic aesthete, we can resolve to be open to the future in light of the necessarily limited possibilities which are part of our heritage. As Heidegger's thinking developed, he spent less time considering authenticity in ways having immediate bearing on ordinary individuals. Instead, he turned his attention to the world-historical changes in the way in which Being reveals itself. Such changes, however, presuppose a world-historical individual who is "cleared" for this revelation.

Toward the end of his essay, Heidegger remarks that the idea of the eternal return is comprehensible only in light of Nietzsche's fundamental position. Each philosopher has such a position, an answer given to the leading metaphysical question *(Leitfrage)*, viz., "What is being?" The more important because more fundamental question *(Grundfrage)*, viz., "What is Being as such?", was posed early in Western thinking and has since been forgotten. Nietzsche's answer to the *Leitfrage* is that all being is Will to Power, and that man's Will to Power turns everything into an object for domination. Hence, Nietzsche's thinking is the high point of Western subjectivism. Yet, it is possible to understand Nietzsche in a non-subjectivistic way. It is possible, moreover, that Nietzsche did have insight into what Heidegger calls Being—the cosmic play of revelation and concealment.[27] If Heidegger is grudging in his acknowledgement of Kierkegaard's importance, he is also hesitant to give credit to Nietzsche.

Heidegger does admit, however, that Nietzsche "ends" metaphysics by returning to its sources; he thus points the way for Heidegger to re-appropriate the fateful revelation which occurred to Heraclitus and Parmenides. Only by re-experiencing the insight that Being means unconcealment and manifestness can an alternative be found to the metaphysical interpretation of Being. Nietzsche goes back to the pre-Socratics to find answers to the following two questions: What is the constitution *(Verfassung)* of the whole of being? What is the way in which the whole of being is? The two early Greek answers to the *Leitfrage* (What is being?) are: 1) being is permanent presence (Parmenides), and 2) being is becoming (Heraclitus). Nietzsche unites these two answers in his idea of creating, which requires both permanence (standpoint) and changes (movement beyond the standpoint). According to Heidegger, we can conclude from this that for Nietzsche the *constitution* of the whole of being is the Will to Power; whereas the *way* in which the whole of being *is*, is the Eternal Return of the Same. Creating imprints being (permanence) on becoming (change), as well as letting being become. This imprinting

> is the informing of becoming in its highest possibilities, wherein (as it measures and makes room) it clarifies itself and wins subsistence. This imprinting is creating. As creating out over itself, creating is in the innermost way: to stand in the *Augenblick* of decision. In this *Augenblick*, what has gone before and what is now also given are raised in the pre-projected *Augenblick* and are thus preserved. This *Augenblick*-aspect of creating is the essence of real, actual eternity, which wins its highest sharpness and breadth as the *Augenblick* of the eternal return of the same. The imprinting of becoming on being—the Will to Power in its highest form—is in its deepest essence *Augenblick*-like, i.e., the eternal return of the same. The Will to Power as the *constitution* of being is as it is only on the basis of the *way* to be on which Nietzsche projects the whole of being. (NI, 466-467)

The Will to Power (creating) is in effect the will to eternity, the will to bring forth the highest possibilities already slumbering in what is. The highest form of the Will to Power is thus not to imprint being on becoming, but to imprint becoming on being; that is, to disclose beings as elements in the great wheel of eternity, the endless unfolding of past in terms of future. Such disclosure-willing is *amor fati*, defined by Heidegger in the following manner. "Love *[amor]* is to be understood as Will, as the Will which wills that the beloved is in its essence what it is. The highest and most decisive Will of this kind is Will as 'clarifying' *[Verklärung]*, which places what is willed into the highest possibility of its Being." (NI, 470) *Fatum*, on the other hand, is not rigid necessity; the eternally self-circling movement (becoming) of the whole of being. "*Amor fati* is the radiant will to the relationship to what is most real in being *[zum Seiendsten des Seienden]*." (NI, 471) *Amor fati* is not the will to dominate but the will to *release* beings to be what they can be. Put in Heidegger's terms, man's understanding of Being changes according to the *Geschick* (destiny) determining each historical epoch. History *(Geschichte)* is a non-teleological happening *(Geschehen)* which is guided by the destiny of Being *(Seinsgeschick)*. The heroic-authentic self stands between past and future as the location where such epoch-altering *Geschicken* are first received. Great thinkers and poets are receptive to what can be because they hearken to the tradition. By loving fate they make possible the changes in the world which accord with genuine historical possibilities. Creating is always conditioned by the historical circumstances. Yet creating is also always a kind of free giving.

"All creating is im-parting [*Mit-teilen*: 'communicating'] . Therein lies the fact that creating grounds, sets forth, or—as Hölderlin says— founds *[stiftet]* in itself new possibilities of Being. Creating as such... is bestowing *[Verschenken]*." (NI, 389) The eternal return of the same is itself a kind of loving bestowal.

> Precisely through the fact that the thinking of the most difficult thought becomes the highest knowing, it is in itself a creating and as creating an imparting, bestowing, loving, and therewith *the fundamental form of the holy and 'religious'*. (NI, 391—emphasis mine)

The idea of the eternal return is a holy one even though it does away with the Platonic-Christian notion of a heavenly afterlife. The notion of heaven springs from a self-hatred which accuses temporal existence of being unreal. The holy, however, does not include hatred and revenge. Holiness means acceptance and thankfulness. To accept thankfully means to let destiny unfold in the manner which best accords with the "good" in destiny; that is, with revealing a novel way of understanding what it means to be.

As we shall see later, there is a problem with this conception of thanking as "thinking" or "openness for Being". The history of Being can seem arbitrary and violent in the manner in which it uses man for the purpose of disclosing itself. Such an extra-human, transcendent interpretation of the meaning of history can be dangerous when applied to the political realm as we shall see in the next chapter. Moreover, talk of the destiny of Being and of the fact that Being conceals and reveals itself tends to reify Being in a way similar to how theology has reified God. Through the concept of *Ereignis* Heidegger attempts, without complete success, to avoid such reification and thus to avoid the dualistic idea of a relation between man and Being.

The idea of authentic temporality as the *Augenblick* is part of the philosophical tradition. Plato describes the moment of vision in his myth of the cave, when the truth-seeker catches a glimpse of the eternally present *agathon*. For Aristotle, God is the eternal circle of pure thought thinking itself. Man becomes God-like when the "circles" of his head become attuned to the cycles of the cosmos, for the cosmos, too, yearns to emulate God's circular perfection. As is well-known, Spinoza also said that the blessed life follows from seeing things *sub specie aeternaetatis*. Kant's idea of freedom is an ethical interpretation of *amor fati*: self-binding to the eternally valid moral law. Hegel tried to explain the presence of eternity in the finite through a historically-oriented, Christianized interpretation of Aristotle. Kierkegaard's critique of Hegel led him to re-appropriate the New Testament conception of *kairos*. And Nietzsche's *amor fati* brought thinking back to its origins in the pre-Socratics. Heidegger's interpretation of authentic temporality is guided by the question left unposed by his predecessors: what is the sense of Being? Continuing meditation on the history of philosophy led him to change his approach to this question from the analysis of the Being of man as Dasein to the analysis of the self-disclosure (truth) of Being through history.

In his lectures in the mid-1930s Heidegger developed his idea that man is an element in an inscrutable cosmic play. The hero is the one who, accepting the loss of his own ego, risks his life to hold himself open for a revelation in this play. In his Schelling-lectures, Heidegger comments on such heroism:

> These highest forms of decision are enthusiasm, heroism, and belief. Their forms are manifold and cannot be explained here. But always in every form of authentic decision is the essential knowledge *[Wissen]* which underlies it and which shines through it. For example, in heroism the following are characteristic: the clearest knowledge of the uniqueness of the Dasein which has been taken over; the longest resoluteness to bring the road of this Dasein over its apex; the certainty which remains unaffected over against its own greatness; and finally and foremost, the ability to remain silent; never to say what the Will authentically knows and wills. (SA, 189)

My analysis in this chapter suggests that Heidegger's concept of authenticity shares the following themes with the Western spiritual tradition: life is a great cycle; fate is not iron necessity but a challenge to which we can respond; freedom lies in choosing to be aligned with fate; only a few are destined to gain enlightenment, and they must endure great hardship; evil–doing arises from self-assertion and egoism, whose roots are self-ignorance; the enlightened person does not act according to a table of commandments (heteronomy), but in accordance with fate. Being fully human means being the thankful witness to, and participant in, the display of life. It is my contention that Heidegger's own life was a journey toward self-understanding. His writings reflect the development of that self-understanding, although he sought to give voice to Being, not to personal experience. This ontological aim distinguishes him from Kierkegaard. In the next chapter, I examine a great crisis in Heidegger's journey—his involvement with National Socialism. This crisis helped lead to a change in his concept of authenticity.

CHAPTER SIX

National Socialism, Voluntarism, and Authenticity

IN THE previous chapter, I argued that Heidegger moved toward his mature concept of authenticity as releasement in the process of developing his notion of the *Augenblick*. Releasement minimizes the role played by individual will in becoming authentic and emphasizes instead that releasement from self-will is a gift. I believe that Heidegger was led to this conclusion not only as the result of intellectual reflection, but also because of insight resulting from his engagement with National Socialism in 1933-1934. In Part One of this chapter, I show that as rector of the University of Freiburg, Heidegger called on the German people to reappropriate their heritage in order to avoid spiritual and social disaster. He was convinced for a short time that Hitler had the "practical wisdom" to direct events in light of Heidegger's philosophical pronouncements about that reappropriation. Although he discovered the error of his ways, Heidegger seems to have been guilty of *hubris* in presuming he had enough political knowledge to speak out in this confused period. In Part Two, which analyzes Heidegger's lectures on metaphysics from 1935, I demonstrate that even after resigning as rector in 1934, he continued to use provocative language to warn Germany about its violent encounter with modern technology. Although critical of National Socialist "philosophy," he still hoped to affect the direction of Germany's "revolution." It did not take him long, however, to realize that events were beyond his control. In Part Three, I draw

169

some conclusions about how recognition of his *hubris* may have helped Heidegger to arrive at his non-voluntaristic conception of authenticity as releasement.

PART ONE: Authenticity, Historicality, and National Socialism.

Heidegger's direct involvement with National Socialism lasted about ten months during 1933-34. As rector, he made speeches not only supporting Hitler and his candidates, but many of their policies as well. Partly due to his refusal to fire two anti-Nazi professors, he resigned as rector in 1934. He continued for a time however, to try to guide the political movement in speeches and lectures. By 1936, he realized that it was impossible to have a positive influence on the regime. This brief political episode disgraced Heidegger in the eyes of many people. For years, ugly rumors and outright lies caused people to believe that his actions during this period were more reprehensible than they actually were. Fortunately, research in recent years has laid many of these claims to rest.[1]

It is difficult for us to imagine the social and political upheaval which affected Germany in the early 1930s. The Great Depression was only a symptom of the industrialization which was destroying culture, family, and countryside in the process of turning human beings into the faceless mass. Industrial "progress," whether it took the form of capitalism or communism, was widely condemned for uprooting the people *(das Volk)* from the soil (earth, tradition). *"Volkish"* philosophers preached the need for returning to the land as a way of preventing the destruction of German *Geist.*[2] Many respectable Germans longed for a "third way" between the political left and right. The German people appeared to be at a crossroads. On the one hand, they could summon their strength to meet the challenge of industrialization without being overwhelmed by it. On the other hand, they could give in to the industrial onslaught, in which case mankind would be totally organized according to what Ernst Jünger has called the *"Gestalt* of the laborer."[3] This cultural crisis was on Heidegger's mind when, in his inaugural address "What Is Metaphysics?" (1929), he called for unification of the quest for knowledge at the university, as opposed to the splintering of knowledge into a myriad of separate disciplines. His personal and professional standing was such that his colleagues elected him unanimously as rector in 1933. He claims that he tried to avoid being nominated for the position, because of the demands which the rectorship involved during those troubled times. Once elected, however, he hoped to prevent the total "politicalization" of the university by the newly-installed regime of National Socialism. Hence, he called his rector's address "The Self-Assertion of the German University"—a daring title during the time when Hitler expected the universities to submit to what he asserted to be the demands of *das Volk*. Breaking with university tradition, Heidegger appointed students to responsible posts and named as deans several young professors who agreed with his desire that the university re-commit itself to a unified quest for truth. (Sp, 201/273) He also resisted demands that he post anti-Jewish signs and that he remove books by Jewish authors from the library.

Had Heidegger's collusion with National Socialism extended only to his acquiescence to the requirement that rectors become party members, his reputation would not have suffered so badly. Unfortunately, however, he did not join the party merely *pro forma*; he informs us that he really believed that Hitler promised the "greatness and glory" of a "new dawn." (Sp, 196/269) As rector, Heidegger supported *Nationalsozialistische Deutsche Arbeiterpartei* (NSDAP) candidates and political positions, including the demand that Germany withdraw from the League of Nations.[4] He also spoke of the complete change of "our German Dasein" which would follow from National Socialist rule. Further political usage of his philosophical vocabulary is found in a remark, quoted in the *Freiburger Zeitung*, that authentic political action occurs in the *Augenblick*. Only then can the needs of the historical situation be disclosed. For Germany in 1933, the situation seemed to call for Hitler's leadership.[5] He affirmed the importance of the military in German society both in his rector's address and on the tenth anniversary of the death of Leo Schlageter.

Schlageter, who had been killed by French occupation forces in the Rhineland in 1923, had become a martyr in Germany's push to reject the "unjust" terms of the Treaty of Versailles.

Heidegger's supporters have sometimes explained his political action as an aberration or a mistake. Paul Hühnerfeld, however, a former student of Heidegger's, asserts that his mentor's deed was not accidental:

> Rather, it was consistent and necessary. The common roots of German fascism and of Heideggerean thinking lie too clearly before all who can see. It was the same irrationalism, the same dangerous romanticism, mixed with nationalism and intolerance against different thinking. In National Socialism, misled Germany found its most unscrupulous mass movement, in Heidegger, its subtlest genius. Their difference is in fact powerful—it is the difference between mass hysteria and creative individualism. But it is nevertheless only a difference of *degree* not of *kind*.[6]

Unfortunately, Hühnerfeld is close to the mark in several of his observations. He is also guilty of some exagerration. Certain echoes of fascism are indeed present in Heidegger's claim that an individual's fate is intimately connected with the historical destiny of his people. Individuals in a community become authentic when they act in concert to reappropriate their common heritage. Just as an individual must struggle to free himself from domination by the "they," so, too, a people must struggle against alien influences which prevent genuine possibilities. Failure of a community to act appropriately leads to decadence, the inauthenticity of a people. Heidegger is hardly the only thinker to have spoken in these terms about the relation of individual to community. His analysis does emphasize voluntarism, however, in a way which must have been appealing to those demanding that Germany make forthright decisions.

Authenticity involves two interrelated moments: resoluteness and fate. The former refers to the individual's will to act in light of truth. The latter refers to an individual's limited possibilities which must be revealed and chosen if they are to be actualized. A person cannot create his possibilities; they are given to him. Heidegger extended this model of authenticity to *das Volk*, because he believed that a group of people can act analogously to a single individual. Setting aside the question of the legitimacy of such an analogy, I repeat that for Heidegger the resolute people discloses and acts on its destiny just as the resolute individual discloses and acts on his fate. Such a view of authenticity becomes dangerous under certain circumstances. Although he insisted that authenticity involves the interplay between its active element (resoluteness, freedom) and its passive element (fate, necessity), he sometimes overemphasized the former. When Hitler offered himself as the decisive leader who would succeed where the Weimar Republic had failed so badly, Heidegger supported him personally and philosophically. That he could have been duped by such a man can be explained in part by his belief that it was time to decide—the risk of choice was preferable to the risk of continued inaction. If Heidegger was not intoxicated by the desire to will for the sake of willing, to decide to act even if the decision might be the wrong one, other people were. His political rhetoric did not cool the inflammatory condition in Germany. A dispassionate reader today might find in Heidegger's rhetoric the balance needed between resoluteness and fate, between will and acceptance, but a person seized by the delirium of 1933 would probably have heard only the summons to decision. He might have been convinced that the free exercise of German will, presently hemmed in by the French and British, should not be fettered by ethical or religious restrictions.

Although Heidegger seems at times to have yielded to this voluntaristic attitude, more often he insisted that Germany had to meet this challenge of historical forces *wisely* as well as resolutely. The crisis was ontological not merely political; human deeds alone could not solve the problem. Supposedly it was Western man's destiny to undergo a change in his understanding of Being. Man had now become the power-seeking subject for whom everything is an exploitable object. Heidegger tried to link this ontological destiny with the historical destiny of the German people. The only hope they had of avoiding the spiritual death caused by industrialization was to decisively revitalize their heritage in a way which could incorporate industrialization. It was one thing for Heidegger to offer philosophical pronouncements about the ontological origins of the crisis of the West. It was another thing for him to offer political recommendations for how this crisis should be met. In so doing, he went beyond the limits of his competence. It is possible that he wanted to be the philosophical prophet for Germany in the 1930s that Fichte had been in the early 1800s. It is also possible that his peasant origins led him to develop a narrow-minded nationalism justified by his philosophical rhetoric. What is undeniable is that he found himself thrown into a situation calling for a major decision. He never publicly "apologized" for the decision he finally made because he did what he thought was best. It is likely, however, that after 1935 he meditated on the connection between *hubris* and resoluteness, particularly as they were manifest in his own actions.

Heidegger's personal reasons for supporting Hitler were accompanied by philosophical ones. As might be expected, he turned to ancient Greek thinking to provide political guidance for Germany in 1933. Other commentators have pointed out the striking parallels between his description of authentic social organization under National Socialism and Plato's description of society in *The Republic*.[7] Neither Heidegger nor Plato were democrats; both recognized that human life cannot be perfected. Yet both thinkers acknowledged that political action is a requisite for authentic human life. Just as Plato apparently tried to educate a philosopher-king at Syracuse, so, too, Heidegger tried to guide the political leader of Germany. Although we are uncertain about the political results of Plato's actions, we know that Heidegger assisted an evil movement. The extent of his influence is not clear. We know that National Socialist idealogues at first ignored him and later castigated him. Hühnerfeld reminds us, however, that Heidegger did damage the opposition by actively supporting Hitler.

> And we recognize without difficulty that Heidegger, from the experience of Hölderlin and Nietzsche, with the excessive pathos of the 20s and the immoderate self-consciousness of a personal and national mission, plays out [the role] of the strong elect against the bourgeois, primordial thinking against common sense, and the courage unto death of the extraordinary against the usualness of the secure: the one elevating, the other damned. It is superfluous to remark that such a man must have the effect of an ideological whip under the conditions of the twentieth century, of a prophet under the exalted conditions of 1935.[8]

Along with Plato's political writings, Aristotle's *Nichomachean Ethics* also sheds light on Heidegger's political thinking. Aristotle distinguishes between the scientific and the deliberative modes of understanding. The former contemplates things whose originating causes are invariable, necessary, and thus eternal. The latter, called "practical wisdom" *(phronesis)*, contemplates things whose originating principles are variable, not necessary, and thus historical. Practical wisdom is distinguished from skilled making *(techne)*. The end or goal of *techne* lies beyond itself, while the end of *phronesis* is in large measure internal. Professor Gadamer recalls that in the 1920s Heidegger spoke of Aristotle's *phronesis* as a kind of knowing which is irreducible to an ultimate objectivity; it, rather, is a "knowing in the concrete existence situation."[9] Once, several of Heidegger's students were trying vainly to interpret the following passage from Aristotle's *Ethics*: "a state of that sort [a reasoned state] may be forgotten but practical wisdom cannot." Finally, Heidegger exclaimed: "That is conscience!"[10] Practical wisdom, which might also be translated as "prudence," is not identical with calculative, discursive rationality. Instead, it is an autonomous capacity to know how to act in a particular (variable) situation. Some individuals are endowed with more of it than others. Practical wisdom has to do with knowing how "to act with regard to human goods."[11] If the noble person follows practical wisdom in making choices, the ignoble person follows desire. The noble person acts virtuously because he is naturally gifted with prudence. Like a great archer, his choices and actions are always on the mark. Aristotle remarks:

> It is for this reason that we think Pericles and men like him have practical wisdom, viz., because they can see what is good for themselves and what is good for men in general; we consider that those can do this who are good at managing households or states.[12]

Unlike philosophical wisdom, which is primarily contemplative and hence not "useful," practical wisdom discloses what is to a man's advantage. The man who deliberates well aims not only at what is best for him, however, but also at what is actually within his power to achieve. Such a man must know what is possible for him in particular situations, and must not get lost in dreaming, wishing, or self-delusion. As Aristotle points out,

> we credit men with practical wisdom in some particular respect when they have deliberated well with a view to some good end which is one of those which is not the object of any art. It follows that in the general sense also the man who is capable of deliberating has practical wisdom. Now no one deliberates about things that are invariable, nor about things that it is impossible for him to do.[13]

Although practical wisdom is important in accomplishing one's own good, "perhaps one's own good cannot exist without household management, nor without a form of government. Further, how one should order one's own affairs is not clear and needs inquiry."[14] Heidegger agreed with Aristotle's observation. For both, the "good life" (authenticity) is possible only within a community which is organized to support the good life. Heidegger also agreed that one should always be ready to question the way one "orders one's affairs." Politics involves public debate concerning how human beings are to live together.

Although practical wisdom is an inborn capacity, Aristotle suggests that it can be nurtured. Because it involves an intuitive sensibility, it is a kind of "aesthetic" capacity. Just as some people have better taste than others, so others know how to act more appropriately. Since practical wisdom always applies to concrete situations, it is not like a science, which deals with the universal, but like perception, which concerns the particular. Aristotle knew that the best life is one guided by moral virtue as well as practical wisdom. Moral virtue causes us to choose the right target; practical wisdom causes us to use the right means to hit the mark. In a helpful essay, Herbert Gold has suggested that Aristotle was critical of Socrates for having tried to make practical wisdom a universal science attainable by all.[15] Aristotle agreed that through training and discipline good character could be developed in most people. But he still maintained that the highest character belongs to those who have intuitive understanding of the good; those who know how to act appropriately to realize the good in particular situations. To be truly virtuous, one must not simply perform right actions, but perform them in the right frame of mind, as the result of deliberate choice and for the sake of the acts themselves, not for ulterior motives. All may be capable of learning the universal norms for acting, but only a few can "see" directly how to act. One cannot be good without practical wisdom, nor prudent without moral virtue. Still Aristotle claimed that, given practical wisdom (the aesthetic-particular capacity, not the ethical-universal skill), all other virtues follow.[16] The practical wise man can develop theoretical principles in light of his excellent particular acts, but if one is lacking the sensibility necessary to act appropriately, ethical theory will be of little value. Let us now explore how Heidegger's political actions can be interpreted in light of Aristotle's idea of practical wisdom.

To many Germans in the early 1930s, the situation seemed to call for a practical wise man capable of making choices designed to accomplish a high purpose: saving Germany from destruction. For a time, Heidegger believed that Hitler was just such a man, an effective political leader to whom Germans could entrust their destiny. Such trust was not blind, of course; individuals had to understand the context in which their decision had to be made.[17] Choosing Hitler, however, involved the risk that, in the confused situation, the strong man could become a tyrant. Heidegger had little confidence that the liberal democracy of Weimar could steer Germany through the difficult days ahead. With the support of the German people, he believed Hitler might be better able to chart a course which would preserve German *Geist* and heritage from the ruinous influence of both industrial capitalism and communism.

Aristotle believed that the aristocratic leader, the man most capable of making and carrying out decisions, offers a model of behavior to those who are naturally less than excellent. The aristocrat is born with a fine character which needs only to be cultivated, while ordinary people require training to develop the character needed for a good community. Heidegger called for the common people to submit to rigorous educational, occupational, and military training designed to develop their German character. The ideal of training was directly opposed to the ideology of "individualism" promoted by the liberal democrats and industrialists. What passed for individualism, however, was usually a form of consumerism which catered to the herd instinct. Instead of developing the character of the German people, mass culture and industrialization enhanced their lower instincts. Heidegger felt that a strong ruler could institute the kind of social hierarchy needed to develop individual character. Just as the young person should look for guidance to the wise adult, so too the German people—in Heidegger's view—would do well to look for guidance to the leader with practical wisdom: Hitler.

If he looked upon Hitler as the prudent leader required to save Germany, Heidegger apparently believed that he himself was chosen to reveal the goals by which Hitler was to make his decisions. At times, however, Heidegger also made political pronouncements betraying an extraordinary lack of practical wisdom. His major philosophical effort, nevertheless, was laudable: he tried to move National Socialism away from its racism and social Darwinism toward a spiritually profound self-conception. Heidegger soon saw how naive he had been to believe that he could influence National Socialism. It turned out to be only a virulent form of modern subjectivism. After 1936, in his lectures on Nietzsche, he publicly criticized National Socialist "philosophy." Thirty years later he observed that "Anyone with ears to hear heard in these lectures a confrontation [Auseinandersetzung] with National Socialism." (Sp, 204/274) Already in his 1934-1935 lectures on Hölderlin, he was attacking such "intellectuals" as Kolbenheyer, who tried to provide a biological basis for the "revolution." Otto Pöggeler describes how Heidegger displayed contempt for such people in a lecture read in the mid-1930s.

> The essence of poetry [Dichtung], as it is called, gets missed if one reduces poetry to the experience of an individual, or grasps it collectively as expression of a culture's soul (Spengler) and finally of a race's soul (Rosenberg). "The author Kolbenheyer says: 'Poetry is a biologically necessary function of a people [Volk].' Not much understanding is needed to say: that is also true of digestion, it, too, is a biologically necessary function of a people, primarily of a healthy one. And if Spengler grasps poetry as expression of the current culture's soul, then this is also true of the production of bicycles and automobiles. This is true [das gilt] of everything— that is, it is not true. Right from the start, this definition brings the concept of poetry into a region where the slightest possibility of an essential apprehension is hopeless. This is all so drearily superficial that we only speak of it with reluctance." At that time to speak

publicly in this way of Rosenberg and Kolbenheyer, to this belonged
more courage than was necessary for all the fellow-travelers of the
ideologies of the past years who have put Heidegger together with
Kolbenheyer. Heidegger could rightly demand that one recall not
only his short-lived, if fateful, activity as rector, but also the soon
following attempt to expose the "spiritual," viz., unspiritual foundation of National Socialism.[18]

After 1935 Heidegger was bitterly and personally attacked in the
writings of ideologically "pure" National Socialists, who regarded
him as being at odds with the true aims of the movement. Heidegger,
like many other intellectuals at the time, hoped to find an alternative to spiritual destructiveness of mass culture and industrialization.
The National Socialists, however, merely talked against industrialization and capitalism. In practice, they supported the industrial establishment and used all of its means (including mass-media propaganda)
to maintain political power. In the late 1930s Heidegger was denied
permission to go to Paris for an international symposium on Descartes. In his own classes, he was spied on by informants and had at
least one seminar shut down by the Gestapo. In 1944, he was labeled
the most expendable professor and, at the age of 58, was sent to work
on the Rhine dikes.

As Heidegger came to see National Socialism as a particularly dangerous form of the Will to Power, he also came to see that his own
thinking was colored by subjectivism. This subjectivism is apparent
in his 1935 lectures on metaphysics, where his violent language seems
to have corresponded well with the times. The lectures claim that
historical change requires a resolute individual who risks everything
to make way for a new revelation of Being. Heidegger's goal here
was both theoretical-ontological and practical-political. He shared
Aristotle's conviction that politics is one of the highest human activities. Toward the end of the *Ethics*, however, Aristotle concludes that
contemplation *(theoria)* is even more worthy of man than politics,
since contemplation is an end in itself. *Theoria* is god-like activity.
Heidegger, too, regarded his philosophical activity as more fundamental than his political activity. Let us consider now this attempt to explain European history and politics in terms of what Heidegger calls
the "history of Being."

PART TWO: *An Introduction to Metaphysics* as an Interpretation of World-Historical Heroism.

Heidegger's lectures on metaphysics, presented in 1935, are noteworthy for several reasons. First, they exhibit Heidegger's assessment of Germany's spiritual-cultural situation. Second, they show his willingness to use violent language to express the magnitude of the challenge facing his country. His message was, in effect: choose rightly or be destroyed. Third, they contain an insightful account of the relation between Being *(legein)* and thinking *(noein)*, which helps form the basis for the concept of *Ereignis*. The lectures are a kind of turning point in Heidegger's own spiritual journey. Although they emphasize resoluteness and risk, they also point toward the overcoming of will in *Gelassenheit*. Sometimes he seems to identify German destiny with the destiny of Being. Other times he makes it clear that the destiny of Being transcends human actions, and that man's fundamental task is to learn how to receive that destiny in the most appropriate manner.

Heidegger is ambiguous about the role of philosophy in these lectures. On the one hand, he says that philosophy cannot directly provide the energy needed for historical change. On the other hand, he asserts that the philosopher is the one "who initiates profound transformations." (EM, 8/8-9) Far from facilitating the ordinary way of doing things, philosophy seeks to make things more difficult by challenging what is accepted. He claims: "the challenge is one of the essential prerequisites for the birth of all greatness, and in speaking of greatness we are referring to the works and destinies of an historical people *[eines geschichtlichen Volkes]*." (EM, 9/9) Remarks such as these give the impression that history is the history of self-actualizing peoples, not the history of Being. The philosopher takes the risks needed to win insight into the extraordinary. Heidegger, who quotes Nietzsche's statement that "Philosophy... is a voluntary living amid ice and mountain heights" (EM, 10/11), apparently saw himself as one of the creators fated to open up new vistas for the German people. Hence, he defines philosophy as

a thinking that breaks the paths and opens the perspectives of the knowledge which measures and ranks, in which and by which a

people conceives its Dasein in the historical-cultural world and ful-
fills itself, the knowledge that kindles and threatens and necessi-
tates all inquiring and appraising. (EM, 8/9)

In trying to make his thinking "relevant" for the political situation
of the day, Heidegger seems to contradict what he said about his
work fourteen years earlier:

I do ... what I must and what I hold as necessary, and do it as I can—
I don't tailor my philosophical work to cultural tasks for a general
today....I work from my "I am" and from my factical origin
[Herkunft]. With this facticity, existing rages on.[19]

Although Heidegger admitted that the creative genius is ultimately
in the service of transcendent destiny, he emphasized that the genius
must struggle mightily to let these movements properly unfold. Unlike the creator who actively wills to know, most people merely
wish to find an answer.

He who wills, he who puts his whole Dasein into a will, is resolved.
Resoluteness does not shift about; it does not shirk, but acts from
out of the Augenblick and never stops. Re-soluteness is no mere
decision to act, but the crucial beginning of action that anticipates
and reaches through all action. To will is to be resolved. (EM, 16/17)

When he published these lectures in 1953, Heidegger added to the
passage just cited. He explained that resoluteness must be understood
as the opening-up of human Dasein into the clearing of Being. We are
informed that, although it seems strange to common sense, all willing
is a "letting-be." In 1935, however, he said that this letting-be requires
a violent removal of concealments. He implied at times that the Being
of beings is enabled to present itself because of the resolute action of
the thinker-hero. One can hardly avoid wondering whether Heidegger
had himself in mind as one of these world-historical figures.

After considering the role of the hero, Heidegger discusses how
industrialization has caused the spiritual destruction of Europe:

This Europe, in its wretched delusion, forever on the brink of stab-
bing itself, lies today in a great pincers, squeezed between Russia
on one side and America on the other. From a metaphysical point

of view, Russia and America are the same: the same desperate
frenzy of unchained technology *[Technik]*, the same unrestricted
organization of the average man. At a time when the furthermost
corner of the globe has been conqured by technology and opened
up to economic exploitation; when any incident whatever...can be
communicated in the rest of the world at any desired speed...;
when a boxer is regarded as a great man; when mass meetings attended by millions [including Hitler's Nuremburg rallies] are looked
on as a triumph—then, yes then, through all this turmoil a question
still haunts us like a specter: What for?—Whither?—and what then?
(EM, 28-29/31)

Heidegger's indirect critique of Hitler's propaganda methods is
coupled here with a critique of mass culture in general. Mass culture is itself linked to the technological frenzy gripping both America (capitalist) and Russia (communist). Technology, though not yet
well defined, is understood here as the reduction of the globe to an
object for economic exploitation. It is in light of this understanding
that we must interpret the following statements:

The works that are being peddled about nowadays as the philosophy
of National Socialism but have nothing to do with the inner truth
and greatness of this movement (namely, the encounter between
planetary-determining technology and modern man)—have all been
written by men fishing in the troubled waters of "values" and "to-
talities." (EM, 152/166)

In 1966 Heidegger admitted that in 1935 he did not read aloud
the crucial passage in parentheses. He chose not to do so because,
as he himself said, "I was convinced that my audience was understanding me correctly. The dumb ones, the spies, and the snoopers
wanted to understand me otherwise, and would, no matter what."
(Sp, 206/276) The "correct" understanding is apparently this: The
true greatness of National Socialism is not its racism but its claim to
offer an alternative to capitalism and communism, which are different expressions of industrialization and technology. Technology
is the challenge to modern man in general and to German people in
particular. The real issue is not one of establishing better values, but
of learning how to be open to ways of revitalizing German heritage
in the face of the technological challenge. Philosophies which talk

of values are themselves reflections of the technological age which regards values as instruments for increasing a nation-state's economic or political might.[20] In the present age, we experience "the darkening of the world, the flight of the gods, the destruction of the earth, the transformation of man into a mass, the hateful suspicion of everything creative and free...." (EM, 29/31) Germany, the most "metaphysical" of all countries, was particularly threatened by the technological challenge. Heidegger's solution to the spiritual crisis was

> to restore the historical Dasein of man—and that is always likewise our own future in the whole of the history determined for us—to the power [Macht] of Being which is originally to be opened. All this, to be sure, in the limits within which philosophy can accomplish anything. (EM, 32/34)

Restoring human Dasein to the power of Being means renewing man's primal possibility of letting beings manifest themselves in the most appropriate way. This is another way of saying that it is necessary to reawaken the question of the sense of Being. One can readily see how far removed this "solution" is from the ones proposed by the real leaders of National Socialism, and in fact by other leading political ideologies and movements. Heidegger believed that the humanistic basis of most modern political movements leads to the "demonic." Humanism is demonic because it puts human spirit in the service of merely human plans; for example, when spirit becomes interpreted as "intelligence" or as a tool. Spirit is thus abused by Marxism, positivism (which Heidegger associated with capitalism), and also by National Socialism, which applies spirit "to the organization and regulation of a people's vital resources and race...." (EM, 36/39) Humanism ends by reducing human life to the process of production without acknowledging any higher possibility. Humanism leads to rampant industrialization, communist as well as capitalist. Mass production deflates spirit and thereby robs human life of its creativity and beauty. Heidegger remarks that "all true power and beauty of the body, all sureness and boldness in combat, but also all purity and inventiveness of the understanding, are grounded in the spirit and rise or fall only through the power or impotence of spirit." (EM, 36/39) He defines "spirit" as "a fundamentally attuned, knowing resoluteness toward the essence of Being." (EM, 37-38/41)

Europe and Germany will survive the technological challenge only
if they let spirit rise; that is, only if they resolve to hold themselves
open for the new revelation of what it means to be. The new revelation has something to do with technology, but up to this point
Europeans have simply made use of the technological disclosure of
beings as a means for exploiting man and Nature. In so doing, they
have nearly succeeded in destroying their culture. What they require
is insight into how to cultivate their heritage in the industrialized
world. Such insight is said to occur through creators who hold themselves open for truth. Heidegger claims that this human struggle is
part of a larger, cosmic battle. That is, human history is conditioned
by forces which transcend it. Some critics maintain that by taking
this "cosmological turn," Heidegger abandoned philosophy and
began to write mythology. They accuse him of projecting onto
"Being" the creative activity which belongs only to human beings.
He would reply that his critics are humanists who fail to understand
that human beings do not own the universe but, instead, are owned
by it. Our historical activity is a reflection of, and in the service of,
ageless cosmic battles. The primordial struggle *(Kampf)* between
the elements of the cosmos eventually leads to the emergence of
human "contenders," creative individuals who strive to bring order
into the cosmic fray.

> Against the overwhelming chaos they set up the barrier of their work,
> and in their work they capture the world thus opened up. It is with
> these works that the elemental power, *physis*, first comes to stand
> in presencing *[im Anwesenden]*. Only now do beings come into being
> as such *[Das Seiende wird jetzt erst also solches seiend]*. This world-
> building is authentic history. (EM, 47-48/51)

In his essay "The Origin of the Work of Art" (1936), Heidegger
describes the cosmological struggle as involving "world" and "earth."[21]
As we remember from his previous essays, Being (to be manifest) always involves an interplay between manifestness and concealment,
presence and absence. "World" corresponds to the clearing where
manifesting occurs, while "earth" corresponds to what always
remains concealed even in the midst of the most decisive disclosure.
In the language of Jung, earth might mean the archetypal contents of

the unconscious. Because these contents are not themselves rational but the very source of rationality, they can never be fully comprehended. The impossibility of the full disclosure of the aboriginal sources for world-symbols is analogous to the impossibility of absolute self-understanding on the part of an individual. We can draw an analogy between the development of an individual and the emergence of a new world-symbol: just as the authentic individual opens himself up to previously unseen possibilities, so too the creative hero is the place for the "self-disclosing openness of broad paths of simple and essential decisions in the destiny of an historical people." (Hw, 37/48) The world opened up by such creators is always limited by the earth, "the spontaneous forthcoming of that which is continually self-secluding and to that extent sheltering and concealing." (Hw, 37/48) What most conceals itself, according to Heidegger, is manifestness and the emptiness where manifestness can happen. The creative hero gains a glimpse of this all-pervading dialectic between Being and nothingness. Because his insight is necessarily only partial, and because he must use words and other symbols to express that insight, he always offers a particularized expression of his insight. Eugen Fink suggested that we never see light itself but only things which it illuminates. Hence, we understand light indirectly, in terms of the non-visual. So, too, with respect to Being and beings: we never see Being directly but only the beings which are manifest. Hence, we understand Being indirectly, in terms of the things which are. The thinker and poet must use language which is primarily suited for beings, not for Being.

In accounting for the possibility of world-founding revelations, Heidegger tries to demonstrate the hidden unity of *logos* and *physis*, which have long been interpreted as "thinking" and "Being." He hopes to show that there is an intrinsic relation between human existence (thinking) and the event of manifestness-concealment (Being) which has been overlooked by modern philosophy. He points out that the term *logos* stems from *legein*, which means to gather or to collect. *Physis* refers to the power that emerges, the self-presencing of what is. A plant *is* because it stands-forth or grows. *Physis* means to be manifest: Being. Because the power of self-presencing is also the gathering and assembling which are essential to *logos*, *physis* (Being) and *logos* (thinking) are said to be "the same." (EM, 100/110) Being means the gathering and assembling of opposing aspects of the enduring cosmic conflict. For a plant to grow, it must struggle constantly to remain unconcealed, or else it will disappear again into nothingness. Light struggles against the dark, but both require each other. This dynamic interaction of conflicting opposites is what Heraclitus meant by *logos*. Because *physis* and *logos* bring about order, Heidegger concludes that "rank and domination are implicit in Being." (EM, 102/112) Being as *logos* "does not show itself as one pleases. The true is not for every man but only for the strong." (EM, 102/112) By talking in this way, Heidegger gave comfort to those who wanted to divide human beings into ranks (including the rank of expendables) in the new Germany. He was right, of course, that people are *not* equally endowed. The great danger lies in assigning people to different ranks on the basis of political or social "imperatives."

Heraclitus, then, defined *logos* as the ordering principle of the cosmos, not as the rational faculty of the human ego. Human understanding is but an instance of the gathering and ordering which constitute the activity of the cosmos. Although Heraclitus suggests that there is an inner relation between human *legein* and *logos*, between thinking and Being, Parmenides was the first to say explicitly that Being and thinking are the same: *"To gar auto noein estin te kai einai."* (cf. EM, 104/115) Heidegger translates *noein* not by "thinking" but by "apprehending" *(Vernehmen)*, a term having a twofold meaning. Apprehending means accepting something, letting come to oneself that which shows or offers itself. Apprehending also means interrogating someone or investigating a situation in order to learn the facts:

> To apprehend in this twofold sense means to let something come to one, not merely accepting it, however, but taking a receptive attitude toward that which shows itself. When troops prepare to receive the enemy, it is in the hope of stopping him at the very least, of bringing him to a stand. This receptive bringing-to-stand is meant in *noein*. (EM, 105/116)

Being and apprehending do not belong together as an empty identity but in a dynamic, reciprocating relation. The event of Being requires the event of apprehending.

> Being means: to stand in the light, to appear, to enter into unconcealment. Where this happens, that is, where Being prevails, apprehension prevails and happens with it: the two belong together. Apprehension is the receptive bringing-to-stand of the intrinsically permanent that manifests itself. (EM, 106/177)

Being and apprehending, however, do not share equal "footing": "Apprehension occurs for the sake of Being." (EM, 106/117) Mankind does not have apprehension as a characteristic, but rather *"apprehension is the happening [Geschehnis] that has man."* (EM, 108/119—emphasis mine) Man can be this apprehension resolutely or indifferently.

> Only as a questioning, historical being does man come to himself and is a self. The selfhood of man means this: he must transform the Being that discloses itself to him into history and bring himself to stand in it. Selfhood does not mean that he is primarily an "ego" and an individual. This he is no more than he is a we, a community. (EM, 110/121)

In returning to Heraclitus' doctrine of the *logos*, Heidegger hoped to find a non-subjective way of explaining human understanding. He maintained that prior to the emergence of human existence, the cosmic play of revelation/concealment was taking place. Natural beings manifest themselves to each other without the aid of man— the ocean is affected by the sun's hot rays. What man adds to the enormous natural display is *awareness* of the play itself. In order to survive, he must establish a world for himself within the natural order. Aboriginal man, however, did not regard his world-founding activity in a purely utilitarian way; instead, he thought he was replicating the original world-founding activity of the gods. His home was thought to be stable only as long as he remembered that his life was dependent on and in the service of the transcendent. Preserving this awareness required a struggle both against his own tendency to forget his primary duty to the transcendent cosmic play, and against the tendency of the cosmos itself to conceal and obliterate man.

To elaborate on his notion that authenticity means struggling to establish a world, Heidegger interprets the first chorus from Sophocles' *Antigone*. Sophocles describes man as the *deinotaton*, the "strangest" of beings. The word *deinon* means awe-inspiring, over-powering order. It also means the powerful in the sense of one who disposes of power *(Gewalt)* violently *(gewalt-tätig)*. *Deinon*, the violence intrinsic to human existence, can be understood in terms of the clash between *techne* and *dike*. *Techne* is the power of the artist to let things be revealed in a particular way. The heroic poet or creator must fight against the forgetfulness of his fellow men in order to help them gain a more profound understanding of themselves and the world. *Deinon* refers not only to human existence but also to the overpowering order or governing structure of the cosmos: "Being, *physis*, as power, is basic and original togetherness: *logos*; it is governing order *[fugender Fug]: dike*." (EM, 123/135) A great clash occurs when *deinon* as overpowering destiny *(diké)* meets *deinon* as man's violent attempt to establish a world.

> The basic trait of the *deinotaton* lies in the interrelation between the two meanings of *deinon*. The knowing man sails right into the middle of the dominant order *[Fug]*; he tears it open and violently carries Being into beings, and yet he can never master the overpowering. Hence he is tossed back and forth between structure and the structureless, order and mischief *[Fug und Un-fug]*, between the evil and the noble. Every violent curbing of the powerful is either victory or defeat. Both, each in its different way, unfold the dangerousness of achieved or lost Being. Both, in different ways, are menaced by disaster. The *violent one*, the creative man, who sets forth into the unsaid, who breaks into this violent one stands at all times in venture.... Since he ventures to master Being, he must risk the assault of the un-being, *me kalon*; he must risk dispersion, instability, disorder, mischief. The more towering the summit of historical Dasein, the more yawning will be the abyss for the sudden plunge into the unhistorical, which merely thrashes around in issueless and placeless confusion. (EM, 123/135)

One reason Heidegger was considered dangerous by the National Socialists was because he regarded talk of a "thousand year Reich" as foolish. All world-founding inevitably ends in forgetfulness and loss. "The Dasein of historical man means: to be posited as the breach into which the preponderant power of Being bursts in its appearing, in order that this breach itself should shatter against Being." (EM, 125/137) Heidegger once again sounds like Nietzsche in saying that the violent creator scorns all normal success: "In willing the unprecedented, he casts aside all help. *To him disaster [Untergang] is the deepest and broadest yes to the overpowering.*" (EM, 125/137—emphasis mine) The authentic man recognizes that his efforts are not merely for his own sake but for the sake of the cosmos of which he is a part. He accepts the possibility of disaster because he sees the relative insignificance of his own brief life, and he acknowledges the importance of letting Being manifest itself in a way it cannot do without human beings. In establishing a world, the creative hero must be attuned to the mysterious, dark, dangerous, hidden: the "earth." Carl Jung has described the torrent of images which swept him away in the years before World War I. These revelations, which are interpreted as manifestations of archetypes of the collective unconscious, inspired much of his subsequent effort to develop a richer understanding of human life. Heidegger's favorite poet, Hölderlin, and his favorite painter, Van Gogh, both went mad. If Heidegger is right, they went mad not merely for psychological reasons, but because they were worn out by their struggle to hold themselves open for the revelations coming through them. In 1936 Heidegger said that

> It is precisely in great art—and only such art is under consideration here—that the artist remains inconsequential as compared with the work, almost like a passageway that destroys itself in the creative process for the work to emerge. (Hw, 29/40)

Erich Neumann, a student of Jung's, interprets the cultural hero in a way very similar to Heidegger and Nietzsche:

The true hero is one who brings the new and shatters the fabric of old values, namely the father-dragon which, backed by the whole weight of tradition and the power of the collective, ever strives to obstruct the birth of the new.

The creators form the progressive element in a community, but at the same time they are the conservatives who link back to the origins. In ever-renewed fights with the dragon they conquer new territory, establish new provinces of consciousness, and overthrow antiquated systems of knowledge and morality at the behest of the voice whose summons they follow, no matter whether they formulate their task as a religious vocation or as practical ethics. The depth of the unconscious layer from which the new springs, and the intensity with which this layer seizes upon the individual, are the real criteria of this summons by the voice, and not the ideology of the conscious mind.[22]

Notice that Neumann's hero, like Heidegger's, struggles to renew the same tradition which he attacks. The hero must fight against his desire to conform to a moribund tradition. He

stands between two worlds: the inner world that threatens to overwhelm him, and the outer world that wants to liquidate him for breaking the old laws. Only the hero can stand his ground against these collective forces, because he is the exemplar of individuality and possesses the light of consciousness.[23]

Besides creative heroes, a community requires individuals who will preserve what the heroes have revealed. Hence, there are degrees of heroism or authenticity. (Hw, 54/66) In one of his essays on Hölderlin (1943), Heidegger says that those who hearken to the word of the poet are participants in the process of reappropriating their heritage.

Out of these deliberate ones will come the slow ones of the long-enduring spirit, which itself learns again to persevere with the still-continuing failure of the god. The deliberating ones and the slow ones are for the first time the careful *[sorgehaftig]* ones. Because they think of that which is written of in the poem, they are directed with the singer's care toward the mystery of the "sparing nearness" *[der sparenden Nähe]*. Through this single turning towards the same object the careful hearers are related with the care of the speaker, "the others" are the "kindred" of the poet. (EHD, 28/267)

The tone of this passage differs from that found in *An Introduction to Metaphysics*, composed eight years earlier. While the lectures on metaphysics emphasize the violence needed to found a world, the essays on Hölderlin speak of Dasein as the preserver of messages sent from the realm of the "holy." The hero is no longer depicted as the powerful agent of disclosure but as the meditative individual who receives revelation. Authenticity is interpreted less from the perspective of the resolute individual and more from the perspective of an historical event in which an individual is appropriated *(vereignet)* by the event of appropriation *(Ereignis)*. In speaking of the "holy," Heidegger tries to endow the cosmic play of revelation/concealment with certain of the characteristics which theology attributes to God. The hero is the one who is fated to be opened up for insight into the transcendent, just as the saint is the one who is chosen to be opened up for insight into God. With the development of the idea of *Ereignis*, the cosmic play of revelation/concealment, Heidegger leaves behind much of the humanism and subjectivism which influenced him in 1935. Before turning to a discussion of *Ereignis* in the final two chapters, I would like to assess Heidegger's relation to National Socialism.

PART THREE: Heidegger's Decision in 1933.

Heidegger was not a supporter of the racist elements of National Socialism; in fact, he initially hoped to focus the movement on higher goals. Yet he remains responsible for helping Hitler to consolidate his position at a crucial point. He did what he felt was necessary. He tells us that in the winter of 1932-1933, he and his colleagues

> spoke often of the situation, not only of the political situation but especially that of the universities, and of the situation of the students which appeared in part to be hopeless. My judgment was this: insofar as I could judge things, only one possibility was left, and that was to attempt to stem the coming developments by means of the constructive powers which were still available. (Sp, 193/268)

In his interview with *Der Spiegel*, Heidegger spoke stiffly and briefly about his human failings; he was a proud, even arrogant man. One can imagine how difficult it must have been for him to reply to his interviewers, who asked him to comment on these remarks he made as rector: "Do not let doctrines and ideas be the rules of your Being. The *Führer* himself and he alone is present and future of German reality and its rule." (Sp, 198/271) Heidegger's reply is a study in understatement:

> These sentences are not found in the rectorial address, but only in the local *Freiburg Students Newspaper*, at the beginning of the 1933-34 Winter Semester. When I took over the rectorship, it was clear to me that I would not see it through without some compromises[!]. I would today no longer write the sentences you cite. Even by 1934 I no longer said such things. (Sp, 198/217)

Heidegger knew first-hand something of what it means to shatter against destiny. Yet the millions of people who were systematically slaughtered by those "true" leaders of German destiny were shattered much more.

For anyone capable of making sound conceptual distinctions, it was evident that Heidegger did not agree with the cruder views of National Socialism, even though his idea of the heroic creator did share some superficial similarities with Hitler's ideas about the Overman (a burlesque of Nietzsche's vision). In his lectures on Nietzsche in 1936-1937, Heidegger sharply criticized the decadent conception of human "greatness" propounded by the Wagnerians so popular with Hitler. Heidegger was not an aristocratic German reactionary yearning for Valhallah; he was a philosopher who was also intensely loyal to the "fatherland." If to the *cognoscentes,* however, Heidegger seemed to side with Nietzsche against the corrupt elements of National Socialism, to ordinary people he probably sounded very much like Hitler, Rosenberg, and others like them. Let us consider how Heidegger's conceptions of destiny and sacrifice come perilously close to similar National Socialist ideas.

We have already examined his claim that man must make a world for himself in the face of "overwhelming cosmic order." Supposedly, our greatness as human beings lies in our courageous response to the challenges we encounter. In 1941, Erich Fromm described Hitler's views in the following way:

> Usually Hitler tries to rationalize and justify his wish for power. The main justifications are the following: his domination of other peoples is for their own good and for the good of the culture of the world; the wish for power is rooted in the eternal laws of nature and he recognizes and follows only those laws; he himself acts under the command of a higher power—God, Fate, History, Nature; his attempts for domination are only a defense against the attempts of others to dominate him and the German people. He wants only peace and freedom.[24]

Fromm believes that Hitler's appeals to fate and nature were so successful because the German people wanted to escape from the intolerable burden of freedom. With the rise of capitalism, European peoples were freed from the bonds of medieval society. Medieval society provided security and meaning, however, which were not to be found so easily in the competitive new society governed by capitalism. Fromm follows Weber and Tawney in suggesting that the authoritarian forms of Protestantism emerged as a response to the widespread sense of helplessness, inferiority, and anomie brought about by the collapse of the old order. Capitalism brought freedom but failed to provide the security necessary for people to make creative use of that freedom. Europeans in general, and Germans in particular, developed an authoritarian character-structure: they wanted both to be dominated by someone stronger and to dominate someone weaker. Because of their lack of the feeling of self-worth, they were unable to relate with others on an equal basis. The economic disasters in Germany in the 1920s and 1930s reinforced their sense of powerlessness and isolation. They were ripe for a leader such as Hitler who would call for them to submit to him as the instrument of a cosmic destiny. In *Mein Kampf*, Hitler remarks: "Idealism alone leads men to voluntary acknowledgement of the privilege of force and strength and thus makes them a dust particle of that order which forms and shapes the entire universe."[25] Many people abandoned the difficult effort to become genuine individuals, and readily accepted the identities provided for them by National Socialism.

Hitler called for the people to be ready to make the ultimate sacrifice. Fromm says:

> In speaking of the instinct for self-preservation, which for Hitler... is more or less identical with the drive for power, he says that with the Aryan the instinct for self-preservation has reached the most noble form "because he willingly subjects his own ego to the life of the community and, if the hour should require it, he also sacrifices it."[26]

Hitler urged his people to become "unselfish," because "in the hunt for their own happiness people fall all the more out of heaven and into hell."[27] Although Heidegger's critique of selfishness (egoism) has nothing to do with the social Darwinism behind Hitler's thinking, this distinction escaped many people. Heidegger's talk about struggle and sacrifice, his critiques of mass culture, liberal democracy, progress, industrialization, his praise of the German spirit, his idea of the violent creator-hero as the guide for an historical people, his exaltation of the "powers of the soil," his emphasis on decision—all of this moved Heidegger too close to Hitler's language.

If Heidegger himself was an authoritarian personality, his support of Hitler had unconscious emotional motives as well as philosophical-political ones. This conjecture is supported by Karl Jaspers, who had frequent philosophical discussions with Heidegger in the 1920s. Although they were friendly in private, Jaspers contends that Heidegger would criticize him harshly behind his back. In 1933, their relationship ended. In 1951, Jaspers wrote an essay, only recently published, in which he makes some provocative claims about his former friend from Freiburg. He says, for example, that Heidegger gave a "masterful" speech at Heidelberg in 1933 (the rector's address originally delivered at Freiburg) about the need for the total regeneration of German spiritual life and the corresponding need to change radically the structure of the German university. After the speech, at dinner, Heidegger supposedly exclaimed that "there is an international conspiracy [Verbindung] of Jews," raved on about there being too many philosophers in Germany, and, in answer to Jaspers' query about how an uneducated man such as Hitler was going to rule Germany, replied: "Education is completely irrelevant, just look at his wonderful hands!"[28] Jaspers continues:

> Heidegger seemed to have changed. A tone arose that separated us right from the moment he arrived. National Socialism had become an intoxication to the people. I came to greet Heidegger upstairs in his room. "It is just like 1914...," I began, and was about to say, "once again this deceitful mass intoxication." But in response to my first words Heidegger agreed so enthusiastically that the last words stuck in my throat.[29]

If we can trust Jaspers, it would appear that Heidegger was taken in by a strong man posing as the savior of *das Volk*. He submitted for a time to Hitler. But the authoritarian personality wants to dominate as well as to be dominated. There is not much doubt that in 1933 Heidegger wanted to impose his vision of man and destiny on the National Socialist revolution. It was not the "voice of Being" speaking through Heidegger when he mounted podium after podium to support Hitler: it was Heidegger himself who spoke out under the mantle of the "destiny of Being." Possessing a high estimation of the historical timeliness of his thinking, he believed it worth the risk to try to channel National Socialism according to it.

Heidegger's appeal to destiny was offensive to many of his contemporaries who, as heirs of the ideals of the Enlightenment, believed that reason could allow man to take control of his fate. It came as a shock to them that the author of *Being and Time* could have succumbed to a "manifest primitivism."[30] Heidegger turned against National Socialism when he found it was only a monstrous version of the subjectivism responsible for industrialization and technological "progress." Herbert Marcuse, who fled Nazi persecution in 1933, supports the idea that National Socialism was not a regression to primitivism or barbarism but was a form of technological totalitarianism:

> The view that the growth of repression in contemporary society manifested itself, in the ideological sphere, first in the ascent of irrational psuedo-philosophies (*Lebensphilosophie*; the notions of Community against Society, Blood and Soil, etc.) was refuted by

> Fascism and National Socialism. These regimes denied these and
> their own irrational "philosophies" by the all-out technical rationali-
> zation of the apparatus. It was the total mobilization of the material
> and mental machinery which did the job and installed its mysti-
> fying power over the society. It served to make the individuals
> incapable of seeing "behind" the machinery those who used it,
> those who profited from it, and those who paid for it.[31]

For those who were spared the test in 1933, it is easy to condemn
Heidegger. Understanding is more difficult. Marcuse, who worked
closely with Heidegger from 1928 to 1932 and who was astonished
by what he considered Heidegger's "betrayal" of philosophy, confronted Heidegger in 1946 for an explanation of his actions in 1933.
Although dissatisfied with his explanation, Marcuse did not entirely
discredit it. In a 1974 interview he said:

> He refused (and I think that somehow I find this rather sympathe-
> tic), he refused any attempt to deny it or to declare it an aberration,
> or I don't know what, because he did not want to be in the same
> category, as he said, with all those of his colleagues who suddenly
> didn't remember any more that they taught under the Nazis, that
> they ever supported the Nazis, and declared that actually they had
> always been non-Nazi.[32]

Commentators on Heidegger's philosophy often choose to ignore
his political involvement, as if the "matter of thinking" unfolds
quite independently of the personal events in the life of the thinker.
This attitude displays ignorance about thinking in particular and
human life in general. Life affects thought. Heidegger, above all,
recognized this. His political engagement, in my opinion, did affect
the development of his concept of authenticity. It would be wrong,
of course, to say that the notion of "releasement" was the product
of a psychological change brought about by his political blunder.
Thinking does have its own way, and Heidegger's thinking was well
underway before 1933. It was not merely intellectual curiosity,
however, which led Heidegger to his eight-year (1936-1944) study
of Nietzsche's Will to Power. At least two factors influenced him.
First, the movement of National Socialism toward totalitarianism
reinforced his belief that the West is dominated by a subjectivistic

understanding of Being. That he once believed National Socialism might alleviate this domination convinced him that he had underestimated the powerful grip of subjectivism. Much of the rest of his career as a thinker was spent in trying to understand the essence of subjectivism as *Technik*. As I explain in the following chapter, he concluded that individuals in industrialized cultures are inauthentic not because of lack of personal fortitude but because they have become commodities, objects to be manipulated for gain.

The first factor which led Heidegger to analyze the Will to Power was a philosophical-cultural one. The second factor was personal. In his self-confident resoluteness in 1933-1935, he had given assistance to the very subjectivism to which he was opposed. His own moment of truth was colored by elements of the Will to Power, of subjectivism, of egoism. He meditated on Nietzsche's idea of the Will to Power partly in order to clarify his own understanding of the relation of will to authenticity. He found he could not separate his thinking from his personal self-understanding. In his later writings, we find fewer discussions about selfhood and resoluteness. He recognized that his earlier work had sometimes embraced aspects of voluntarism, subjectivism, and humanism. He had focused his thinking too much upon man and too little on the event of revelation *(Ereignis)*. In turning away from his existentialist ontology, Heidegger found his way back to his original spiritual-religious path. His mature conception of authenticity can be understood in light of an a-theistic, yet spiritual, interpretation of man as the place in which the event of revelation/concealment (Being) can be manifest. In a way analogous to what Christianity describes as the advent of grace, the authentic self is released from self-will by and for this cosmic event.

CHAPTER SEVEN

Inauthenticity, Technology, and Subjectivism

HEIDEGGER'S CONCEPT of authenticity underwent a process of maturation, not a metamorphosis. His later version of this concept claims that will power cannot lead to authenticity; instead, it comes as a gift. Although he sometimes speaks of releasement as an individual occurrence, more often he regards it as a world-altering event. Presently, we live in a world where everything (including people) appears to be a commodity. In a world where efficiency in production is the major social standard, inauthenticity is not a matter of individual decision; rather, it is almost unavoidable. According to Heidegger, we are destined to understand things primarily as exploitable objects. Supposedly, Being has "hidden itself" from us more and more since the time of Plato. As Being withdraws, we no longer notice the manifestness (Being) of beings, nor do we recall that we are the openness for that manifestness. Because we lose all sense of the transcendent, we assume that we are the foundation for value, reality, and truth. The self-concealment of Being is the ontological analogue to the death of God. Technological culture is egoism on a planetary scale. We cannot liberate ourselves from the Will to Power which impels us toward total mobilization of all things. We can only prepare ourselves for a new revelation of what it means to be. Only such a revelation will enable Western humanity to be what it most properly can be: openness for the Being of beings.

198

In *Being and Time*, Heidegger suggested that by resolving to accept the call of conscience, an individual chooses to be authentic. Every individual, moreover, is in principle capable of deciding for authenticity. This voluntaristic-individualistic interpretation of authenticity owes much to Nietzsche and Kierkegaard. Yet *Being and Time* also explains that an individual's fate is tied up with his people's destiny. Hence, it would appear that an individual can only be as authentic as his historical community. An historical community or people becomes authentic by revitalizing its heritage, that is, by actualizing its particular possibilities. Occasionally *Being and Time* implies that the truly authentic person is the hero who leads his people in the right direction. In the 1920s, Heidegger had not yet worked out fully the relation between the destiny of Being and the destiny of historical peoples. He knew that historical epochs differ because Being is understood in different ways, but he often talked as if changes in ontological understanding resulted from the unfolding of a people's destiny. Later, he made it clear that the destiny of a people is ultimately conditioned by the play of Being, a play that transcends human control. When discussing the creative *hero*, even in his later writings, Heidegger introduced voluntaristic and individualistic themes. The hero must struggle to let the truth break through him. When discussing Western *humanity*, however, Heidegger denied the efficacy of will for bringing about any significant change in the prevailing understanding of Being. Heroes arise only if they are fated to do so. As I demonstrate in the next chapter, Heidegger at times spoke of releasement neither in terms of the world-historical hero, nor in terms of Western humanity, but in terms of the individual who seeks to be released from self-will. In such cases, we find evidence that his youthful religious concerns never left him; they became only more profound.

   In the present chapter, I analyze Heidegger's mature concept of *in*authenticity, now understood to be an almost inescapable condition of contemporary mankind. Part One takes up the claim that inauthenticity results from nihilism: the increasing self-concealment of Being during the course of Western history. The history of philosophy from Plato to Nietzsche reflects the rise of nihilism. Part Two considers Heidegger's concept of *Technik*. *Technik* does not mean technological skills or instruments, but the disclosure of beings as objects which can be manipulated in technological ways. A technological world is possible because everything seems to be an object for domination by the self-certain human Subject. In concluding, I suggest that Heidegger's analysis of inauthentic Western man is analogous in certain respects to Plato's analysis of society in *The Republic*. Just as for Plato the state is the individual soul "writ large," so, too, for Heidegger, inauthentic Western man is the individual self "writ large." Western mankind as self-willed subject exhibits collectively the characteristics belonging to the inauthentic self as depicted in *Being and Time*.

PART ONE: **Nihilism, Inauthenticity, and the History of Being.**

Although he usually insists that mankind has been destined to become the self-certain Subject, Heidegger occasionally talks as if human will played a role in bringing about the present age. Yet he criticizes the humanism which believes that reason enables man to determine his own destiny and lets him take the place of God, not only as an object of worship (Feuerbach) but also as the source of value (Marx, Nietzsche). Seen from Western man's viewpoint, the struggle to dominate Nature has led to great improvements in his "standard of living." The idea that Nature is an object which we can dominate arose only because Being hid itself from us. As we lost sight of the transcendent, we no longer concerned ourselves with conforming to it; instead, we became enamored of controlling the beings revealed by it. Becoming oblivious to our essential dependence and finitude, we eventually assumed that we were self-created and self-grounding— a God. We now justify our assault on the natural world by saying that human beings are all-important and that natural objects have only the value we choose to assign to them.

When Heidegger says that Being conceals itself or withdraws, he tends to "personify" it. If Being (presencing, manifesting) *is not* a being, however, how can it *do* anything, including *withdrawing*?

Hearing such mythological language, we might conclude that Being means a transcendent agent who guides human history according to a pre-established plan. Heidegger did think that he had found a pattern in history: the continuing decline in our understanding of Being. This decline is called "nihilism," because we have become oblivious to the nothingness or absence which allows beings to be revealed to us.[1] Unlike Hegel, Heidegger denied that the cosmos is ordered according to a plan discernable by human reason. Indeed, he maintained that the cosmos "happens" as a kind of play whose rules are unknown to us. The cosmic play of revelation/concealment is transcendent in at least three senses. First, it transcends beings because it "is not" a being, but the on-going event in which beings manifest and conceal themselves. Second, it transcends our experience since we are usually focused on beings, not on their manifestness, nor on the emptiness in which this manifestness happens. Third, it transcends human history. Although we can only use figurative language to describe how it happens, Western history is somehow determined by the "destiny of Being." Above all, Heidegger wanted to avoid talking about a Supreme Being who is the ground of it all, but his choice of words sometimes suggests that Being is a kind of "agency."

Our age is nihilistic not because we don't believe in anything, but because we have lost our awareness of *das Nichts*: the nothingness which lets beings be revealed. In *Being and Time*, Heidegger wrote that Dasein's temporal horizons determine the various ways in which beings can be manifest. These horizons are themselves concealed or absent; they are determinate modes of nothingness. Gradually he stopped talking about the temporality of *human* Dasein and turned his attention to the temporality (absence, nothingness) of Being as such. For something to be manifest, a self-concealing absence is required. Being presupposes nothingness. Truth (un-concealment, *a-letheia*, Being) is made possible by un-truth (self-concealing absence, *-lethe*, nothingness). *Being and Time* makes this point when it explains that Dasein does not notice the self-concealing temporality which lets beings be manifest as tools. Yet because of its subjectivistic vocabulary, *Being and Time* sometimes implies that Being belongs to beings, while temporality belongs to human Dasein. Later on, Heidegger maintained that Being and time are fundamentally the same; *we* separate them conceptually because our understanding is inherently dualistic. He no longer spoke as if human beings possessed temporality. Instead, he asserted that mankind is a necessary element in the unpredictable dialectic of "Time/Being." Just as an individual fails to notice the temporality which lets beings be present as tools, so, too, Western humanity does not notice the self-concealing absence which has allowed beings to present themselves in one way for the Greeks, in another way for medieval man, and in still another way for us.

Heidegger calls the historical tendency of Being to conceal itself the *"epoche"* of Being. (Hw, 311/26) The word *epoche* means "suspending", "bracketing", "holding-back". Each epoch of Western history is different because Being holds itself back more and more. As it does so, beings manifest themselves differently. Heidegger said in 1946:

> In this way, by illuminating them, Being sets beings adrift in errancy. Beings come to pass in that errancy by which they circumvent Being and establish the realm of error (in the sense of a prince's realm or the realm of poetry). Error is the space in which history unfolds. In error what happens in history bypasses what is like Being. Therefore, whatever unfolds historically is necessarily misinterpreted.... Man's inability to see himself corresponds to the self-concealing tendency of the lighting of Being. (Hw, 311/26)

By now, we know it is misleading to say that Being "illuminates" beings, because Being is not a light which shines on beings. Beings manifest themselves: Being always refers to the Being (un-concealment) of beings. Illuminating beings means establishing a clearing *(Lichtung)* or absence in which they can present themselves. *Being and Time* describes this clearing as temporal ecstases of human Dasein. Heidegger later wrote that human temporality is an aspect of a more fundamental "world-time." The Western world is historical because world-time has continually altered itself; that is, the absence needed for presencing has become more and more concealed from us. As a result, we have fixed our attention solely on beings, which now seem to be merely objects for us.

The passage quoted above says that beings are set adrift into "errancy," a term Heidegger used as early as 1930 in "On the Essence of Truth." The talk of errancy does not mean that a mistake has been made in history, or that mankind has flunked some sort of cosmic exam. The "error" lies in the fact that as long as only *beings* are revealed, and then in a particular way for each epoch, and as long as Being conceals itself, mankind will fail to see that its own essence (*Wesen*, "way of being present) is as openness for the manifestness of beings. When Heidegger says that "Man's inability to see himself corresponds to the self-concealing of the light of Being," he means that our tendency toward self-concealment (falling) is analogous to the tendency of Being to conceal itself. Indeed, our obliviousness with respect to Being is not our fault but happens because Being has disappeared from our view. "The fundamental trait of presencing *[Anwesen]* itself is determined by remaining concealed and unconcealed." (VA, III, 58/106-107) In previous ages, mankind was destined to have a deeper sense of the transcendent, but in the present age this sense has vanished altogether.

Because the cosmic play of revelation/concealment has become more and more hidden from mankind, there have been important differences in the ancient, medieval, and modern worlds. Heidegger is saying in his ontological language what other people have been saying for a long time: modern man has become arrogant and self-centered; hence, he has forgotten that he has certain obligations to the universe which gave birth to him. For Plato, "Being" meant permanent presence: idea, *eidos*, the unchanging realm of forms which transcended the realm of becoming. For Aristotle, "Being" meant being present in relative permanence, as dynamic emergence from unconcealment: *physis*. God, the highest instance of self-actualizing activity, transcends the world of change, but draws all beings to emulate divine self-perfection. For medieval man, "Being" meant being present as a creature in the great chain of Being, whose apex was God. God's absolutely permanent presence (Supreme Being) guaranteed the contingent presence of his creatures. For modern man, "Being" means being representable as an object for the rational Subject. Only modern man lives without any sense of the transcendent. Heidegger interprets the history of philosophy to show how it reflects the increasing disappearance of the transcendent in Western civilization.

The distinction between Being and beings, between presencing as such (transcendence) and the beings which are present, was vaguely apparent to some early Greek thinkers. Heidegger claims that Heraclitus' glimpse of the Being of beings is the hidden source of the destiny of the West. (VA, III, 23/76) This glimpse can be re-experienced indirectly if we interpret Heraclitus' *logos*-doctrine in a certain way. As mentioned earlier, Heidegger points out that *logos* is the stem for the word *legein*, which means "gathering" and "sheltering," although it is usually translated as "saying" and "talking." Sheltering something means letting it be, making a place for it. *Legein* can thus refer to the human activity of founding a world in which beings can be manifest. This human gathering and ordering functions best when it is attuned to the cosmic *logos*, the primordial gathering which governs the universe.

> Because the *logos* lets lie before us what lies before us as such, it discloses what is present in its presencing. But disclosure is *Aletheia*. This and *logos* are the Same. *Legein* lets aletheia, unconcealment as such, lie before us.... All disclosure releases what is present from concealment. Disclosure needs concealment. The *A-letheia* rests in *lethe*, drawing from it and laying before us what remains deposited in *lethe*. *Logos* is in itself and at the same time a revealing and concealing. It is *aletheia*. Unconcealment needs concealment. (VA, III, 16-17/71)

Although Heraclitus saw that revealing/concealing are intrinsic to the manifestness of things (VA, III, 76-77/120-121), and although he was in the vicinity of the "twofold" (distinction between Being and beings), Heidegger asserts that his Greek predecessor never voiced any of this explicitly. Heraclitus often interpreted the interplay of concealment and unconcealment as a kind of being; indeed, the ultimate instance of being. Heraclitus *(logos)*, Parmenides *(moira)*, Anaximander *(chreon)*, Plato *(eidos)*, and Aristotle *(energeia, ousia)* all try to express the Same: "the unity of the Unifying One." (Hw, 432/56; VA, III, 36-37/86-87)

Heidegger regards Plato's thinking as so decisive that he once said: "All Western thinking is Platonism." (NII, 220) In his controversial essay "Plato's Doctrine of Truth," he tries to show that Plato initiated subjectivistic thinking (metaphysics) in two ways. First, he turned attention away from Being *(presencing)* and toward *eidos* (that which is premanently *present).* Second, he suggested that the crucial element in knowing is for the knower to get an adequate vision of the *eidos.* This emphasis on the knower later led to the subjectivistic turn. Elsewhere, Heidegger writes that Plato's notion of the *agathon,* that which makes beings possible, also contributed to the unfolding of subjectivism. Kant used Plato's *agathon* and *eidos* as models for his notion of the a priori, that which makes experience possible. And Nietzsche turns the a priori into "values" which make possible the increase of power of those who posited the values. (NII, 213-255) Heidegger goes so far as to say that "the metaphysics of Plato is no less nihilistic than the metaphysics of Nietzsche." (NII, 343) Their thinking is nihilistic in that they have become oblivious to the *nihil,* the nothingness required for beings to be present. Heidegger admits that Plato still had some insight into the play of revelation/concealment, however, since *"The intepretation of Being as eidos, presence [Anwesen] in appearance, presupposed the interpretation of truth as aletheia, un-obstructedness."* (NI, 212)

Aristotle's notion of *energeia,* the movement of *ousia* to bring itself from concealment into appearance, includes a faint echo of the distinction between Being (presencing) and beings (things that are present). This distinction was utterly lost, however, with the Latin translation of *energeia* as *actualitas.*[2] (Hw, 342/56-57; NII, 413/12-13) Philosophers eventually interpreted *actualitas* as "reality"; finally, they understood reality as "objectivity." "To be" ends up meaning to be an object for the knowing subject.

Medieval theologians, influenced by Greek metaphysics, interpreted God as the ground of reality. God guarantees the presence of His creatures. Already in Greek times,

Being becomes present as *logos* in the sense of ground, of allowing to let lie before us. The same *logos,* as the gathering of what unifies,

> is the *En*. This *En*, however, is twofold. For one thing, it is the unifying One in the sense of what is everywhere primal and thus most universal; and at the same time it is the unifying One in the sense of the All-Highest (Zeus). (ID, 137/69)

The ontological thinking which unites *logos*-philosophy (the quest to discover the ultimate ground) with theology, Heidegger calls "onto-theo-logical thinking." Both philosophy and theology were damaged in this merger. Theology was hurt because it was diverted from its original calling—assisting the faithful to a deeper level of faith. Metaphysical theology replaced the *mysterium tremendum* with a concept: God as ground of reality. This is hardly a God to whom one can sing and dance. (ID, 140/72) By the end of the Middle Ages, God had become weak enough for man to consider taking His place as measure of everything. Hence, a significant development in the course of Western metaphysics (the subjectivistic turn, Descartes' *ego cogito*) helped bring about the death of God. Philosophy was hurt by the merger with theology because the authoritarianism of the Church forbade free and open inquiry.

Like Kierkegaard, Heidegger distinguishes between Christianity and "Christendom," which refers to Christianity as a socio-political institution. Genuine Christianity lasted only for the short duration between the death of Christ and the beginning of Paul's "propaganda" missions. (Hw, 202/63) Heidegger speaks for himself when he says of Nietzsche:

> Christendom for Nietzsche is the historical-world-political phenomenon of the Church and its claim to power within the shaping of Western humanity and its modern culture. Christendom in this sense and the Christianity of the New Testament are not the same. (Hw, 202-203/63)

According to Heidegger, real faith means giving up hope for security in life, letting go of egoism and self-will, and accepting the grace which brings salvation. Most people find the life of faith to be very difficult. Early on, the Church learned that it could maintain and increase its flock only by promising them an easier road to salvation. Christendom offered methods (sacraments, penance, indulgences, and other "good works") which guaranteed eternal life to those who used them. In setting itself up as the paternal authority for the faithful, Christendom misinterpreted the teaching that we "must become again as little children." The point is not to *become* little children, but to become *as* they are: filled with wonder, open to possibilities.[3] Children must obey, too, but not just anyone who claims to represent their father. Christendom defined truth as belief in the "infallibility of the written word and doctrine of the Church." (Hw, 75/122) Knowing meant understanding correctly "the authoritative Word and the authorities proclaiming it." (Hw, 75/122) Instead of being the abandonment of security, faith degenerated into its guarantee.

Heidegger claims that Platonic thinking had a dire effect on aboriginal Christianity. Indeed, he even calls it "Platonism for the people." (EM, 80/90) Like neo-Platonism, Christendom depicted earthly life as a sojourn in a world of mere appearances. Ultimate reality was found only when bodily death freed the soul for its return to the unchanging realm of heaven. Christendom played down the possibility that "eternity" might mean *kairos* (redemption here and now), instead of a heavenly afterlife. Plato's metaphysics of presence suggested that the "really real" is that which is always present and unchanging. Christendom, interested in finding philosophical support for its views about the afterlife, adopted neo-Platonic doctrines and claimed that the human soul shares in God's permanent presence. By turning the person into a permanent object (soul), Christendom both denied human mortality and promoted the very egoism from which genuine Christianity promised to save us. Salvation came to mean the eternal continuation of "me."

Luther's Reformation attacked the worst excesses of Catholic Christendom, including the sale of indulgences which promised to alleviate punishment in the afterlife. He asserted that only God's grace, not human works, brings salvation. In proclaiming that man cannot save himself, Luther initiated sweeping questions about the possibility of "justification."

> At the beginning of the modern age the question was freshly raised
> as to how man, within the totality of what is, i.e., before the ground
> of everything in being (God), can become certain and remain certain
> of his own sure continuance, i.e., his salvation. This question of the
> certainty of salvation is the question of justification, i.e., of justice
> *(iustitia)*. (Hw, 226/90)

Heidegger maintains that Luther played an important role in the
history of subjectivism. Luther denied that priests or sacraments are
needed to mediate between an individual and God. Each person is
endowed with a conscience which, as the voice of God, is the ultimate
authority and guide. Protestantism destroyed the basis for a religious
community by claiming that each person is alone before God, and by
making each person the final judge concerning religious truth. Many
people have pointed out how difficult it was for Protestants to endure
the isolation and insecurity produced by the doctrine of "election"
or predestination. While the Catholic Church had guaranteed salvation for those who practiced its methods, the Protestant Church
asserted that salvation is a gift from an inscrutable and apparently
despotic God. The growing inability of religion to deliver the security
and certainty man needed helped to promote a movement begun in
the Italian Renaissance: the drive to achieve security and satisfac-
tion in *this* life, apart from any consideration of the afterlife.

Descartes, who was—ironically—a Catholic, gave expression to
the humanistic desire for man to justify himself, to become master
of his own fate, to free himself from dependence on authority,
tradition, and revelation. Heidegger remarks that

> What is new in the new era, over against the medieval, Christian era,
> rests in that fact that man prepares from out of himself and with
> his own capacities to become certain of and secure about his being-
> human in the midst of the whole of beings. The essentially Christian
> thought of the certainty of the Holy is taken over, but the "Holy"
> is not the other worldly eternal salvation: the way thereto is not
> self-abnegation *[Entselbstung]*. The Holy and the healthy get sought
> exclusively in the free self-unfolding of all creative capacities of man.
> As a result, the question arises *how* a certainty—sought for his this-

worldly life—about this being human and the world is to be won and grounded. (NII, 133)

Descartes changed the traditional metaphysical question, "What is being?" to the an inquiry about the method in which "an unconditioned certainty and security get sought by man himself and for man, and in which the essence of truth gets delimited." (NII, 142) To gain complete self-certainty, at least in this life, man had to discover an absolutely certain foundation within himself. (Hw, 98-100/148-149) Such self-certainty is only found in the *ego cogito*, which affirms the fundamental importance of the human subject. Until Descartes' time, the word "subject" was understood as *hypokeimenon*, that which stands on its own and supports its qualities. All creatures were considered to be subjects, supported by the permanently present God. Influenced as he was by scholasticism, Descartes also thought in terms of foundation (ground) and subject. He secularized the Christian quest for certainty by claiming that the self-thinking ego is the guarantor of its own permanent presence. He asserted moreover, that the *ego cogito* is the ground for determining the reality and truth of everything it encounters. Descartes reduced beings to ideas or representations, whose validity is determined according to the standards imposed by the ego-subject. The self-validating subject (the ego is certain of its own existence), which is permanently present because it accompanies all its representations, now becomes the ground and standard for everything. Man assumes God's place in the great chain of being.

For Descartes, only those ideas are true which are as "clear and distinct" as the *ego cogito*. Since only mathematical ideas approach this degree of certainty, only the quantifiable can be judged as real and true. What cannot be so measured becomes an object of superstition, fancy, or at best "common sense." To be real means to be an object for the subject. The word "object" comes from the Latin *ob-iacere*, "to throw over or against," a meaning which is more apparent in the German word for object: *Gegenstand*, "something which stands over against." After Descartes, "to be" means to stand over against the knowing subject as something placed there by and for the subject. The subject places before itself, re-presents, or posits *(vor-stellt)* its objects. Things now appear primarily in ways amenable to the projects of scientific research. In 1940, when commenting on the meaning of the *cogito sum*, Heidegger wrote:

> The proposition speaks of a connection between *cogito* and *sum*. It says that I am as the representer *[Vorstellende]*, that not only is my Being essentially determined through this representing *[Vorstellen]* but that my representing—as the authoritative *repraesentatio*—decides about the presence *[Präsenz]* of everything represented *[Vorgestellten]*, i.e., about the presence *[Anwesenheit]* of what is meant in it, i.e., about its Being as a being. The proposition says: representing, which is itself essentially represented *[vor-gestellt]* posits Being as representedness and truth as certainty. (NII, 162)

Because the subject makes its own self-certainty the ultimate standard for truth, the nature of truth changes. Formerly, a statement was said to be true if it conformed to what the statement is being made about. Now, however, an idea is true or correct only if it is "certain"; that is, only if satisfies the self-validating and self-securing standards of the subject.

> The representing is now correct when it is right in relation to this claim to secureness. Proved correct *[richtig]* in this way, it is, as "rightly dealt with" *[recht gefertigt]* and as at our disposal, made right, justified *[gerechtfertigt]*. The truth of anything that is in being, in the sense of the self-certainty of subjectness is, as secureness *(certitudo)*, fundamentally the making-right, the justifying, of representing and of what it represents before representing's own clarity. Justification *(justificatio)* is the accomplishing of *justitia* [justice or rightness] and is thus justice *[Gerechtigkeit]* itself. Since the Subject is forever Subject, it makes itself certain of its own secureness. It justifies itself before the claim to justice that it has itself posited. (Hw, 225-226/89-90)[4]

Although Luther may have been right in saying that man cannot justify himself before God, Descartes countered him by saying that man could justify himself before himself. Heidegger maintains that we are not to understand the word "subject" in terms of an individual ego. (Hw, 101/150-151; NII, 451/56) Modern egoism does not make possible the subjectivistic understanding of Being; rather, such egoism is made possible because man's essence has been changed into that of the subject. Individuals in the modern world understand themselves and other beings primarily in accordance with the subjectivistic understanding: rational man is the measure of all things, Nature is a stockpile of resources whose value lies only in gratifying human desires. Western man, under the domination of this subjectivistic understanding of Being, seeks to gain security not just by *knowing* reality, but by *mastering* it.

The Renaissance and Enlightenment led to man's self-deification, but only because Christianity had degenerated into Christendom.

> The fact that the transformation of reality to the self-certainty of the *ego cogito* is determined directly by Christianity...only proves how Christian faith adopted the fundamental trait of metaphysics and brought metaphysics to Western domination in this form. (NII, 472/67)

In place of God, who used to determine the truth and presence of all things, man now posits human *reason*, whose major expression is the Principle of Sufficient Reason. In the early 1950s, Heidegger observed that many people regard the "Europeanization" of the earth as the "triumphal march of Reason," which was proclaimed a goddess during the French Revolution. "Indeed, the idolization of that divinity is in fact carried so far that any thinking which rejects the claim of reason as not originary, simply has to be maligned today as unreason." (US, 103-104/15) According to Heidegger, however, the Principle of Sufficient Reason is itself without a "sufficient reason" or ground. This principle cannot give adequate reasons for its own reasonableness. Its self-evidence to modern man testifies that we are blind to alternative ways of thinking.

Sometimes Heidegger talks as if Descartes' notion of the self-assertive ego introduces will into the notion of the subject. (IIw, 225/88) Elsewhere, however, he claims that Leibniz, with whom "the metaphysics of subjectivity executes its decisive beginning," makes will an explicit element of the subject. (NII, 237) Leibniz regarded all beings as subjects or "monads." Monads contain within themselves the totality of their experiences. Each monad is driven by *appetitio* or *conatus* to actualize its possibilities or to unfold its possible experiences. (NII, 298) Leibniz introduced Aristotelean dynamism into Descartes' static metaphysics of the subject. He concluded that all beings have the *will* to become what they are, the will to self-actualization.

> Only when we conceive Beingness as actuality *[Wirklichkeit]* does their open a connection with doing and effecting *[Wirken und Erwirken]*, i.e., with the empowering to power as the essence of the Will to Power. Accordingly, there subsists an inner relation between Beingness as subjectivity and Beingness as Will to Power. (NII, 236-237)

Kant was influenced by Leibniz's notion that space and time are not constituents of external reality but are principles of order for human experience. For both Leibniz and Kant, the human subject is endowed with the capacity to organize for itself its own experience. Although Kant thus participated in the subjectivistic turn, he also caught a glimpse beyond it. He did assert that objects of experience (natural beings) must be determined by the a priori categories of the understanding. Hence, for him Being still meant "objectivity." In his first *Critique*, however, he also suggested that the rational categories are themselves determined by what is non-rational: the modes of temporality. Heidegger, of course, maintains that it is only a short step from here to his own view: that the prevailing rational understanding of Being is determined by the way world-time allows beings to manifest themselves to us. Kant's subject is finite and receptive, not entirely self-grounding in the manner of Descartes'.

Hegel, who neglected Kant's insistence on the finitude of the human subject, led subjectivism toward its culmination. According to Heidegger, Hegel's concept of Absolute Spirit striving to appropriate its object (Nature) unites Leibniz's thinking (Being as the striving to bring forth one's representations) and Kant's (Being as the condition for the possibility of):

> Being as such condition, however, cannot be conditioned by a being, i.e., something which is still conditioned, but only through itself.

Only as the unconditioned self-law-giving is representing, i.e., reason, in the dominating, completely unfolded fullness of its essence, the Being of all beings. But self-law-giving characterizes the "will," insofar as its essence is determined in the range of pure Reason. *Reason, as striving representing, is in itself at the same time Will.* The unconditioned subjectivity of reason is willful self-knowledge. This means: reason is absolute spirit. As such, reason is the absolute actuality of the actual, the Being of beings. (NII, 299—emphasis mine.)

By making human reason absolute, Hegel was a key figure in the Faustian drive for human self-deification so characteristic of nineteenth century German philosophy. Robert Tucker has given the name "epistemological aggrandizement" to the violent effort by the subject to reveal everything as rational and, hence, as an aspect of itself (reason).[5] Hegel depicted the march of reason to recognize itself in and thus to appropriate otherness (Nature) as a ruthless drive which tramples "many an innocent flower." History is the "slaughter-bench" on which people and ideals are annihilated in Spirit's drive to end its alienated condition.[6]

Hegel restricted will by making it an essential aspect of the struggle of Absolute Spirit to achieve unconditioned and total self-manifestation. Only in Nietzsche's thinking did subjectivism reach its pinnacle, since Nietzsche regarded will itself as its own highest aim. Will is the unconditioned subjectivity of life which strives to become ever stronger. "Will is no longer only the self-law-giving re-presenting...to commanding, the pure empowering of power." (NII, 301) While Hegel stressed the rational in man, Nietzsche emphasized the animal in him:

Thus the unconditioned essence of subjectivity unfolds itself necessarily as the *brutalitas* of the *bestialitas*. At the end of metaphysics stands the proposition: *Homo est brutum bestiale.* Nietzsche's word of the "blond beast" is not an incidental exaggeration, but the characterization and motto for a context in which he knowingly stands, without penetrating its essential historical relations. (NII, 200-201)

Nietzsche exhausted the essential possibilities of metaphysical-subjectivistic thinking. (VA, I, 75-76/95-96) His "value-philosophy"

214 Eclipse of the Self

expresses the nihilism of the modern age. For him, nihilism has more than one meaning. On the one hand, there is "passive nihilism," which means the de-valuation of the highest values. On the other hand, there is "active nihilism," which means the destruction of decaying values to make way for new ones. In passive nihilism, people identify the *symptoms* of decline with the problem itself, namely, the exhaustion of the dominant system of values. Instead of trying to create new values, a decadent culture props up the old ones. Hence, according to Heidegger, in modern times, the tottering ideals of Plato's forms and the Christian heaven were secularized through "doctrines regarding world happiness, through socialism, and equally through Wagnerian music, i.e., everywhere where 'dogmatic Christendom' had 'become bankrupt'." (Hw, 208/69) Heidegger, whose own views are difficult to disentangle from Nietzsche's, summarizes the decay of the West since the sixteenth century:

> Into the position of the vanished authority of God and the teaching office of the Church steps the authority of conscience, obtrudes the authority of Reason. Against these the social instinct rises up. The flight from the world into the supersensory is replaced by historical progress. The otherworldly goal of everlasting bliss is transformed into earthly happiness of the greatest number. The careful maintenance of the cult of religion is relaxed through enthusiasm for the creating of a culture or the spreading of civilization. Creativity, previously the unique property of the biblical god, becomes the distinctive mark of human activity. Human creativity finally passes over into business enterprise. (Hw, 203/64)

In contrast to the "sickly" view of life propounded by the Christian-Platonic system of values, Nietzsche asserted that all life seeks to become stronger. Hence, values are not pre-existing standards found in some heavenly realm, but perspectives necessary for the enhancement of human power. Will does not will something external, but wills itself. In willing itself, will strives for what is essential to it: power. Hence, will is always the Will to Power. Power remains powerful only if it continues to become more powerful. Hence, the Will to Power is the Will to Will. (Hw, 216-217/77-78) The Will to Power describes the fact that everything strives to assert itself, to become what it already is, to actualize its potential. Heidegger says that if the Will to Power is the *essentia* of what is, the Eternal Return of the Same is the *existentia*; that is, the way in which the Will to Power exists. (Hw, 219/81-82) As pure Will to Will, the Will to Power unfolds in a spiral out of itself. The constant becoming of the Will to Power achieves permanence (presence, Beingness) as Will to Will: the Eternal Return of the Same. Life wills to be the living will which it already is.

For human beings to preserve the stage of power already achieved, they must establish a domain of truth. Nietzsche remains true to the metaphysical tradition by using the term "Being" to describe the stable realm of truth necessary for human will to will itself to a higher stage. For Nietzsche, life is worth more than truth, however, because art opens up the new perspectives (values) needed for passing to a higher stage of power. While truth maintains Being, art wills Becoming. Nietzsche claimed that Descartes' quest for cognitive certainty in the form of the *ego cogito* was a disguised form of the Will to Power. Hence, Descartes was a kind of artist, a creator who opened a new perspective which increased man's power. Subsequent thinkers continued to develop this perspective, which eventually enabled man to become his own highest value. With the death of God, "the self-consciousness in which modern humanity has its essence completes its last step. It wills itself as the executor of the unconditional Will to Power." (Hw, 231/95) In willing out beyond its present form, mankind wills to become the Overman.

Heidegger's interpretation of the doctrine of the Overman is ambiguous. On the one hand, he regards the Overman as the highest expression of subjectivism. On the other hand, he regards the Overman as pointing beyond subjectivism to a new beginning. By the Overman,

> Nietzsche does not mean a type of existing man, only super-dimensional. Nor does he mean a type of man who casts off "humanity," to make sheer caprice the law and titanic rage the rule. The Overman is the man who first leads the essential nature of existing man over into its truth, and so assumes that truth. (WHD, 25-26/59)

The Overman can be interpreted as humanity released from its drive to dominate the earth in order to gain "security." "The thing that the Overman discards is precisely our boundless, purely quantitative nonstop progress." (WHD, 67/69) Modern man seeks to increase his power by mastering himself. Mastering himself requires that he accept his finitude and affirm the eternal return of the same.

The subjectivistic side of Nietzsche's value-philosophy, however, expresses the same theme which belongs to all modern thinking: everything is an object for the Subject. "Being has been transformed into a value." (Hw, 238/102) To degrade Being to the level of a value for man is the true consummation of nihilism, understood as man's complete oblivion to the transcendent character of Being and man's dependence on it. The transcendent is so hidden from man, that he even turns God into a "value," although the "highest" one. In *The Gay Science*, Nietzsche asks how mere humans could have killed God: "How could we drink up the sea? Who gave us the sponge to wipe away the entire horizon? What were we doing when we unchained this earth from its sun?"[7] Heidegger interprets the "sun" in this passage to refer to Plato's *agathon*, that which makes beings possible. The "horizon" refers to the suprasensory world as the world which truly is. But once the earth, man's home, is unchained from the sun,

> The realm that constitutes the suprasensory, which as such, *is* in itself, no longer stands over man as the authoritative light. The whole field of vision has been wiped away. The whole of that which is as such, the sea, has been drunk up by man. For man has risen up into the I-ness of the *ego cogito*. Through this uprising, all that is, is transformed into object. That which is, as the objective, is swallowed up into the immanence of subjectivity. The horizon no longer emits light of itself. It is now nothing but the point-of-view posited in the value-positing of the Will to Power. (Hw, 241/107)

Once man has assumed the highest position and has swallowed everything up, "The earth can show itself only as an object of assault.... Nature appears everywhere...as the object of technology." (Hw, 236/100) The subjectivism which was developing in Western thinking from the very beginning finally led to the technological age.

Before I examine what Heidegger means by technology, the following observations about his interpretation of the history of philosophy are in order. He easily could have written a traditional "history of philosophy," but others have already done so. He chose, instead, to interpret philosophy in light of the idea that its history reflects the history of Being: the gradual self-concealment of the play of revelation/concealment. Such an interpretation leads to distortions. Yet Heidegger took his predecessors seriously. He believed that they could really speak only to those willing to engage them in a creative dialogue, an attempt to arrive at a new position. Above all, Heidegger emphasized the importance of struggling with the text of a great thinker. Once, after condemning Heidegger's political engagement, Herbert Marcuse remarked:

> I want to add, after all criticism (and I still stick to every word I said), I want to stress that I did learn from the early Heidegger. And if I should say what I did learn—thinking, but mainly, reading a text, reading a text and being serious with a text, even if and when you violate the traditional interpretation of the text.[8]

Here are some questions which might be asked of Heidegger's interpretation of the history of philosophy: (1) In general, does he not twist the meaning of previous thinkers, especially when they seem to be anticipating his own insights? (2) Does he succumb to "word mysticism" when he provides etymologies more suitable to his own ideas than to the text in which they are found? (3) When he claims that medieval man regarded God as a mere being by turning Him into the metaphysical ground, does he not ignore the *via negativa* taken toward God by some medieval theologians and mystics? (4) Why does he pay so little attention to Spinoza, who—though part of the metaphysical tradition—seems to have pointed beyond the anthropocentrism of that tradition?[9] (5) When Heidegger says that Nietzsche's thinking exhausts the possibilities of metaphysics, the implication is clear that Heidegger hopes to initiate a new beginning, one made possible by Nietzsche and others. In suggesting that the history of philosophy leads up to his own thinking, does Heidegger make the same mistake as Aristotle and Hegel? (6) Does he take seriously enough the material factors in history; namely, the socioeconomic conditions which made possible the culture in which metaphysical thinking could flourish? It is not enough to *claim* that a change in man's understanding of Being is responsible for the rise of science, industry, and technology, as well as for the development of metaphysics. He does not advance arguments which are strong enough to convince those who say that historical changes come about as the result of changes in the methods of material production.

PART TWO: *Technik* and the Desolation of Modern Man.

In the 1930s and 1940s, in conjunction with his interpretation of nihilism, Heidegger was developing the notion that *Technik* is an expression of the Will to Power.[10] In his definitive essay on the topic, "The Question Concerning Technology" (1955), he defines *Technik* as the disclosure of all beings as raw material for exploitation by the human subject. He distinguishes between *Technik* and what I call "machine technology," including the systems of production, distribution, governance, transportation, calculation, communication, research, planning, and mass-culture which we usually think of when we hear the word "technology." Conventional wisdom claims that machine technology began with the application of scientific discoveries to production methods in the late eighteenth century. Modern science is commonly regarded as the predecessor of technology. Chronologically speaking, this description is accurate; essentially speaking, however, it misses the point. The mathematical sciences arose in response to the fact that man's understanding of Being changed to "objectivity." As Heidegger demonstrated in his 1936 lectures, "The Question Concerning the Thing," modern science is projective in that it leaps ahead of its possible objects; it reveals them in terms of a priori hypotheses. Early modern scientists could investigate Nature using mathematical hypotheses because—in advance of their investigations—Nature manifested itself as a mathematical field which they could learn to understand. The machine technology of the eighteenth century is not merely a scientifically-boosted version of the previous mode of production, but a new kind of *praxis* determined by the new understanding of Being.

Industrialization arises only in a society which understands Nature solely as an object which can be known by and manipulated for man. *Technik* refers to a challenging disclosure of the Being of beings. As might be expected in the age of the Will to Power, what *Technik* provokes beings to reveal is energy.

> The challenging *[Heraus-fordern]* happens in that the energy concealed in Nature is unlocked, what is unlocked is transformed, what is transformed is stored up, what is stored up is, in turn, distributed, and what is distributed is switched about ever anew. Unlocking, transforming, storing, distributing, and switching about are new ways of revealing. (VA, I, 16/16)

The German words for these new ways of revealing are all variations on the verb *"stellen,"* meaning to place, posit, arrange, or set. *Technik* refers to the way that everything now presents *(west)* itself as "placed before" *(vor-gestellt)* the subject for disposal. Heidegger calls this subjectivistic attitude toward beings *"vorstellend Denken."* The disclosure of beings as energy for man is not the result of a human decision. The essence *(Wesen)* of *Technik* is nothing human or merely "technical." That is, *Technik* refers not to technical objects or to the activity of making and planning them, but to the understanding of Being which makes such activity possible. Heidegger maintains that man himself is challenged and claimed by the "enframing" *(Ge-stell)*, the way in which the current revelation of Being leads man to strive to harness the earth, which now appears as "standing reserve" *(Bestand)*. (VA, I, 19-20/19-20) Once everything is understood exclusively as a stockpile of raw material, man can treat himself as raw material, too. Even when he reduces himself to the status of a thing, however, "man...exalts himself to the posture of lord of the earth. In this way the impression arises that everything man encounters exists only insofar as it is his construct." (VA, I, 25-26/26-27) Reason ends up as instrumental-technological rationality which, as Herbert Marcuse has pointed out, is the "logic of domination."[11]

Heidegger's attitude toward *Technik* is ambivalent. On the one hand, he regards it as necessary; our destiny is to understand things as raw material. *Technik* is not the "work of the devil." (VA, I, 27-

28/28-29)[12] It even includes the possibility of bringing man to maturity, although it is not clear how this might happen. Moreover, he admits that we cannot do without the technical devices and increased productivity which *Technik* has made possible. On the other hand, he believes that, as a result of being challenged by *Ge-stell*, mankind has entered a "world-night," a "time of destitution," and is threatened with an "endless winter." (Hw, 248/91-92) In 1946, he remarked that in our age the gods have fled, so that "no god any longer gathers men and things unto himself, visibly and unequivocally, and by such gathering disposes of the world's history and man's sojourn in it." (Hw, 248/91) The absolutely destitute character of our time can be seen in the fact that it "is no longer able even to experience its own destitution." (Hw, 249/92-93) Just as Kierkegaard declared that a man is most desperate when unaware of his despair, so too Heidegger maintains that mankind is most destitute when oblivious to its destitution.

In 1951 Heidegger noted that Spengler's idea of the "decline of the West" is "only the negative, though correct, consequence of Nietzsche's word, 'the wasteland grows'." (WHD, 14/38) Spengler's estimation is negative because it only describes the symptoms of decay, not the origins. Recalling the destruction caused by World War II, Heidegger asserted that the present spiritual devastation is more uncanny than physical destruction. "The devastation of the earth can easily go hand in hand with a guaranteed supreme living standard for man, and just as easily with the organized establishment of a uniform state of happiness for all men." (WHD, 11/29-30) He denied that he was part of the "chorus of voices" which condemned the "sickness" of Europe. While some writers took the easy road of describing the absurdity of modern life, Heidegger sought to discover the source of this absurdity. This source turns out to be: our destiny to understand ourselves as absolute subjects in a universe of commodities. Life in such a world cannot help but be absurd or, to use Heidegger's early terminology, inauthentic.

Although technological culture is supposedly our destiny, Heidegger is not pleased with its traits—the self-sustaining, constantly expanding, and ultimately aimless systems of mass production and consumption; power politics; global warfare; mass-culture; and the collapse of great art, literature, philosophy, and religion. Already in "The Age of the World Picture" (1938), he writes that once the world becomes a mere picture *(Bild)* for the human subject, men contend for the "right" to organize the picture as it suits them. There arises the struggle of "world views," for whose sake "man brings into play his unlimited power for the calculating, planning, and molding of all things. Science as research is an absolutely necessary form of this establishing of self in the world...." (Hw, 87/135) Each competing world-view declares that its system of values best promotes human life; that is, the life of the people of the nation promoting the particular world-view. Values become nothing more than the "objectification of needs as goals." (Hw, 94/142) Refusing to acknowledge anything transcendent, nation-states try to dominate each other in their quest for markets, raw material, and *"Lebensraum."* Anything which enhances the power of the state, including the politicalization of education, art, religion, and science, is justified. (NII, 28, 362-363) Production and consumption are, of course, organized as part of the push for total power. In a public lecture in 1939, Heidegger said that people expect that this drive for power necessarily establishes life-enhancing values,

> as if total mobilization were something in itself and not the organiza-
> tion of unconditioned senselessness for and from the Will to Power.
> Such power-empowering positings no longer direct themselves ac-
> cording to "masses" and "ideals," which could still be grounded in
> themselves; they stand "In the service" of the pure expansion of
> power and are evaluated only according to the thus esteemed econo-
> mic value. The age of fulfilled senselessness is thus the time of the
> power-like discovery and accomplishment of "world-views," which
> drive all reckoning of re-presenting and re-producing *[Vor- und
> Herstellens]* to the uttermost extreme, because according to their
> essence they arise from a self-posited self-directing of mankind into
> beings and its [mankind's] unconditioned domination over all means
> of power of the earth and over [the earth] itself. (NII, 21-22)

The analysis of the clash of world-views was directed primarily against Germany under National Socialism, but against other Western nations as well. This is evident in a comment Heidegger made in 1940 concerning how one nation "justifies" all actions, so long as they promote greater power: "For example, if the English thoroughly blast the French fleet anchored in the harbor of Oran, this is from *their* power-standpoint wholly 'justified' *[gerecht]*; for 'justified' means only: what is useful for power-enhancement." (NII, 198) This remarkable statement anticipated by almost two years the Japanese attack on the American fleet at Pearl Harbor. The statement was made around the time Hitler ordered the invasion of Poland for reasons of "national security."

When Heidegger said in 1951 that World War II "decided nothing" (WHD, 65/166), he did not mean that it was unimportant for Hitler to have been defeated. His point was that world wars are only offshoots of the industrialization and "planetary imperialism" (Hw, 102/152-153) which are the key symptoms of the modern age. In a marginal note found in his own copy of his "Letter on Humanism," Heidegger wrote: "Industrial society as the authoritative subject—and thinking as 'politics'."[13] World wars are ways of shoring up faltering economies; wars provide "the stability of a constant form of using things up." Leaders of power-hungry nations are not merely individuals caught up in the "blind rage of a selfish egoism," but are instruments of world-destiny. (VA, I, 84-85/104-105) Everything is planned for the sake of accelerating the process of production and consumption, as Ernst Jünger pointed out in the 1920s.[14] The push for power will finally lead to attempts to "breed" human beings in factories, because humans are the most important raw material.

> The increase in the number of masses of human beings is done explicitly by plan so that the opportunity will never run out for claiming more "room to live" for the large masses whose size then requires correspondingly higher masses of human beings for their arrangement. This circularity of consumption for the sake of consumption is the sole procedure which distinctively characterizes the history of a world which has become an unworld. (VA, I, 88/107)

The Will to Power manifests itself primarily, therefore, in economic terms. Self-willed man turns everything into a commodity. Man himself, along with everything else, is turned into a "calculated market value" of a world-wide market. (Hw, 270/114-115) Heidegger was aware of the international corporations which ignore national boundaries in the search for cheaper material, labor, and new markets.[15] In the world run by corporate interests, everyday life becomes the effort to succeed in the marketplace. (Hw, 290/136) Heidegger sounds like Marx in saying:

> Self-willed man reckons everywhere with things and men as with objects. What is so reckoned becomes merchandise. Everything is constantly changed about into new orders.... Self-assertive man lives by staking his will. He lives essentially by risking his essence *[Wesen]* in the vibration of money and the currency *[Geltens]* of values. As the constant trader and middleman, man is the "merchant." He weighs and measures constantly, yet does not know the real weight of things. He also does not know what in himself has authentic weight *[Gewicht]* and prevails *[überwiegt]*. (Hw, 289/ 135)

Everyday life is determined according to the demands of the economic system. In this hectic world, we no longer understand death, pain, or love. (Hw, 253/96) We are uprooted and alienated; great masses move across continents in search of "better opportunities," "personal improvement," and a "higher standard of living"; the self disappears in the process of production (ZSF, 74/ 75); rivers and streams become sewers; the air is poisoned; forests are annihilated; mountains are flattened for their ore, or to make room for highways; farms become "agri-business" operations which degrade the soil with the imposition of artificial fertilizers and pesticides; homes become high-rise apartment complexes; work becomes repetitive, simplified, and boring; biochemists study how to manipulate man's genetic structure; and all of this happens under the *aegis* of self-development, self-emancipation, and progress. No human action can bring about a change in the technological impulse, for "Self-assertive man...is the functionary of *Technik*." (Hw, 271/ 116)[16] The momentum of the technological Will to Power has outstripped man's capacity to control it. (G, 19/51) Before World War II, Heidegger speculated that "Before Being can occur in its primal truth, Being as the will must be broken, the world must be forced to collapse and the earth must be driven to desolation, and man to mere labor." (VI, I, 65/86) But even the devastation of the wars did not essentially change the situation in the modern world.

Human life in the technological age bears important similarities to what Heidegger called "inauthentic everydayness" in *Being and Time*. There he suggested that inauthenticity resulted when an individual chose to conceal the truth. In his later work, he argues that inauthenticity reigns because humanity has become the self-certain subject who yearns to dominate everything. Heidegger personifies the subject, talking as if it were a conscious agent manipulating individuals to act according to its dictates. He makes individuals appear to be functions of the subject in a way analogous to how Marx makes them appear to be functions of "Lord Capital." In *Capital*, we read:

> As the conscious bearer of this movement [of capital], the possessor of money becomes a capitalist. His person, or rather his pocket, is the point from which the money starts, and to which it returns. The objective content of the circulation we have been discussing— the valorization of value—is his subjective purpose, and it is only insofar as the appropriation of ever more wealth in the abstract is the sole driving force behind his operations that he functions as a capitalist, i.e., *as capital personified and endowed with consciousness and will.* Use-values must therefore never be treated as the immediate aim of the capitalist; nor must the profit of any single transaction. This boundless drive for enrichment, this passionate chase after value, is common to the capitalist and the miser, but while the miser is merely a capitalist gone mad, the capitalist is a rational miser.[17]

Capital is not a thing, according to Marx, but a system of social relations which allows one class to exploit another. For Heidegger, too, the subject is not a thing, but the self-understanding which conditions the behavior of everyone in Western culture. We have not chosen this self-understanding; instead, we are possessed by it. We do not elect to look at the world as an exploitable object; instead, natural beings *disclose themselves* as objects for us. As long as beings appeared to be creatures of God, or appeared to be valuable other than as raw material for man, technological culture did not arise. Human greed and egoism used to be constrained by a sense of the transcendent operating in the cosmos. When this sense vanished there was nothing standing in the way of unleashing human desire. Marx, too, recognized this important change when he says that in capitalist society,

> For the first time, nature becomes purely an object for humankind, purely a matter of utility; ceases to be recognized as a power for itself; and the theoretical discovery of its autonomous laws appears merely as a ruse so as to subjugate it under human needs, whether as an object of consumption or as a means of production.[18]

Marx focuses not so much on the individual, but on the social class which determines individual consciousness and behavior. Changing the individual requires changing the social relationships which condition him. Freud also claimed that entire civilizations can exhibit the same pathological symptoms which characterize a neurotic individual. Examining the norms, values, and structures of society can provide insight into the workings of the sick person. Plato was probably the first to advise that we can learn about the self by analyzing the structure of society. We recall that in *The Republic* he explains that the three major social classes (rulers, warriors/administrators, producers) correspond to the three aspects of the individual soul (reason, will, desire). Heidegger, too, concluded that individuals could be interpreted in terms of their culture, which is necessarily conditioned by a particular way of understanding Being. Hence, we find that modern man as self-certain subject shares many of the traits belonging to the inauthentic (self-objectifying, egoistical) self depicted in *Being and Time*. Modern mankind is the inauthentic individual "writ large."

Being and Time says that an individual becomes inauthentic when he flees from the truth about his finitude. Inauthenticity intensifies the egoism which is characteristic of everyday life. The inauthentic individual desperately tries to conceal his mortality by losing himself in distractions; he tries to avoid death by gaining power, wealth, or fame. His life becomes ambiguous, filled with idle chatter, and guided by curiosity. He is caught in the throw of falling, which is tempting, tranquillizing, alienating, self-entangling, and turbulent. Experiencing time as a guilt-ridden past or as an anxiety-ridden future, he can never be satisfied with the present. He yearns for more security and gratification, for more revenge against his limitations. These same traits belong to modern mankind as self-willed subject.

As self-certain subject, mankind is basically egoistical: the natural world appears merely as an object for domination. Given the fact that the primary goal of the subject is greater and greater power, we can conclude that the subject values security and certainty above all else. Mankind as subject can be secure only if the entire cosmos can be subjugated to the unending quest for power. Total mobilization of the entire earth gives the impression that mankind has finally become the master of destiny. Mankind acts in this way because it no longer has insight into its most proper way to act—as openness for the Being of beings. This openness is concealed beneath the constantly expanding cycle of production and consumption. Since the "meaning" of life is now defined in terms of an ever increasing standard of living, it becomes dangerous to think of mankind other than as a natural species with the capacity to gratify its infinite desires. Life becomes ambiguous because people act in the "accepted" way even though they have the vague feeling that the prevailing standards are destructive of life. Mankind, however, cannot bear the thought that its world is based on a lack of understanding about human life; hence, it loses itself in distractions. Just as the inauthentic self becomes seized by curiosity, mankind as self-certain subject engages in research to reveal the secrets of everything. The information explosion resulting from scientific research reassures us that we know more and more, although in fact we know less and less about what is most important. Idle chatter abounds in the innumerable discussions convened to promote world peace or to arrange more equitable exploitation of the earth's resources. In 1951, when discussing Nietzsche's idea of the "last man" who blinks while the old values collapse, Heidegger asked: "The congresses and conferences, committees and sub-committees—are they anything other than the blinking organizations of blinking arrangements of distrust and treachery?" (WHD, 32/84) Idle chatter is also found in the gloss of publicity, showmanship, mass-communication, and mass-culture which legitimates the enterprise of global "management." The very idea that mankind can "dominate" Nature shows to what extent mankind has become oblivious to his finitude and dependence.

Mankind as self-certain subject is caught in the throw of falling. It is tempting for the subject to organize the planet for the sake of "security"; the goal of happiness and security for all tranquillizes the populous which must be uprooted, exploited, and abused in the process of bringing about that happiness; mankind is alienated from itself as the openness for the Being of beings; entangled in the enormous process of production and consumption, mankind experiences a turbulence which threatens to destroy it. The inauthentic person feels fragmented because he experiences time as a series of disconnected episodes; his life has no sense of development and unity. Modern mankind also experiences time as a series of instants in the process of production and consumption. Life becomes fragmented in the industrial plant, office, home, and even in recreation, which has now been "colonized" by the "leisure-time industry."[19] Instead of being cultivated and revitalized, Western man's heritage is either forgotten altogether or else is trivialized by being turned into a commodity. Western mankind, therefore, ends up like the "Flying Dutchman." Rootless and homeless, we restlessly prowl the planet and outer space; we are deluded in thinking that being master sailors is enough to find the harbor for which we desperately seek.

Although Heidegger maintains that man is destined to be homeless as the self-willed subject, he sometimes talks as if man is not wholly blameless for this unhappy condition. For if Being has hidden itself from us, we, too, seem to have stopped being open for it. Given Heidegger's enduring interest in religion, it is not surprising to learn that his account of the fall of Western man into the role of the self-deifying subject resembles the Old Testament account of the fall of the ancient Israelites into greed and idolatry. One major difference between the two accounts, of course, is that Heidegger speaks of impersonal Being while the Old Testament speaks of a personal God. Just as the Hebrews were the people chosen by God to participate in realizing His divine plan, so too Western man was destined to be the site for playing out the destiny of Being. The Hebrews fell into greed, pride, and idolatry when they forgot about God. Western man also fell into greed, pride, and self-idolatry when he became oblivious to

Being. Like the Hebrews, who required divine intervention to rescue them from their selfish ways, modern man needs to be released from his selfish ways. Just as God chose prophets to remind his fallen people of their proper relation to Him, so too thinkers and poets are fated to remind self-assertive man of his proper relation to Being. The Hebrews suffered for as long as God hid His face from them. Modern man must also suffer for as long as Being continues to hide from us.[20]   As Professor Caputo has pointed out, the major problem with such religious analogies to Heidegger's thinking is that God is supposed to be loving and judgmental, while the "destiny of Being" does not admit of such characteristics.[21] If there is no assurance that the historical play of Being is benevolent, however, why should we try to become open to it? How are we to understand Heidegger's claim that we become authentic *(eigentlich)* by letting ourselves be appropriated *(vereignet)* by the event of appropriation *(Ereignis)*?

CHAPTER EIGHT

The Mature Concept of Authenticity

HEIDEGGER'S MATURE concept of authenticity develops in a manner different from the subjective elements of *Being and Time*. This early work considered the question of the sense of Being by analyzing the Being of the authentic self; an approach suffering from two kinds of subjectivism. First, it was influenced by transcendental philosophy's notion of the "subjectivity of the subject." On occasion, *Being and Time* implied that temporality, the absence needed for beings to be present, was a projection of *human* Dasein. Heidegger later insisted that temporality (absence) is intrinsically connected with Being (presencing). Human temporality, therefore, is to be understood as an aspect of the "temporality of Being." Human history is conditioned by the history of Being as such. Second, the earlier concept of authenticity overemphasized the role played by individual resoluteness, will, and courage in disclosing the truth. Many readers of *Being and Time* received the impression that authenticity meant "self-actualization." In spite of this emphasis on "works," however, *Being and Time* also maintained that resoluteness is primarily a response to the summons of conscience. Conscience is the call of Dasein's own Being to be open for Being as such. In his later writings, Heidegger stressed that authenticity or openness comes unexpectedly as a kind of gift. He continued to maintain, however, that courage is required to accept this gift. In order to overcome the subjective elements in his earlier work, Heidegger began to speak of *Ereignis*, a concept which describes the relations among truth (unconcealment), Being (presencing), and Dasein. The idea of *Ereignis*

229

is relatively free of the anthropocentrism implicit in the former claim that Being occurs only insofar as human Dasein exists. Man's "understanding" of Being is only one of the ways in which Being manifests itself. *Ereignis* has at least three senses.

First, *Ereignis* refers to the self-organizing play of Nature in which beings are constantly appearing and disappearing, revealing and concealing themselves. As the science of ecology has tried to show in recent years, everything in Nature is interrelated. Microbes manifest themselves as food for insects; insects, in turn, appear as food for the small animals which appear as food for larger ones. When the larger animals die, they decay into microbes—food for insects, and the cycle begins once more. The complex and dynamic interactions of Nature demonstrate that the play of revealing/concealing happens quite independently of human life. Without mankind, however, this play would not itself be manifest. In more familiar terms: without mankind, Nature would be unaware of itself. The second meaning of *Ereignis* is that man is appropriated *(ver-eignet)* as the clearing or absence in which the cosmic play can manifest itself. Just as cosmic absence (world-time, self-concealing nothingness) allows natural beings to emerge from unconcealment and to appear to each other, so, too, human absence (temporality) lets this cosmic event *(Ereignis)* be revealed. Human temporality is a specific modality of cosmic temporality. At present, man is oblivious to his role as awareness of the cosmic spectacle. Only when released from his subjectivistic understanding of Being can he become open for *Ereignis*. The third meaning of Ereignis, then, is for man to be authentically appropriated *(eigentlich vereignet)* for the cosmic play.

In Part One of this chapter, I discuss the first two meanings of *Ereignis*: (1) the self-unifying cosmic play of manifestness and concealment; (2) the appropriation of man for the revelation of this play. In Part Two, I analyze the third meaning: the authentic appropriation made possible when an individual is released from self-will. The released thinker or poet is fated to offer to us his more profound understanding of Being as *Ereignis*. Part Three considers some similarities between Zen Buddhism's idea of enlightenment and Heidegger's idea of releasement. Both suggest that authenticity means being cleared of ego so that the Being or "suchness" of beings can be manifest through us. Heidegger's thinking remains different from Zen because he was influenced by the metaphysical-eschatological Western understanding of Being. Although he points beyond the subjectivism of the metaphysical tradition, his thinking retains traces of anthropocentrism.

PART ONE: *Ereignis*, Mankind, and Language.

Although Heidegger developed the concept of *Ereignis* between 1936 and 1938, the seeds for this idea were planted in *Being and Time* and began to sprout in his 1930 essay, "On the Essence of Truth." Here we are told that freedom constitutes the essence of truth or disclosedness. Freedom is not an arbitrary human power.

> Man does not "possess" freedom as a property *[Eigenschaft]*. At best, the converse holds: freedom, ek-sistent, disclosive *Da-sein*, possesses man—so originally that only *it* secures for humanity that distinctive relatedness to being as a whole as such which first founds all history. Only ex-sistent man is historical. "Nature" has no history. (WGM, 85/219)

Already in this essay we can detect a shift from the notion of authenticity as self-appropriation *(Eigentlichkeit)* to the notion of authenticity as being appropriated *(vereignet)*. In 1962, however, Heidegger claimed that *Being and Time* itself was already beyond the sphere of subjectivism, and that it is

> strikingly clear that the 'Being' into which *Being and Time* inquired cannot long remain something that the human subject posits. It is rather Being, stamped as presence by its time-character [that] makes the approach to Dasein. As a result, even in the initial steps of the Being-question in *Being and Time* thought is called upon to undergo a change whose movement cor-responds with the turn *[Kehre]*. (LR, xix/xviii)

In another evaluation of *Being and Time*, this one written in 1946, he admitted that the "language of metaphysics" prevented that early work from moving from the Being of human Dasein to Being as such. (WGM, 159/208) The language of metaphysics is subjectivistic. Even if he began to find his way beyond metaphysical thinking in 1930, for years thereafter he continued to talk of will as necessary to tear the veil away from Being. Overcoming subjectivism requires more than abandoning transcendental philosophy; voluntarism, too, is a form of subjectivism.

In his later work, Heidegger continued to develop the idea that human existence is not merely for itself but has a cosmic function. Man is "thrown" into the truth of Being; he is called on to guard this truth or openness. Heidegger even calls man "the shepherd of Being." (WGM, 161-162/210) When he speaks of the fact that Being "needs" man (NII, 483), his point is twofold. First, without human openness beings would not be able to reveal their intelligible aspect. Second, without the authentically appropriated human being, the cosmic play of revelation/concealment *(Ereignis)* would not be revealed. Since Being means presencing, and since Dasein means the location where this presencing presents (reveals) itself, Being and Dasein are intimately related. Around 1945 Heidegger described this relation:

> This "where" *[Wo]*...belongs to Being itself, *"is"* Being itself, and is thus called *Da-sein.*
>
> "The Dasein in man" is the essence which belongs to Being itself, in which essence, however, man belongs, indeed such that he has this Being to be. *Da-sein* concerns *[geht...an]* man.... Man becomes essentially [himself] when he enters properly into his essence. He stands in the un-hiddenness of being as the hidden place, at which Being is present *[west]* from its truth. (NII, 358)

Heidegger found it difficult to express the relation between Being and Dasein because of the limitations of German's subject-predicate ("metaphysical") grammar. It is even misleading to speak of a "relation" between them because this suggests that they are two things bound together by some external bond. The idea of *Ereignis* attempts, in part, to express the intimate correspondence between human existence *(Da-)* and Being or presencing *(-sein).* Heidegger gained insight for this idea in his examination of the thinking of Heraclitus, who claims that man is most properly himself when he is attuned to the *Logos*, the self-gathering play of concealment and manifestness. Heidegger interprets *Logos* to mean both Being and truth. As Being, *Logos* refers to the presencing or self-manifesting of beings. As truth, *Logos* refers to the gathering activity which clears the place needed for this presencing. *Logos*, then, plays the role of the temporal ecstases described in *Being and Time*. In that book, however, temporality was assigned only to human existence. Hence, Heidegger concluded that beings could be present or manifest only insofar as human Dasein exists. Later on, Heidegger tried to avoid the subjectivistic implications of this attitude by saying that beings manifest themselves to each other even if Dasein does not exist. (US, 254/ 123) When the carrot shoots emerge from the earth, they display themselves for the rabbit as well as for the gardener. The difference is that the gardener *understands* that the carrots *are* carrots; he can be aware of their manifestness as such in a way the rabbit cannot. *Logos* refers to the self-governing activity of the natural world, where beings continually affect each other. The interaction of natural beings is possible only because they "appear" to each other.

All disclosure releases what is present from concealment. Disclosure needs concealment. The *A-letheia* rests in *Lethe*, drawing from it and laying before us whatever remains deposited in *Lethe*. *Logos* is in itself and at the same time a revealing and a concealing. It is *Aletheia*. Unconcealment needs concealment, *Lethe*, as a reservoir upon which disclosure can, as it were, draw. (VA, III, 16-17/71)

Does *Lethe* as "reservoir" mean something like Plato's "receptacle" *(Timaeus)*? Can *Lethe* be understood as the inexhaustible Void from which beings constantly emerge? Natural beings come to be, or manifest themselves, only because *Lethe* does not manifest itself; that is, because it gathers the absence in which natural events can transpire. The temporality of Dasein is a modification of this cosmic *Lethe*. Indeed, human existence is authentic when it allows the cosmic play of revealing/concealing to manifest itself.

For the most part, we are unaware that we are "openness." Once we become so aware, it dawns on us that this openness is not simply for us, but is in the service of the transcendent. According to Heidegger, a person who was possessed with this awareness was called a "seer." The seer is "the one who has already seen the totality of what is present in its presencing." (Hw, 321/36) Although all of us are appropriated by the *Logos*, the seer in particular sees the *Logos* itself. He is one who, like the *Logos* itself, reveals what is hidden. While *Logos* reveals the beings of the cosmos to each other, the seer reveals *Logos* itself. When the seer is "appropriated" by *Logos*, *homolegeín* (conformity, correspondence) occurs:

> Mortal *legein* lies secured in the *Logos*. It is destined to be appropriated *[ereignet]* in the *homolegein*. Thus it remains appropriated *[vereignet]* to the *Logos*. In this way mortal *legein* is fateful. But is it Fate itself, i.e., *En Panta* as *o Logos*. (VA, III, 20/74)

Just by virtue of being human, men and women have some understanding of the Being or presencing of beings. Usually, however, we are victims of *hubris*, so that we are not in tune with Being or *Logos*. The seer is released from *hubris* so that he can experience the "lightning flash" of a more profound revelation of *Logos*. Because the seer then knows that real freedom lies in conforming to the *Logos*, he tries to explain to his fellow mortals what he has seen. His message, however, is not just for them, but is more importantly the self-manifestation of the *Logos*. (VA, III, 22/75) Human beings become most themselves when they become like the revealing/concealing force of *Logos*. Heidegger makes this point when interpreting fragment 16 of Heraclitus: "How can one hide himself before that which never sets?" *Logos* means the self-concealing event of gathering and clearing which enables beings to present themselves to each other as a cosmos. Hence, the cosmos is governed by a "fire" (self-concealing gathering) which never ends. Gods and men cannot hide from this fire, "Because their relation to the lighting is nothing other than the lighting itself, in that this relation gathers men and gods into the lighting and keeps them there." (VA, III, 74/120) What is peculiar about gods and men is that they are not only present as beings in the cosmos, but "they are luminous in their essence. They are enlightened *[er-lichtet]*; they are appropriated into the event of lighting, and therefore never concealed." (VA, III, 74/120) "Lighting" does not mean "illuminating" but "light-ening" or "opening up." (H, 224-228, 260)

Heidegger appeals to everyday experience to show the similarity between human existence and the cosmic *Logos*. Just as beings appear and disappear, so too in our experience events occur and are then forgotten. We not only forget the event, however; we forget the forgetting itself. (VA, III, 60-61/108) We forget our own existence. We forget that Being means to be manifest. Fortunately, we do not have to look far for something which will help us to remember. Heidegger claims that the *Logos* manifests itself in the simplest of things, such as a jug.

Normally, I see a jug in terms of cultural standards. It appears as an object of a certain size and weight, made for a certain purpose, and composed of certain materials. As an object, the jug stands over against me, the constituting subject. Hence, I tend to overlook its independent presence. I must suspend this "natural (subjective) standpoint" to allow the jug to reveal itself from itself. Heidegger claims that we can learn about the jug by considering how it is used. We use the jug to pour liquids. In this pouring, the jug gathers together: (1) the earth, from which spring the grapes for the wine in the jug; (2) the sky, from out of which comes the sunlight needed for the grapes to grow; (3) the gods, to whom a libation of wine is offered; and (4) the mortals, whose thirst is quenched by the wine. The jug, a mere "thing," gathers together the four elements of the world. That the gods are absent from our world means that it has become a "non-world," a place where things cannot display themselves in the proper way.

Note that as an image of the cosmos, the thing organizes itself. Although made by a person, the jug is independent; it gathers a world around and through itself. A world is a context of meaningful interrelations. Each thing mirrors these interrelations from its own standpoint. Note, too, that the world gathers itself together as an interrelated cosmos. It is not a construction of the transcendental subject. Heidegger remarks that "Thinging, the thing stays the united four, earth and sky, divinities and mortals, in the simple onefold of their self-unified fourfold *[Geviert]*." (VA, II, 50/178) The world is a unity because its elements reflect each other.

> Each of the four mirrors in its own way the presence of the others. Each therewith reflects itself in its own way into its own, within the simpleness of the four. The mirroring does not portray a likeness. The mirroring, lightening each of the four, appropriates their own presencing into simple belonging-together. Mirroring in this appropriating-lightening way, each of the four plays to each of the others. The appropriative mirroring sets each of the four free into its own, but it binds these free ones into the simplicity of their essential being toward one another. (VA, II, 52/179)

Albert Hofstadter's etymological analysis of the word *Ereignis* shows the following. First, *Ereignis* contains the sense of the verb *eignen*, to make something one's own. Hence, *Ereignis* refers to the mutual appropriating of the elements of the world. Second, *Ereignis* also stems from an early verb-form, *eräugnen*, to place before the eyes *(Augen)*, to show. Professor Hofstadter then summarizes the dual meaning of *Ereignis*:

> Thus *ereignen* comes to mean... the joint process by which the four of the fourfold are able, first, to come out into the light and clearing of truth, and thus each to exist in its own truthful way, and secondly, to exist in appropriation of and to each other, belonging together in the round dance of their being; and what is more, the mutual appropriation becomes the very process by which the emergence into the light and clearing occurs, for it happens through the sublimely simple play of their mutual mirroring. The mutual lighting-up, reflecting, *eräugnen*, is at the same time the mutual belonging, appropriating, *ereignen*; and conversely, the happening, *das Ereignis*, by which alone the meaning of Being can be determined, is this play of *eräugnen* and *ereignen*; it is an *Eräugnen* which is an *Ereignen* and an *Ereignen* which is an *Eräugnen*.[1]

The notion that the world is constituted by the mutual mirroring of its elements is reminiscent of Leibniz's notion that each monad reflects the world from its own point of view. As early as 1926, Heidegger criticized Leibniz's description of monads as "windowless." They cannot be windowless, Heidegger asserted, because they are "not housed [in a subject] to begin with." (GP, 426-427) Monads are self-gathering openness in which the world can mirror itself. The world as such is the self-gathering totality of these self-reflecting, self-gathering centers of spiritual activity. In 1928 Heidegger pointed out that, for Leibniz, the monad is a *speculum vitale*:

> A mirror *(speculum)* is a letting see: *miroir actif indivisible* (G. IV, p. 557; S.I, p. 146), a thrusting, indivisible, simple mirror. This letting-see comes about in the way of monadic being, where there is accomplished the unveiling of the world. The mirroring is not a rigid portrayal, but itself thrusts as such to new prefigured possibilities of itself. In anticipating the one universe in a viewpoint from which the manifold first becomes visible, it is simple. (ALM, 506/331)[2]

Heidegger found Leibniz so compelling partly because both thinkers owed so much to Aristotle. From Aristotle, Heidegger may have derived the idea that the ringing, circling play *(Ereignis)* unifies the elements of the world and lets them be manifest to each other. Aristotle conceived of God as the self-circling, self-complete thinking which lures individuals to imitate its activity by manifesting the stages in their own cycle of becoming. For Aristotle, without God things would not "actualize their potential." For Heidegger, without the ringing play of the world things would not bring themselves into mutual presencing. Yet *Ereignis* does not refer to a super-thing which causes other things to be, any more than Aristotle's God refers to the creator of substances. As self-concealing absence which lets beings present themselves as a cosmos, *Ereignis* is not a ground or foundation but an abyss *(Ab-grund)*. Aristotle's notion that God is *actus purus*—the necessity which explains why the contingent world exists—pointed away from this abyss, however. Metaphysical thinking developed according to the idea that there must be an ultimate foundation for reality. In the modern age, Leibniz claimed that this foundation is the Principle of Sufficient Reason *(Der Satz vom Grund)*. God is no longer the ground for reality; instead, we now say that a thing is "real" if human reason can provide sufficient "grounds" for it. Everything now orients itself around man. We have seen, however, that such self-deification has led to the age of *Technik*.

To develop an alternative to the current understanding of Being, Heidegger calls on Angelius Silesius' phrase:

> The rose is without why; it blooms because it blooms;
> It cares not for itself, asks not if it's seen. (SG, 68)

The rose, like other natural beings, offers no reason for its Being; it blooms because it blooms, just as the universe happens because it happens. The world goes on whether or not human beings are around to discover the "reasons" for natural events. Modern man regards himself as the ultimate *arche* or first principle of everything because he wants self-certainty and security. Heidegger claims, however, that there is no ultimate basis, ground, or reason for the universe. Our drive to find such a basis, and even to *be* it, leads us away from our openness for the play of revealing/concealing. To become open, we must become more like the other beings of the world. Heidegger says that "man, in the most hidden depths *[Grunde]* of his being *[Wesens]* first truly is when he is in his own way like the rose— without why." (SG, 73) To find our way out of the technological age, we need a non-subjective, non-representational, non-anthropocentric understanding of human existence. Instead of assuming that the world must be explained in terms of the history of man, we must learn that the human world is an aspect of the world as such. Moreover, we must learn to see that "The 'world' is swallowed up in the play. The play is without 'why'. It plays because it plays. It remains only play: the highest and deepest." (SG, 188) In agreeing with Heraclitus that the world is like a child at play, Heidegger strikes against the very foundations of Western rationality. Against the audacious supposition that human reason can understand the meaning and purpose of the cosmos, Heidegger argues that human reason is essentially finite and dependent. A consideration of Heidegger's later concept of temporality will show man's proper relation to the cosmos.

Once again, Heidegger turns to Heraclitus in saying that the cosmic play *(logos, Ereignis)* includes the world-time which makes human temporality possible. He explains:

> Heraclitus names that which addresses itself to him as *logos*, as the sameness of Being and ground: *aeon*. The word is difficult to translate. One says: world-time. It is the world which worlds and temporalizes. For as *cosmos*, it brings the structuring of Being to a lus-

trous shine. According to what is said in the words *logos, physis, cosmos,* and *aeon,* we should hear what is unsaid, which we call the destiny of Being. (SG, 187)

Ereignis refers to the world-play in which time is "given" to Being and Being is "given" to time. (ZS, 20/21) In the 1920s, Heidegger was unable to specify adequately the "relation" between time and Being, nor was he able to say much about the "origin" of time, primarily because his thinking was restricted by the vocabulary of transcendental philosophy. Eventually, he interpreted Being as both un-concealment (*a-letheia,* truth) and as presencing *(Anwesen)*; and he interpreted temporality as *lethe,* the self-concealing absence needed for un-concealment. In his lecture "Time and Being" (1962), he describes temporality in a way which resembles the account in *Being and Time,* with at least one important exception: the lecture makes no reference to the "self." Time is discussed simply as the absence needed for presencing. In *Being and Time* the unity of the temporal horizons was bound up with the unity of the authentic self. In "Time and Being," Heidegger says that

> the unity of time's three dimensions consists in the interplay *[Zuspiel]* of each toward each. This interplay shows itself as the authentic reaching, which plays in the ownness *[Eigenen]* of time—not only "as it were," but from the matter *[Sache]* itself. (ZS, 16/15)

To explain how the three dimensions of time are both united and differentiated, Heidegger introduces a fourth dimension called "nearness" *(Nahheit).* The mutual appropriating of the various dimensions of temporality is what Heraclitus meant by *aeon*: world-time. "Nearhood" or "world-time" refers to the *Logos* which organizes temporal absence so that beings can manifest themselves to each other as a cosmos. Heidegger adds that *Ereignis* "gives" time and Being, but *Ereignis* itself "is not," and hence cannot be a "giver" in any ordinary sense. Since *Ereignis* means the mutually appropriating cosmic play, what "it gives" *(es gibt)* is a play of appearance (Being) and concealment (time). A pure description of experience shows that it involves one event after the next: a feeling appears, then disappears; an idea comes up, then fades away; eating takes place, then is forgotten when writing begins. We find it almost impossible, however, to regard our experience just as a series of happenings; instead, we filter it through all sorts of projections and interpretations, including scientific theories about the structure of "reality," and religious claims about the "meaning" of it all. We tend to be so purposive and willful that the world appears only as a set of goals and obstacles. In viewing the world this way, we are shut off from its primal mystery: that events are constantly happening, that the play of appearance is going on at all. These happenings (beings, events) require a place (time, absence) to happen (to be manifest). The place does not come from outside of the happening, but is intrinsic to it. Presencing and absencing happen together, or "give" themselves to each other. The play plays because it plays. We are most ourselves when we participate in this play.

> Insofar as Being and time are there only in appropriating, there belongs to appropriating the peculiar property [Eigentumliche] of bringing man into his own [in sein Eigenes] as the one who perceives [vernimmt] Being, since he stands in authentic time. Thus appropriated [geeignet], man belongs to Ereignis. (ZS, 24/23)

The beings of the cosmos mutually appropriate each other because they "make way" for each other. The dry earth lets the rain be moist, and the rain lets the earth be absorbent. If there is no reason for things, there is yet a temporal rhyme. Beings make way for each other according to their own seasons. Hence, the world displays mutual ordering, not merely chaos. Unlike other beings, however, man is able to make way for the Being of all beings. He is akin to the *Logos*, so he can reflect the world more profoundly than other beings can. Human time is an aspect of world-time, an aspect which lets world-time itself be manifest. Heidegger seems to suggest otherwise when he remarks that "There is no time without man." (ZS, 17/16) This remark from 1962 can be regarded as reiterating what he implied in 1927; namely, that man alone possesses time. Heidegger's discussions of Heraclitus, however, clearly show that world-time is prior to, and independent of, human time. The sentence, therefore, must mean this: world-time cannot *be revealed* without man. World-time *happens*, however, whether or not man exists.

In trying to explain *Ereignis*, Heidegger attempts the impossible. Since *Ereignis* "is not," we cannot talk about it propositionally. Heidegger himself says that "Everything—statements, questions, and answers—presupposes *the experience of the matter itself.*" (ZS, 27/ 25-26) Yet in discussing *Ereignis*, he maintains that man is called on to bring it to language. Mortal *legein* is supposed to gather and shelter the cosmic *Logos*. In his 1936 essay, "Hölderlin and the Essence of Poetry," he described language as a gift. For Hölderlin, man becomes himself when he affirms that he belongs to the things that are. We belong to everything because we can understand them. We can be universal because language allows us to transcend the immediate environment. Hölderlin suggests that language is rooted in "innerness" *(Innigkeit)* which—much like the *Logos* of Heraclitus—means the setting-apart which binds together the beings of the cosmos. We become most human when we affirm that we belong to this innerness. "This attesting to belonging to the whole of being happens as history. But so that history is possible, language is given to man. It is the 'good' of man." (EHD, 34/275) Western history has been conditioned by the various ways in which Western man has "attested" to belonging to the whole of being. In the modern age, man has concluded that the whole of being belongs to *him*! We have forgotten that "Language is not a tool at [man's] disposal, rather it is that *Ereignis* which disposes of the highest possibility of humanity." (EHD, 35/276) Man becomes attuned to cosmic necessity when he responds to the silent appeal of *Logos* or "Saying" *(Sagen)*. (US, 152-153/52-53) We can speak only because *Logos* endows us with that power. "Authentically language speaks, not man. Man only speaks insofar as he cor-responds to language." (HH, 34) Since the essence of language lies in unconcealing, and since language is distinctive to man, then genuine human existence means disclosing things through language. "Man is that being *[Wesen]*, who—by speaking—lets what is present lie forth in its presence, and perceives that lying forth." (WGM, 271)

In his essay "The Way to Language" (1959), Heidegger interprets the word Saying much as he does the word *Logos*—as a cosmological word.

Saying is in no way the linguistic expression added to the phenomena after they have appeared—rather, all radiant appearance and all fading

> away is grounded in the showing Saying. Saying sets all present beings free into their given presence, and brings what is absent into their absence....
>
> Saying is the gathering that joins all appearances of the itself-manifold showing which everywhere lets all that is shown abide with itself. (US, 257/126)

Saying refers to the cosmic "owning" which gathers beings together to abide in themselves and with other beings as a cosmos. "This owning which brings them there, and which moves Saying as showing in its showing, we call *Ereignis*." (US, 258/127) Human existence becomes authentic *(eigentlich)* when it is appropriated *(vereignet)* by Saying, so that Saying *(Logos, Ereignis)* can be revealed in language. It is not possible to capture Saying in a statement; Saying must be experienced. (US, 266/134-135) Heidegger maintains that his lectures on language are

> intended to bring us face to face with a possibility of undergoing an experience with language. To undergo an experience with something—be it a thing, a person, or a god—means that this something befalls us, strikes us, comes over us, overwhelms us and transforms us. When we talk of "undergoing" an experience, we mean specifically that the experience is not of our own making; to undergo here means that we endure it, suffer it, receive it as it strikes us, and submit to it. (US, 159/57)

In submitting to the claim of *Logos*, we respond to the play or dialogue of which we are a part. (WHD, 83/118-119) Professor Caputo has reminded us, however, that this play is nothing trivial but a "high and dangerous game" whose stakes are our very existence.[3] We are not only ignorant of the rules of this game—we don't even know when the next move will come. The moves occur as new revelations of what it means "to be." In suggesting that the next revelation will lead man to become "like the rose," that is, without self-justification, Heidegger implies that we are in store for a fundamental alteration of traditional concepts of law, responsibility, and social order.[4] Elsewhere, I have shown how Herbert Marcuse's political theory is guided by the idea that man is most himself when at play.[5] Even if we would like to live in a world where play predominates, we cannot initiate the change of understanding required for such a world. We can only remain open for it.

We have seen that *Ereignis (Logos,* Saying) refers to the self-concealing abyss which lets beings present themselves to each other as a self-organizing cosmos. Just as *Logos* refers to the nothingness (world-time) which allows beings to manifest themselves to each other, so, too, human Dasein refers to the embodied nothingness (temporality) which allows *Logos* itself to be revealed. Human existence is truly "owned" when it is appropriated for the self-revelation of *Logos.* Before turning to the next part of this chapter, which explains that appropriation occurs only when humanity is released from self-will, I would like to comment on the relation between *Ereignis* and Western history. Heidegger was always interested in the meaning and development of Western history. In his early thinking, conditioned by transcendental philosophy, he tended to interpret history as if it involved the self-actualization of mankind. Later, when he began studying the cosmological doctrines of the pre-Socratics, he discovered that Heraclitus' notions about *Logos* and *legein* offered a way of describing the relation between the history of Being and human history. Heraclitus, of course, knew nothing of the eschatological-historical tradition established by the Old and New Testaments, and developed by Augustine, Hegel, Dilthey, and others. When Heidegger interprets Heraclitus, therefore, he makes him say things which are probably foreign to his own way of thinking. As we shall see in the last part of this chapter, Heidegger never manages to completely escape the sphere of anthropocentrism. He tends to overemphasize the importance of human history as the vehicle for the self-expression of the history of *Ereignis.* Indeed, the concept of history as such is intrinsically human and subjective; it cannot be readily applied to *Logos.*

PART TWO: **Releasement as the Mature Concept of Resoluteness.**

For the purposes of my study, it would be helpful if I could say of Heidegger's thinking: In his early work, authenticity is a matter of will-power; in his later work, authenticity is a matter of being released. Unfortunately, however, the matter is not so simple. I have already pointed out that even in *Being and Time*, which does emphasize the importance of courage and will, Heidegger claims that we are *called* to authenticity. Moreover, the term "resoluteness" itself can be understood as "being unlocked" or "being opened up." In his later work, he minimized the voluntaristic theme but did not abandon it altogether. He speaks of releasement in three different contexts. First, there is the *individual* who is released from self-will. Here, Heidegger explains that only a trace of willing is required to allow oneself to be redeemed from willing. Second, there is the *world-historical hero* who is appropriated as the place in which *Ereignis* or *Logos* can manifest itself in a decisive new way. In describing the struggle of the hero to remain open for such a revelation, Heidegger sometimes resorts to the voluntaristic language of his early thinking. Even here, however, the hero struggles not so much to conquer himself as to allow himself to be appropriated. Third, there is *Western humanity* which may be released at some point from the technological Will to Power. Human will and action can neither change the prevailing mode of understanding Being, nor accelerate the advent of a new understanding. What we can do, however, is prepare ourselves to hear *Logos* if and when it happens to speak to us anew. Let us consider in turn each of these modes of releasement.

Heidegger's most extensive treatment of releasement concerns the release of the individual from self-will and objectifying thinking. This discussion is found in his essay "Towards the Elucidation of Releasement: From a Dialogue on a Country Path about Thinking" (1944-1945). This dialogue among a scientist, a scholar, and a teacher (who appears to represent Heidegger) contends that genuine "thinking" begins only when an individual is released from the willfulness inherent in representational thinking. (G, 29-30/58-59) Representational thinking is willful because it discloses beings only in accordance with standards it imposes. That Heidegger once engaged in such thinking is evident from the following remark he made in 1927:

In *ontology*, i.e., in philosophy, Being becomes [an] explicitly and thematically grasped object *[Gegenstand]*. [Philosophy] is accordingly the freely grasped task of the illumination and formation of the understanding of Being belonging to human existence. (PIK, 38)

In apparent reference to such earlier statements in general, and to the subjectivistic orientation of *Being and Time* in particular, one of the interlocutors confesses that "Previously we had come to see thinking in the form of transcendental-horizonal re-presenting." (G, 36/63) The transcendental horizon refers to the field in which an object can appear. In knowing things and dealing with them, we forget the conditions necessary for the possibility of encountering them at all. Common sense supposes that the horizon opens up just because we open our eyes, while philosophy knows that looking presupposes an horizon. While *Being and Time* suggests that Dasein projects horizons for itself, however, the dialogue makes clear that Dasein is neither source nor center of the horizon. Instead, the horizon is "the side facing us of an openness which surrounds us; an openness which is filled with views of the appearances of what to our re-presenting are objects." (G, 37/64) This openness is called the *"Gegend"* or *"Gegnet,"* terms etymologically connected with the preposition *"gegen,"* meaning "towards," "in the direction of," or "against." *Gegend* seems to mean much the same as *Ereignis*. *Gegend* gathers together the clearing in which beings can manifest themselves to each other. This clearing is not a subjective projection, but the openness in which "subjectivity" itself can first occur.

Under the domination of egoism and self-will, an individual regards himself as the self-grounding vantage point around which everything else is organized as an object for him. In fact, however, we are born into a play of appearances which has no "center" and no "interiority." Only if we are released from the isolation imposed by self-willed egoism, however, can we become fully open for this play. In releasement, the playful region "appropriates the presence *[Wesen]* of man for its own regioning...." (G, 62/83) The released individual no longer experiences himself as looking out on objects; instead, he feels that beings are appearing to each other *through* him! How is this extraordinary releasement accomplished?

First of all, since representational or objectifying thinking is itself a kind of willing, we can hardly expect to stop such thinking by an act of will. Willing only reinforces will. Yet the release does not occur unless one is somehow ready for it. Hence, the scientist says to the teacher: "You want a non-willing in the sense of renouncing of willing, so that through this we may release, or at least prepare to release, ourselves to the sought-for essence of a thinking that is not a willing." (G, 31/59-60) Renouncing will, however, requires a "trace" of willing which disappears entirely in releasement. This "trace of willing" is how we are to "think 'resoluteness' as it is thought in *Being and Time*: as the properly *[eigens]* undertaken self-opening of Dasein for the open...." (G, 59/81) Since releasement lies beyond willing, it stands outside of the ordinary distinction between activity and passivity. In the context of this dialogue, "doing" means acting to achieve a goal posited by the ego. The "not-doing" characteristic of the released individual, however, "is in no way a matter of weakly allowing things to slide and drift along." (G, 33/61). Instead, such not-doing is "something like the power of action and resolve." (G, 58/80) Releasement means resolving to let the nature of truth (un-concealment) be revealed. This resolve, a kind of "endurance" *(Ausdauer)* which increases as releasement itself increases, is called "constancy" *(Instandigkeit)*. (G, 59/81) Releasement is a noble-mindedness *(Edelmut)* which humbly awaits the disclosure of the Being of beings. Awaiting the manifestation of Being can involve practical activity. As released, we are open for the possibilities of beings. Instead of subjecting things to our will, we seek to let them be what they already are. There are two ways of tilling the soil, for example. Subjectivistic man treats the earth merely as raw material to be exploited for profit; hence, he uses chemicals which dramatically improve crop "production" for a time, but which ultimately degrade the earth. Released man regards the earth as the source of life; hence, in tilling it, he takes care that the soil remains fertile and healthy. "Waiting" on Being can mean nurturing and caring. True nobility resides in such waiting. If the noble is that which has origins *(Herkunft)*, and if our origin as human beings is the region of regions *(Ereignis)*, we are noble when we let ourselves be appropriated by that region. (G, 61/83) When appropriated, the ego gives way to what is more fundamental—openness.

TEACHER: A patient noble-mindedness would be pure resting in itself of that willing, which, renouncing willing, has released itself to what is not will.

SCHOLAR: Noble-mindedness would be the essence of thinking *[Denken]* and thereby of thanking *[Danken]*.

TEACHER: Of that thanking which does not have to thank for something, but only thanks for being allowed to thank. (G, 64-65/85)

"Thinking" does not mean deductive reasoning, calculating, or categorizing. These dualistic operations reduce beings to objects for the subject. In genuine thinking, the "self" or "subject" disappears. In the released individual, there is no longer a self-conscious ego; instead, *Ereignis* is aware of itself through the cleared individual. The ego-subject is eclipsed by the self-manifesting play of appearances. Heidegger remarks in his essay, "The Turning":

> Only when the human essence, in the *Ereignis* of the insight by which he himself is beheld, renounces human self-will *[Eigensinn]* and projects himself toward that insight and away from himself, does he correspond in his essence to the claim of that insight. In thus corresponding man is gathered into his own *[ge-eignet]*, so that he, within the safeguarded element of world, may, as mortal, look out toward the divine. (TK, 45/47)

Thinking is a kind of thanking. In thanking, we accept the gift of existence. In accepting ourselves, we become ourselves. As released, we gratefully enter into the play of which we are already a part. Releasement means "homecoming" (Hölderlin). Thinking as thanking means loving. In *What Is Called Thinking?*, Heidegger cites Hölderlin's line: "Who the deepest has *thought, loves* what is most alive." (WHD, 9/20) Thinking as thanking means being "poor in spirit," seeking nothing, and submitting to the necessity of the play of appearances. The "thinking which recalls" *(andenkendes Denken)* preserves, gathers, and reveals the cosmic play analogously to how the cosmic play gathers the absence *(aeon)* in which beings can appear to one another. In a poem called "Thanks," written for René Char, Heidegger says: "Giving thanks: announcing one's belonging to/the needy, appropriating event." (D, 87) Because we always belong to the appropriating event, we are always open for it. Releasement means becoming aware of our openness. Because Heidegger wants to avoid describing *Ereignis* as an agent, he cannot quite say that *Ereignis* releases us. The release simply comes unexpectedly as a gift, in a way similar to the advent of what Christianity calls "grace."

As John D. Caputo and Reiner Schürmann have demonstrated, Heidegger's concept of releasement *(Gelassenheit)* resembles the Christian mystic Meister Eckhart's concept of releasement *(Gelâzenheit).*[6] According to Caputo, the following "analogy of proportionality" holds between Heidegger's concept and that of Eckhart: Being is to Dasein as God is to the soul. For both thinkers, releasement (redemption) is not an achievement of the self; rather, it is a matter of becoming what we already are. For Heidegger, this means becoming the clearing in which the cosmic play can display itself; for Eckhart, this means becoming the clearing for the birth of Jesus (the advent of God) in the soul. Eckhart explains that the soul is the "image" of God insofar as God gives birth to His Son (hence, to Himself) in it. This divine birth, however, requires that the soul be cleared and prepared through grace. God does not give birth to Himself in a soul seized with self-will. Self-will includes being attached to worldly affairs. Hence, for Eckhart, releasement is detachment *(Abgeschiedenheit)* from things. So free is the released soul from purposive or willed activity that it does not even act in order to please God. It cannot please Him, for it is united with Him. Indeed, it is united with the Godhead *(Gottheit),* the abyss which lies beyond the personal God of Creation.

Although Eckhart never says that God needs the human soul to be brought into His own, Heidegger says that *Ereignis* needs man to reveal himself. Heidegger, moreover, hesitates to speak of the "unity" of Dasein and *Ereignis*; instead, he talks of their mutual "appropriating." Caputo adds another distinction between the two thinkers: unlike Eckhart, Heidegger is not a mystical thinker in the religious sense, for there is no element of love or hope in his notion of *Ereignis.* "Heidegger's 'Being' cannot be determined personalistically.... And in my view this must be counted as the most decisive difference of all between Eckhart and Heidegger."[7] Yet we have already seen that Heidegger's releasement is a gift or "loving bestowal" which allows us to think, thank, and love. He refused to personalize *Ereignis*, because this would have the effect of treating it as a being. Even for Eckhart, the Godhead lacks the personal characteristics we attribute to God as Father, Son, and Holy Spirit. The Godhead refers to the Absolute Void from whence all beings appear; we become the image of the Godhead when we become the absence in which the Void itself can be revealed. By replacing the word "Godhead" in the previous sentence with the word *"Ereignis,"* the sentence approximates Heidegger's view. We might use the word "Love" to describe this Void which lets beings be.

In the dialogue we have been discussing, Heidegger minimizes the need for will or effort in becoming released. In focusing on the individual making his way toward releasement, or toward being ready for releasement, Heidegger speaks in a way very similar to how a religious person would describe the journey toward salvation. In other of his later works, however, particularly those which discuss the world-historical hero, he re-introduces the theme of violent struggle ("works") along with the theme of appropriation ("grace," "election"). Individuals do not *choose* to be prophets or creators, of course; they are sent on their way. (WHD, 61/46) In support of his own view that creative individuals are rare and noble, Heidegger refers to Eckhart:

> Unless man first establishes himself beforehand in the space proper to his essence and there takes up his dwelling, he will not be capable of anything essential within the destiny now holding sway. In pondering this, we pay heed to a word of Meister Eckhart, as we think it in keeping with what is most fundamental to it *[aus seinem Grunde]*. It reads: "Those who are not of a great essence, whatever work they perform, nothing comes of it." (*Reden der Unterscheidung*, no. 4) (TK, 34/39)

In "What Are Poets For?", Heidegger observed that, although *Technik* brings danger, it also contains within itself the possibility of rescue. This rescue will not take place, however, unless "there is a turn with mortals in their essence." (Hw, 273/118) To begin this turning, some mortals must venture into the "abyss of the destitute." Heidegger calls this venturing the highest form of will, since the venturer allows himself to be willed by the play of *Ereignis* or Being itself. Such willing is beyond the normal dichotomy of willing and non-willing.

> The more venturesome ones do not venture themselves out of self-ishness, for their own personal sake. They seek neither to gain an advantage, nor to indulge their self-interest. Nor, even though they are more venturesome, can they boast of any outstanding accomplish-ments. For they are more daring only by a little, "more daring by a breath." (Hw, 274/119)

These chosen individuals gain fulfillment precisely through self-renunciation. (US, 168-171/65-68) They are "more daring by a breath" because they catch the scent of death; they let their own emptiness be revealed. Although death and *Angst* are seldom dis-cussed in Heidegger's later writings, they remain important under-lying themes. In his 1943 "Afterword" to "What Is Metaphysics?," for example, he sounds much as he did in *Being and Time*.

> Readiness for *Angst* is to say "yes" to constancy, to fulfill the highest claim, through which alone is the essence of man touched....
> The clear voice of *Angst* guarantees the most mysterious possibility: the experience of Being....
> To the degree that we degrade this essential *Angst* and the rela-tion cleared in it of Being to man, we devalue the essence of courage. But [courage] makes it possible to endure nothingness. Courage recognizes in the abyss of terror the all but untrodden realm of Being, from the clearing of which each steps back into what it is and can be. This lecture neither puts forward a "philosophy of *Angst*," nor seeks to give the false impression of being a "heroic philosophy." It only thinks what has, since the beginning, arisen for Western thinking to think, but which nevertheless remains forgotten: Being. But Being is not a product of thinking. Quite the opposite: essential thinking is an *Ereignis* of Being. (WGM, 103/355-356)

The one chosen for revelation is not the self-willed conqueror, but the one who has sacrificed himself in order to be open for that revelation. Courage is not a straining, but a letting be. Only when we have been enabled to let things be does there occur the "lightning flash" of revelation. "We see this lightning only when we station ourselves in the storm of Being. Yet everything today betrays the fact that we bestir ourselves only to drive storms away." (VA, III, 25/78) The greatest storm for us is the disclosure of our mortality. To station ourselves in the storm means to let this disclosure occur.

> The essence of mortals calls upon them to heed a call which beckons them toward death. As the outermost possibility of mortal Dasein, death is not the end of the possible but the highest keeping (the gathering sneltering) of the mystery of calling disclosure. (VA, III, 52/101)

Although only a few are gifted with the linguistic talent needed to express the revelation of Being, each of us has the possibility of experiencing that revelation. From the beginning, we have all been witnesses to the miracle of the play of revealing/concealing, yet it usually remains invisible to us. "All we need is the plain, sudden, unforgettable and hence forever new look into something which we—even though it is familiar to us—do not even try to know, let alone understand in a fitting manner." (US, 257-258/127) Thinking (openness for Being) does not result from the steady work so familiar to those striving to achieve a specific goal. Nor does thinking happen when one *reads* about it, any more than one swims when one reads about swimming. (WHD, 9/21) Thinking begins with a leap out of the framework *(Gestell)* of representational thinking. In this leap, we jump onto the soil on which we already stand. A strange kind of leap! Trying to gain enlightenment by reflecting one's way out of reflection (Hegel) keeps us in the circle of representational thinking. The thirst for Absolute Knowledge is a form of will. (US, 100/13)

We often imagine that the moment of enlightenment must occur in circumstances befitting a movie epic. In fact, however, every moment of everyday life, every cup of coffee we drink, every word we offer others, involves the revelation of Being. When sunk in inauthentic everydayness, we cannot see the "golden gleam" which shines through us but not for us. Yet we are drawn to this mystery, "the splendor of the simple." (AED, 13/7) The mystery cannot be explained by representational thinking, for such thinking involves grasping and manipulating. But "the golden gleam of the lightning's invisible shining cannot be grasped because it is not itself something grasping. Rather, it is the pure *Ereignen.*" (VA, III, 77/ 127) What shines forth is precisely nothing: the absence necessary for beings to be manifest. These moments of vision do not last forever. Even the released individual slips back into everydayness. (WHD, 108/175)

So far we have examined releasement with respect to both the individual released from self-will and the world-historical figure who is fated to express the revelation of Being granted to him in the moment of release. Had Heidegger focused more on the released individual, he might have gone down the religious way, but his major interest remained the origin of changes in the way in which Being reveals itself. These changes condition the historical existence of Western mankind. Presently, Being reveals itself to Western man as objectivity. Heidegger claims that man is incapable of acting to change this revelation; we must somehow learn to live with our destiny while remaining open for a change in it. Against Marx, Heidegger denies the efficacy of human *praxis* in bringing about the fully human world. The highest form of action is thinking—opening ourselves to a new manifestation of Being. Thinking prepares us for the release, which will allow us to "let technical objects enter our daily world and at the same time leave them outside; that is, let them alone, as things which are nothing absolute but which remain dependent on something higher." (G, 23/54) As if to emphasize the impotence of man in the face of destiny, however, Heidegger once asserted that "Only a God can save us." (Sp, 209/277) He refused to offer detailed recommendations for social or political action, not only because he doubted the efficacy of such action, but also because genuine thinking lacks authority to give instructions. The predominant technological rationality has denied that thinking has practical "relevance." In his interview with *Der Spiegel* he also remarked: "I cannot [speak out on such issues], because the questions are so difficult that it would be contrary to the meaning of the task of thought to step up publicly, as it were, to preach and to impose moral judgment." (Sp, 212/280) This statement implies that Heidegger's political actions in 1933-1934 were contrary to the task of thinking. Given the outcome of his last political efforts, it would have been surprising had he offered political advice in 1966!

Although the task for man is to ready himself for a new revelation, Heidegger recognized the urgency of the present situation: technological change threatens our moral standards and social bonds. In 1946 he asked: "Should we not safeguard and secure the existing bonds even if they hold human beings together ever so tenuously and merely for the present? Certainly." (WGM, 183/232) Genuine thinking must go on at the same time, however, since man is not really prepared to assume technological dominion over the earth. Heidegger was aware of the problem of finding a political system compatible with man's ontological nature as well as with the emerging technological order. In his view, democracy was not promising. (Sp, 206/276) He agreed with Nietzsche that something like a "will to tradition" is necessary. To let our destiny meet us from the future means that we must not lay waste to the planet. Otherwise, our progeny cannot participate in the play of life in which we are but passing moments. (WHD, 65-67/67-69) The gigantic cycle of production and consumption resembles in certain ways the Eternal Return of the Same, but we are not yet capable of comprehending this. (WHD, 47/109) Heidegger had hopes for the future, but he was convinced that the earth will never be a paradise for us mortals. Suffering is not only unavoidable but necessary, especially to temper the technological Will to Power. Heidegger intimated that the transformed man of later centuries might resemble Nietzsche's Overman: "Caesar, with the soul of Christ." (WHD, 67/69) Since mankind is under the sway of the unpredictable play of Being, however, it is difficult to see why Heidegger would have any hope at all. His hopeful acceptance of destiny contrasts with Herbert Marcuse's fiery "Great Refusal" to accept one-dimensional society. Yet even Marcuse, who sided with Marx concerning the efficacy of human action, could not offer adequate practical guidelines for bringing man out of the present situation.[8]

Let me summarize the major distinctions and similarities between authenticity as resoluteness and as releasement. Both forms of authenticity involve a kind of steadfastness: a gathering together of one's openness, a self-focusing. *Being and Time* emphasizes courage and will to the point that resoluteness almost seems to be a kind of self-actualization. Yet resoluteness is also said to be in the service of

254 Eclipse of the Self

temporality, the unifying sense of Dasein's Being. Dasein's conscience calls it to allow temporality to generate itself authentically, so that beings might reveal themselves in themselves, not merely for us. Heidegger's later works claim that the released individual is owned or appropriated not by and for itself, but by the cosmic play of *Ereignis*. Just as *Ereignis (Logos)* refers to the world-time which gathers itself as the absence where beings can manifest themselves, so, too, the released individual (image of the *Logos*) is gathered together as the absence needed for the cosmic play to manifest itself. Both resoluteness and releasement involve the loss of egoism (self-objectification); both involve a kind of self-sacrifice; both claim that the truth is usually hidden but always somehow available in everyday life; and both claim that Being reveals itself in a moment of vision or a lightning flash. Releasement is the mature version of resoluteness. Releasement is relatively free of the two aspects of subjectivism which characterize resoluteness: (1) voluntarism, and (2) transcendental-horizonal thinking. The resolute individual *wants* to have a conscience, *wants* to actualize its particular possibilities. But "every will wants to actualize, and to have actuality as its element." (G, 58/80) The purposive striving of the resolute individual is foreign to the released one. Although releasement requires steadiness, the released individual is above all patient and accepting; he knows that light breaks in at its own time.

Just as each fruit ripens according to its own pre-figured plan, so each human being matures according to internal necessity. In the present age, most of us never ripen fully; we remain closed up in egoism. Yet just as the blooming flower is drawn toward the sun, so, too, a few individuals are drawn to *Ereignis*: the golden gleam which is present in every moment of everyday life. The cleared individual matures in harmony with the movement of *Logos*. The fruit of that maturation is language, which allows *Logos* itself to be revealed, even if only tenuously. In the cleared individual, language blooms. "Language is the flower of the mouth. In language the earth blossoms toward the bloom of the sky." (US, 206/99) The final question for this study is: was Heidegger's own way a way of releasement? Did his philosophical venture correspond with a personal one?

PART THREE: Zen, Releasement, and the Limitations of Heidegger's Way.

In this final portion of my essay, I compare Zen Buddhism's notion of *satori* ("enlightenment") with Heidegger's idea of releasement in order to: (1) elaborate further on releasement; (2) show how Zen is compatible with Heidegger's suggestion that in releasement we are thankful not to God but simply for being part of the great play of life; (3) show how the Zen master might question Heidegger's attachment to the concept of the "history of Being"; (4) exhibit how Heidegger's own way to enlightenment seems to have been inextricably involved with meditation on the history of Being; (5) demonstrate that he became detached at times from the "fruits" of his thinking, which he came to regard as a kind of play; and (6) show that his thinking both reveals the limits of Western understanding of Being and calls on us to be open for a new understanding. Although his vocabulary changed over the years, he never separated the dramatic issue of human existence from the theoretical issue of the sense of Being. Indeed, the concept of "thinking" unites practice and theory in a remarkable way. Heidegger eventually saw that the spiritual-religious concerns which initiated his thinking continued to draw him along all the time. For him, meditation on the event of thinking (openness to what is) turned out to be a way of life.

Heidegger, who was often visited by Japanese and Indian students who came to work with him as early as 1927, seems to have had a favorable attitude toward Eastern "thinking." In 1966, however, he said that the change needed in Western man's understanding of Being

> cannot happen because of any takeover of Zen Buddhism or any other Eastern experience of the world. There is need for a rethinking which is carried out with the help of the European tradition and of a new appropriation of that tradition. Thinking itself can be transformed only by a thinking which has the same origin and calling. (Sp, 214-217/281)

His major objection to the possibility of a "meeting of East and West" was that we live in different "houses of Being" because of

our totally different languages. (US, 90/5) Yet his dialogue with
Professor Tezuka (Tokyo) suggests that there are ways for us to
enter each other's houses, even if only tentatively. Let us take an
example. The preceding part of this chapter ended with Heidegger's
remark that "In language the earth blossoms toward the bloom of
the sky." This statement reminds us of how, in their dialogue,
Heidegger and Professor Tezuka interpret the Japanese words *"Koto
ba."* *Koto* refers to the "grace" which occurs when an individual is
cleared of ego and filled with the manifestness of what is:

> JAPANESE: But *Koto* always at the same time names what itself
> gives delight, that which uniquely in each unrepeatable *Augen-
> blick* comes to appearance in the fullness of its graciousness.
> INQUIRER: *Koto*, then, would be the *Ereignis* of the clearing tidings
> of graciousness. (US, 142/45)

Koto clears the individual who is then able to express something of
the wondrous emptiness from which the multitude of beings spring
into appearance. Of *Koto ba* the Japanese concludes: "Language
[Sprache], heard through this word is: the petals that stem from
Koto." (US, 144/47) For both Heidegger and Tezuka, language is
an event as wonderful and purposeless as the blooming of a flower.
Only in this particular flower, blooming becomes aware of itself.

Heidegger's interest in Eastern thinking can be seen elsewhere, too.
In "The Nature of Language," for example, he calls the *Tao* "a
great hidden stream which moves all things along and makes way for
everything. All is way." (US, 198/92) *Tao* might be analogous to
Logos. "Perhaps the mystery of mysteries of thoughtful Saying
conceals itself in the word 'way', *Tao*, if only we let these names
return to what they leave unspoken, if only we were capable of this,
to allow them to do so." (US, 198/92) To follow the *Tao* and to
hearken to the *Logos* mean "the same": to be cleared of ego and
attuned to the cosmic play which is hidden from the rational intellect. In 1958 Heidegger observed:

> Lao Tzu says (Ch. 17), "one aware of his brightness keeps to the
> dark." To this we add the truth that everyone knows but few
> realize: Mortal thinking must descend into the dark of the depths

of the well if it is to view the stars by day. It is harder to preserve
the clearness of the dark than to produce a brightness which would
seem to shine as brightness only. What would seemingly only shine
does not illuminate. (GD, 40/56)

The darkness referred to here seems to mean *"-lethe,"* the hidden
absence which lets beings be manifest. Heidegger sometimes speaks
of this absence as illumination but he does not mean a light which
shines. Rather, illumination means the clearing in which the manifest
can first be encountered. "The openness for the light in general is
the condition for [a man] seeing something like the candle-shine."
(H, 224) Earlier, I showed that, for Heidegger, *-lethe* can be understood as a kind of "reservoir" on which *a-letheia* (un-concealment)
can draw. In his book, *The Tao of Physics*, Fritjof Capra speaks of
the Eastern idea of the Void in a similar way:

> Buddhists express the same idea [as the Hindus, for whom Brahman
> is the Void] when they call the ultimate reality Sunyata—'Empti-
> ness' or 'the Void'—and affirm that it is a living Void which gives
> birth to all forms in the phenomenal world. The Taoists ascribe a
> similar infinite and endless creativity to the *Tao* and, again, call it
> empty. "The *Tao* of heaven is empty and formless," says the *Kuan-
> tzu*, and Lao Tzu uses several metaphors to illustrate this emptiness.
> He often compares the *Tao* to a hollow valley, or to a vessel which
> is forever empty and thus has the potential of containing an infinity
> of things.[9]

Capra goes on to claim that what contemporary physicists call
the "field" corresponds to the Void. The field is the non-visible,
non-detectible source from which elementary particles draw their
organization and energy, and hence their reality. As fascinating as
these connections among Heidegger, Taoism, and modern physics
might be, more remarkable still is the similarity between Heidegger's
thinking and Zen Buddhism.

Zen Buddhism is not a theistic religion since it does not involve
worship of a transcendent deity. Nor is it philosophy, although Zen
Buddhists can and do discuss sophisticated philosophical issues.
What Zen seems most to resemble is what Heidegger calls thinking—

openness to the manifestness of beings. Zen is not a system of philosophy, but a practical way of life. The master of Zen is the completely human being who is similar to Heidegger's released individual. Keeping in mind the characteristics of the relased individual, let us consider the way to enlightenment according to Zen.

First of all, there is no "way" to enlightenment, although the Zen master is always "on his way." There is no way because there is no goal to be accomplished; we already are the emptiness which constitutes our "Buddha-nature." Enlightenment *(satori, kensho)* occurs when we are liberated from the delusion that we are permanent substances (selves, egos) over against other enduring objects. The Buddha pointed out that human life involves suffering because we strive to cling to a constantly changing world. The cure for this ailment is a way of life devoted to gaining direct insight into the fact of our own insubstantiality and hence into the fact that "security" is impossible. Enlightenment involves revelation of the fact that the true "self" is "no-self" or "no-mind" *(wu-hsin)*. Yasutani-roshi has remarked that "man grasps for the world because intuitively he longs to be rejoined with that from which he has been estranged through delusion."[10] The suffering produced by the dualistic experience of the world cannot be alleviated by any action taken by the ego, but only by releasement from egoistical self-understanding. At first, one's motives for practicing Zen are usually colored by the view that Zen may succeed in producing "success" where the pursuit of wealth, power, or sensual gratification has failed. Looking upon enlightenment as a goal to be achieved by the efforts of the ego, however, is self-defeating. Gradually, through the practice of what Zen calls "mindfulness," the hard knot of one's ego begins to dissolve—and one forgets about the desire to achieve enlightenment. The enlightened person acts freely and spontaneously, without being dominated by a goal or idea. Only when as un-self-conscious as a flower can one be the pure emptiness in which the presence or "suchness" *(tathata)* of things can be manifest. Once one is free from the greed, hate, and delusion which accompany egoistical self-understanding, one is open to the world in a compassionate way. The Zen master is not interested in dominating others, but in relieving their suffering. Suffering is relieved, however, only when the other has direct insight into the source of his suffering: egoism. Zen is a religion insofar as it points the way to salvation or redemption from the pain which permeates human life, but for Zen this redemption includes an ontological dimension.

Thomas Merton, whose familiarity with Meister Eckhart, Heidegger, and Zen makes his observations particularly important for the present study, notes that *satori* means becoming the "light" which we already are.[11] This light is not a physical light, but "no-light," the Void. *Satori*, which means the most profound possible awareness, is an ontological event. The enlightened man sees where there is no "object." He sees the "golden gleam," the manifestness or Being of beings. Instead of experiencing himself as an ego looking out on the world, he lets the world look out on itself through him. He *becomes* the fragrance of the flower, the brightness of the moon. There is no "inner" sphere for Zen. The feeling and sensations "within" us are just as manifest as trees and people "without" us. To the question "Who or what, then, *am* I?", Zen answers: the openness where the play of appearances happens.

A Tibetan Buddhist writer has emphasized that the self is the openness in which beings can be present. "Our most fundamental state of mind, before the creation of the ego, is such that there is basic openness, basic freedom, a spacious quality; and we have now and have always had this openness."[12] We dance freely in this space until we separate ourselves from it by interpreting ourselves as something solid—ego. Separateness makes us feel awkward, so we try to secure a "ground" for ourselves. In looking for security, we begin reacting to our projections rather than seeing things as they really are. "There is no situation of 'letting be' at all, because one is ignoring what one is [openness] all the time. This is the basic definition of ignorance."[13] As separate egos, we want "to confirm our experience, to interpret weakness as strength, to fabricate a logic of reality, to confirm our ignorance."[14]

Rational speculation and scholarship cannot replace the direct experience of the manifestness of beings and of oneself as the mortal emptiness where this manifesting occurs. It may be, however, that all great thinking involves the attempt to give expression to the Void *(Tao, Logos, Ereignis, Sunyata)*, which seeks to manifest itself in language. D.T. Suzuki observes that:

> We can talk of *sunyata* only because we are it. If this were not the case, there would be no philosophy in this world. It is entirely due to *sunyata* that we can reason, although reasoning itself cannot lead us to *sunyata*....*Sunyata* wants to see itself, to know itself, and it is this want on the part of *sunyata* that leads to reasoning, and reason, not knowing this cause of its activity, defeats itself in spite of its ambitious claim for omniscience. *Sunyata* knows itself through us, because we are *sunyata*.[15]

Because we already *are* emptiness, Zen enlightenment does not occur in some exceptional circumstances, but is always available in everyday life. We need only become aware of the miracle of manifestness. Even the most trivial incident can be the occasion for the "lightning flash." Shunryu Suzuki tells us in his lectures on Zen practice:

> When you know everything, you are like a dark sky. Sometimes a flashing will come through the dark sky. After it passes, you forget all about it, and there is nothing left but the dark sky. The sky is never surprised when all of a sudden a thunderbolt breaks through. And when the lightning does flash, a wonderful sight may be seen. When we have emptiness we are always prepared for watching the flashing.[16]

Practicing Zen means being constantly mindful of, and open to, each moment of life. Only in being open can we see things as they are, and not as they are set up by intellect and imagination. Each moment is a new and different episode in the play of life.

> Everyone comes out from nothingness moment after moment. Moment after moment we have true joy of life. So we say *shin ku myo u*, "from true emptiness, the wondrous being appears." *Shin* is "true"; *ku* is "emptiness"; *myo* is "wondrous"; *u* is "being"; from true emptiness, wondrous being.[17]

In the moment of enlightenment, one dwells in the great openness in which beings can be manifest. D.T. Suzuki describes this moment in a way similar to how Heidegger, Kierkegaard, Bultmann, and Tillich describe *kairos*, the moment when eternity breaks into the finite. Experience of the eternal *(ekaksana)* means "the bursting of time out of eternity....but there is no eternity as such; it is always to be in the time process."[18] Abe Masao, in commenting on the work of the great Zen master Dogen, says that "To realize time as time is to attain the Buddha nature. For Dogen time is the Buddha nature and the Buddha nature is time."[19] Experiencing time in the ordinary way leads to the egoism which regards life as a series of unending nows to be crammed with gratification. Experiencing time authentically, however, coincides with direct insight into one's finite openness, i.e., into one's Buddha-nature. Authentic temporality thus involves the *uncovering* of what has been forgotten and the *recovery* of what one already is. As D.T. Suzuki says with regard to resolute-mindedness.

> It is not a question of developing what has already been developed but of recovering what has been left behind, though this has been with us, in us, all the time and has never been lost or distorted except for our misguided manipulation of it.[20]

Experiencing time authentically means being so open and attuned to our situation that we live without leaving a trace of life as it happens—we live spontaneously.[21] In being opened to the interplay of the world, the enlightened person always knows how to act appropriately. Hence, he is endowed with what Aristotle calls *phronesis*. In a remarkable discussion of Zen and Japanese swordsmanship, D.T. Suzuki explains that resoluteness in the face of death is the key to great swordfighting.

> When one is resolved to die, that is, when the thought of death is wiped off the field of consciousness, there arises something in it, or rather, apparently from the outside, the presence of which one has never been aware of, and when this strange presence begins to direct one's activities in an instinctual manner wonders are achieved.[22]

Wiping away the thought of death is possible only through the confrontation with and acceptance of it. In Japan's middle ages, samurai swordsman would train for years with Zen masters in hopes of having direct insight into their own finitude, so that they would be liberated from the delusions of egoism. Freed from the egoistical self-understanding which separates self from world, the master of swordfighting becomes one with his opponent. Hence, he can anticipate his every move and act without hesitation. He effaces himself so that the *Tao* can work through him. Performers in the arts and athletics tell us that they are at their best precisely when they are not *trying* to be so. Although much training has prepared them for such moments, it is only when they are unexpectedly void of second-guessing reflection that they can move freely in accordance with the possibilities of the situation. We do not have to resort to extreme examples to understand the spontaneity associated with openness. D.T. Suzuki says that

> When Heavenly Reason is present in us it knows how to behave on every occasion; when a man sees fire, his Reason knows at once how to use it; when he finds water, it tells him at once what it is good for; when he meets a friend, it makes him greet him; when he sees a person in a dangerous situation, it makes him go right out to the rescue. As long as we are one with it, we never err in our proper behavior however variable the situation may be.[23]

In Heidegger's terms, the authentic individual has been cleared of objectifying thinking so that he allows beings to show themselves as they are. No longer trapped in an isolated sphere of subjectivity, the authentic person "ek-sists" in the sense of being "ec-centric": non-egocentric.[24] Instead of seeing things from his self-centered viewpoint, he somehow becomes the viewpoint for the entire situation. This extraordinary openness is somehow ordinary; it is always with us, though we are usually forgetful of it. The enlightened person is aware yet not dualistically aware; he is there yet not there; he is in a state of relaxation and receptivity, yet he is always prepared; he both does and does not do. It is difficult to understand how these apparently contradictory kinds of behavior can be reconciled in practice. D.T. Suzuki warns us, however, that "It is a great mistake to adjust everything to the Proceustean bed of logic and a greater mistake to make logic the supreme test in the evaluation of human behavior."[25] According to Heidegger, the principle of sufficient reason, along with other logical principles, are expressions of the metaphysical understanding of the West, an understanding which is not absolute but historical. Metaphysical-logical thinking has enormous practical consequences, but it leads to a dualistic experience: Being comes to mean objectivity, the capacity to be known and controlled by the subject. In both Heidegger's thinking and in Zen, however, the primordial is not what results from the categorizing, judging activities of the subject. Instead, the primordial is the givenness or manifestness of beings. Both Heidegger and Zen reject the metaphysics of substance; they affirm a kind of phenomenalism. If we are able to put our calculating intellects to rest for a time and simply observe, we see that the phenomenal content of our experience arises from nowhere: thoughts, feelings, perceptions, memories, projections keep appearing. Judgments about the causal factors which "explain" these phenomena are themselves further phenomena. Life is a happening for which we can find no adequate explanation. "All things come out of an unknown abyss of mystery...."[26] By having direct insight into this phenomenal play of presence and absence, we learn that the ego, too, is just another (though complex) phenomenon. This changed self-understanding helps lead to the end of suffering caused by greed, hate, and delusion—the major forms of egoism.

Two of the major sects of Zen, Rinzai and Soto, recommend different ways for becoming free from greed, hate, and delusion. In some measure, these two sects are different ways of responding to the enduring puzzle of Buddhism: if we already *are* Buddha-nature, why must we *do* anything to be enlightened? The Rinzai sect, which emphasizes the self-reliant, courageous struggle to become free from delusion, is reminiscent of the young Heidegger's claim that authenticity requires resoluteness. The Soto sect, which emphasizes patient waiting for truth to happen, is reminiscent of Heidegger's later claim that authenticity requires releasement. It would appear that Rinzai Zen stresses "works," while Soto Zen stresses "grace," although common to both is the theme that egoism must be directly intuited as the source of suffering if one is to be liberated from it.[27]

The Rinzai sect often employs a *"koan,"* a puzzle assigned to a student by his master. This puzzle, which is to be worked on at all times but particularly while in sitting meditation *(zazen)*, cannot be solved by the discursive intellect. Indeed, struggle with the *koan* supposedly reveals the limitations of reason. Eventually, reasoning reveals itself as one of the activities of the ego. Zen holds that real sanity begins when one sees that reasoning is inherently dualistic, and hence can never provide insight into the truth: that the world is not divided into subjects and objects. D.T. Suzuki claims that *koan*-study involves a fierce effort which demands a "reconstruction of one's character."[28] This process

> is stained with tears and blood. But the height the great masters have climbed cannot otherwise be reached; the truth of Zen can never be attained unless it is attacked with the full force of personality. The passage is strewn with thistles and brambles, and the climb is slippery in the extreme. It is no pastime, but the most serious task of life; no idlers will ever dare attempt it. It is then indeed a moral anvil on which your character is hammered and hammered. To the question, "What is Zen?" a master gave this answer, "Boiling oil over a blazing fire."[29]

Given these remarks, it is not surprising to hear D.T. Suzuki call Zen (at least as practiced by the Rinzai sect) "a religion of the will."[30]

The rational ego clings fiercely to its attempt to explain the world in terms of concepts and ideas. Because the world is an impenetrable mystery, however, the ego is ultimately frustrated in its yearning for absolute knowledge. Thomas Merton has described the *koan* as an *epoche* in which purposive-rational categories must be bracketed.[31] Although effort is a prerequisite for unravelling the ego, even the Rinzai sect admits that effort alone is sometimes not sufficient to bring enlightenment. Patience, too, is crucial. Enlightenment comes if it comes. Indeed, too much is usually made of having the experience of *satori*. More important is learning to live everyday life in as mindful a way as possible.

The patient way of *zazen* is recommended by the Soto sect. We should recall, however, that "Zen" is the Japanese translation of the

Chinese *"Ch'an,"* which itself stems from the Sanskrit *"Dhyana,"* meaning "meditation." All Zen practice, therefore, involves long hours of *zazen*. In *zazen*, one learns just to sit. Surprisingly, it is very difficult to do nothing but sit. Most of the time when sitting, we are engaged in talking, wishing, thinking, imagining—anything but "just sitting." Sitting provides the opportunity for one to examine the workings of the ego and to see that experience is constantly in flux. The insight that everything changes leads toward detachment from things, and in particular from the misguided belief that there is such a thing as a stable, permament ego. Because striving and self-will are aspects of egoism, to grasp at enlightenment is a sure way to miss it. Yet Shunryu Suzuki says that we must make a kind of effortless effort to let ourselves be open and calm. This effort must be forgotten once it has been made.[32] Suzuki's words remind us of Heidegger's claim that although our own efforts cannot guarantee success, we need a "trace of willing" to be released from objectifying thinking. (US, 147, 161/48, 59) The Zen master Yasutani says that "since you sit with the conviction that your essential nature is no different from Buddha's, there is no *purposeful* striving for satori."[33] The Soto sect suggests that enlightenment occurs gradually and spontaneously, almost as a kind of ripening. Heidegger supports this view when he cites from Nietzsche: "Thus man grows out of everything that once embraced him; he has no need to break the shackles—they fall away unforeseen, when a god bids them...." (WHD, 75/80) While the Zen master often describes enlightenment as the moment one becomes aware of one's own Buddha-nature, Christian mysticism describes enlightenment as the sudden awareness of one's essential union with God. Such awareness comes as the gift of grace. St. John of the Cross remarks that

> however greatly the soul itself labors, it cannot actively purify itself so as to be in the least degree prepared for the Divine union of perfection of love, if God takes not its hand and purges it not in that dark fire....[34]

Although influenced by Christian mysticism, Heidegger sought to interpret the mystical experience in non-theistic terms. Just as he developed his concept of authenticity from his de-mythologizing interpretation of the New Testament, so, too, he developed his notion of releasement in part from his de-mythologizing treatment of Christian mysticism. The mystic, Zen master, and Heidegger all seem to agree that the aspirant must prepare himself in some way for the advent of truth. Zen emphasizes meditation and the *koan*, while Christian monasticism emphasizes prayer and devotion. We can assume that as a Jesuit novice, Heidegger became acquainted with the rigorous thirty-day spiritual exercises known as the Ignatian Way. He was well aware of the importance of *practice* in preparing for releasement, but he never describes the form such practice should take. Perhaps he considered this an "existentiell" matter to be decided by each person; perhaps he recognized (as does the Zen master) that spiritual guidance must flow in a direct personal relation between master and student. It is also possible, of course, that Heidegger considered his major task to be that of intepreting the experiences he underwent, not showing others how to have such experiences. This choice of tasks may have turned him away from the priesthood and toward philosophy. Yet he became a masterly teacher whose influence on many brilliant students is well-known.

Heidegger did not fail to point out the importance of the direct experience of openness and *Ereignis*, and he hoped that his words would be of some assistance in bringing his hearers to such experience. With regard to his own lecture, "Time and Being," he remarked that

> it had to attempt to prepare the participants for their own experience of what was said in terms of an experience of something which cannot openly be brought to light. It is...the attempt to speak of something that cannot be mediated cognitively, not even in terms of questions, but must be experienced. The attempt to speak of it with the intention of preparing for this experience essentially constituted the daring quality of the seminar. (ZS, 27-28/26)

Heidegger's point is that we must not depend upon him to tell us what we ourselves can and must experience first-hand. Analogously, being a true Christian requires more than reading Scriptures or attending church; one must try to imitate the life of Christ just as the Zen aspirant must emulate the life of Buddha. Such imitation is possible only because in a profound sense one already *is* Christ or Buddha. As Merton has suggested, this is what Paul may have had in mind when he said that "I live, now not I, but Christ lives in me."[35] For Christian, Buddhist, and for the released individual, enlightenment (*satori*, redemption) involves the discovery that one is totally *accepted*—that one can just be what he already *is*. Such a discovery brings with it an overwhelming sense of gratitude.[36]

Not only Western philosophers, but Zen masters, too, have felt the need to bring to language the manifestness (*tathata*) of things which is revealed in *satori*. D.T. Suzuki informs us that

> *Tathata* cannot remain expressionless and undifferentiated; it has to that extent to be conceptualized. While to utter, "Oh, the morning glory!" is to come out of the identification [with *tathata*], and hence, to be no more of *tathata*, this coming out of itself, this negating itself in order to be itself, is the way in which we are all constituted.[37]

Haiku, the Japanese form of poetry which was so influenced by Zen, offers considerable insight into what Zen regards as the true power of language. D.T. Suzuki offers as an example of *haiku* the following, which was written by the founder of modern *haiku*, Bashō (1643-94):

> The old pond, ah!
> A frog jumps in:
> The water's sound![38]

Within the limitations of seventeen syllables, *haiku* attempts to provide a direct expression of the miraculous presence or suchness of beings. It is important to see that *haiku* does not use metaphors or similes; it is not a "representation" of anything. Instead, the images of *haiku* "directly point to original intuitions, indeed, they are intuitions themselves. When the latter are attained, the images become transparent and are immediate expressions of the experience."[39] We can see here certain similarities to Heidegger's view of language. Although language must have some physical manifestation (sounds, written words), it is not a thing; rather, it is truly a phenom-enon in the sense of what lets things be present while it somehow conceals itself. The great poem is self-effacing; it opens up a clearing in which things manifest themselves as they ordinarily do not do. The words slide away so the things may be. If we let ourselves be used properly by language (as *Logos*), we give voice to the sound-less Word without which no thing could be. D.T. Suzuki says this very well when he describes how Bashō was transformed when he experienced the presence of the frog, the pond, and the water's sound. The sound of the frog landing in the water filled the entire universe; everything was absorbed into the sound. No longer was there a subject confronting an object.

> An yet this could not be a state of absolute annihilation. Bashō was there, the old pond was there, with all the rest. But Bashō was no more the old Bashō. He was "resurrected." He was "the Sound" or "the Word" that was even before heaven and earth were separated. He now experienced the mystery of being-becoming and becoming-being.[40]

Haiku can be a direct expression of the presence of things only insofar as the author is so cleansed of egoism that he can "be an altogether passive instrument for giving an expression to the inspira-tion."[41] As Heidegger might say, only when appropriated by the *Logos* can the poet become sufficiently released from representa-tional thinking to give voice to the *Logos*. It should be clear that the *Logos* does not refer to a separately existing substance which is analogous to a metaphysically-conceived God. *Logos* refers to the ultimately inexpressible absence which is somehow present in all of our experience. When a person experiences the self-concealing pre-sence of things, he realizes that what is most significant is right there in that very experience. It is always here, not elsewhere. Using his own language, D.T. Suzuki makes this point by saying that "this intuitive grasp of Reality never takes place when a world of Emptiness is assumed outside of our everyday world of the sense; for these two worlds, sensual and supersensual, are not separate but one."[42]

Zen masters do not deny that speculative thinking has a place, but they discourage the attempt to use concepts to understand that which can only be experienced immediately. For centuries, Zen masters have answered metaphysical inquiries with statements such as "The full moon in the autumnal sky shines on the ten thousand houses," or "The green bamboos are swaying in the wind; the cold pine trees are shivering in the moonlight."[43] These rather cryptic replies make more sense if one realizes that they were addressed to students who had been practicing mindfulness for many years. These students were on the brink of "seeing" without relying on dualistic concepts. By pointing directly to the appearances which constitute the play of experience, the Zen master hopes his students will finally see for themselves that metaphysical questions are not only unanswerable by the finite human mind, but miss the point entirely.

Although in his lecture "Time and Being," Heidegger encourages his readers to experience *Ereignis* for themselves, his language is still largely theoretical. He still speaks as a "philosopher," although as one trying to find his way beyond the limitations of philosophy. On other occasions, however, Heidegger seems to try to give direct expression to the presence of things. In so doing, he sounds much like a Zen master or the author of *haiku*. Consider, for example, the following passages from *Out of the Experience of Thinking*:

When on a summer's day the butterfly
settles on the flower and, wings
closed, sways with it in the
meadow-breeze....

When the evening light, slanting into
the woods somewhere, bathes the three
trunks in gold....

Forests spread
Brooks plunge
Rocks persist
Mist diffuses

Meadows wait
Springs well
Winds dwell
Blessing muses

(AED, 16, 24, 27/9, 13, 14)

This language is not theoretical, nor is it meant to be merely descriptive. It is, instead, an attempt to let the Being of natural beings be manifest. In the simple things of everyday life, the *Logos* always shines. The mysterious play of presence and absence always goes on. We only need to wake up to it; we only need to stop dreaming. Yet perhaps it is better not to speak of what *we* need to do, as if the problem were somehow on the side of the "subject." According to Heidegger, the presence of things withdraws *itself (sich ent-zieht)*; hence, we must always be ready for the unexpected "lightning-flash." The "play" of life in which we find ourselves is not frivolous; it includes sickness, old age, and death. These cannot be avoided. Only in accepting, and even affirming their necessity, can we become detached from our delusions concerning them. In such detachment, we become free from the cycle of pleasure and pain. The gift of detachment lets us see what transcends our little egos: the mysterious beauty of the presence of things.

From what has been said, the similarities between Heidegger's idea of releasement and Zen's notion of *satori* should be evident. Peter Kreeft summarizes this similarity by saying: "A remarkably 'Zennish' character, Heidegger's 'released' man: patiently noble-minded, willessly steadfast, voidedly joyful, objectlessly grateful, unattached to ideas or things, ordinary in the here and now, and as worldly as a plant."[44] Both the Zen master and Heidegger would acknowledge that releasement occurs when one is emptied of ego and filled with the presence of what is. If mysticism necessarily involves a theistic concept of God, neither Heidegger's thinking nor Zen is mystical. But if mysticism means being emancipated from egoism and opened up to the mysterious presence of things, then both Heidegger's thinking and Zen are mystical. Perhaps Zen's *satori* and Heidegger's releasement can be understood as "de-theologized" mysticism.[45]

There are differences, of course, between Zen and Heidegger's thinking. An obvious one, supposedly, is that Zen is religious while Heidegger's thinking is philosophical. I think I have shown, however, that Zen is no ordinary religion and that Heidegger's thinking is no ordinary philosophy. Both emphasize the importance of first-hand insight into what it means *to be*; hence, for both, good theory ultimately depends on right practice. Heidegger's reflections on practice are infrequent and usually somber, like the rest of his work. Zen lore and literature, however, are replete with humorous anecdotes about the bumbling attempts of students to find their way out of the snares of self-deception. *Satori*, too, is sometimes accompanied by explosive laughter when one suddenly sees one's own self-concealments.

Professor Charles Wei-hsun Fu points out another difference. He claims that Heidegger's notion of *Ereignis*—despite its proximity to the naturalism of Taoism—is colored by the eschatological tradition of Christianity, as mediated by Hegel and Dilthey, Nietzsche, and Heraclitus.[46] By asserting that Western man has been appropriated for the unfolding of the history of Being, Heidegger seems to practice anthropocentrism as well as ethnocentrism. That is, he concentrates on explaining how *Western* mankind's understanding of Being has changed, and he fails to give adequate attention to the natural world of which man is but a small, if crucial, part. Professor Fu suggests that Heidegger continued to cling to the ideal of *Logos*-philosophy: to bring to language the *historical* sense of Being. He did try to overcome the metaphysical-eschatological concept of man and history when he introduced the notion of *Ereignis* as the cosmic play in which man is an element. Yet he sometimes sounded like Hegel, who claimed that man is needed so the universe can be aware of itself. According to Professor Fu, who is interested in showing how Eastern thinking really does lie beyond the framework of metaphysics, both the human being and Western history remain too important in Heidegger's thinking.[47] Although I agree with much of Professor Fu's assessment concerning the metaphysical traces in Heidegger's thinking, I also believe that Heidegger's proximity to Zen demonstrates how far he was able to move beyond the limits of metaphysics.

I also do not think we must agree with Heidegger's claim that our experience of Being is *wholly* determined by language. Although we are children of a particular language, we are *first* human beings. Heidegger's work has long been considered important by the Japanese because, despite the fact that it is written in German, they understand something of what is is saying. When D.T. Suzuki and

Shunryu Suzuki came to the West, they did so with the confidence that they could make themselves understood in a foreign tongue. This confidence rests in the fact that they themselves had had some direct experience of the presence of things and knew that Japanese, too, could not express that presence adequately; it could only point to it. No words can express the Word. Even Greek and German, Heidegger's favorite languages, are inadequate to the task. The most fundamental communication occurs in silence. Our efforts to express what has been given to us in that silence are as disappointing as they are necessary.[48]

Unless we simply ignore Heidegger's claim that experience of the play of presence and absence is all-important, we must conclude that his intellectual journey beyond the limitations of Western metaphysics was bound up with his personal journey toward self-understanding. He once pointed out that the only way to find out about thinking is to go that way. "But it takes the devotion of almost a lifetime." (WHD, 71/75) His word "thinking" includes two interrelated meanings. First, it refers to the immediate experience of the manifestness of beings. Thinking, thus, means being free from discursive, categorizing activity and open for Being. Second, it refers to meditation on the historically-decisive changes in the Western understanding of Being. These two meanings of "thinking" correspond to Heidegger's distinction between the dramatic change required for a revelation of Being and the philosophical venture required to express that revelation. Although his self-understanding and philosophical vocabulary changed, his way always led through the area opened up by practical-dramatic and theoretical-ontological themes. He discovered that the more deeply he understood his own Being, the more profoundly he was able to understand the history of Being and vice-versa. Thinking was his way of life.

He offers us insight into this way in his autobiographical essay "The Pathway" (1947), which describes his long walks in the Black Forest as a youth. On those walks he sensed that if he could understand the living forest, he would have immediate access into what even the greatest thinkers and poets could only express inadequately. For it is impossible to name the "way."

The oak itself spoke: Only in such growth is grounded what lasts and fructifies. Growing means this: to open oneself up to the breadth of heaven and at the same time to sink roots into the darkness of the earth. Whatever is genuine thrives only if man does justice to both: ready for the appeal of the highest heaven, and transformed [aufgehoben] in the protection of the sustaining earth. (FW, 3/89)

Like many other German thinkers, Heidegger interpreted the history of Western man along the lines of the development of the self. Just as the self unfolds in a spiral which keeps returning to the source (dynamis) which guides and nourishes it, so, too, the history of Western man unfolds in a spiral which keeps returning to its own roots in early Greek thinking.[49] Heraclitus' insight into the Logos opened up the possibility for metaphysical thinking—the quest for the ultimate ground for reality. Metaphysical thinking, which leads to technological cultures, is not the only way to appropriate Heraclitus' thinking, however. Heidegger's own longing for roots led him to try to find a way to return Western mankind to its own proper soil. Perhaps his philosophical way can be understood as that of a therapist or healer for Western man in the grips of despair. The desperate individual is one who interprets himself solely as an ego to be defended and gratified at all costs. Not only are total security and gratification impossible, however, but the quest for them prevents the individual from gaining a genuine self-understanding. The more he strives for security, the more desperate and alienated he becomes. Because he is often unaware of his suffering, and because he can only see himself in terms of his neurotic categories, he cannot heal himself. He needs someone to point out that he is suffering and to explain its source. This theoretical insight, however, will not itself bring change. The individual has to experience for himself the truth expressed by the theory. Heidegger offered some insight to modern Western man who strives so desperately for total security by the industrial mobilization of the earth. This insight will be of no help to us, however, unless we become directly aware of our suffering and its cause. No one can say when we are destined to become so aware any more than one can predict when an individual will finally become aware of his own suffering and delusion. Heidegger knew that his words might be of no help, but he continued to speak, just as we continue to offer whatever insight we can to a desperate friend, even though we know he may not hear us.

In "The Pathway" Heidegger speaks of the "Simple" *(Einfache)*, the source of life for things growing along the pathway *(Tao, Logos, Ereignis)*. These things—trees, shrubs, flowers, sky, clouds, earth, mortals, and gods—speak to us along the way. "In what remains unsaid in their speech is—as Eckhardt, the old master of letter and life, says—God, only God." (FS, 4/89) Although the message of the pathway is always there for those who can hear it, modern man is deaf to it. Contemporary men "have ears only for the noise of media, which they consider almost the voice of God. So man becomes distracted and path-less." (FW, 4-5/90) As a noted Buddhist scholar has remarked, "The Dharma [cosmic ordering] cannot be heard in a world dominated by modern science and technical progress."[50] Like the self-ignorant man distracted by extraneous affairs, Western mankind is distracted by the activity of production for its own sake. We are presently on a wayward path, but can return if we hearken to those who call us back to the right way.

In his younger days, Heidegger was apparently convinced that his philosophical activity was destined to have world-historical importance. In 1927 he described philosophy in a manner which reflected his own will to achieve an understanding of Being: "[Philosophy] is the independent, free, fundamental struggle *[grundsätzliche Kampf]* of human existence with the darkness constantly breaking out within it." (PIK, 2) His heroic self-conception led to his engagement with National Socialism, an engagement which helped modify that self-conception. The philosopher, too, must learn about the meaning of life by experiencing it, not just by reading about it. Heidegger might have been speaking for himself when, in his "Dialogue on a Country Path about Thinking," he has the scientist say:

> As I see more clearly just now, all during our conversation I have been waiting for the arrival of the nature of thinking. But waiting itself has become clearer to me now and therewith this too, that presumably *we all become more waitful along our path.* (G, 43/69—emphasis mine)

In the same dialogue, the interlocutors speak of the difficulty of weaning themselves from will. The teacher remarks: "If only I possessed already the right releasement, then I would soon be freed from that task of weaning." (G, 32/60) Heidegger's personal growth inevitably affected his philosophical thinking. As he matured, his youthful brashness was tempered. In "Dialogue on Language," he responds in the following way to the suggestion that he was gifted with the quest for language and Being: "Who would have the audacity to claim that such a gift had come to him?" (US, 93/7) Yet he was not audacious enough to deny his real gifts; he knew both that he was a rare thinker and that he had been in some measure released from his earlier willfulness. In "The Pathway," he speaks of a "serene knowing," and remarks that "No one wins it who does not have it. Those who have it, have it from the pathway." (FW, 5/90) Serenity does not come easily or quickly, even for those who are sent along the pathway. "This knowing serenity is a gate to the eternal. Its door turns on hinges once forged out of the puzzles of Dasein by a skilled smith." (FW, 5/90) Heidegger forged those hinges; that is, he gained insight, by his struggle to understand what it means to be human. He learned that struggle must be transformed into detachment. What he knew only dimly became more apparent as he went along. Along the path of serene knowing, "Winter's storm encounters harvest's day, the agile excitation of Spring and the released dying of Autumn meet, the child's game and the elder's wisdom gaze at each other." (FW, 506/90)

In saying that the child's game and the elder's wisdom gaze at each other, Heidegger suggests that his philosophical activity was on its way to becoming a kind of play. In the end his thinking was not purposeful; he did not seek to change the world, or to lead a revolution. He thought just because he thought; he remained open to that which called him. His writing came to resemble the Zen master's art of archery, painting, calligraphy, or flower-arranging.[51] Painstakingly, the Zen student gains familiarity with his tools; he studies the master's work; he concentrates single-mindedly on his activity. Yet self-will continues to affect his painting or shooting, thereby spoiling the spontaneity which gives the effect which cannot be produced by sheer talent alone. Finally, after long years, he paints explosively, freshly, without a trace of ego or purpose, yet in a way which is somehow informed by the tradition. In Heidegger's case, his art was that of interpreting the tradition of Western philosophy. He was a conceptual artist. His later essays sometimes seemed to be playing with the tradition, teasing it to see what novel configurations lie hidden in it. To put it more in his language: gathered together by the stillness of the *Logos*, he became the lens through which the *Logos* could manifest itself. Heidegger hoped to burnish Western thinking, which hitherto had only let *Logos* shine "as in a glass darkly."[52] He did not come to thoughts; they came to him. He was drawn along the paths which lead nowhere *(Holzwege)*, and he left signs along the way *(Wegmarken)* for those who want to go along the way, too. Each must go his own way, however. Hence, one does Heidegger an injustice by treating his thinking as merely an object of scholarship. "Few are experienced enough in the difference between an object of scholarship and a matter of thought." (AED, 9/5) Thinking only occurs when one takes the risk of undergoing an experience with thinking. This means that one must be prepared to sacrifice his "self" in order to be open for Being. In the eclipse of the self there occurs the dawning of Being. According to Heidegger, who has been aptly called the "planetary thinker in the age of *Technik*,"[53] the eclipse of subjectivism is necessary if there is to be a new dawn for the evening-land (West: *Abendland*). Rebirth requires that we become again as children—ready for play, but with wisdom—ready to listen. There is no guarantee that rebirth will come. But in the darkness of despair, who of us believed he would ever recover? To recover means to become whole, holy, and healthy once again. Recovery comes on its own, although our efforts are somehow also necessary. Releasement from the suffering caused by egoism comes from a source so deep that, when it touches us, we are led to exclaim:

> That a thinking is, ever and suddenly—
> whose amazement could ever fathom it?
> (AED, 21/11)

Appendix: Authenticity in Light of Heidegger's *Gesamtausgabe**

ALTHOUGH HEIDEGGER was never an existentialist in the way Sartre was, and even though already in the 1920s he was seeking a way beyond the subjectivism of modern philosophy, nevertheless he regarded authentic existence as a crucial aspect of ontology. During his years at the University of Marburg (1923–28), he claimed that anticipatory resoluteness or authentic Being-towards-death is a necessary condition for experiencing Being in a philosophically primordial way. Authenticity is a prerequisite for genuine ontology! If some particular individual does not make the *existentiell* (concrete) decision to endure the anxiety involved in becoming open for Being, no ontology is ever achieved. If human *Dasein* were pure intellect or absolute spirit, there would be no need for this *existentiell* element in ontology. Since *Dasein* is essentially finite, individual, and historical, however, the existential-ontological can only be reached by way of the *existentiell*-ontical. To be sure, "authenticity" (*Eigentlichkeit*) primarily means the "moment of truth" (*Augenblick*) when Being manifests itself in a decisive way, but "authenticity" also refers to what occurs when a particular *Dasein* resolves to become the site for that "moment of truth."

Joseph P. Fell remarks that even if the later Heidegger was right in saying that even *Being and Time* was Being-centered and not man-centered, "this cannot mean that the human being can be left out of an ontological study, for it is the human being who asks about Being and the human being to whom beings appear as beings, i.e., in their Being."[1] What is essential to

*A slightly altered version of this Appendix appeared in *International Philosophical Quarterly*. XXIV, No. 3 (September, 1984), pp. 219–236. Grateful acknowledgement is made to the journal's editor, W. Norris Clarke, for allowing the essay to be reprinted in its present form.

the human being is not ego, personality, or psychological traits, but *Dasein* as the temporal-historical opening or clearing for Being. Yet since Being is always the Being of *a* being, *Dasein* is always yours or mine. For Heidegger, this fact means that philosophy always stems from concrete life-concerns: "A philosophical reflection neither falls from heaven nor is it an arbitrarily thought-out undertaking; rather, it arises, as does all knowledge, from factical Dasein and its everydayness" (L, 248).[2] Moreover, "One can never philosophize 'in general', but instead every genuine philosophical problem is always an individually determined one" (MAL, 8). For Heidegger, the *existentiell* dimension of *Dasein* is not reducible to the merely psychological or subjective, but constitutes the way *Dasein* really exists: as this or that concrete individual. As an aspect of the very Being of human *Dasein*, the *existentiell* element must be taken into account when doing fundamental ontology, i.e., when interpreting the conditions necessary for the possibility of understanding Being.

Heidegger's concern for factical life-experience reflects in part his early religious interests. Though he imported de-mythologized religious notions into his philosophical work, he also rejected his former submission to religious doctrine. In so doing, however, he overemphasized the role of the individual's will in attaining authentic openness for Being.[3] This is true in spite of the fact that during his Marburg years, he talked as if authenticity means submission to the claims of one's own Being and, hence, to the claims of Being as such. The "subjectivistic" dimension of his early thought lies not only in its debt to transcendental philosophy, but also in its voluntaristic tone. During the 1920s, he spoke at times as if the loss of meaning brought about by the death of God could only be restored "without ground by a transcendental-subjective faith, will, or choice in independence of any past."[4] Karl Löwith, a student of Heidegger's during the 1920s, reports that

> . . . it was no mere misunderstanding when so many hearers of Heidegger's lectures and readers of *Being and Time* understood the author at that time other than he understands himself today [1953], namely as the composer—attuned to Kierkegaard, Pascal, Luther, and Augustine—of an irreligious [*ungläubigen*] "analytic of Dasein," and not as a mystic of Being who, supposedly already in *Being and Time*, had left all "subjectivity" of man behind him.[5]

In opposition to his colleagues who regarded philosophy as the cognitive activity of a worldless ego-subject, Heidegger insisted that philosophy radically transforms the philosopher. He understood philosophy not only in the context of "scientific" (*wissenschaftlich*) discipline, but also in the context of the spiritual quest for wholeness and redemption. Indeed, he believed that philosophical rigor is only possible for the one who exists authentically. For example, the phenomenological *epoché*—as Heidegger understood it—can only be carried out by a phenomenologist who is prepared to remain in the disclosive mood of *Angst*. In *Angst*, as worldly involvements with entities fall away against the background of no-thingness, Being manifests itself. For Heidegger, of course, the true "object" of phenomenology is Being. Those who pursue Being must be prepared to face the truth about their own mortality. Scholars who come to Heidegger's work through Husserl's are often uncomfortable with talk about authenticity and Being-towards-death. They prefer to see him in terms more consistent with the detached, scholarly life-style and bearing of the dignified German Professor. But Heidegger was not cut from this mold. The fact is that he regarded most of his professional colleagues somewhat contemptuously as being incapable of hearing the truth about Being. For him, many were called to be philosophical scholars, but few were chosen to be true thinkers. Conceptual hairsplitting can be done from nine to five without ruffling one's suit-coat, but real philosophy demands a change in one's very existence.

The young Heidegger's existentialist-sounding insistence on *existentiell* resolve as a pre-condition for ontology arises in part from his debt to transcendental philosophy and to humanism in general. He spoke at times as if the disclosure of Being were an achievement of *human* history, instead of as an event within the "history of Being." And in one set of lectures from the 1920s, he even says that it is for the sake of human *Dasein* itself or "human life" (*menschliches Leben*) that *Dasein* poses the questions of Being and truth (L, 50). But Heidegger's interest in authenticity cannot be explained solely in terms of his early work with transcendental philosophy and historicism. If he later shifted emphasis from human *Dasein* to Being as such, he did not thereby simply abandon his interest in the issue of "authenticity." Instead, he reformulated it in a non-voluntaristic, non-humanistic way. It is this voluntarism and self-assertiveness that gives an existentialist flavor to his early concept of authenticity developed during the Marburg years. No matter how much his thought may have changed over the years and in spite of his own claims about what he really meant during the 1920s, the fact remained that he spoke at that time as if decisiveness and resoluteness were an integral aspect of doing genuine philosophy.

The voluntaristic tone of his early conception of philosophy is discernible in all his Marburg lectures. One day, for example, he announced that philosophy

> . . . is a matter of the highest personal *freedom*. . . . [O]ne can freely seize upon [philosophy] as the most radical necessity of human existence, however, only when the individual existence understands itself—but that always means: has resolved to understand itself (L, 39).

Paradoxically, true freedom is a kind of self-assertive decision to be who we already are. Authenticity means owning oneself, taking responsibility for being this particular mortal openness. In becoming who I already am, I become engaged in my own finite possibilities. The existential-ontological dimension of authenticity, then, is always linked with the existential-ontological, though in a way that is difficult to specify. One writer concludes that authenticity

> . . . suggests either one's own true, but hidden, and not faced, way of being or a form of self-coincidence in which a human being's particular *existentiell* actions are brought into explicit accord with one's own real *existential* structure, which is the very possibility of those particular actions.[6]

Philosophy is the highest form of human existence because the philosopher chooses existentielly to disclose the existential conditions needed for the possibility of such a choice. Hence, the existence of the authentic philosopher constitutes the hermeneutic circle. For the young Heidegger, the true philosopher risks everything in the attempt to understand what it means "to be."

With regard to Heidegger's concept of authenticity during his years at Marburg, I argue a two-fold thesis: first, that his concept of authenticity included a voluntaristic strain that explains how he could have been labeled an "existentialist"; second, that already in the late 1920s he was casting about for a way beyond such voluntarism, though it was to be some time before he found an adequate way of expressing himself. Eventually, he replaced the notion of authenticity as resolute disclosedness (*Entschlossenheit*) with the notion of authenticity as releasement (*Gelassenheit*). The latter lacks the element of self-will found in the former. In his later years, Heidegger at times seemed to acknowledge this subjectivistic or voluntaristic strain, but at other times he denied it was ever there. I shall let the lectures from the 1920s speak for themselves in support of my thesis.

At least two objections can be raised against my thesis. The first is that Heidegger was never interested in authenticity, if understood as the resolute decision of the individual *Dasein*;[7] the second is that even if he did have such an interest, it certainly did not include any voluntaristic or existentialistic dimension. The first group of critics often approach Heidegger's thought in light of structuralism, post-structuralism, language theory, and semiotics, most of which are influenced by Heidegger's later thought and which minimize the importance of the individual. The "deconstruction" of the metaphysics of the subject initiated in *Being and Time*, and later played out in post-structuralism, is used by many commentators to justify the view that Heidegger's early account of authentic individuation is really an oblique way of speaking about events in the "history of Being." Such commentators, however, confuse the young Heidegger's deconstruction of the Cartesian ego with the outright volatilizing of the individual *Dasein*. As we shall see, during the 1920s he was very concerned with the relation between authentic individuation and the possibility of genuine ontology. Throughout his career, moreover, he insisted that understanding Being requires an *experience* that cannot be gained from conceptual thought which is inherently dualistic. If such experience does not happen to an ego or subject, nevertheless it happens through an individual chosen as the site for the self-disclosure of Being. While discussing Heraclitus' thought in 1943, Heidegger remarked that

> . . . we can never take this knowledge of the essence of truth from the text of the first thinker of the Greeks as from a [seminar] protocol. If we ourselves have not first arrived in the nearness of Being from originary experiences [*Erfahrungen*], our ear remains deaf for the originary Word of the originary thinkers (H, 176).

The second group of critics acknowledges that Heidegger did speak about authenticity, but never in a voluntaristic way. They correctly note that the "turn" in his thought was a maturing and not an abrupt about-face, but they refuse to admit that there are any differences between pre- and post-turn Heidegger. Yet I contend that one such difference is the voluntarism which is apparent from the way he spoke in his Marburg lectures. While *Entschlossenheit* can be interpreted as an earlier expression of *Gelassenheit*, as Heidegger himself tries to do in his later reflections on his earlier work, the fact remains that during the 1920s he emphasized the *decisional* character as well as the disclosive character of *Entschlossenheit*.

The first part of this essay explains how Heidegger's early religious concerns helped give rise to his conviction that there is an intrinsic relation between rigorous philosophy and authentic existence on the part of the philosopher. The second part will consider the difference between the submissiveness of the religious person and the self-assertiveness of the philosopher. In part three, we shall see that in the late 1920s Heidegger was seeking a non-voluntaristic way of expressing the nature of the decision that permits a new disclosure of Being. Taking his cue in part from religious doctrine, he suggested that the initiative for the disclosure of Being comes not from the human individual, but from Being itself. While trying to move beyond the voluntaristic-humanistic Scylla, he also hoped to avoid the nihilistic Charybdis. One of his aims in the 1920s was to find a way out of the nihilism arising from the destruction of the Christian-Platonic table of values ("God"). His solution, however, calls for resolute disclosure of one's own mortality—disclosure of the no-thingness that would seem to render meaningless all worldly aims and deeds. It is not clear that Heidegger completely eschewed the path later taken by Sartre and Camus, who call for heroic self-assertion in the face of the meaninglessness exposed by mortality. In the final part of this essay, I raise some questions about the notion that a true philosopher must exist authentically.

I. Heidegger's Move From Religion To Philosophy

The young Heidegger was concerned about how to exist authentically in relation to the transcendent, whether this was God or Being.[8] Torn between submitting to the Word of God or striking out on the road of free philosophical inquiry, he chose to train for a time with the Jesuits, famous for their religious and intellectual discipline. Although he eventually abandoned his faith when he concluded that it impeded his quest to disclose the "sense of Being," he nevertheless imported into his philosophical life an interest in authenticity analogous to his desire for religious justification. Between 1916 and 1919, he apparently moved from Catholicism to Protestantism. For a while liberal Protestantism proved more satisfactory to the intellectually curious Heidegger than had Catholicism. What he said in 1925 about Franz Brentano could probably just as well have been said about himself:

> Inner difficulties of the Catholic system of belief, above all the mystery of the Trinity and in the seventies the declaration of the infallibility of the Pope, drove him out of his spiritual world. He took with him, however, a wholly determined horizon and a reverence for Aristotle and lived now in the direction of a free, not bound, philosophical science (ZB, 23).

Heidegger was attracted to Protestantism partly because it renounced the need for sacramental-priestly mediation between the individual and God. While Catholicism promises that the use of the sacraments ("good works") leads to salvation, Protestantism claims that only God's grace can save. Yet while at first emphasizing the saving power of grace, Protestant theology eventually had to provide some role for human volition in accepting this divine gift. In the 1920s, Heidegger's colleague at Marburg, Paul Tillich, proclaimed that decision "is the fundamental activity of Protestantism."[9] The young Heidegger believed that decisiveness and resoluteness are just as important in philosophy as they are in faith. Access to ontological truth is possible "only where the individual in the core of his Dasein, from inner choice and penetrating struggle or from an inconceivable inner struggle, has won a fundamental relation to this context" (L, 15). Philosophical knowledge is only as valid as is the philosopher's insight into the limits of his own mortal existence.

By the early 1920s, influenced by the Christian skepticism of Hans Oeverbeck, Heidegger had lost his faith altogether and began asserting his independence from theological structures.[10] Those familiar with his later writings, which suggest that genuine thinking may prepare the way for a renewal of the experience of the divine, would have been surprised to hear him say in 1925:

> *Philosophical investigation is and remains atheism;* for this reason it can achieve for itself the "measure of thinking." Not only will it achieve this for itself, but it is the inner necessity and authentic strength of philosophy. And precisely in this atheism will it become what a great thinker once said, a "joyful science" (ZB, 109)

Despite asserting that philosophy is atheism, he nevertheless tried to extract universal philosophical truths from their religious contexts. He felt justified in doing so because theology and philosophy had been intertwined for so long:

> Not only in the Middle Ages, but the whole of modern philosophy is incomprehensible in its problematic and would be absolutely impossible without the doctrinal content of Christian dogmatics. On the other hand, the doctrinal content of this Christian dogmatics—with regard to its conceptual nature and its scientific character—is wholly and absolutely determined by philosophy and by that of current philosophy (L, 233).

During the 1920s Heidegger claimed that St. Paul's notion of *kairos* ("time of fulfillment") presupposes the ontological event of authentic temporality;[11] he studied Luther, Calvin, Zwingli, Barth, Kierkegaard, Scotus, Aquinas, and Augustine, the last-named of whom provided him with the idea of care (*Sorge*) (ZB, 418) and curiosity (*Neugier*) (ZB, 379–380); he worked closely with Rudolf Bultmann to explain the ontological conception of human existence presupposed by the New Testament;[12] and he noted approvingly that for Augustine and Pascal love and hate are more fundamental than knowledge (ZB, 222; MAL, 169). Yet despite these, and many more, debts to theology, he distinguished it sharply from philosophy. In his 1925 lectures, while discussing the phenomena of falling and inauthenticity, he proclaimed:

> It is to be stressed here that the explication of these structures of Dasein has nothing to do with a doctrine of the sinfulness of human nature or any theory of original sin. What is set forth here is a purely structural consideration which lies *before all* other kinds of considerations. It is to be set apart wholly and sharply from a theological consideration. It is possible, perhaps necessary, that all these structures be turned back into a theological anthropology, but I cannot judge how, because I understand nothing about such things [!] (ZB, 391).

Later in the same lectures, he claims that both Husserl and Scheler neglected *die Seinsfrage* because of the hidden influence of theological themes on their work. Husserl was led astray by Descartes, whose Scholastic tendencies were far removed from the Greek origins of the Western understanding of Being. Scheler was also misled by Christian theology which defined man as transcendent only in the sense that he reaches out for or is made in the image of the transcendent God. Scheler's "theomorphism," like Kant's rational definition of the person, takes up "the old Christian definition of man, only de-theologized in a certain way" (ZB, 182). We are told that this development results not so much from the failings of particular thinkers, but from the fact that historical *Dasein* tends to conceal the truth (ZB, 179). Yet Heidegger also suggests that individuals are expected to struggle against this tendency. Hence, he asserts that

> This merely rough characterization [of the decline of awareness about the question of the sense of Being] is provided simply to let the omission concealed in the critique be understood—not as an easily correctible "failure," but as the power of historical Dasein which we are damned or called to be. To the last named alternative, one can only answer from personal conviction; no scientific judgment is possible here. Perhaps even the alternative is not a pure one (ZB, 182).

One way of interpreting this cryptic passage is as follows: according to Christian theology, a person is damned if he fails to submit to the Will of God; he is saved if he accepts God's law and, thereby, renounces his rebellion against God. In contrast, however, Heidegger implies that a philosopher is damned ontologically (cut off from the experience of Being) if he submits to Christian theology, and is saved only if he renounces it. Atheism is salvation for the philosopher; faith is his damnation. Because theology captured ontology so long ago, the history of metaphysics has concealed the primordial Greek experience of Being. Thus, paradoxically, metaphysics is the history of philosophical damnation. Renewing philosophy requires that theological impediments be removed.

In his Kant-lectures from 1927–28; Heidegger makes an assertion that contrasts starkly with Christian man's presuppositions: "The understanding of Being makes possible the existing relations of Dasein to its current world and to itself. The understanding of Being is accordingly the most primordial condition of the possibility of human *existence*" (PIK, 38; cf. also MAL, 20). If the understanding of Being (*not* the creating act of God) is the primordial condition for the possibility of human existence, then understanding that understanding—i.e., the very act of doing philosophy—must be the highest form of human existence: "Philosophy belongs to the most primordial human efforts [*Bemühungen*] (PIK, 1).

> In *ontology*, i.e., *philosophy*, Being becomes explicitly, purposely, and thematically grasped as an object. That is, accordingly, the freely seized task of the il-

luminating and structuring of the understanding of Being belonging to the essence of human existence. Precisely because, however, the understanding of Being in general, be it pre-ontological or ontological, is the most primordial and necessary condition of the possibility of human existence, precisely for this reason is the seizing of the task of its illumination, i.e., philosophy, the freest possibility of human existence. Only where the most primordial necessity binds, only there is the highest freedom possible (PIK, 38).

True freedom is the freedom to bind oneself to necessity, i.e., the freedom to choose to be who one already *is*. For Heidegger, we *are* always already openness for Being. We are "lost" (inauthentic) if we flee from or conceal this openness, and "saved" (authentic) if we choose it. He left religious faith behind once he realized that it did not permit him to make a sufficiently *radical* choice. His desire to proclaim his independence from dogma partly explains the self-assertiveness that one finds in his Marburg lectures. This self-assertiveness, however, sprang not only from his rejection of faith, but also from his conviction that only decisive resolve could enable someone to stand up to the *Angst* necessary for the revelation of Being. Yet since resolute decision to be open for one's own mortal no-thingness is a choice to be who one already is, this decision is one of choosing to submit to one's own Being. In the next part of this essay, we shall see that Heidegger's 1928 lectures analyze the struggle needed for the philosopher to live up to his calling to be open for Being. Although much of Heidegger's concept of authentic decision was derived from de-mythologized religious doctrines, he omitted the doctrine of "grace," the divine gift that offers justification. In part three, we shall learn that in the same 1928 lectures he began looking for something like an ontological analogue to grace, an analogue that eventually became *Gelassenheit*.

II. Genuine Philosophizing and Authentic Existence

Heidegger's most sustained account of the relation between philosophy and authenticity is found in his 1928 lectures, which are ostensibly devoted to the metaphysical origins of logic with special reference to Leibniz. In these lectures, which often seem to be replying to criticisms of *Being and Time* (1927), he begins by reaffirming the need for resoluteness on the part of the individual philosopher; then he warns us not to confuse the attainment of personal authenticity with the true goal of philosophy—ontology;

finally, he seeks a non-voluntaristic way of expressing how it happens that *Dasein* can experience the Being of beings in an originary or authentic way.

He begins by noting that a truly philosophical logic is impossible unless we have an adequate understanding of philosophy:

> To create for the hearer a preview [of the nature of philosophy] we will do well to acquaint ourselves in a wholly preparatory way about the idea of philosophy. This is demanded not only with regard to the particular course of these lectures, but still more with reference to the fact that you have made your own Dasein ready for the sciences and that always means, whether explicitly or not, for philosophy. How far that happens and has happened from inner freedom, whether behind this decision stands a real will, how far in general the realm of this form of Dasein in the university as such is clear, or is consciously left in darkness and indifference—all that is a matter for individuals (MAL, 9).

The activity of philosophy, we are told, occurs within the "moment of truth" (*Augenblick*) that recalls the ontological origins of the Western metaphysical tradition. The term "moment of truth" is used in *Being and Time* to describe the authentic temporality needed for Being to manifest itself primordially. But if philosophy itself takes the form of a moment of vision, the *explanation* of philosophy as such

> . . . is also one that recollects within the moment of truth. Here there stands a primordial unity, namely *that of the temporality of the factical Dasein doing the philosophy*. The whole problem must be expounded from this unity. For what is to be recollected, only the properly free project is suitable . . . (MAL, 10— my emphasis).

To gain insight into the truth, the individual philosopher must exist as authentic temporality. Radical self-change is needed for the one who pursues the deepest insight: "Philosophy . . . is not the name for any knowing that could be passsed around arbitrarily; no possession of men of knowledge and teachers. Philosophy must be sought essentially, i.e., its objects must be fundamentally 'hard-earned' [*erworben*]" (MAL, 15). Philosophy's proper "object" is, of course, Being as such, but from Parmenides to Hegel the *self* is always involved in this effort to understand.

> The struggle for Being drives itself onto the field of thinking, of asserting, of the soul, of subjectivity. . . . Human Dasein moves into the center! Why that? Is it an accident that the struggle is shoved onto this field? . . . Is it a particular

rapture for the interiority of the soul or a particularly high estimate of the free personality, or a blind subjectivism which is this fundamental problem chooses human Dasein as such for the battleground? None of these! But instead, the content of the fundamental problem itself and only this demands this battleground, makes human Dasein itself the exemplary field (MAL, 19).

Ontology is a kind of warfare occurring within the realm of human existence, for it is only in and through such existence that Being can manifest itself. It human existence is not purged of impediments to the truth, Being cannot reveal itself primordially. The issue here is not a psychological one, but an ontological one. The philosopher must be willing to move from self-objectifying subjectivism to openness that submits to Being. For Heidegger, those guilty of psychologizing are precisely the ones who think that the rational ego-subject is the foundation for ontological truth. Only acceptance of one's mortality can break the tenacious grip of the ego, whose primary aim is survival, *not* disclosure of the truth. Heidegger proclaims dramatically:

That in the fundamental ontological question of philosophy it is, in some sense, a question about the whole of being and also about human existence, so that therein is always decided the existence of the one doing the philosophizing, this is expressed in Aristotle by saying that 'first philosophy' is also *theologica*. Philosophy is in its innermost ground the most radical, universal, and most strictly conceived knowledge—but the truth of this knowledge is no free-floating, arbitrarily knowable proposition about just any state of affairs. The touchstone of philosophical truth lies only in the fidelity of the individual philosopher to himself.

We do not philosophize in order to become philosophers, but just as little to create for ourselves and others a saving world-view that one can don like a hat and coat. The goal of philosophy is not a system of science, nor a sentimental edifice for vacillating souls. Only he can philosophize who has already decided to grant to Dasein in its radical and universal-essential possibilities the free dignity which alone makes it appropriate to withstand the constant insecurity and the rift torn open . . . (MAL, 21–22).

Philosophy does not provide insight into how to live, but is *itself* the authentic way of life for the philosopher. The philosopher is all that a human being can be: resolutely open for Being. The true philosopher gains ontological insight through free resolution: "(1) philosophy is rigorous conceptual knowledge of Being. (2) But it is such only if this conceiving is in itself the philosophical grasping of Dasein in freedom" (MAL, 23).

Later in his 1928 lectures, Heidegger considers in more detail the relation between the *existentiell* decision of the philosopher to do philosophy, and the existential-ontological results gained thereby. Although convinced that the individual must in some sense choose to become the site for the revelation of Being, Heidegger also wanted to avoid the charge that his philosophy was a heroic, but nihilistic "existentialism." The philosopher does not merely choose to be who he already is, but does so in order to become open for what transcends him or her: Being as such. Authentic self-choosing is a revelation not of one's particular psychological make-up, personality, or subjective preferences, but instead a revelation of the *Being* of human Dasein as such. Resolute *Dasein* gains insight into this "neutral-ontological" dimension of its Being. But Heidegger adds that "This neutral Dasein is never the one existing; Dasein always only exists in its factical concreteness" (MAL, 172). Put in language that is not entirely accurate: Heidegger, the heir of Aristotle, insisted that the ontological "form" is always instantiated in some particular individual. In the following passage, he informs us of how the particular philosopher gains insight into this neutral-ontological structure;

> Because Dasein always exists as itself, and [because] self-Being as existing *is* only in its execution, accordingly the project of the ontological-fundamental constitution of Dasein must always arise from the construction of a most extreme possibility of an authentic and whole possibility of the Being of Dasein. The direction of the project concerns Dasein as a whole and the fundamental determination of its wholeness, although ontically it is only as existing. Otherwise put: the winning of metaphysical neutrality and the isolating of Dasein is in general possible only on the basis of the existentiell *beginning* of the one doing the projecting (MAL, 175–176).

Inquiry into the Being of *Dasein*, or into Being as such, must begin with someone who actually does the inquiring. In his own way, Heidegger criticizes the "idealistic" view of philosophy that Marx also condemned in his critique of Hegelianism. Yet Heidegger also warns us not to confuse the *existentiell* resolution with the ontological goal:

> The concreteness of the analysis of the phenomenon of Dasein . . . easily leads [one] to take this concrete phenomenon of Dasein first for itself, and second, in its extreme fundamental-ontologically conditioned constitution: to absolutize it on the reverse side as existentiell. The more radical the existentiell beginning,

the more concrete the ontological-metaphysical project; the more concrete, however, this interpretation of Dasein, the easier the principal misunderstanding—that the existentiell beginning as such is the essential and primary thing, while the project it reveals itself precisely in its personal unimportance (MAL, 176).

Later on, Heidegger repeats the claim that understanding *Dasein*'s Being is not merely a personal endeavor, but is the task to which *Dasein* as such is summoned:

If we say: Dasein is essentially always mine, and if the task is to determine Dasein ontologically on the basis of this character, this does not mean the essence of myself as this factical individual or of somebody else should be investigated. *The object of the question is not the individual essence of myself, but the essence of mineness and selfhood in general* . . . (MAL, 242).

Yet philosophy can only move toward its ontological goal by way of the particular individual who seeks to understand his own existential-ontological (not psychological) constitution. The *existentiell* emphasis in *Daseinanalysis* leads only to the *appearance* or *semblance* of "an extremely individualistic, radical atheism . . ." (MAL, 177). Resoluteness, then, is not "a solipsistic-egoistic drawing back in upon oneself . . ." (MAL, 244). Indeed, the authentic individual "chooses authentic *Mitsein* with others, and its *Sein-bei* other non-Daseinlike beings" (MAL, 244). But Heidegger hastens to add that "How far that [choosing of Dasein] succeeds is not a question of metaphysics, but a question of and matter for individuals . . ." (MAL, 245). And earlier he remarked that "To what extent . . . in the metaphysical project and the *existentiell* beginning of philosophy there also lies an existentiell achievement, and indeed an indirect one, that is a proper problem" (MAL, 175).

The issues here are reminiscent of the ones faced by monks seeking to discover the Divine within themselves. They must begin by working on themselves just as they are, in their own concrete situation, but their aim is not to dwell upon their particular traits and preferences. Instead, they seek the Divine present in *all* human beings. In surpassing the limits of ego, they attain true openness that includes ego within it. The enlightened monk becomes himself or herself (as openness) only by surpassing himself or herself (as ego). Something of the same problem faces the individual who sets out to do philosophy. Hence, Heidegger says that only the one who understands "the art of existing" can discover the universal truth that manifests itself within mortal limits (MAL, 201).

We can draw this parallel between Heidegger's philosophical way and the religious way because he himself drew inspiration from what he learned as a practicing Christian. The difference is that while the philosopher becomes fully human only in choosing to submit to his or her own ontological possibility, the religious individual becomes fully human only in choosing to submit to the Creator. According to the theologian, we are motivated to make such a choice by our innate love of God, a love that is always threatened by willful love of self. According to Heidegger, however, the motive for choosing to be oneself is ontological, not religious. Speaking in the tradition of Kant and Aristotle, he asserts that

> . . . metaphysics belongs to the nature of man. And thus human Dasein, in accordance with its essence, has a pre-love for metaphysics. We can even say: all existing is already philosophizing. Philosophy . . . is not to be derived from somewhere else, but grounds itself. This happens, however, such that *philosophy belongs essentially to the selfhood of Dasein* (MAL, 274).

The philosopher is fully himself: finite-mortal openness for Being. This means that the individual philosopher is not merely open for Being as such, considered as some sort of abstraction, but is open to the Being of the beings in his or her own particular situation. True philosophizing brings one right into the concreteness and exigencies of everyday life.

At this time, Heidegger's conception of the decisional character of philosophy was characterized by a curious ambivalence. On the one hand, he noted that resoluteness means submitting to our highest calling: to let beings be; on the other hand, and in contrast to the religious tone of the talk of "letting be," he insisted that resoluteness is the free self-assertion of Dasein. The following passage reveals the submissive aspect of his notion of resoluteness:

> . . . should Dasein win itself in its authenticity, and thus exclusively and primarily be fallen into the world, it is necessary that Dasein—in order to win itself—must have already lost itself; it must have lost itself namely in the sense that it stands in the possibility of being able to give up all worldly gains and possessions.

> This peculiar ontological connection that subsists between the authenticity of the Being of Dasein and falling concern has experienced a particular determination in Christianity and in the Christian interpretation of Dasein. But this structure should not be understood as if it belonged specifically to the consciousness of Christian Dasein, but instead lies in the things themselves [*die Dingen*]. Insofar as Dasein in itself *qua* care has this structure, there subsists the possibility of a specifically Christian interpretation of Dasein, and accordingly the working out of these structures, which we do not follow further here, is completely isolated from all orientation to any dogmatic whatsoever (L, 232).

Here Heidegger appropriates the New Testament notion that in order to gain everything, one must give up everything. To be authentic *Dasein* must stop clinging to beings and submit to its own essential no-thingness. *Dasein* is called to authenticity by its conscience, which no one can command to call. One can only resolve to be ready to respond if it does call. Authenticity occurs when *Dasein* lets temporality generate itself authentically, just as, for the Christian, regeneration involves a transformation of time (*kairos*) with which the individual is summoned to cooperate.[13]

The religious overtones of "letting be" seem to disappear in Heidegger's 1927 lecture on "Phenomenology and Theology." Here we learn that the philosopher makes a self-assertive response to conscience that is quite foreign to the faithful person's response to grace. While faith demands unquestioning submission, philosophy involves "the free questioning of purely self-reliant [*auf sich gestellten*] Dasein."[14]

> . . . *faith*, as a specific possibility of existence, is in its innermost core the mortal enemy of the form of existence that is an essential part of philosophy and which is in fact everchanging. Faith is so absolutely the mortal enemy [*der Todfeind*] that philosophy does not even begin to want to do battle with it![15]

Heidegger later recognized that in his notion of self-affirmative freedom, he had overemphasized not only human will but also humanity itself. By saying in 1928 that *Dasein* wills to uncover the being of beings, that "The question of Being . . . is at bottom the correctly understood question about man," and that "Human Dasein bears in itself, in its most proper history, the fate of philosophy itself" (MAL, 20)—in saying all this, he overestimated the role of humanity in the history of Being. Eventually he made it clear that the history of Being is guided by Being itself, not by humanity. Human beings cannot resolve or will to disclose Being; instead,

Being reveals itself in its own time, independently of human initiative. But in the 1920s, as the following passage plainly shows, Heidegger was still torn between defining resoluteness as wilfull uncovering and as letting-be:

> *Scientific* knowledge . . . is determined by the fact that the existing Dasein posits for itself as a freely chosen task the uncovering of the already somehow accessible being *in order to will its being-uncovered.* The free seizing of the possibility of such an uncovering—as a task of existence—is, as a seizing of the uncovering of the being in itself, a free self-binding to the uncovered being as such. . . . In this case, the struggle is directed solely to the being itself and solely in order to tear it from its hiddenness and thereby precisely to help it into its own, i.e., to let it be the being which it is in itself (PIK, 26).

In the final portion of his 1928 lectures, Heidegger searches for a non-voluntaristic way of explaining how Dasein can freely choose to bind itself to being who it already is: openness for Being.

III. Toward the Non-Voluntaristic Concept of Freedom and Authenticity

Partly as the result of abandoning his faith, the young Heidegger over-emphasized the importance of will in the attainment of authenticity. He suggested that human *Dasein* could become authentically human by dint of its own resolve, without divine assistance. Even to theologians sympathetic to Heidegger, his concept of authenticity had the earmarks of pride. Rudolf Bultmann remarked:

> If the authentic life of man is one of self-commitment, then that life is missed not only by the blatantly self-assertive but also by those who try to achieve self-commitment by their own efforts. They fail to see that self-commitment can only be received as a gift from God.
> . . . In Heidegger's case the perversity of such an attitude is less obvious because he does not characterize resolve as self-commitment. But it is clear that the shouldering of the accident of his destiny in the face of death is really the same radical self-assertion on man's part.[16]

Though it would take several more years before Heidegger would be free from this voluntaristic point of view, he already knew that the key to authenticity lies in the fact that *Dasein* is most free when affirming the necessity of what transcends *Dasein*—Being. The affirmation of necessity or the

love of fate (*amor fati*), a Stoic notion revitalized by Nietzsche, bears important similarities to the Christian notion of submission to the Will of God.
Still missing in Heidegger's concept of authenticity as free affirmation of
one's mortal openness was the philosophical analogue to grace, though the
concept of conscience pointed in the right direction. In his later writings,
the analogue to grace appears as *Gelassenheit*, which is linked to the idea of
Ereignis. *Ereignis* refers, in part, to the appropriation (*Vereignen*) of human existence by and for Being.[17] After the "turn" in his thinking, Heidegger maintained that authenticity (*Eigentlichkeit*) occurs when a thinker
or poet is released from subjectivism-voluntarism and is appropriated or
enowned (*ereignet*) by and for *Ereignis*.

According to Medard Boss, the Swiss psychiatrist for whose students
Heidegger gave seminars for seventeen years, Heidegger's insight into
Ereignis was not merely a conceptual event, but a personal enlightenment
experience as well. Boss informs us that for years, Heidegger repeatedly
dreamed that at his high school matriculation exam a group of teachers
grilled him mercilessly. By working with Boss, he gradually came to see
that his dream expressed in a disguised way that

> . . . he had long been examined out of the center of his being, which consisted
> primarily of a fundamental ability to think. It brought him suffering enough,
> that in his waking state he was exposed to the never slackening demand emanat-
> ing from this center of this being that he endure and pass the maturity examina-
> tion of his philosophizing. However, his dreaming vision was so highly con-
> stricted that of all possible examinations of maturity only that of his high school
> matriculation examination could occur to him. His own proper and fundamen-
> tal self-realization was evidently reached with his waking discernment of that
> state of affairs which revealed itself to him as "*das Ereignis*". . . . If this
> lightning-like revelation of "*das Ereignis*" had not corresponded to the true
> completion of his selfhood, how could it be at all comprehensible that Hei-
> degger forthwith not only never again dreamt of having to stand the scrutiny of
> his examining high school professors, but, now waking, found his way out of
> his earlier constant pressure to think, and into a wise, serene composure in the
> depths of his heart.[18]

If Boss is correct, Heidegger's early account of philosophy was influenced by his fear of failure. He drove himself relentlessly because he felt that
a great deal was expected of him. Finally, the "lightning-like" event of
releasement freed him from his compulsiveness. As I have argued earlier,

the "turn" in his thinking corresponded with a decisive "turn" in his life.[19] Let us now see to what extent his final lectures at Marburg point the way toward that turn.

Human *Dasein*, Heidegger informed his students in 1928, is not an abstract clearing for Being; instead, *Dasein* is always individualized— "mine." *Dasein* is transcendent not only in the sense that it stands out from itself (ek-sists) toward Being, but also in the sense that it transcends its present situation toward its own potentiality. *Dasein* is always an issue for itself; it is purposive, future-oriented, potentiality-for-Being (*Seinkönnen*). Because each individual is his own "for-the-sake-of-which" (*Umwillen*), each individual acts according to his or her own perception of his or her life-situation. Hence, I experience the world as a meaningful arena in which my own life-possibilities are to be worked out. My freedom lies in the fact that I can understand and fulfill my potentiality. Only because I transcend myself, i.e., because I open up the clearing in which I can act, am I free to choose myself or neglect myself. Freedom is not license. Real freedom is freedom to bind myself to my own finite possibilities. Authentic self-limitation enables me to do what is within my power and thus act in accordance with my fate. Heidegger summarizes all this by saying:

In other words: the world, primarily characterized by for-the-sake-of-which, is the primordial totality of that which Dasein as free gives itself to understand. Freedom gives itself to understand; it is the *Ur*-understanding, i.e., the *Ur*-project of that which makes it possible. In the project of for-the-sake-of-which as such, Dasein gives itself primordial *binding*. Freedom makes Dasein bound to itself in the ground of its essence, or more precisely: gives itself the possibility of binding. The whole of the binding lying in the for-the-sake-of-which is the world. According to this binding, Dasein binds itself as a potentiality-for-Being to itself as co-potentiality-for-Being with others, and in potentiality-for-Being with things present-at-hand. Selfhood is the free bindingness for and to oneself (MAL, 247).

The self to which one binds oneself is not the ego-subject, but the mortal openness in which subject and object can first appear. For the most part, *Dasein* chooses to bind itself not to its mortal openness, but to beings that appear in it. Worldly beings tempt *Dasein* to escape from the burden of openness for Being. Resolute *Dasein*, however, discloses its own mortality and thereby enables itself to understand what it itself and other beings really *are.* Yet because *Dasein's* existence is always an issue for itself, it is plagued by the question of *why* beings—including itself—*are. Dasein* always seeks the ground or reason for what is:

> Why is there something like a why and therefore? Because Dasein exists, i.e., because transcendence temporalizes itself! But transcending is the ecstatical to-be-itself in the mode of its for-the-sake-of-which. For-the-sake-of-which, as the primary character of the world, i.e., transcendence is *the Ur-phenomenon of ground in general.* (MAL, 276)

No one chooses to create himself or herself; instead, each of us is *thrown* into existence. Yet we are called on to be this temporal openness. My choice is either to be who I already am, or to conceal who I am by identifying with worldly interests. Supposedly, religious individuals choose to let Scripture tell them who they are and thus provide them with a "reason" or "basis" for life. The philosopher discovers, however, that the ultimate "reason" for his existence is not a being (God as ultimate ground or basis), but nothingness, openness, transcendence—the abyss (*Abgrund*). Only in the temporal absence of human existence can beings manifest themselves. Science gives reasons for the ways in which beings act; philosophy discloses the groundless "ground" (*Abgrund*) for all reasons. For Heidegger, "To philosophize means existing from the ground [*Grund*]" (MAL, 285), i.e., becoming the radical openness one already is. *Dasein* as the for-the-sake-of-which is the "*Ur*-phenomenon of ground in general," but this does not mean that egoistic self-interest is the highest form of human life. Quite the opposite. It means that *Dasein* is authentic only when it exists as openness in a responsible and responsive way. We are not the source of the openness into which we have been thrown; but we are called on to exist as the beings that we are. *Dasein* is the location of, but not the origin of freedom:

> The *Ur*-phenomenon of ground is the for-the-sake-of-which. The origin of "ground" lies in freedom as freedom to ground. For-the-sake-of-which, however, is the primary character of the world. World-projection in freedom is nothing other than the temporalizing of the understanding of Being. Accordingly, if ground as the for-the-sake-of-which is the primary character of the world, but if world is the Being (understood in the understanding of Being) which creates the world-entry for being, i.e., lets it be understood as being, then *"ground" belongs essentially to Being* (MAL, 282).

As Heidegger was to say many years later, freedom has nothing to do with human voluntarism but refers to the clearing that we are summoned to hold open:

> The essential nature of freedom is *originally* not coordinated with the will nor with the causality of human volition at all. Freedom governs the free in the sense of the cleared or illuminated, that is, of the unconcealed. It is the happening of unconcealing, that is, of truth, with which freedom stands in closest and most intimate affinity.[20]

Yet if true philosophy means existing from and as the *Abgrund* or abyss, how can the philosopher avoid the charge of being a nihilist? Many critics have charged that at least the early Heidegger is really no different from Sartre and Camus who called for "engagement" in the face of the absurdity of death and nothingness. Karsten Harries says that Heidegger's

> . . . view of authentic existence may suggest a heroic nihilism, a faith in the meaning of life in spite of, or perhaps rather because of a lucid awareness of the nothingness that governs human existence and that dooms man and all his projects to establish a secure dwelling place for himself to certain defeat. Perhaps this attempt to salvage victory from defeat, meaning from nothing, is peculiarly German. *Being and Time* reads in places as if Heidegger had been inspired by the *Nibelungenlied*, as if its hero were dark Hagen, who stands beyond good and evil, whose life is shadowed by death, who possesses the strength to accept the certainty of defeat, responding to it with an affirmation of the situation into which he has been cast, and who discovers meaning in this affirmation.[21]

Despite all this, however, Heidegger never quite veers into nihilism because he insists that we are obligated to exist responsibly as mortal openness—and that our decisions become clear in light of what is called for by the concrete situation in which we find ourselves. Yet there is ultimately no "reason" or "basis" for a resolute decision: each choice is made simply because it is made. Authentic existence acts from out of the *Abgrund*; each authentic decision is a new event within a historical situation. Because such decisions are not "grounded" in any-thing, but rather arise from the free choice to be who we are responsibly, such decisions are anxiety-provoking. Authentic *Dasein* acts not in the service of its security- and approval-craving ego, but in the service of the clearing as such: openness for Being. The "meaning" of such existence, then, results neither from belief in a transcendent God-thing, nor from an arbitrarily chosen "project," but *from existing itself,* i.e., from being who we already are. If the "meaning" of the plant's life is to bloom, the meaning of *Dasein*'s life is to be responsively open to what is. As Charles M. Sherover has demonstrated, in such responsive openness lies the groundless ground for a genuine ethics.[22]

If in his early writings Heidegger preserved the importance of the individual but overemphasized self-assertiveness, in his later writings he played down voluntarism but also spoke much less about the individual human being. Everything eventually hinges on events within the "history of Being," with which humanity can "cooperate" in some way that Heidegger never specified. Yet even during the Marburg years, he interpreted human existence as standing out from within the history of Being. At this time, however, he suggested that human decision played a more decisive role in shaping that history than he was later to say. He was always convinced that real "nihilism" is not so much the collapse of values, for such is only the symptom for the true source of nihilism: the self-concealment of *das Nichts,* the no-thingness or clearing in which Being manifests itself. In a way foreign to some "existentialists," he viewed human existence as playing a crucial role within the drama of the history of Being. By indicating that human existence springs from and is indebted to what both transcends it and yet is also intimately involved with it, Heidegger sought to disclose the relation between history and the transcendent by interpreting the Judaeo-Christian notion of historicality in light of Greek thought. Like Hegel, Dilthey, and others who also went this way, Heidegger found that there were unexpected obstacles. One is the tendency to remythologize the transcendent as an agent, thereby attributing to it some of the characteristics that Heidegger had removed from his earlier conception of authentic human existence.

IV. Concluding Remarks

If Heidegger's lectures at Marburg do not show that he was an existentialist in the way in which Sartre or Camus was, they at least show that his interest in such existentialist-sounding themes as resoluteness and Being-towards-death was far from incidental. Yet if something like authenticity is required for ontological understanding, how is one to ascertain whether he or she has arrived at the truth? During the Marburg years, Heidegger would have said—taking his cue from the Protestant idea of justification—that the individual's own experience of openness is self-confirming. But is there any "outward" sign that one has undergone this experience? What is the "standard" against which to measure the findings of someone who has heard the truth and of someone who has not? Can such truth ever be communicated, or is it ineffable? Long after *Being and Time* appeared, Heidegger gave a lecture that tried to speak what cannot be spoken. This lecture, he later remarked,

> . . . had to attempt to prepare the participants for their own experience of what was said in terms of an experience of something which cannot openly be brought to light. It is . . . the attempt to speak of something that cannot be mediated cognitively, not even in terms of questions, but must be experienced. The attempt to speak of it with the intention of preparing for this experience essentially constitutes the daring quality of the seminar (ZS, 27–28/26).

Although many contemporary philosophers seem to find it difficult to comprehend Heidegger's claim that knowledge demands a change of behavior on the part of the knower, virtually all wisdom traditions—West and East—agree that the truthseeker must prepare for the metamorphosis necessary for insight. The seeker must be released from the subject-object paradigm and admitted into the hidden intimacy of self as openness and Being as what manifests itself therein. One writer has argued that even modern science, which began by adopting the subject-object paradigm, is now in the process of transcending it:

> Recall the essential insight of the work of Heisenberg, Schroedinger, and Einstein that the texture of reality is one in which the observer and the event, the subject and the object, the knower and the known, *are not separable.* To deeply comprehend this therefore requires a comparable mode of knowing, a mode of knowing whose nature it is to be undivided from what it knows.[23]

Throughout his career, Heidegger sought a way beyond philosophical dualism. His early emphasis on the responsibility of each individual for living the truth gives his work an existentialist flavor which, its voluntarism and human-centeredness notwithstanding, is so compelling. We often hear that his later work leaves behind consideration of the theme of "authenticity," but anyone familiar with his lectures from the 1930s and 1940s knows that this is not the case. In 1941, for example, well after the alleged turn in his thought, Heidegger remarked that philosophy demands an unusual kind of character on the part of the philosopher. Knowledge of the *Grund* (meaning *Ab-grund* here) "*is* character itself, the feature of man without which all tenacity of will remains merely blind obstinacy, all deeds remain merely fleeting results, all activity remains merely self-consuming bustle, all 'experiences' merely self-deception" (GB, 3). But how can such knowledge be gained? What must one do to understand the truth? In 1941, Heidegger remarked that

> Presumably . . . an individual can never come upon such knowledge from the accidents of his capacities and his possessions. Neither he himself nor others can force open such knowledge by decree [*Machtspruch*]. The relation to the essential, wherein historical man becomes free, can only have its origin in the essential itself (GB, 6).

Just what the "essential" means, and how we can dwell appropriately within it—all this remains the enduring mystery of human existence.[24]

Notes

INTRODUCTION

1. On this issue, cf. Thomas J. Sheehan's excellent essay "Heidegger's 'Introduction to the Phenomenology of Religion,' 1920-21," in *The Personalist*, 60 (July, 1979), p. 316.

2. William J. Richardson's monumental work, *Heidegger: Through Phenomenology to Thought* (The Hague: Martinus Nijhoff, 1963), remains the most sustained account of the change in Heidegger's thinking which began about 1930.

3. Richard Schmitt, in *Martin Heidegger on Being Human* (New York: Random House, 1969), translates *Eigentlichkeit* as "genuine self-possessedness." My thanks to John D. Caputo for reminding me of this.

CHAPTER ONE

1. At this time, there exists no complete biography of Martin Heidegger. His insistence on preserving the integrity of his private life discouraged those who sought his assistance in the preparation of a biography during his lifetime. Heidegger's most explicit autobiographical reflections are infrequent, but cf. "My Way to Phenomenology" (ZS, 81-90/74-82), "The Pathway," (FW), and "Heidelberg Inaugural Address" (AR). There are a number of helpful sketches on Heidegger's life and character. Cf. Thomas J. Sheehan, "Heidegger's Early Years: Fragments for a Philosophical Biography," *Listening*, XII (Fall, 1977), pp. 3-20. Sheehan is preparing what promises to be a definitive account of Heidegger's philosophical life in the mid-1920s, to be called: *The Genesis of "Being and Time."* David Farrell Krell's "General Introduction: 'The Question of Being'" to *Martin Heidegger: Basic Writings*, ed. by Krell (New York: Harper & Row, 1977) is quite helpful. See also: Hannah Arendt, "Martin Heidegger at Eighty," trans. by Albert Hofstadter in *Heidegger and Modern Philosophy*, ed. by Michael Murray (New Haven: Yale University Press, 1978), pp. 293-303; Hans-Georg Gadamer, *Philosophical Hermeneutics*, especially Part Two, "Phenomenology, Existential Philosophy, and Philosophical Hermeneutics," trans. and ed. by David E. Linge (Berkeley: University of California Press, 1976); Karl Löwith, *Heidegger: Denker in dürftiger Zeit*, 2d ed. (Göttingen: Vandenhoek & Ru-

precht, 1960) and "The Nature of Man and the World of Nature for Heidegger's 80th Birthday," trans. by R. Phillip O'Hara in *The Southern Journal of Philosophy*, VIII (Winter, 1970), pp. 309-318 (Here Löwith shares passages from Heidegger's letter to him in the 1920s.); Otto Pöggeler, "Heidegger Today," *The Southern Journal of Philosophy*, VIII (Winter, 1970), pp. 273-308, and "Zum Tode Martin Heideggers," *Research in Phenomenology*, VII (1977), pp. 31-42. References to Heidegger's political activities (1933-34) will be found in Chapter Six.

2. The theme of "rootedness" as a pre-condition for authentic human existence is common to the Germanic philosophical tradition. Heidegger, in a remarkably candid autobiographical statement called "Why We Remain in the Province" (WBW), explained that his philosophical work was directly akin to the work of the peasants tilling the soil and hewing wood in the Black Forest. Cf. Chapter Four.

3. Cf. Herbert Marcuse and Frederick Olafson, "Heidegger's Politics: An Interview," *Graduate Faculty Philosophy Journal*, VI (Winter, 1977), p. 37.

4. Walter Biemel, *Martin Heidegger: An Illustrated Study*, trans. by J.L. Mehta (New York: Harcourt, Brace, Jovanovich, 1976).

5. Karl Jaspers, "On Heidegger," trans. by Dale L. Ponikvar, *Graduate Faculty Philosophy Journal*, VII (Spring, 1978), pp. 107-108. In a footnote, the translator remarks: "From the new expanded edition of the *Philosophische Autobiographie* (R. Piper and Co. Verlag, 1977), pp. 92-111. The original draft, written in the 1950s, included this chapter on Jaspers' relation to Heidegger, and was excluded from the first edition on the urging of his wife and friends, who thought that the piece should not be published during Heidegger's lifetime." Cf. David Farrell Krell, "The Heidegger-Jaspers Relation," *The Journal of the British Society for Phenomenology*, IX (May, 1978), pp. 126-130.

6. Paul Hühnerfeld, *In Sachen Heidegger: Versuch über ein deutsches Genie* (Hamburg: Hoffmann und Campe, 1959), p. 55. Translation my own.

7. C. G. Jung, *Memories, Dreams, Reflections*, recorded and edited by Aniela Jaffé, trans. by Richard and Clara Winston (New York: Vintage Books, 1965), pp. 4-5. There are many interesting parallels between the lives and thinking of Jung and Heidegger, some of which will be touched on in later chapters.

8. Bernhard Welte, "Seeking and Finding: The Speech at Heidegger's Burial," trans. by Thomas J. Sheehan, *Listening*, VII (Fall, 1977), pp. 106-109.

9. Cf. Thomas J. Sheehan's excellent essay "Getting to the Topic: The New Edition of *Wegmarken*," *Research in Phenomenology*, VII (1977), pp. 299-313.

10. Cited in Sheehan, "Heidegger's 'Introduction to the Phenomenology of Religion,' 1920-21," p. 313.

11. *Ibid.*, p. 313.

12. *Ibid.*, pp. 313-314.

13. For a very helpful discussion of Heidegger's *Habilitationsschrift*, cf. Roderick M. Stewart, "Signification and Radical Subjectivity in Heidegger's

Habilitationsschrift," Man and World, 12 (3), 1979, pp. 360-384. Stewart's essay includes a translation of the *Schluss* of the *Habilitationsschrift*.

14. Cf. Edward G. Ballard, *Man and Technology* (Pittsburgh: Duquesne University Press, 1978), pp. 156-157. I am indebted to Professor Ballard for much insight into Heidegger's thinking.

15. Cf. Richard E. Palmer, *Hermeneutics: Interpretation Theory in Schleiermacher, Dilthey, Heidegger, and Gadamer* (Evanston: Northwestern University Press, 1969).

16. Jaspers, "On Heidegger," p. 110.

17. Calvin O. Schrag, *Existence and Freedom: Toward an Ontology of Human Finitude* (Evanston: Northwestern University Press, 1961), p. vii. This fine book was of considerable help to me in understanding Heidegger's debt to his philosophical predecessors.

18. George J. Stack, *Kierkegaard's Existential Ethics* (University, Alabama: The University of Alabama Press, 1977), p. 136. Although Stack has something of an axe to grind against Heidegger, his book is first-rate.

19. Schrag, *Existence and Freedom*, p. 14.

20. Stack, *Kierkegaard's Existential Ethics*, pp. 122-123.

21. Quoted on p. 23 of Rudolf Bultmann's "New Testament Mythology," in *Kerygma and Myth*, ed. by Hans-Werner Bartsch, trans. by Reginald H. Fuller (London: SPCK, 1960).

22. *Ibid.*, p. 24. The original letters are found in *Briefwechsel zwischen Wilhelm Dilthey und Dem Grafen Paul Yorck von Wartenburg, 1887-97* (Halle: Niemeyer, 1923), pp. 154, 158.

23. Otto Pöggeler, *Der Denkweg Martin Heideggers* (Pfullingen: Günther Neske, 1963), pp. 36-45; Sheehan, "Heidegger's 'Introduction to the Phenomenology of Religion,' 1920-21." Because both Pöggeler and Sheehan have had access to Heidegger's still unpublished lectures from 1920-21, these well-written pieces are invaluable.

24. *Ibid.* pp. 319-323. The following several lines are much in debt to Sheehan.

25. *Ibid.*

26. Otto Pöggeler, "Being as Appropriation" ("Sein als Ereignis"), trans. by Ruediger Hermann Grimm in *Philosophy Today*, XIX (Summer, 1975), p. 156.

27. Pöggeler, *Der Denkweg Martin Heideggers*, p. 42. Translation my own.

28. Cf. James M. Robinson's "Introduction" to *The Future of Our Religious Past: Essays in Honor of Rudolf Bultmann*, trans. by Charles E. Carlston and Robert P. Scharlemann (New York: Harper & Row, 1971).

29. Bultmann, *Kerygma and Myth*, p. 24.

30. Karl Barth, "Bultmann: An Attempt to Understand Him," in *Kerygma and Myth*, II, ed. by Hans-Werner Bartsch, trans. by Reginald H. Fuller (London: SPCK, 1962), p. 114.

31. Ballard, *Man and Technology*, pp. 38-40.

32. Sheehan, "Heidegger's Early Years."

33. On Heidegger's relation to Husserl, cf. Ernst Tugendhat, *Der Wahrheits-begriff bei Husserl und Heidegger* (Berlin: Walter de Gruyter & Co., 1970); J.L. Mehta, *Martin Heidegger: The Way and the Vision* (Honolulu: The University of Hawaii Press, 1977); Frederick Elliston, "Phenomenology Reinterpreted: From Husserl to Heidegger," *Philosophy Today*, XXI (Fall, 1977), pp. 273-283; Edward G. Ballard, "On the Pattern of the Phenomenological Method," *The Southern Journal of Philosophy*, VIII (Winter, 1970), pp. 421-431; John D. Caputo, "The Question of Being and Transcendental Phenomenology: Reflections on Heidegger's Relationship to Husserl," *Research in Phenomenology*, VII (1977), pp. 84-105; John D. Scanlon, "The Epoché and Phenomenological Anthropology," *Research in Phenomenology*, II (1972), pp. 95-110; Sheehan, "Heidegger's Early Years" and "Heidegger's 'Introduction to the Phenomenology of Religion." Volume XX of Heidegger's *Gesamatausgabe, Prolegomena zur Geschichte des Zeitbegriffs* (Frankfurt an Main: Vittorio Klostermann, 1979), contains a lengthy and far-reaching criticism of Husserl's phenomenology. This volume (consisting of lectures from 1925) was not available to me until this essay was completed.

34. Jaspers, "On Heidegger," p. 116.

35. Robert Sokolowski, *Husserlian Meditations: How Words Present Things* (Evanston: Northwestern University Press, 1974), pp. 34-42. This book and another one by Sokolowski, *The Formation of Husserl's Concept of Constitution* (The Hague: Martinus Nijhoff, 1970) are two of the finest analyses of Husserl in English.

36. Edmund Husserl, *Logical Investigations*, II, trans. by J.N. Findlay (New York: Humanities Press, 1970), p. 785. Cf. Frederick A. Olafson, "Consciousness and Intentionality in Heidegger's Thought," *American Philosophical Quarterly*, 12 (April, 1975), pp. 91-103. Cf. also Jacques Taminiaux's remarkable article "Heidegger and Husserl's *Logical Investigations*, trans. by Jeffrey Stevens in *Radical Phenomenology: Essays in Memory of Martin Heidegger*, ed. by John Sallis (Atlantic Highlands, N.J.: Humanities Press, 1978).

37. Schrag, *Existence and Freedom*, p. 55. On the issues raised by Heidegger's critique of the view of self as substance, cf. Aron Gurwitsch, "A Non-Egological Conception of Consciousness," *Studies in Phenomenology and Psychology* (Evanston: Northwestern University Press, 1966), pp. 287-300; Christopher P. Smith, "Heidegger's Critique of Absolute Knowledge," *New Scholasticism*, 45 (Winter, 1971), pp. 56-86; Charles E. Scott, "Self-Consciousness without an Ego," *Man and World*, IV (May, 1971), pp. 193-201; Jean-Paul Sartre, *Being and Nothingness*, trans. by Hazel Barnes (New York: Philosophical Library, 1956).

38. Cf. Sheehan, "Heidegger's Early Years." as well as his "Time and Being: 1925-27," *Proceedings* of the Heidegger Conference, Villanova University, May, 1978.

39. Jürgen Habermas, "Martin Heidegger: On the Publication of Lectures from the Year 1935," trans. by Dale Ponikvar, *Graduate Faculty Philosophy Journal*, VI (Fall, 1977), p. 156.

40. Cf. Scanlon, "The Epoche and Phenomenological Anthropology."

41. Sheehan, "Getting to the Topic: The New Edition of *Wegmarken*."

42. On the self-referential character of *Being and Time*, cf. James R. Watson's outstanding essay, "Heidegger's Hermeneutic Phenomenology," *Philosophy Today*, XV (Spring, 1971), pp. 30-43; Fridolin Wiplinger, *Wahrheit und Geschichtlichkeit* (München: Karl Alber Verlag, 1961), p. 165; Peter Fürstenau, *Martin Heidegger: Das Gefüge seines Denkens* (Frankfurt am Main: Vittorio Klostermann, 1958), p. 24.

43. Cf. Watson, "Heidegger's Hermeneutic Phenomenology." Also cf. Stephen Erickson, "Martin Heidegger," *The Review of Metaphysics*, XIX (March, 1966), pp. 462-485.

44. John Sallis, *The Concept of World: A Study in the Phenomenological Ontology of Martin Heidegger* (Tulane University: Unpublished Ph.D. Dissertation, 1964), p. 66.

CHAPTER TWO

1. Alberto Rosales, *Transzendenz und Differenz* (The Hague: Martinus Nijhoff, 1970). Cf. my essay "On Discriminating Everydayness, Unownedness, and Falling in *Being and Time*," *Research in Phemomenology*, V (1975), pp. 109-128.

2. Cf. C.B. Macpherson, *The Political Theory of Possessive Individualism* (Oxford: Clarendon Press, 1962).

3. Erich Fromm, *Escape from Freedom* (New York: Avon Books, 1969), pp. 134-137. This book, along with many others by Fromm, has provided me with considerable insight into the meaning of "authenticity."

4. Søren Kierkegaard, *The Present Age*, trans. by Alexander Dru (New York: Harper & Row, 1962).

5. Norman Fruchter, "Movement Propaganda and the Culture of the Spectacle," *Liberation* (May, 1971), p. 5. On the topic of mass culture and its effect on consciousness, cf. Donald Lazere's essay, "Mass Culture, Political Consciousness, and English Studies," which introduces the special issue of *College English*, 38 (April, 1977), edited by Lazere on this occasion. The reader is invited to consult the extensive bibliography provided by Lazere at the end of this issue. The "Frankfurt Critical School" has devoted much attention to the idea that critical-revolutionary (Marxist-socialist) activity among the working class has been defused by the increased production of consumer goods and by the mass culture characteristic of advanced capitalistic societies. A detailed history of this school can be found in Martin Jay's work, *The Dialectical Imagination* (Boston: Little, Brown, and Company, 1973). Probably the classic work in this area is Herbert Marcuse's *One-Dimensional Man* (Boston: Beacon Press, 1964). On Heidegger's relation to the Critical School, cf. Fred R. Dallmayr, "Phenomenology and Critical Theory: Adorno," *Cultural Hermeneutics*, 3 (July, 1976), pp. 367-405, and Otto Pöggeler, *Philosophie und Politik bei Heidegger* (Frei-

burg/München: Verlag Karl Alber, 1972), pp. 38-40, 111-112. Cf. also my essay,
"Heidegger and Marcuse: Technology as Ideology," in *Research in Philosophy
and Technology*, Vol. II, ed. by Paul T. Durbin and Carl Mitcham (Greenwich,
Conn.: Jai Press, 1979). Cf. also Bruce Brown, *Marx, Freud, and the Critique
of Everyday Life* (New York: Monthly Review Press, 1973); Henri Lefebvre,
Everyday Life in the Modern World, trans. by Sacha Rabinovitch (New York:
Harper & Row, 1971); Stanley Aronowitz, *False Promises: The Shaping of
American Working Class Consciousness* (New York: McGraw Hill, 1973); Philip
Slater, *The Pursuit of Loneliness* (Boston: Beacon Press, 1970).
    6. Rudolf Bultmann, "Romans 7 and the Anthropology of Paul," in *Existence
and Faith*, trans. by Schubert M. Ogden (New York: Meridian Books, Inc.,
1960), p. 150.
    7. *Ibid.*, p. 152.
    8. *Ibid.*, p. 156.
    9. Rudolf Bultmann, "The Meaning of Christian Faith in Creation," in *Exis-
tence and Freedom*, p. 216. On Heidegger's relation to Bultmann, cf. Schubert M.
Ogden, *The Reality of God*, especially "The Temporality of God" (London:
SCM Press, 1967), and also Ogden's *Christ without Myth* (New York: Harper &
Row, 1961). For a bibliography of literature on Heidegger and theology, cf.
Thomas F. O'Meara's essay, "Heidegger on God," *Continuum*, V (1968), pp.
686-698. Cf. also the essays in Otto Pöggeler's collection of essays, *Heidegger*
(Cologne—Berlin: Kiepernheuer & Witsch, 1969), including Helmut Franz,
"Das Denken Heideggers und die Theologie," and Oskar Becker, "Para-Existenz."
Also cf. the extensive bibliographical references in the notes to *The Piety of
Thinking: Essays by Martin Heidegger*, trans. by James G. Hart and John C.
Maraldo (Bloomington: Indiana University Press, 1976).
    10. Matthew, 26:39. Cf. also John, 5:30-34. All Biblical quotations are taken
from *The Holy Bible: Revised Standard Version*, ed. by Herbert G. May and
Bruce M. Metzger (New York: Oxford University Press, 1973).
    11. Bultmann, "The Meaning of Christian Faith in Creation," p. 216.
    12. John, 3:19.
    13. Rudolf Bultmann, "The Eschatology of the Gospel of John," *Faith and
Understanding*, ed. by Robert W. Funk, trans. by Louise Pettibone Smith
(New York: Harper & Row, 1969), p. 170.
    14. Paul, II Corinthians, 3:15.
    15. Luke, 14:7-11.
    16. Luke, 9:23-24.
    17. Bultmann, *Faith and Understanding*, p. 170.
    18. Hans-Georg Gadamer, *Philosophical Hermeneutics*, trans. and ed. by
David E. Linge (Berkeley: University of California Press, 1976), p. 141.
    19. Blaise Pascal, *Pensées*, trans. and ed, by A.J. Krailsheimer (Middlesex:
Penguin Books, 1979), pp. 67-68.
    20. *Ibid.*, p. 69.
    21. *Ibid.*, pp. 71-72.

22. *Ibid.*, p. 95.

23. Wilhelm Friedrich von Herrmann, *Die Selbstinterpretation Martin Heideggers* (Meisenheim am Glan: Anton Han, 1964), p. 183. Translation my own.

24. *Ibid.*, p. 187.

25. Two books in particular helped me to see that Heidegger's notion of everydayness is a way of talking about egoism. The first is *Be Here Now* (New York: Crown Publishers, Inc., 1971). Although authorship is credited to the "Lama Foundation," the book was largely written by Ram Dass, formerly a professor of psychology at Harvard, Richard Alpert. The second is *The Art of Loving* (New York: Harper & Row, 1956) by Erich Fromm. Neither book refers to Heidegger, but each expresses in its own way a similar point of view: inauthenticity is selfishness, authenticity is openness.

CHAPTER THREE

1. Gadamer, *Philosophical Hermeneutics*, p. 139.

2. Cf. Søren Kierkegaard, *The Concept of Dread*, trans. by Walter Lowrie (Princeton: Princeton University Press, 1957). Heidegger is not always fair to Kierkegaard.

3. Schrag, *Existence and Freedom*; Stack, *Kierkegaard's Existential Ethics*; and Michael Wyschogrod, *Kierkegaard and Heidegger: Ontology of Existence* (New York: Humanities Press, 1969).

4. Søren Kierkegaard, *Concluding Unscientific Postscript*, trans. by David F. Swenson and Walter Lowrie (Princeton: Princeton University Press, 1969), pp. 116, 119.

5. Kierkegaard, *Either/Or*, II. trans. by Walter Lowrie (New York: Doubleday & Company, Inc., 1959), p. 173.

6. *Ibid.*, p. 199.

7. Kierkegaard, *Concluding Unscientific Postscript*, p. 133.

8. Kierkegaard, *Either/Or*, p. 220; *Concluding Unscientific Postscript*, pp. 90-97.

9. Kierkegaard, *Either/Or*, pp. 220-223.

10. Cf. Stack, *Kierkegaard's Existential Ethics*, p. 122; Kierkegaard, *Either/Or*, p. 210.

11. Kierkegaard, *Either/Or*, p. 333; *Concluding Unscientific Postscript*, p. 113.

12. An attempt at a critique of Heidegger's conception of Being-towards-death has been made by Paul Edwards, "Heidegger and Death: A Deflationary Critique," *The Monist*, 59 (April, 1976), pp. 161-186. Lawrence M. Hinman, in his essay "Heidegger, Edwards, and Being-toward-death," *Southern Journal of Philosophy*, XVI (Fall, 1978), pp. 193-212, systematically demonstrates the serious flaws in Edwards' arguments.

13. Gadamer, *Philosophical Hermeneutics*, p. 49.

14. Plato, *Phaedo*, trans. by Hugh Tredennick in *The Collected Dialogues of Plato*, ed. by Edith Hamilton and Huntington Cairns (New York: Pantheon Books, 1963), p. 61 (77e-78b).

15. Cf. Martin Heidegger, "Review of Ernst Cassirer's *Mythical Thought*," trans. by James G. Hart and John C. Maraldo, in *The Piety of Thinking* (Bloomington: Indiana University Press, 1976). Cf. WHD, 6-7/10. Karsten Harries in "Fundamental Ontology and the Search for Man's Place," *Heidegger and Modern Philosophy*, ed. by Michael Murray (New Haven: Yale University Press, 1978), p. 78, remarks about Heidegger's conception of authenticity: "Such a view of authentic existence may suggest a heroic nihilism, a faith in the meaning of life in spite of, or perhaps rather because of a lucid awareness of the nothingness that governs human existence and that dooms man and all his projects to establish a secure dwelling place for himself to certain defeat. Perhaps this attempt to salvage victory from defeat, meaning from nothing, is peculiarly German. *Being and Time* reads in places as if Heidegger has been inspired by the *Nibelungenlied*, as if its hero were dark Hagen, who stands beyond good and evil, whose life is shadowed by death, who possesses the strength to accept the certainty of defeat, responding to it with an affirmation of the situation into which he has been cast, and who discovers meaning in this affirmation."

16. Erik H. Erikson, *Gandhi's Truth: On the Origins of Militant Nonviolence* (New York: W.W. Norton & Co., Inc., 1969), p. 397.

17. *Ibid.*, p. 398.

18. Joseph Campbell, *The Hero with a Thousand Faces* (Princeton: Princeton University Press, 1972), pp. 45-46. Since this work was first published in 1949, it has been both praised and criticized. It is probably true that Campbell's attempt to provide a single overriding scheme for interpreting the hero myths of all cultures does not succeed. Nevertheless what he says is highly suggestive and opens up the realm of myth in a way important for modern man. Campbell forms part of the tradition of depth psychology developed by C.G. Jung, whose great work, *Symbols of Transformation*, trans. by R.F.C. Hull (Princeton: Princeton University Press, 1976) is in many ways more profound than Campbell's. Probably the most insightful and penetrating study of the structure of the myth of the hero and its relation to the modern psyche is Erich Neumann's remarkable *The Origins and History of Consciousness*, trans. by R.F.C. Hull with a foreword by C.G. Jung (Princeton: Princeton University Press, 1970). I have elected to use Campbell's model for the structure of the hero myth because it is somewhat less complicated and depends less on the psychological theories of Jung and Neumann.

19. Schrag, *Existence and Freedom*, p. 192.

20. Friedrich Nietzsche, *The Will to Power*, trans. by Walter Kaufmann and R.J. Hollingdale (New York: Vintage Books, 1967), pp. 272, 380. Cf. also Nietzsche's *Beyond Good and Evil*, trans. by Walter Kaufmann in *The Basic Writings of Nietzsche* (New York: The Modern Library, 1968), pp. 201, 209,

211, 236, 261, 326; *The Gay Science*, trans. by Walter Kaufmann (New York: Vintage Books, 1974), pp. 163-164, 171-172, 176-177, 219. Cf. my essay "A Comparison of Nietzsche's Overman and Heidegger's Authentic Self, *The Southern Journal of Philosophy*, XIV (Spring, 1976), pp. 213-231.

21. Nietzsche, *The Will to Power*, p. 453; *Beyond Good and Evil*, pp. 262-263.

22. Friedrich Nietzsche, *Thus Spoke Zarathrustra*, trans. by Walter Kaufmann in *The Portable Nietzsche* (New York: The Viking Press, 1968), p. 176.

23. *Ibid.*, pp. 200-202 and *passim*. Cf. also *The Gay Science*, pp. 88, 176.

24. Nietzsche, *Beyond Good and Evil*, p. 273; also pp. 259, 308; cf. also *Thus Spoke Zarathustra*, pp. 139, 236.

25. *Ibid.*, p. 170.

26. Nietzsche, *The Geneology of Morals* in *The Basic Writings of Nietzsche*, p. 531; cf. also *The Gay Science*, p. 324.

27. Nietzsche, *Thus Spoke Zarathustra*, pp. 149-152.

28. *Ibid.*, p. 269.

29. For Heidegger's views on *das Man*, cf. SZ, 126-130, 166-180/163-168, 210-224; for examples of Nietzsche on the herd, cf. *Thus Spoke Zarathustra*, pp. 163-166; *The Will to Power*, p. 467.

30. Richard Lowell Howey, *Heidegger and Jaspers on Nietzsche* (The Hague: Martinus Nijhoff, 1973). This fine work has been very helpful in my understanding of Heidegger's relation to Nietzsche. Lawrence Lampert offers an incisive critical appraisal of this relation in his essay "Heidegger's Nietzsche Interpretation," *Man and World*, VII (November, 1974), pp. 353-378. I also call the reader's attention to Harold Alderman's insightful work, *Nietzsche's Gift* (Athens, Ohio: Ohio University Press, 1977).

31. In a forceful paper delivered at the Heidegger Conference at Tulane University, May, 1977, "Pre-scientific Truth and *Aletheia*: A Reconsideration of Heidegger's Relationship to Nietzsche," P. Christopher Smith argues that Nietzsche is much closer to the idea of disclosedness and manifestness than Heidegger admits.

32. Tugendhat, *Die Wahrheitsbegriff bei Husserl und Heidegger*, p. 322. Translation my own.

33. *Ibid.*, p. 327.

34. Cf. Krailsheimer's Introduction to Pascal's *Pensées* for an insightful account of the Jansenist controversy. A good explanation of the history of the major issues involved in the theological controversy concerning grace can be found in Oscar Hardmann, *The Christian Doctrine of Grace* (London: The Centenary Press, 1946).

CHAPTER FOUR

1. Charles M. Sherover, *Heidegger, Kant, and Time* (Bloomington: Indiana University Press, 1971), p. 209. This fine work was most helpful to me in

coming to some understanding of Heidegger's idea of temporality.

2. *Ibid.*, p. 209.

3. Friedrich-Wilhelm von Herrmann, *Subjekt und Dasein* (Frankfurt am Main: Vittorio Klostermann, 1974), pp. 90-91. Translation my own.

4. Karel Kosik, *Dialectics of the Concrete*, trans. by Karel Kovanda with James Schmidt, Vol. LII, Boston Studies in the Philosophy of Science, ed. by Robert S. Cohen and Marx W. Wartofsky (Dordrecht: D. Reidel Publishing Company, 1976), p. 121. This remarkable book, first published in Czechoslovakia in 1961, attempts to appropriate important elements of Heidegger's thinking for a renewed Marxism. Kosik's critique of Heidegger, who is hardly ever mentioned by name but who in fact is the major thinker under consideration in the first part of the book, cannot conceal his admiration for Heidegger's analysis of human existence.

5. *Ibid.*, p. 122.

6. Schrag, *Existence and Freedom*, pp. 136-137. Cf. Also Schrag's insightful essay "Heidegger on Repetition and Historical Understanding," *Philosophy East and West*, XX (July, 1970), pp. 287-295.

7. Cf. Hannah Arendt, *The Life of the Mind*, Vol. II, *Willing* (New York: Harcourt, Brace, Jovanovich, 1978), p. 178.

8. James M. Demske, *Being, Man, and Death* (Lexington: The University Press of Kentucky, 1970), p. 50. I have changed the words in brackets to correspond with the way I have been translating Heidegger's vocabulary. Demske's book is probably the best available treatment on the theme of death in Heidegger's thinking.

9. Schrag, *Existence and Freedom*, pp. 133-136.

10. *Ibid.*, p. 133.

11. Stack, *Kierkegaard's Existential Ethics*, p. 68.

12. *Ibid.*, p. 136.

13. *Ibid.*, p. 136.

14. Sheehan, "Getting to the Topic: The New Edition of *Wegmarken*." Sheehan has written several brilliant essays designed to demonstrate the enormous importance of Aristotle for the development of Heidegger's thinking. Cf. for example "Heidegger, Aristotle and Phenomenology," *Philosophy Today*, XIX (Summer, 1975), pp. 87-94; "Heidegger's Interpretation of Aristotle: *Dynamis* and *Ereignis*," *Philosophical Research Archives*, IV, No. 1253 (1978). Cf. also Sheehan's exceptional translation of Heidegger's crucial essay "On the Being and Conception of *Physis* in Aristotle's *Physics* B, 1", *Man and World*, IX (August, 1976), pp. 219-270. It is difficult to overestimate my debt to Sheehan for helping me to understand many difficult aspects of Heidegger's thinking. His Aristotle-Heidegger essays provided insight for much of the present chapter, as well as for others.

15. Sheehan, "Getting to the Topic: The New Edition of *Wegmarken*," p. 310.

16. *Ibid.*, p. 311.

17. Hugh Prather, *Notes on Love and Courage* (New York: Doubleday and Company, Inc., 1977), no page numbers.

18. I Corinthians, 13

CHAPTER FIVE

1. Edmund Husserl, *The Phenomenology of Internal Time Consciousness*, ed. by Martin Heidegger, trans. by James S. Churchill, with an introduction by Calvin O. Schrag (Bloomington: Indiana University Press, 1964). On the topic of "horizon," cf. Helmut Kuhn's essay, "The Phenomenological Concept of 'Horizon'," in *Philosophical Essays in Memory of Edmund Husserl*, ed. by Marvin Farber (Cambridge: Harvard University Press, 1949).

2. Karl Lehmann, "Christliche Geschichtserfahrung und ontologische Frage beim jungen Heidegger," in Pöggeler, *Heidegger*, pp. 144-145. Cf. also Helmut Franz, "Das Denken Heideggers und die Theologie," *ibid*, pp. 179-216.

3. Sigmund Freud, *Civilization and Its Discontents*, trans. and ed. by James Strachey (New York: W.W. Norton & Company, Inc., 1961), p. 21.

4. I refer the reader once again to the excellent works by Sheehan ("Heidegger's 'Introduction to the Phenomenology of Religion,' 1920-21") and Pöggeler *(Der Denkweg Martin Heideggers)*.

5. For a helpful theological interpretation of this passage, cf. Schubert M. Ogden, "The Temporality of God" in his book *The Reality of God*. John S. Dunne in *The Way of All the Earth* (New York: Macmillan Publishing Co., Inc., 1972) has discussed the relation of God's temporality to human temporality within the context of an interpretation of the development of religious consciousness in East and West. This fine book is highly recommended.

6. Cf. for example, Matthew, 24:43; Luke 12:39f; 12:35-38; Mark 13:33-37; Rev. 3:3; II Peter, 3:10.

7. Lehmann, "Christliche Geschichtserfahrung und ontologische Frage beim jungen Heidegger," p. 145.

8. Romans, 13:11-12.

9. II Corinthians, 5:17.

10. II Corinthians, 6:1-12.

11. I Corinthians, 15:26.

12. Schrag, *Existence and Freedom*, p. 133.

13. *Ibid.*, pp. 133-136.

14. *Ibid.*, pp. 135-136.

15. *Ibid.*, p. 138.

16. Karl Jaspers, *Psychologie der Weltanschauung* (Berlin: Springer-Verlag, 1954), p. 112. Translation my own. Cf. my essay "Heidegger and Nietzsche on Authentic Time," *Cultural Hermeneutics*, IV (1977), pp. 239-264.

17. Bultmann, "The Eschatology of John," in *Faith and Understanding*, p. 170. On the relation of Heidegger and Bultmann, cf. John Macquarrie, *An Existentialist Theology: A Comparison of Heidegger and Bultmann* (London:

S.C.M. Press, 1955). Cf. also Heinrich Ott, *Denken und Sein: Der Weg Martin Heideggers und der Weg der Theologie* (Zollikon: Evangelischer Verlag, 1959).

18. Bultmann, "Bultmann Replies to His Critics," *Kerygma and Myth*, I, p. 205.

19. I Corinthians, 15:54-56.

20. Luke, 17:20-21; also 19:9-10.

21. Paul Tillich, "Kairos II: Ideen zur Geisteslage der Gegenwart," in his *Gesammelte Werke*, Vol. VI, *Der Widerstreit von Raum und Zeit* (Stuttgart: Evangelisches Verlagswerk, 1963), p. 33. I am thankful to Professor Walter Eisenbeis of Denison University for having pointed out to me the connection between Heidegger and Tillich. Translation my own.

22. Paul Tillich, "Kairos und Logos: Eine Untersuchung zur Metaphysik der Erkenntnis," in his *Gesammelte Werke*, Vol. IV, *Philosophie und Schicksal*, p. 50. Translation my own.

23. *Ibid.*, p. 64.

24. Lehmann, "Christliche Geschichtserfahrung und ontologische Frage beim junge Heidegger," pp. 159-160.

25. *Ibid.*, pp. 145-146.

26. The following quotation from Mack Singleton, "Morality and Tragedy in *Celestina*," *Studies in Honor of Lloyd A. Kasten* (Madison, Wisconsin: Hispanic Seminary of Medieval Studies, 1975), p. 258, draws together many of the themes discussed by Schelling and Heidegger:

"In order to be be free we must submit. This is demanded by the Great Morality which is the creator of the splinters of law and code that proceed from it. When we romantically rebel in the name of the (false) freedom of the ego, we violate the ordained scheme of the world, which is derived from the Forms of Order living in the core and center of the Godhead (the One within, as mystics know)—an Order dedicated eternally to the task of achieving the immortality of life. So it is that, when we wound the order of world-without, we wound the Order of world-within, because what we decisively know concerning the world-without has been projected onto it from the world of Order within. If, therefore, we in our Pride have attempted to shatter Order within or its projection which is Order without, we have committed the wickedest hubris and must pay for so vile an outrage by being ourselves shattered beyond pity. We may previously be warned about this by conscience and nightmare. When these fail to impress, we are then destroyed in the realm of the Unconscious."

My thanks to Professor Thomas Spaccarelli of the University of the South for having pointed out this remarkable passage to me.

27. P. Christopher Smith, in his excellent essay "Pre-scientific Truth and *Aletheia*," delivered at the Heidegger Conference, May, 1977 at Tulane University, points out that Heidegger did not always give Nietzsche adequate credit for having anticipated what Heidegger himself saw decades later.

CHAPTER SIX

1. Cf. Alexander Schwan, *Politische Philosophie im Denken Heideggers* (Köln und Opladen: Westdeutscher Verlag, 1965); Otto Pöggeler, *Philosophie und Politik bei Heidegger* (Freiburg und München: Karl Alber, 1972); Jean-Michel Palmier, *Les écrits politique de Heidegger* (Paris: l'Herne, 1968); Karsten Harries, "Heidegger as a Political Thinker," *The Review of Metaphysics*, XXIX (June, 1976), pp. 642-669; Reiner Schürmann, "Political Thinking in Heidegger," *Social Research*, 45 (Spring, 1978), pp. 191-221. The bibliographical references in these works are invaluable. Cf. also my essay "Heidegger, Ethics, and National Socialism," *The Southwestern Journal of Philosophy*, V (Spring, 1974), pp. 97-196. Karl A. Moehling has written a remarkable dissertation called *Martin Heidegger and the Nazi Party: An Examination* (Northern Illinois University: Unpublished Ph.D. Dissertation, 1972), which—in addition to insightful analyses of Heidegger's relation to National Socialism—includes transcripts of the hitherto unavailable documents on Heidegger "de-nazification" hearings held after the war. Although Moehling has not yet completed the book version of this dissertation, the reader is invited to read his essay taken from the dissertation, "Heidegger and the Nazis," *Listening*, special issue on "Heidegger: The Man and the Thinker," 12 (Fall, 1977), pp. 92-105.

2. George L. Mosse, *The Crisis of German Ideology: Intellectual Origins of the Third Reich* (New York: Grosset & Dunlap, 1964). This book provides a wealth of information concerning the origin and development of *Volkish* thinking in Germany. Cf. also the very helpful background provided by Peter Gay in *Weimar Culture: The Outsider as Insider* (New York: Harper & Row, 1968), especially Chapter Six, which tries to link Heidegger to German abstract expressionism as well as to *Volkish* thinking. In a book of the present scope, it is impossible to describe adequately the enormous changes and complex social-political-economic-cultural episodes which happened in Germany from 1914 to 1933. The bibliographical listings on Weimar Culture alone are enormous. Anyone familiar with this period in Germany and with Heidegger's political views will understand that Heidegger was, at least to some extent, "reactionary" insofar as he opposed the degradation of German life through industrialization.

3. Cf. Ernst Jünger, *Der Arbeiter* (1932), and much of the rest of Jünger's extensive works. The crucial parallels between Jünger and Heidegger on industrialization, technology, and the transformation of German humanity in the twentieth century are handled very well by Palmier in *Les écrits politiques de Heidegger*, especially pp. 167-293. Heidegger clarifies his position with respect to Jünger in *Die Seinsfrage* (Frankfurt am Main: Vittorio Klostermann, 1956). This essay was first published as part of a *Festschrift* for Jünger in 1955.

4. Cf. the documents assembled in Guido Schneeberger's biased *Nachlese zu Heidegger: Dokumente zu seinem Leben und Denken* (Bern: 1962). Even

though Schneeberger is clearly interested in portraying Heidegger in the worst possible light, such bias in itself does not comfort readers who admire Heidegger's thinking and who come across some of his political statements in this book.

5. *Ibid.*, p. 195.

6. Hühnerfeld, *In Sachen Heidegger*, p. 93. Translation my own. Cf. also the very instructive chapter "'Professor NSDAP': The Intellectuals and National Socialism," in Joachim C. Fest, *The Face of the Third Reich*, trans. by Michael Bullock (Middlesex: Penguin Books, 1970).

7. On this topic, cf. Leon Goldstein, "Heidegger and Plato on the Good," *Philosophy Today*, XXII (Winter, 1978), pp. 332-354. In her remarkable book *The Human Condition* (New York: Doubleday & Company, Inc., 1959), Hannah Arendt provides a Heideggerean-influenced interpretation of the difference between the classical Greek world and the modern world. I refer the reader to this book for further insight into Heidegger's reaction against industrialization.

8. Hühnerfeld, *In Sachen Heidegger*, p. 105.

9. Gadamer, *Philosophical Hermeneutics*, p. 201.

10. *Ibid.*, p. 201. The quotation from Aristotle is found in *Nichomachean Ethics*, trans. by W.D. Ross in *The Basic Works of Aristotle*, ed. by Richard McKeon (New York: Random House, 1941), p. 1027 (1140b29-30).

11. *Ibid.*, p. 1027 (1140b20).

12. *Ibid.*, p. 1026 (1140b8-11).

13. *Ibid.*, p. 1026 (1140a29-33).

14. *Ibid.*, p. 1029 (1142a9-10).

15. Howard B. Gold, "Praxis: Its Conceptual Development in Aristotle's *Nichomachean Ethics*," *Graduate Faculty Philosophy Journal*, VI (Winter, 1977), pp. 106-130. This essay provided me considerable insight into Aristotle's practical thinking.

16. Aristotle, *Nichomachean Ethics*, p. 1036 (1144b30-36−1145a1-7).

17. On this topic, cf. Harries, "Heidegger as a Political Thinker."

18. Cited by Otto Pöggeler in "Zum Tode Martin Heideggers," *Research in Phenomenology*, VII (1977), p. 37. Translation my own.

19. Hühnerfeld, *In Sachen Heidegger*, p. 51.

20. Cf. my essay, "Dewey, Heidegger, and the Quest for Certainty," *The Southwestern Journal of Philosophy*, IX, No. 1 (1978), pp. 87-95. For an alternative approach to Heidegger and Dewey, cf. Richard Rorty, "Overcoming the Tradition: Heidegger and Dewey," in *Heidegger and Modern Philosophy*, ed. Michael Murray, pp. 239-258.

21. Cf. Harries, "Heidegger as a Political Thinker," for a helpful treatment of this topic.

22. Neumann, *The Origins and History of Consciousness*, p. 377. There are many profound similarities between Neumann's interpretation of the function of the world-historical hero and Heidegger's interpretation. This extraordinary work deserves the reader's attention.

23. *Ibid.*, p. 380.

24. Erich Fromm, *Escape from Freedom* (New York: Avon Books, 1969), p. 251.

25. Cited by Fromm, p. 258.

26. *Ibid.*, p. 250.

27. Cited by Fromm, p. 258

28. Jaspers, "On Heidegger," pp. 117-118.

29. *Ibid.*, p. 118.

30. Habermas, "Martin Heidegger: On the Publication of Lectures from the Year 1935," p. 156.

31. Marcuse, *One-Dimensional Man* p. 189.

32. Marcuse, "Heidegger's Politics: An Interview with Herbert Marcuse by Frederick Olafson," p. 34.

CHAPTER SEVEN

1. For a critique of Heidegger's views on nihilism, cf. Stanley Rosen, *Nihilism* (New Haven: Yale University Press, 1969). Cf. David A. White's reply, "A Refutation of Heidegger as Nihilist," *The Personalist*, 56 (Summer, 1975), pp. 276-288. Cf. also Christopher Smith, "Heidegger, Hegel, and the Problem of *das Nichts*," *International Philosophical Quarterly*, VIII (September, 1968), pp. 379-405; Alfred Guzzoni, "Ontologische Differenz und Nichts," *Martin Heidegger zum Siebzigsten Geburtstag* (Pfullingen: Günther Neske, 1959). For appraisals of Heidegger's approach to the history of philosophy, cf. Bernard Rollin, "Heidegger's Philosophy of History in *Being and Time*," *The Modern Schoolman*, 49 (January, 1972), pp. 97-112; Thomas E. Wren, "Heidegger's Philosophy of History," *Journal of the British Society for Phenomenology*, III (May, 1978), pp. 126-130; S.L. Bartky, "Originative Thinking in the Later Philosophy of Heidegger," *Philosophy and Phenomenological Research*, XXX (March, 1970), pp. 368-391; Walter Schulz, "Über den philosophiegeschichtlichen Ort Martin Heideggers," *Philosophische Rundschau*, I (1953-54), pp. 65-92, 211-232; Karl Löwith, *Nature, History, and Existentialism*, ed. by Arnold Levison (Evanston: Northwestern University Press, 1966); Otto Pöggeler, "Metaphysik und Seinstopik bei Heidegger," *Philosophisches Jahrbuch*, LXX (1962), pp. 118-137; James L. Perotti, *Heidegger on the Divine* (Athens, Ohio: Ohio University Press, 1974); Donald W. Cress, "Heidegger's Criticism of 'Entitative Metaphysics' in His Later Writings," *International Philosophical Quarterly*, XII (March, 1972), pp. 69-86.

2. I refer the reader once again to the excellent essays by Sheehan on Heidegger and Aristotle.

3. Cf. Rollo May, *Love and Will* (New York: W.W. Norton & Co., Inc., 1969).

4. In a helpful footnote on p. 89 of his translation of Heidegger's essay "The Word of Nietzsche," in *The Question Concerning Technology* (New York: Harper & Row, 1977), William Lovitt points out the interrelation of *Rechtgerti-*

gung, Gerechtigkeit, Iustitia, and justice.

5. Robert Tucker, *Philosophy and Myth in Karl Marx* (Cambridge: Cambridge University Press, 1972). This is an invaluable book for understanding the voluntaristic aspect of Marx's thinking.

6. G.W.F. Hegel, *Reason in History*, trans. by Robert S. Hartman (New York: The Bobbs-Merrill Company, Inc., 1953), pp. 27, 43.

7. Cf. Friedrich Nietzsche, *The Gay Science*, trans. by Walter Kaufmann (New York: Vintage Books), 1974, p. 181. For appraisals of Heidegger's interpretation of Nietzsche, cf. Lawrence Lampert, "Heidegger's Nietzsche Interpretation," *Man and World*, VII (November, 1974), pp. 353-378; F. Leist, "Heidegger und Nietzsche," *Philosophisches Jahrbuch*, 70 (1972-73), pp. 363-394; and cf. the helpful bibliography in Harold Alderman's book, *Nietzsche's Gift*.

8. Marcuse, "Martin Heidegger: An Interview with Herbert Marcuse by Frederick Olafson," p. 37.

9. George Sessions has written some very helpful essays concerning how Spinoza's thinking offers us a new non-anthropomorphic, ecologically-oriented understanding of man's relation to Nature. Cf. his "Spinoza and Jeffers on Man in Nature," *Inquiry*, 20, No. 4 (1977), pp. 481-528, and "Anthropocentrism and the Environmental Crisis," *Humboldt Journal of Social Relations*, II (Fall/Winter, 1974), pp. 1-12.

10. Cf. my essays: "Heidegger on Nihilism and Technique," *Man and World*, VIII (November, 1975), pp. 394-414; "Beyond Humanism: Heidegger's Understanding of Technology," *Listening*, XII (Fall, 1977), pp. 74-83. Cf. also Don Ihde, *Technics and Praxis* (Boston: D. Reidel Publishing Company, 1979), especially pp. 103-129; Harold Alderman, "Heidegger's Critique of Science and Technology," in *Heidegger and Modern Philosophy*, pp. 35-50; William J. Richardson, "Heidegger's Critique of Science," *New Scholasticism*, 42 (Fall, 1968), pp. 511-536; R. Schaeffler, "Martin Heidegger und die Frage nach der Technik, *Zeitschrift für Philosophie Forschung*, 16 (1954), pp. 118-125; K. Grunder, "Martin Heideggers Wissenschaftskritik in ihren geschichtlichen Zusammenhangen," *Archiv für Philosophie*, 11 (1961), pp. 312-335; Simon Moser, "Toward a Metaphysics of Technology," trans. by William Carroll, ed. by Carl Mitcham and Robert Mackey, *Philosophy Today*, XV (Summer, 1971), pp. 129-156;

Readers who find Heidegger's account of the relation between the Will to Power and modern socio-political events hard to follow are urged to consult Hannah Arendt's *The Origins of Totalitarianism* (New York: The World Publishing Company, 1962). For example, she remarks of Hobbes:

"Hobbes was the true, although never fully recognized philosopher of the bourgeoise because he realized that acquisition of wealth conceived as a never-ending process can be guaranteed only by the seizure of political power, for the accumulating process must sooner or later force open all existing territorial limits. He foresaw that a society which had entered the path of never-ending acquisition had to engineer a dynamic political organization capable of a corresponding never-ending process of power generation." (p. 146)

11. Cf. Marcuse, *One-Dimensional Man*. Marcuse was definitely influenced by Heidegger. Indeed, in 1928 he was able to write an essay in which he claimed that *Being and Time* provided the ontological underpinning for Marx's theory of history. Cf. "Beiträge zu einer Phänomenologie des Historischen Materialismus," *Philosophische Hefte*, I (1928), pp. 45-68, and "Ueber konkrete Philosophie," *Archiv für Sozialwissenschaft und Sozialpolitik*, 62 (1929), pp. 111-128. On the relation of Heidegger and Marcuse, cf. my essay "Heidegger and Marcuse: Technology as Ideology," *Philosophy and Technology*, Vol. II; Reinhart Maurer, "Der angewandte Heidegger: Herbert Marcuse und das akademische Proletariat," in *Philosophisches Jahrbuch*, LXX (1970), pp. 238-259; Hans Sachsse, "Die Technik in der Sicht Herbert Marcuses und Martin Heideggers," in *Proceedings of the XVth World Congress of Philosophy*, 1973; "Entretien avec Heidegger," *l'Expresse*, No. 954 (October 20-26, 1969), pp. 78-85; Alfred Schmidt, "Existential-Ontologie und historischer Materialismus bei Herbert Marcuse, in *Antworten auf Herbert Marcuse*, ed. by Jürgen Habermas (Frankfurt am Main: Suhrkamp, 1968). A classic example of a travesty of scholarship is Paul Piccone and Aleander Delfini's simplistic critique, "Herbert Marcuse's Heideggerean Marxism," *Telos* (Fall, 1979), pp. 36-46. For a fine account of the development of the idea that man is lord of Nature, cf. William Leiss, *The Domination of Nature* (Boston: Beacon Press, 1974).

12. Cf. also *Martin Heidegger in Gespräch*, ed. by Richard Wisser (Freiburg/München: Karl Alber, 1969), p. 73; G, 22/53.

13. Cf. the *Gesamtausgabe* edition of *Wegmarken* (Frankfurt am Main: Vittorio Klostermann, 1977), p. 341. My thanks to Thomas J. Sheehan for pointing out this gloss.

14. Cf. Jünger, *Der Arbeiter*; also Palmier, *Les écrits politiques de Heidegger*.

15. Cf. Richard J. Barnet and Ronald E. Müller, *Global Reach: The Power of the Multinational Corporations* (New York: Simon and Schuster, 1974).

16. Cf. VA, I, 34/33-34; WHD, 31-32/83-84; WGM, 191-194/240-242; G, 21/52. On the question of *praxis* in Heidegger's thinking, cf. Reinhart Maurer, "From Heidegger to Practical Philosophy," trans. by Walter E. Wright, *Idealistic Studies*, III (May, 1973), pp. 133-162; Alexander Schwan, "Martin Heidegger, Politik und Praktische Philosophie: Zur Problematik neuerer Heidegger-Literatur," *Philosophisches Jahrbuch*, 81 (1974), pp. 148-172; Bernard Dauenhauer, "Renovating the Problem of Politics," *The Review of Metaphysics*, XXIX (June, 1976), pp. 626-641.

17. Karl Marx, *Capital*, trans. by Ben Fowkes (New York: Vintage Books, 1976), pp. 254-255. Emphasis mine.

18. Karl Marx, *Grundrisse: Foundations of the Critique of Political Economy*, trans. by Martin Nicolaus (New York: Vintage Books, 1973), p. 410. I am indebted to Professor John Clark of Loyola University of New Orleans for

pointing out this passage, and for his help in understanding Marx's thinking. On the relation between Marx and Heidegger, cf. my essay, "A Comparison of Marx and Heidegger on the Technological Domination of Nature," *Philosophy Today*, 23 (Summer, 1979), pp. 99-112; Kostas Axelos, *Alienation, Praxis, and Techne in the Thought of Karl Marx*, trans. by Ronald Bruzina (Austin: The University of Texas Press, 1976); Axelos, *Einführung in ein künftiges Denken* (Tübingen: Max Niemeyer, 1966); Jean Beaufret, "Le 'Dialogue avec le Marxisme' et la 'Question de la Technique'," in *Dialogue avec Heidegger*, Vol. II, *Philosophie Moderne* (Paris: Les Editions de Minuit, 1973); Gajo Petrovic, "Der Spruch des Heideggers," *Durchblicke: Martin Heidegger zum 80. Geburtstag* (Frankfurt am Main: Vittorio Klostermann, 1970).

19. Cf. the references in note 6, Chapter Two, *supra*.

20. My thanks to William and Harriet Lovitt for suggesting the comparison between Heidegger's later thinking and the Old Testament.

21. Cf. John D. Caputo, *The Mystical Element in Heidegger's Thought* (Athens, Ohio: Ohio University Press, 1978).

22. Although I have suggested that there are important parallels between Heidegger's later thinking and the prophetic writings of the Old Testament, important critics as Paul Ricoeur have asserted that Heidegger ignores the Hebraic root of Western culture and focuses solely on the Greek root. This issue and other important topics are treated in the following collection of essays published too late to be integrated into my text: *Heidegger et la Question de Dieu*, edited by Richard Kearner and Joseph Stephen O'Leary (Paris: Bernard Grasset, 1980).

CHAPTER EIGHT

1. Albert Hofstadter in his Introduction to his translation of a group of Heidegger's essays called *Poetry, Language, Thought* (New York: Harper & Row, 1971), p. xxi. On the idea of *Ereignis*, cf. Ken Maly, "Toward *Ereignis*," *Research in Phenomenology*, III (1973), pp. 63-93; James Street Fulton, "The Event of Being," *Southwestern Journal of Philosophy*, VI (Winter, 1975), pp. 7-13; Pöggeler, "Being as Appropriation," *Philosophy Today*; John D. Caputo, "Time and Being in Heidegger," *The Modern Schoolman*, 50 (May, 1973), pp. 324-349.

2. Secondary literature on Heidegger has not paid sufficient attention to the influence of Leibniz on Heidegger's thinking.

3. Caputo, *The Mystical Element in Heidegger's Thought*, pp. 214-215. Cf. also David Farrell Krell, "Towards an Ontology of Play," *Research in Phenomenology*, II (1972), pp. 63-94; Eugen Fink, *Spiel als Welt-Symbol* (Berlin: Walter de Gruyter & Co., 1968), Ingeborg Heidemann, *Der Begriff des Spieles* (Berlin: Walter de Gruyter & Co., 1968), especially Chapter Three, "Die Problematik des Spielbegriffs bei Heidegger," pp. 278-372; John D. Caputo, "Being, Ground, and Play in Heidegger," *Man and World*, 3 (1971), pp. 26-48.

4. Cf. John D. Caputo, "Heidegger's Original Ethics," *The New Scholasticism*, 45 (Winter, 1971), pp. 127-138; John D. Caputo, "The Rose is Without Why: An Interpretation of the Later Heidegger," *Philosophy Today*, XV (1971), pp. 3-15; Bernard Dauenhauer, "Renovating the Problem of Politics," *The Review of Metaphysics*, XXIX (June, 1976), pp. 626-641; Bernard Dauenhauer, "Heidegger, Spokesman for the Dweller," *The Southern Journal of Philosophy*, XV (Summer, 1977), pp. 189-200; Reiner Schürmann, "Principles Precarious: The Origin of the Political in Heidegger," in *Heidegger, The Man and the Thinker*, ed. by Thomas J. Sheehan (Chicago: Precedent Publishers, Inc., 1979); Reiner Schürmann, "Questioning the Foundation of Practical Philosophy," *Human Studies*, I (1979), pp. 357-368. Schürmann is also preparing a book which should prove to be a significant contribution to the topic of Heidegger's political thinking. The book will be called *Politics and Deconstruction: Heidegger and Practical Philosophy*.

5. Zimmerman, "Heidegger and Marcuse: Technology as Ideology," in *Philosophy and Technology*.

6. Caputo, *The Mystical Element in Heidegger's Thought*, especially Chapter Four, "Heidegger and Meister Eckhart." This book is an elaboration of a two-part essay called "Meister Eckhart and the Later Heidegger: The Mystical Element in Heidegger's Thought," *The Journal of the History of Philosophy*, XII (October, 1974), pp. 479-494, and XIII (January, 1975), pp. 61-80. By a remarkable coincidence, Reiner Schürmann submitted an excellent two-part study on Heidegger, Eckhart, and Suzuki to the same journal at about the same time. Cf. Schürmann, "Trois penseurs de délaissement: Maître Eckhart, Heidegger, Suzuki," *Journal of the History of Philosophy*, XII (October, 1974), pp. 455-478, and XII (January, 1975), pp. 43-60. Cf. also Reiner Schürmann, "Heidegger and Meister Eckhart on Releasement," *Research in Phenomenology*, III (1973), pp. 95-119. Finally, cf. Schürmann's *Meister Eckhart: Mystic and Philosopher*, (Bloomington: Indiana University Press, 1978).

7. Caputo, *The Mystical Element in Heidegger's Thought*, pp. 248-249.

8. Cf. Marcuse, *One-Dimensional Man*; also *An Essay on Liberation* (Boston: Beacon Press, 1969). For attempts to use Heidegger's thinking to develop a non-anthropocentric understanding of Nature, cf. Hwa Yol Jung, "The Paradox of Man and Nature: Reflections on Man's Ecological Predicament," *The Centennial Review*, XVIII (Winter, 1974), pp. 1-28; Hwa Yol Jung and Petee Jung, "To Save the Earth," *Philosophy Today*, XIX (Summer, 1975), pp. 108-117; also their "Toward a New Humanism: The Politics of Civility in a 'No-Growth' Society," *Man and World*, IX (August, 1976), pp. 283-306. Cf. also S.L. Bartky, "*Seinsverlassenheit* in the Later Philosophy of Heidegger," *Inquiry*, X (1967), pp. 74-88; Frank M. Buckley, "The Everyday Struggle for the Leisurely Attitude," *Humanitas*, VIII (November, 1972), pp. 307-321.

9. Fritjof Capra. *The Tao of Physics*, (New York: Bantam Books, 1975), p. 198.

10. Cited in Philip Kapleau, *The Three Pillars of Zen* (Boston: Beacon Press, 1967), p. 149. My study of Zen has involved "practice" as well as "theory." During the summer of 1979, I spent five weeks as a guest student at Green Gulch Farm and at Zen Moutain Center (Tassajara), both of which are branches of the San Francisco Zen Center. Many people there were very helpful to me in developing insight into myself as well as into the "theory" of Zen. I am particularly grateful to Lew Richmond for his assistance in reading and criticizing the section on Zen in this book. Any errors, of course, are my responsibility. Some of the sources I have consulted include: D.T. Suzuki, *Zen Buddhism*, ed. by William Barrett (New York: Anchor-Doubleday, 1956); D.T. Suzuki, *Zen and Japanese Culture* (Princeton: Princeton University Press/Bollingen Series, 1973); D.T. Suzuki, *Essays in Zen Buddhism* (First Series) (New York: Grove Press, 1961); Eugen Herrigel, *Zen in the Art of Archery*, trans. by R.F.C. Hull (New York: Vintage Books, 1971); Eugen Herrigel, *The Method of Zen*, ed. by Hermann Tausend, trans. by R.F.C. Hull (New York: Vintage Books, 1974); Reiho Masunaga, *A Primer of Soto Zen: A Translation of Dogen's Shobogenzo Zuimonki* (Honolulu: The University of Hawaii Press, 1975); Shunryu Suzuki, *Zen Mind, Beginner's Mind*, ed. by Trudy Dixon (New York: John Weatherhill, Inc., 1977); Katsuki Sekida, *Zen Training*, ed. by A.V. Grimston (New York: John Weatherhill, Inc., 1977); Thomas Merton, *Mystics and Zen Masters* (New York: Dell Publishing Co., Inc., 1967); Thomas Merton, *Zen and the Birds of Appetite* (New York: New Directions Publishing Company, 1967); Nancy Wilson Ross, *The World of Zen* (New York: Vintage Books, 1960); Alan Watts, *The Way of Zen* (New York: Vintage Books, 1957); Dom Aelred Graham, *Zen Catholicism* (New York: Harcourt, Brace, & World, Inc., 1963); Reiner Schürmann, "The Loss of Origin in Soto Zen and Meister Eckhart," *The Thomist*, 42 (April, 1978); pp. 281-312; Caputo, *The Mystical Element in Heidegger's Thought*, pp. 203-217; Peter Kreeft, "Zen in Heidegger's *Gelassenheit*," *International Philosophical Quarterly*, 11 (December, 1971), pp. 521-545; Marco Pallis, "Is There Room for 'Grace' in Buddhism?", in *The Sword of Gnosis*, ed. by Jacob Needleman (Baltimore: Penguin Books, 1974), pp. 274-295; Abe Masao, "Dogen on Buddha Nature," *The Eastern Buddhist*, IV (May, 1971), pp. 28-71; Fritz Buri, "The Concept of Grace in Paul, Shinran, and Luther," *The Eastern Buddhist*, IX (October, 1976), pp. 21-42; Yuho Yokoi, with Daizen Victorio, *Zen Master Dogen* (New York: John Weatherhill, Inc., 1976).

11. Merton, *Mystics and Zen Masters*, p. 27.

12. Chögyam Trungpa, *Cutting Through Spiritual Materialism* (Boulder: Shambhala Publications, Inc., 1975), p. 122.

13. *Ibid.*, pp. 125-126.

14. *Ibid.*, p. 127.

15. D.T. Suzuki, *Zen Buddhism*, p. 263.

16. Shunryu Suzuki, *Zen Mind, Beginner's Mind*, p. 84. This book, based on lectures given by Suzuki when he was the *roshi* (abbot) of the Zen Center of

San Francisco, is highly recommended.

17. *Ibid.*, p. 119.

18. D.T. Suzuki, *Zen Buddhism*, p. 268.

19. Abe Masao, "Dogen on Buddha Nature," p. 68.

20. D.T. Suzuki, *Zen and Japanese Culture*, p. 184.

21. D.T. Suzuki, *Zen Buddhism*, p. 267.

22. D.T. Suzuki, *Zen and Japanese Culture*, p. 197.

23. *Ibid.*, p. 174.

24. This interpretation of "ek-sistence" was suggested to me by William J. Richardson during his lecture on Heidegger and Lacan at City University (London), November 30, 1979.

25. D.T. Suzuki, *Zen and Japanese Culture*, p. 140.

26. *Ibid.*, p. 257.

27. Cf. Buri, "The Concept of Grace in Paul, Shinran, and Luther."

28. D.T. Suzuki, *Zen Buddhism*, p. 17.

29. *Ibid.*, p. 18.

30. D.T. Suzuki, *Zen and Japanese Culture*, p. 61.

31. Merton, *Mystics and Zen Masters*, p. 253.

32. Shunryu Suzuki, *Zen Mind, Beginner's Mind*, p. 37.

33. Cited in Kapleau, *Three Pillars of Zen*, p. 126.

34. St. John of the Cross, *Dark Night of the Soul*, trans. and ed. by E. Allison Peers (New York: Doubleday Image Books, 1959), p. 46.

35. Cited in Merton, *Zen and the Birds of Appetite*, p. 56. Cf. Paul's Letter to the Galatians, 2:19-20; also Romans 1:5-17.

36. Cf. "Eight Contemporary Enlightenment Experiences of Japanese and Westerners," in Kapleau, *Three Pillars of Zen*, pp. 189-268.

37. D.T. Suzuki, *Zen Buddhism*, p. 272.

38. D.T. Suzuki, *Zen and Japanese Culture*, p. 227.

39. *Ibid.*, p. 240.

40. *Ibid.*, p. 229.

41. *Ibid.*, p. 225.

42. *Ibid.*, p. 241.

43. D.T. Suzuki, *Zen Buddhism*, p. 250.

44. Kreeft, "Zen in Heidegger's *Gelassenheit*," p. 545.

45. On the relation between mysticism and philosophy, cf. Rudolf Otto, *Mysticism East and West*, trans. by Bertha L. Bracey and Richenda C. Payne (New York: Meridian Books, 1957).

46. Charles Wei-hsun Fu, "Heidegger and Zen on Being and Nothingness: A Critical Essay in Transmetaphysical Dialectics," in *Buddhist and Western Philosophy: A Critical Study* (New Delhi: Sterling Publishing Co., 1978). Cf. also Professor Wu's essays; "Creative Hermeneutics: Taoist Metaphysics and Heidegger," *Journal of Chinese Philosophy*, 3 (1976), pp. 115-143, and "The Trans-onto-theo-logical Foundations of Language in Heidegger and Taoism," *Journal of Chinese Philosophy*, I (1975), pp. 130-161. Fu's suggestion that Heidegger's

thinking remains colored by metaphysical elements is echoed both by John Steffney's "Transmetaphysical Thinking in Heidegger and Zen Buddhism," *Philosophy East and West*, 27 (July, 1977), pp. 323-335, and Abe Masao's "Dogen on Buddha Nature," p. 71. Cf. also Julia Ching, "'Authentic Selfhood': Wang Yang-Ming and Heidegger," *The Monist*, 61 (January, 1978), pp. 3-27. The entire issue of Philosophy *East and West*, XX (July, 1970), is devoted to a symposium dealing with similarities between Heidegger's thinking and that of Eastern thinkers. On Heidegger's relation to Taoism, cf. Chung-Yuan Chang. "Reflections," in Günther Neske, *Erinnerung an Martin Heidegger* (Pfullingen: Günther Neske, 1977). In the same volume, cf. also Jarava Mehta, "A Western Kind of Rishi."

47. For a helpful analysis of Heidegger's position *vis-à-vis* Marx and others concerning the end of the Western ideal of "humanism," cf. Reiner Schürmann, "Anti-Humanism. Reflections of the Turn Towards the Post-Modern Epoch," *Man and World*, 12 (No. 2, 1979), pp. 160-177. During the past couple of decades, a group of French thinkers (including Roland Barthes, Claude Lévi-Strauss, Michel Foucault, Jacques Lacan, Jacques Derrida, and Louis Althusser), often loosely grouped under the rubric of "structuralists," have tried to overcome the dominance of the subject-orientation of Cartesian thinking by suggesting that deep-lying symbolic structures are determinative for the individual ego. Although influenced by Marx, Freud, and Ferdinand de Saussure, many structuralists are also indebted to Heidegger.

48. For an impressive survey of the problem of translation, cf. George Steiner, *After Babel: Aspects of Language and Translation* (London: Oxford University Press, 1975).

49. Cf. J.L. Mehta, "Heidegger and Vedanta: Reflections on a Questionable Theme," *International Philosphical Quarterly*, 18 (June, 1978), pp. 121-144. For a treatment of Western history and thinking from an Indian viewpoint which often resembles Heidegger's, cf. R. Radhakrishnan, *Eastern Religious and Western Thought* (New Delhi: Oxford University Press, 1974). Cf. also Radhakrishnan's remarkable introduction to, commentary on, and translation of *The Bhagavad-gita* (New York: Harper & Row, 1973).

50. Edward Conze, *Buddhism: Its Essence and Development* (New York: Harper & Row, 1975), p. 68.

51. Cf. D.T. Suzuki, *Zen and Japanese Culture*; Herrigel, *Zen and the Art of Archery*.

52. The phrase in quotation marks is from Paul's First Letter to the Corinthians, 13:12.

53. Cf. Axelos, *Alienation, Praxis, and Techne in the Thought of Karl Marx*, *passim*.

APPENDIX

1. Joseph P. Fell, *Heidegger and Sartre* (New York: Columbia Univ. Press, 1979), p. 63.

2. References to Heidegger's works are keyed to the following abbreviations:
GP, *Die Grundprobleme der Phänomenologie*, ed. by Friedrich Wilhelm von Herrmann, Vol. 24, *Gesamtausgabe*, lectures from summer semester, 1927 (Frankfurt am Main: Vittorio Klostermann, 1976).

GB, *Grundbergriffe*, ed. by Petra Jaeger, Vol. 51, *Gesamtausgabe*, lectures from summer semester, 1941 (Frankfurt am Main: Vittorio Klostermann, 1981).

H, *Heraklit*, ed. by Manfred S. Frings, Vol. 55, *Gesamtausgabe*, lectures from summer semesters 1943, 1944 (Frankfurt am Main: Vittorio Klostermann, 1976).

L, *Logik: Die Frage nach der Wahrheit*, ed. by Walter Biemel, Vol. 21, *Gesamtausgabe* lectures from winter semester, 1925–26 (Frankfurt am Main: Vittorio Klostermann, 1976).

MAL, *Metaphysische Anfangsgründe der Logik im Ausgang von Leibniz*, ed. by Klaus Held, Vol. 26, *Gesamtausgabe*, lectures from summer semester, 1928 (Frankfurt am Main: Vittorio Klostermann, 1978).

PIK, *Phänomenologische Interpretation von Kants Kritik der reinen Vernunft*, ed. by Ingtraud Görland, Vol. 25, *Gesamtausgabe*, lectures from winter semester, 1927–28 (Frankfurt am Main: Vittorio Klostermann, 1977).

ZB, *Prolegomena zur Geschichte des Zeitbegriffs*, ed. by Petra Jaeger, Vol. 20 of *Gesamtausgabe*, lectures from summer semester, 1925 (Frankfurt am Main: Vittorio Klostermann, 1979).

ZS, *Zur Sache des Denkens* (Tubingen: Max Niemeyer, 1969), trans. by Joan Stambaugh as *On Time and Being* (New York: Harper & Row, 1973).

3. Cf. Fell, *Heidegger and Sartre*, p. 97: "Heidegger found [*Being and Time*] in effect too voluntaristic."

4. Fell, *Heidegger and Sartre*, p. 54

5. Karl Löwith, *Heidegger: Denker in dürftiger Zeit* (Frankfurt am Main: S. Fischer Verlag, 1953), p. 21. Written three decades ago, this book remains an outstanding interpretation of Heidegger's thought.

6. Fell, *Heidegger and Sartre*, p. 51. Fell's book is a significant contribution to the literature; I have learned from him.

7. Those who support the view that Heidegger was never really interested in "authenticity" will be encouraged by Albert Hofstadter's fine translation of *Die Grundprobleme der Phänomenologie* as *The Basic Problems of Phenomenology* (Bloomington: Indiana Univ. Press, 1981). Because the lectures are more readable than *Being and Time*, and because they contain so few references to the "existentialist"-sounding themes that figure so prominently in *Being and Time*, some commentators are already touting the lectures as *the* way to gain access to Heidegger's early thought. Before concluding that *Being and Time* has been rendered obsolete, however, we should note carefully what Heidegger says in *The Basic Problems of Phenomenology*: "Before we discuss the basic ontological problem, the existential analytic of the Dasein needs to be developed. This, however, is impossible within the present course, if we wish to pose the basic ontological problem at all. Therefore, we have to choose an alternative

and *presuppose the essential result of the existential analytic of the Dasein as a result already established.* In my treatise *Being and Time,* I set forth what the existential analytic encompasses in its essential result . . ." (my emphasis). *Basic Problems,* pp. 227–228; GP, 322–323.

8. Thanks to John D. Caputo for suggesting this way of formulating Heidegger's life-task.

9. Paul Tillich, "Kairos und Logos: Eine Untersuchung zur Metaphysik der Erkenntnis," *Gesammelte Werke,* VI, *Philosophie und Schicksal* (Stuttgart: Evangelisches Verlagswerk, 1963), p. 50. For an excellent account of how Heidegger's thought both influenced and was influenced by the "decisional" character of politics in Germany during the 1920s and 1930s, cf. Karl Löwith, "Der Okkasionelle Dezionismus von C. Schmitt," in *Gesammelte Abhandlungen: Zur Kritik der Geschichtlichen Existenz* (Stuttgart: W. Kohlhammer Verlag, 1960).

10. On Heidegger's relation to Overbeck, cf. pp. 112–119 of James G. Hart and John C. Maraldo's commentary following their translation of some of Heidegger's essays in *The Piety of Thinking* (Bloomington: Indiana Univ. Press, 1976).

11. Cf. Thomas J. Sheehan, "Heidegger's 'Introduction' to the Phenomenology of Religion,' 1920–21," *Personalist,* 60 (1979), 312–324.

12. Cf. my essay, "Heidegger and Bultmann, Egoism, Sinfulness, and Inauthenticity," *Modern Schoolman,* 58 (1980), 1–20.

13. Cf. my essay, "Heidegger and Nietzsche on Authentic Time," *Cultural Hermeneutics,* 4 (1977), 239–264.

14. Martin Heidegger, "Phenomenology and Theology," *The Piety of Thinking,* p. 20; *Phänomenologie und Theologie* (Frankfurt am Main: Vittorio Klostermann, 1970), p. 31.

15. Heidegger, "Phenomenology and Theology," pp. 20–21; *Phänomenologie und Theologie,* p. 32.

16. Rudolf Bultmann, *Kerygma and Myth,* ed. by Hans Werner Bartsch (London: S.P.C.K., 1960), pp. 29–30.

17. On the topic of *Ereignis,* cf. Albert Hofstadter's excellent essay, "Enownment," *Martin Heidegger and the Question of Literature,* ed. by William V. Spanos (Bloomington: Indiana Univ. Press, 1979).

18. Medard Boss, "Martin Heidegger's Zollikon Seminars," trans. by Brian Kenny, *Review of Existential Psychology and Psychiatry,* 16 (1978–79), 13–20.

19. Cf. *supra,* especially chapters six and eight.

20. Cited by Hofstadter in "Enownment," p. 22. Cf. Martin Heidegger, *The Question Concerning Technology,* trans. by William Lovitt (New York: Harper & Row, 1977), p. 25; Martin Heidegger, "Die Frage nach dem Technik," *Vorträge und Aufsätze,* I (Pfullingen: Günther Neske, 1967), pp. 24–25.

21. Karsten Harries, "Fundamental Ontology and the Search for Man's Place," *Heidegger and Modern Philosophy,* ed. by Michael Murray (New Haven: Yale Univ. Press, 1978), p. 78.

22. Charles M. Sherover, "Founding an Existential Ethic," *Human Studies,* 4 (1981), 223–236.

23. Ken Wilber, *The Spectrum of Consciousness* (Wheaton, Ill.: Theosophical Publishing House, 1979), pp. 42–43.

24. I read an early version of this essay at the Heidegger Conference at Pennsylvania State University in May, 1981. My thanks to the participants for their helpful comments and criticisms.

Bibliography

The following bibliography does not contain the titles which have already been mentioned in the "List of Abbreviations."

I. SECONDARY SOURCES ON HEIDEGGER.

A. *Books*

Axelos, Kostas. *Einführung in ein künftiges Denken.* Tübingen: Max Niemeyer, 1966.

Biemel, Walter. *Le Concept du Monde chez Heidegger.* Louvain: E. Nauwelaerts, 1959.

_____. *Martin Heidegger: An Illustrated Study.* Translated by J.L. Mehta. New York: Harcourt, Brace, Jovanovich, 1976.

Bretschneider, Willy. *Sein und Wahrheit.* Meisenheim am Glan: Anton Hain, 1965.

Caputo, John D. *The Mystical Element in Heidegger's Thought.* Athens: Ohio University Press, 1978.

Declève, Henri. *Heidegger et Kant.* The Hague: Martinus Nijhoff, 1970.

Demske, James M. *Being, Man, and Death.* Lexington: The University Press of Kentucky, 1970.

Fürstenau, Peter. *Martin Heidegger: Das Gefüge seines Denkens.* Frankfurt am Main: Vittorio Klostermann, 1958.

Gadamer, Hans-Georg. *Philosophical Hermeneutics.* Translated by David E. Linge. Berkeley: University of California Press, 1976.

Heidegger and Modern Philosophy, Edited by Michael Murray. New Haven: Yale University Press, 1978.

Heidegger: Perspektiven zur Deutung seines Werks. Edited by Otto Pöggeler. Köln: Kiepenheuer & Witsch, 1969.

Heidegger, The Man and the Thinker. Edited by Thomas J. Sheehan. Chicago: Precedent Publishers, Inc., 1979.

Howey, Richard Lowell. *Heidegger and Jaspers on Nietzsche.* The Hague: Martinus Nijhoff, 1973.

Löwith, Karl. *Heidegger: Denker in dürftiger Zeit.* 2d Ed. Göttingen: Vandenhoek & Ruprecht, 1960.

_____. *Nature, History, Existentialism.* Edited by Arnold Levison. Evanston: Northwestern University Press, 1966.

Macquarrie, John. *An Existentialist Theology: A Comparison of Heidegger and Bultmann.* London: S.C.M. Press, 1955.

Mehta, J.L. *The Philosophy of Martin Heidegger.* New York: Harper & Row, 1971.

_____. *Martin Heidegger: The Way and the Vision.* Honolulu: The University of Hawaii Press, 1977.

Moehling, Karl. *Martin Heidegger and the Nazi Party: An Examination.* Northern Illinois University: Unpublished Ph.D. Dissertation, 1971.

Ott, Heinrich. *Denken und Sein: Der Weg Martin Heideggers und der Weg der Theologie.* Zollikon: Evangelischer Verlag, 1959.

Palmer, Richard E. *Hermeneutics: Interpretation Theory in Schleiermacher, Dilthey, Heidegger, and Gadamer.* Evanston: Northwestern University Press, 1969.

Palmier, Jean-Michel. *Les écrits politiques de Heidegger.* Paris: l'Herne, 1968.

Perotti, James L. *Heidegger on the Divine: The Poet, Thinker, and God.* Athens: Ohio University Press, 1974.

Pöggeler, Otto. *Der Denkweg Martin Heideggers.* Pfullingen: Günther Neske, 1963.

_____. *Philosophie und Politik bei Heidegger.* Freiburg/München: Karl Alber, 1972.

Richardson, William J. *Heidegger: Through Phenomenology to Thought.* The Hague: Martinus Nijhoff, 1963.

Rosales, Alberto. *Transzendenz und Differenz.* The Hague: Martinus Nijhoff, 1970.

Sallis, John. Editor. *Radical Phenomenology: Essays in Memory of Martin Heidegger.* Atlantic Highlands, N.J.: Humanities Press, 1978.

_____. *The Concept of World: A Study in the Phenomenological Ontology of Martin Heidegger.* Tulane University: Unpublished Ph.D. Dissertation, 1964.

Schmitt, Richard. *Martin Heidegger on Being Human.* New York: Random House, 1969.

Schneeberger, Guido. *Nachlese zu Heidegger: Dokumente zu seinem Leben und Denken.* Bern: 1962.

Schrag, Calvin O. *Existence and Freedom: Toward an Ontology of Human Finitude.* Evanston: Northwestern University Press, 1961.

Schwann, Alexander. *Politische Philosophie im Denken Heideggers.* Köln und Opladen: Westdeutscher Verlag, 1965.

Sherover, Charles M. *Heidegger, Kant, and Time.* Bloomington: Indiana University, 1971.

Steiner, George. *Heidegger.* London: Fontana, 1978.

Sternberger, Adolph. *Der Verstandene Tod*. Leipzig: S. Hirzel, 1934.

Tugendhat, Ernst. *Der Wahrheitsbegriff bei Husserl und Heidegger*. Berlin: Walter Gruyter & Co., 1970.

Versenyi, Laszlo. *Heidegger, Being, and Truth*. New Haven: Yale University Press, 1965.

von Herrmann, Wilhelm Friedrich. *Die Selbstinterpretation Martin Heideggers*. Meisenheim am Glan: Anton Hain, 1964.

—————. *Subjekt und Dasein*. Frankfurt am Main: Vittorio Klostermann, 1974.

Wahl, Jean. *Vers la fin de l'ontologie*. Paris: 1956.

Wiplinger, Fridolin. *Wahrheit und Geschichtlichkeit*. München: Karl Alber, 1961.

Wisser, Richard. *Martin Heidegger in Gespräch*. Freiburg/ München: Karl Alber, 1969.

Wyschogrod, Michael. *Kierkegaard and Heidegger: Ontology of Existence*. New York: Humanities Press, 1969.

B. *Articles.*

Alderman, Harold. "Heidegger's Critique of Science and Technology," in *Heidegger and Modern Philosophy*. Edited by Michael Murray. New Haven: Yale University Press, 1978.

Arendt, Hannah. "Martin Heidegger at Eighty," in *Heidegger and Modern Philosophy*.

Ballard, Edward G. "A Brief Introduction to the Philosophy of Martin Heidegger," *Tulane Studies in Philosophy*. XII (1963), 108-151.

—————. "On the Pattern of the Phenomenological Method," *The Southern Journal of Philosophy*. VIII (Winter, 1970), 421-431.

Bartky, S.L. "Originative Thinking in the Later Heidegger," *Philosophy and Phenomenological Research*. XXX (March, 1970), 368-391.

—————. "*Seinsverlassenheit* in the Later Philosophy of Heidegger," *Inquiry*. X (1967), 74-88.

Beaufret, Jean. "Le 'Dialogue avec le Marxisme' et la 'Question de la Technique'," in *Dialogue avec Heidegger*, Volume II. *Philosophie Moderne*. Paris: Les Editions de Minuit, 1973.

Caputo, John D. "Being, Ground, and Play in Heidegger," *Man and World*. 3 (1971), 26-48.

—————. "Heidegger's Original Ethics," *The New Scholasticism*. 45 (Winter, 1971), 127-138.

—————. "'Meister Eckhart and the Later Heidegger: The Mystical Element in Heidegger's Thinking," *The Journal of the History of Philosophy*. XII (October, 1974), 479-494 and XIII (January, 1975), 61-80.

—————. "The Question of Being and Transcendental Phenomenology: On Heidegger's Relation to Husserl," *Research in Phenomenology*. VII (1977), 84-105.

_____. "The Rose is Without Why: An Interpretation of the Later Heidegger," *Philosophy Today*. XV (1971), 3-15.

_____. "Time and Being in Heidegger," *The Modern Schoolman*. 50 (May, 1973), 324-349.

Ching, Julia. "'Authentic Selfhood': Wang Yang-Ming and Heidegger," *The Monist*. 61 (January, 1978), 3-27.

Cress, Donald W. "Heidegger's Criticism of 'Entitative Metaphysics' in his Later Writings," *International Philosophical Quarterly*. XII (March, 1972), 69-86.

Dauenhauer, Bernard. "Heidegger, Spokesman for the Dweller," *The Southern Journal of Philosophy*, XII (Summer, 1977), 189-200.

_____. "Renovating the Problem of Politics," *The Review of Metaphysics*. XXIX (June, 1976), 626-641.

Edwards, Paul, "Heidegger and Death: A Deflationary Critique," *The Monist*. 59 (April, 1976), 161-186.

Elliston, Frederick. "Phenomenology Reinterpreted: From Husserl to Heidegger," *Philosophy Today*. XXI (Fall, 1977), 273-283.

Erickson, Stephen. "Martin Heidegger," *The Review of Metaphysics*. XIX (March, 1966), 462-485.

Fu, Charles Wei-hsun. "Creative Hermeneutics: Taoist Metaphysics and Heidegger," *Journal of Chinese Philosophy*. 3 (1976), 115-143.

_____. "Heidegger and Zen on Being and Nothingness: A Critical Essay in Transmetaphysical Dialectics," in *Buddhist and Western Philosophy: A Critical Study* (New Delhi: Sterling Publishing Co., 1978).

_____. "The Trans-onto-theo-logical Foundations of Language in Heidegger and Taoism," *Journal of Chinese Philosophy*. I (1975), 130-161.

Fulton, James Street. "The Event of Being," *Southwestern Journal of Philosophy*. VI (Winter, 1975), 7-13.

Goldstein, Leon. "Heidegger and Plato on the Good," *Philosophy Today*. XXII (Winter, 1978), 332-354.

Grunder, K. "Martin Heideggers Wissenschaftkritik in ihren geschichtlichen Zusammenhangen," *Archiv für Philosophie*. 11 (1961), 312-335.

Guzzoni, Alfred. "Ontologische Differenz und Nichts," *Martin Heidegger zum siebzigsten Gebürtstag*. Pfullingen: Günther Neske, 1959.

Jaspers, Karl. "On Heidegger." Translated by Dale L. Ponikvar, *Graduate Faculty Philosophy Journal*. VII (Spring, 1978), 107-128.

Jung, Hwa Yol and Petee Jung. "To Save the Earth," *Philosophy Today* (Summer, 1975), 108-117.

Habermas, Jürgen. "Martin Heidegger: On the Publication of Lectures from the Year 1935." Translated by Dale L. Ponikvar, *Graduate Faculty Philosophy Journal*. VI (Fall, 1977), 155-173.

Harries, Karsten. "Fundamental Ontology and the Search for Man's Place," *Heidegger and Modern Philosophy*.

_____. "Heidegger as a Political Thinker," *The Review of Metaphysics*. XXIX (June, 1976), 642-669.

Hinman, Lawrence M. "Heidegger, Edwards, and Being-towards-Death," *Southern Journal of Philosophy*. XVI (Fall, 1978), 193-212.

Kreeft, Peter. "Zen in Heidegger's *Gelassenheit*," *International Philosophical Quarterly*. 11 (December, 1971), 521-545.

Krell, David Farrell. "General Introduction: 'The Question of Being'," in *Martin Heidegger: Basic Writings*. Edited by David Farrell Krell. New York: Harper & Row, 1977.

——————. "The Heidegger-Jaspers Relation," *The Journal of the British Society for Phenomenology*. IX (May, 1978), 126-130.

——————. "Towards an Ontology of Play," *Research in Phenomenology*. II (1972), 63-94.

Lampert, Lawrence. "Heidegger's Nietzsche Interpretation," *Man and World*. VII (November, 1974), 353-378.

Leist, F. "Heidegger und Nietzsche," *Philosophische Jahrbuch*. 70 (1972), 363-394.

Löwith, Karl. "The Nature of Man and the World of Nature for Heidegger's 80th Birthday." Translated by R. Phillip O'Hàra. *The Southern Journal of Philosophy*. VII (Winter, 1970), 304-318.

Maly, Ken. "Toward *Ereignis*," *Research in Phenomenology*. III (1973), 63-93.

Marcuse, Herbert. "Beiträge zu einer Phänomenologie des historischen Materialismus," *Philosophische Hefte*, I (1928), 45-68.

—————— and Frederich Olafson. "Heidegger's Politics: An Interview," *Graduate Faculty Philosophy Journal*. VI (Winter, 1977), 28-40.

——————. "Ueber konkrete Philosophie," *Archiv für Sozialwissenschaft und Sozialpolitik*. 62 (1929), 111-128.

Maurer, Reinhart. "Der angewandte Heidegger: Herbert Marcuse und das akademische Proletariat," *Philosophisches Jahrbuch*. LXX (1970), 238-259.

——————. "From Heidegger to Practical Philosophy." Translated by Walter E. Wright. *Idealistic Studies*. III (May, 1973), 133-162.

Mehta, J.L. "Heidegger and Vedanta: Reflections on a Questionable Theme," *International Philosophical Quarterly*. 18 (June, 1978), 121-144.

Moehling, Karl A. "Heidegger and the Nazis," *Listening*. 12 (Fall, 1977), 92-105.

Morrison, Ronald P. "Kant, Husserl, and Heidegger on Time and the Unity of 'Consciousness'," *Philosophy and Phenomenological Research*. XXXIX (December, 1978), 182-198.

Moser, Simon. "Toward a Metaphysics of Technology." Translated by William Carroll. Edited by Carl Mitcham and Robert Mackey. *Philosophy Today*. XV (Summer, 1971), 129-156.

O'Meara, Thomas F. "Heidegger on God," *Continuum*. V (1968), 686-698.

Petrovic, Gajo. "Der Spruch des Heideggers," *Durchblicke: Martin Heidegger zum 80. Gebürtstag*. Frankfurt am Main: Vittorio Klostermann, 1970.

Piccone, Paul and Aleander Delfini. "Herbert Marcuse's Heideggerean Marxism," *Telos*. (Fall, 1970), 36-46.

Pöggeler, Otto. "Being as Appropriation." Translated by Ruediger Hermann

Grimm. *Philosophy Today.* XIX (Summer, 1975), 152-178.
_____. "Heidegger Today." Translated by R. Phillip O'Hara. *The Southern Journal of Philosophy.* VII (Winter, 1970), 273-308.
_____. "Metaphysik und Seinstopik bei Heidegger," *Philosophische Jahrbuch.* LXX (1962), 118-137.
_____. "Zum Tode Martin Heidegger," *Research in Phenomenology.* VII (1977), 31-42.
Richardson, William J. "Heidegger's Critique of Science," *The New Scholasticism.* 42 (Fall, 1968), 511-536.
Rollin, Bernard. "Heidegger's Philosophy of History in *Being and Time,*" *The Modern Schoolman.* 49 (January, 1972), 97-112.
Rorty, Richard. "Overcoming the Tradition: Heidegger and Dewey," in *Heidegger and Modern Philosophy.*
Sachsse, Hans. "Die Technik in der Sicht Herbert Marcuses und Martin Heideggers," *Proceedings* of the IVth World Congress of Philosophy (1973).
Scanlon, John. "The Epoche and Phenomenological Anthropology," *Research in Phenomenology,* II (1972), 95-110.
Schaeffler, R. "Martin Heidegger und die Frage nach der Technik," *Zeitschrift für philosophische Forschuung.* 16 (1954), 118-125.
Schmitt, Alfred. "Existential-Ontologie und Historischen Materialismus bei Herbert Marcuse," *Antworten auf Herbert Marcuse.* Edited by Jürgen Habermas. Frankfurt: Suhrkamp, 1968.
Schrag, Calvin O. "Heidegger on Repetition and Historical Understanding," *Philosophy East and West.* XX (July, 1970), 287-295.
Schulz, Walter. "Über den philosophiegeschichtlichen Ort Martin Heideggers," *Philosphische Rundschau.* I (1953-54), 65-92, 211-232.
Schürmann, Reiner. "Anti-Humanism: Reflections of the Turn towards the Post-Modern Epoch," *Man and World.* 12 (No. 2, 1979), 160-177.
_____. "Heidegger and Meister Eckhart on Releasement," *Research in Phenomenology,* III (1973), 95-119.
_____. "The Loss of Origin in Soto Zen and Meister Eckhart," *The Thomist.* 42 (April, 1978), 281-312.
_____. "Political Thinking in Heidegger," *Social Research.* 45 (Spring, 1978), 191-221.
_____. "Principles Precarious: The Origin of the Political in Heidegger," *Heidegger, The Man and the Thinker.* Edited by Thomas J. Sheehan. Chicago: Precedent Publishers, 1979.
_____. "Questioning the Foundations of Practical Philosophy," *Human Studies.* I (1979), 357-368.
_____. "Trois penseurs de délaissement: Maitre Eckhart, Heidegger, et Suzuki," *Journal of the History of Philosophy.* XII (October, 1974), 455-478, and XII (January, 1975), 43-60.

Schwann, Alexander. "Martin Heidegger, Politik, und Praktische Philosophie: Zur Problematik neuerer Heidegger Literatur," *Philosophisches Jahrbuch*. 81 (1974), 148-172.

Sheehan, Thomas J. "Getting to the Topic: The New Edition of *Wegmarken*," *Research in Phenomenology*. VII (1977), 299-316.

——————. "Heidegger, Aristotle, and Phenomenology," *Philosophy Today*. XIX (Summer, 1975), 299-316.

——————. "Heidegger's Early Years: Fragments for a Philosophical Biography," *Listening*. XII (Fall, 1977), 3-20.

——————. "Heidegger's Interpretation of Aristotle: *Dynamis* and *Ereignis*," *Philosophical Research Archives*. IV, no. 1253 (1978).

——————. "Heidegger's 'Introduction to the Phenomenology of Religion,' 1920-21," *The Personalist*. 60 (July, 1979), 312-324.

Smith, Christopher. "Heidegger's Critique of Absolute Knowledge," *The New Scholasticism*. 45 (Winter, 1971), 56-86.

——————. "Heidegger's Misinterpretation of Rilke," *Philosophy and Literature*. III (Spring, 1979), 3-19.

——————. "Heidegger, Hegel, and the Problem of *das Nichts*," *International Philosophical Quarterly*. VIII (September, 1968), 379-405.

Steffney, John. "Transmetaphysical Thinking in Heidegger and Zen Buddhism," *Philosophy East and West*. 27 (July, 1977), 323-335.

Stewart, Roderick M. "Signification and Radical Subjectivity in Heidegger's *Habilitationsschrift*," *Man and World*. 12 (no. 3, 1979), 360-386.

Taminiaux, Jacques. "Heidegger and Husserl's *Logical Investigations*." Translated by Jeffrey Stevens. *Radical Phenomenology*. Edited by John Sallis. Atlantic Highlands, N.J.: Humanities Press, 1978.

Watson, James R. "Heidegger's Hermeneutic Phenomenology," *Philosophy Today*. XV (Spring, 1971), 30-43.

White, David A. "A Refutation of Heidegger as Nihilist," *The Personalist*. 56 (Summer, 1975), 276-288.

Wren, Thomas E. "Heidegger's Philosophy of History," *The Journal of the British Society for Phenomenology*. IX (May, 1978), 126-130.

Zimmerman, Michael E. "Marx and Heidegger on the Technological Domination of Nature," *Philosophy Today*. 23 (Summer, 1979), 99-112.

——————. "A Comparison of Nietzsche's Overman and Heidegger's Authentic Self," *The Southern Journal of Philosophy*. XIV (Spring, 1976), 213-231.

——————. "Beyond Humanism: Heidegger's Understanding of Technology," *Listening*. XII (Fall, 1977), 74-83.

——————. "Dewey, Heidegger, and the Quest for Certainty," *The Southwestern Journal of Philosophy*. IX (1978), 87-95.

——————. "Heidegger and Nietzsche on Authentic Time," *Cultural Hermeneutics*. IV (1977), 234-264.

_____. "Heidegger, Ethics, and National Socialism," *The Southwestern Journal of Philosophy*. V (Spring, 1974), 97-106.

_____. "Heidegger and Marcuse: Technology as Ideology," *Research in Philosophy and Technology*. Volume II. Edited by Paul T. Durbin and Carl Mitcham. Greenwich, Conn.: Jai Press, 1979.

_____. "Heidegger on Nihilism and Technique," *Man and World*. VIII (November, 1975), 394-414.

_____. "On Discriminating Everydayness, Unownedness, and Falling in *Being and Time*," *Research in Phenomenology*. V (1975), 109-128.

_____. "Some Important Themes in Current Heidegger Research," *Research in Phenomenology*. VII (1977), 259-281.

_____. "Technological Culture and the End of Philosophy," *Research in Philosophy and Technology*. Volume II. Edited by Paul T. Durbin and Carl Mitcham. Greenwich, Conn.: Jai Press, 1979.

II. OTHER SOURCES REFERRED TO IN FOOTNOTES.

A. *Books*

Arendt, Hannah. *The Human Condition*. New York: Doubleday & Company, 1959.

_____. *The Life of the Mind*. Two Volumes. New York: Harcourt, Brace, Jovanovitch, 1978.

_____. *The Origins of Totalitarianism*. New York: The World Publishing Company, Inc., 1962.

Aristotle. *The Basic Works of Aristotle*. Edited by Richard McKeon. New York: Random House, 1941.

Aronowitz, Stanley. *False Promises: The Shaping of American Working Class Consciousness*. New York: McGraw Hill, 1973.

Axelos, Kostas. *Alienation, Praxis, and Techne in the Thought of Karl Marx*. Translated by Ronald Bruzina. Austin: The University of Texas Press, 1976.

Ballard, Edward G. *Man and Technology*. Pittsburgh: Duquesne University Press, 1978.

Barnet, Richard J. and Ronald E. Müller. *Global Reach: The Power of the Multinational Corporations*. New York: Simon and Schuster, 1974.

Biddis, Michael O. *The Age of the Masses*. New York: Harper & Row, 1977.

Brown, Bruce. *Marx, Freud, and the Critique of Everyday Life*. New York: Monthly Review Press, 1973.

Bultmann, Rudolf. *Existence and Faith*. Translated by Schubert M. Ogden. New York: Meridian Books, Inc., 1960.

_____. *Faith and Understanding*. Translated by Louise Pettibone Smith. New York: Harper & Row, 1969.

Campbell, Joseph. *The Hero with a Thousand Faces*. Princeton: Princeton University Press/Bollingen Series, 1972.

Capra, Fritjof. *The Tao of Physics*. New York: Bantam Books, 1975.

Conze, Edward. *Buddhism: Its Essence and Development*. New York: Harper & Row, 1975.

Dunne, John. *The Way of All the Earth*. New York: MacMillan Publishing Co., 1972.

Erikson, Erik H. *Gandhi's Truth: On the Origins of Militant Nonviolence*. New York: W.W. Norton & Co., Inc., 1969.

Fest, Joachim C. *The Face of the Third Reich*. Translated by Michael Bullock. Middlesex: Penguin Books, 1970.

Fink, Eugen. *Spiel als Welt-Symbol*. Berlin: Walter de Gruyter & Co., 1968.

Freud, Sigmund. *Civilization and Its Discontents*. Translated and edited by James Strachey. New York: W.W. Norton & Company, Inc., 1961.

Fromm, Erich. *The Art of Loving*. New York: Harper & Row, 1956.

_____. *Escape from Freedom*. New York: Avon Books, 1969.

Gay, Peter. *Weimar Culture: The Outsider as Insider*. New York: Harper & Row, 1968.

Graham, Dom Aelred. *Zen Catholicism*. New York: Harcourt, Brace, & World, Inc., 1963.

Hardmann, Oscar. *The Christian Doctrine of Grace*. London: The Centenary Press, 1946.

Ihde, Don. *Technics and Praxis*. Boston: D. Reidel Publishing Company, 1979.

Jaspers, Karl. *Psychologie der Weltanschauungen*. Berlin: Springer Verlag, 1954.

Jay, Martin. *The Dialectical Imagination*. Boston: Little, Brown, and Company, 1973.

Jung, C.G. *Memories, Dreams, Reflections*. Edited by Aniela Jaffé. Translated by Richard and Clara Winston. New York: Vintage Books, 1965.

_____. *Symbols of Transformation*. Translated by R.F.C. Hull. Princeton: Princeton University Press/Bollingen Series, 1976.

Jünger, Ernst. *Der Arbeiter*. Hamburg: Hanseatische Verlaganstalt, 1932.

Hegel, G.W.F. *Reason in History*. Translated by Robert S. Hartman. New York: The Bobbs-Merrill Company, Inc., 1953.

Herrigel, Eugen. *The Method of Zen*. Edited by Hermann Tausend. Translated by R.F.C. Hull. New York: Vintage Books, 1974.

_____. *Zen and the Art of Archery*. Translated by R.F.C. Hull. New York: Vintage Books, 1971.

Husserl, Edmund. *Logical Investigations*. Translated by J.N. Findlay. New York: Humanities Press, 1970.

_____. *The Phenomenology of Internal Time Consciousness*. Edited by Martin Heidegger. Translated by James S. Churchill. Bloomington: Indiana University Press, 1967.

Kapleau, Philip. *Three Pillars of Zen*. Boston: Beacon Press, 1967.

Kerygma and Myth. Edited by Hans-Werner Bartsch. London: S.P.C.K., 1960.

Kierkegaard, Søren. *The Concept of Dread*. Translated by Walter Lowrie. Princeton: Princeton University Press.

_____. *Concluding Unscientific Postscript*. Translated by David F. Swenson and Walter Lowrie. Princeton: Princeton University Press, 1969.

_____. *Either/Or*. Translated by Walter Lowrie. New York: Doubleday & Company, Inc., 1959.

_____. *The Present Age*. Translated by Alexander Dru. New York: Harper & Row, 1962.

Kosik, Karel. *Dialectics of the Concrete*. Translated by Karel Kovanda with James Schmitt. Dordrecht: D. Reidel Publishing Company, 1976.

Lefebvre, Henri. *Everyday Life in the Modern World*. Translated by Sache Rabinovitch. New York: Harper & Row, 1971.

Leiss, William. *The Domination of Nature*. Boston: Beacon Press, 1974.

Lukacs, John. *The Passing of the Modern Age*. New York: Harper & Row, 1970.

Macpherson, C.B. *The Political Theory of Possessive Individualism*. Oxford: The Clarendon Press, 1962.

Marcuse, Herbert. *An Essay on Liberation*: Boston: Beacon Press, 1969.

_____. *Eros and Civilization*. Boston: Beacon Press, 1966.

_____. *One Dimensional Man*. Boston: Beacon Press, 1964.

Marx, Karl. *Capital*. Translated by Ben Fowkes. New York: Vintage Books, 1976.

_____. *Grundrisse: Foundations of the Critique of Political Economy*. Translated by Martin Nicolaus. New York: Vintage Books, 1973.

Masunaga, Reiho. *A Primer of Soto Zen: A Translation of Dogen's Shobogenzo Zusmonki*. Honolulu: The University of Hawaii Press, 1975.

May, Rollo. *Love and Will*. New York: W.W. Norton & Co., Inc., 1969.

Merton, Thomas. *Mystics and Zen Masters*. New York: Dell Publishing Co., Inc., 1967.

_____. *Zen and the Birds of Appetite*. New York: New Directions Publishing Company, 1967.

Mosse, George L. *The Crisis of German Ideology*. New York: Grosset & Dunlap, 1964.

Neumann, Erich. *The Origins and History of Consciousness*. Translated by R.F.C. Hull. Princeton: Princeton University Press/Bollingen Series, 1970.

Nietzsche, Friedrich. *The Basic Writings*. Translated by Walter Kaufmann. New York: Modern Library, 1968.

_____. *The Gay Science*. Translated by Walter Kaufmann. New York: Vintage Books, 1974.

_____. *The Portable Nietzsche*. Translated by Walter Kaufmann. New York: The Viking Press, 1968.

_____. *The Will to Power*. Translated by Walter Kaufmann and R.J. Hollingdale. New York: Vintage Books, 1967.

Ogden, Schubert. *Christ without Myth*. New York: Harper & Row, 1961.

_____. *The Reality of God*. London: S.C.M. Press, 1967.

Ortega y Gasset, José. *The Revolt of the Masses*. New York: Mentor Books, 1956.

Pascal, Blaise. *Pensées*. Translated by A.J. Krailscheimer. Middlesex: Penguin Books, 1979.

Plato, *Phaedo*. Translated by Hugh Tredennick in *The Collected Dialogues of Plato*. Edited by Edith Hamilton and Huntington Cairns. New York: Pantheon Books, 1963.

Prather, Hugh. *Notes on Love and Courage*. New York: Doubleday & Company, Inc., 1977.

Radhakrishnan, R., editor and translator. *The Bhagavadgita*. New York: Harper & Row, 1973.

_____. *Eastern Religions and Western Thought*: Delhi: Oxford University Press, 1974.

Ram Dass, Baba. *Be Here Now*. New York: Crown Publishers, 1971.

Robinson, James M., editor. *The Future of Our Religious Past: Essays in Honour of Rudolf Bultmann*. New York: Harper & Row, 1971.

Rosen, Stanley. *Nihilism*. New Haven: Yale University Press, 1969.

Ross, Nancy Wilson. *The World of Zen*. New York: Vintage Books, 1960.

Sartre, Jean-Paul. *Being and Nothingness*. Translated by Hazel Barnes. New York: Philosophical Library, 1956.

St. John of the Cross. *Dark Night of the Soul*. Translated by Allison Peers. New York: Doubleday Image Books, 1959.

Sekida, Katsuki. *Zen Training*. Edited by A.V. Grimstone. New York: John Weatherhill, Inc., 1977.

Slater, Philip. *The Pursuit of Loneliness*. Boston: Beacon Press, 1970.

Sokolowki, Robert. *The Formation of Husserl's Concept of Constitution*. The Hague: Martinus Nijhoff, 1970.

_____. *Husserlian Meditations: How Words Present Things*. Evanston: Northwestern University Press, 1974.

Stack, George J. *Kierkegaard's Existential Ethics*. University, Alabama: The University of Alabama Press, 1977.

Steiner, George. *After Babel: Aspects of Language and Translation*. London: Oxford University Press, 1975.

Suzuki, D.T. *Essays in Zen Buddhism*, First Series. New York: Grove Press, 1961.

_____. *Zen and Japanese Culture*. Princeton: Princeton University Press/ Bollingen Series, 1973.

_____. *Zen Buddhism*. Edited by William Barrett. New York: Doubleday & Co., Inc., 1956.

Suzuki, Shunryu. *Zen Mind, Beginner's Mind*. Edited by Trudy Dixon. New York: John Weatherhill, Inc., 1977.

Tillich, Paul. *Philosophie und Schicksal. Gesammelte Werke*, Volume IV. Stuttgart: Evangelische Verlagswerk, 1963.

_____. *Der Widerstreit um Raum und Zeit. Gesammelte Werke*, Volume VI. Stuttgart: Evangelische Verlagswerk, 1963.

Trungpa, Chögyam. *Cutting Through Spiritual Materialism*. Boulder: Shambhala Publications, Inc., 1975.

Tucker, Robert. *Philosophy and Myth in Karl Marx.* Cambridge: Cambridge University Press, 1972.

Watts, Alan W. *The Way of Zen.* New York: Vintage Books, 1957.

Yokoi, Yuhu with Daizen Victorio. *Zen Master Dogen.* New York: John Weatherhill, Inc. 1976.

B. *Articles*

Abe Masao. "Dogen on Buddha Nature." *The Eastern Buddhist.* IV (May, 1971), 28-71.

Barth, Karl. "Bultmann: An Attempt to Understand Him." *Kerygma and Myth,* II. Edited by Hans-Werner Bartsch. Translated by Reginald Fuller. London: S.P.C.K., 1962.

Buckley, Frank M. "The Everyday Struggle for the Leisurely Attitude," *Humanitas.* VIII (November, 1972), 307-321.

Buri, Fritz. "The Concept of Grace in Paul, Shinran, and Luther." *The Eastern Buddhist.* IX (October, 1976), 21-42.

Dallmeyer, Fred R. "Phenomenology and Critical Theory: *Adorno,*" *Cultural Hermeneutics.* 3 (July, 1976), 367-405.

Ebeling, Gerhard. "Time and Word." Translated by Charles E. Carlston and Robert P. Scharlemann, in *The Future of Our Religious Past.* Edited by James Robinson. New York: Harper & Row, 1971.

Fruchter, Norman. "Movement Propaganda and the Culture of the Spectacle," *Liberation.* (May, 1971).

Gold, Howard B. "Praxis: Its Conceptual Development in Aristotle's *Nichomachean Ethics,*" *Graduate Faculty Philosophy Journal.* VI (Winter, 1977), 106-130.

Gurwitsch, Aron. "A Non-Egological Conception of Consciousness," in his *Studies in Phenomenology and Psychology.* Evanston: Northwestern University Press, 1966.

Jung, Hwa Yol and Petee Jung. "Toward a New Humanism: The Politics of Civilization in a "No-Growth' Society," *Man and World.* IX (August, 1976), 283-306.

Kuhn, Helmut. "The Phenomenological Concept of 'Horizon'," *Philosophical Essays in Memory of Marvin Farber.* Cambridge: Harvard University Press, 1949.

Lazere, Donald. "Mass Culture, Political Consciousness, and English Studies," *College English.* 38 (April, 1977), 751-767.

Olafson, Frederick A. "Consciousness and Intentionality in Husserl's Thought," *American Philosophical Quarterly.* 12 (April, 1975), 91-103.

Pallis, Marco. "Is There Room for 'Grace' in Buddhism?", in *The Sword of Gnosis.* Edited by Jacob Needleman. Baltimore: Penguin Books, 1974.

Schmitt, Alfred. "Existential-Ontologie und historischen Materialismus bei Herbert Marcuse," in *Antworten auf Herbert Marcuse.* Edited by Jurgen Habermas. Frankfurt: Suhrkamp, 1968.

Sessions, George. "Spinoza and Jeffers on Man in Nature," *Inquiry*. 20 (No. 4, 1977), 481-528.

_____. "Anthropocentrism and the Environmental Crisis," *Humboldt Journal of Social Relations*. II (Fall/Winter, 1974), 1-12.

Scott, Charles E. "Self-Consciousness without an Ego," *Man and World*. IV (May, 1971), 193-201.

Singleton, Mack. "Morality and Tragedy in *Celestina*," in *Studies in Honor of Lloyd A. Kasten*. Madison, Wisconsin: Hispanic Seminary of Medieval Studies, 1975.

Addendum: Received too late to be incorporated in the text, but of special value for understanding Heidegger as a deep ecological thinker, is Dolores LaChapelle's *Earth Wisdom* (Los Angeles: The Guild of Tutors Press, 1978).

Index of Subjects

Abgrund 154
Abgeschiedenheit 248
absence 38, 106, 110, 118, 125, 136, 137, 153, 155, 201, 202, 229, 230, 233, 237, 239-241, 247, 249, 251, 254, 263, 268, 270, 272
Absturz 62
absurdity 220
abyss 93, 143, 152, 154, 237, 243, 249-250, 263
acquisitiveness 49
actualitas 205
actuality 7, 121, 131, 146, 254
actus purus 23, 237
adequatio 22
aeon 238-239, 247
aesthete 78, 120, 122
agape 129
agathon 167, 205, 216
aletheia 21, 201, 204, 233, 239, 257
alienation 52, 225, 273
alreadiness 14, 153
ambiguity 53, 55, 57, 58, 66, 78, 225
amor fati 155-158, 265-267

Angst 54, 56, 62-65, 75, 114, 120, 138-139, 145, 152, 160, 250
animals 107, 115, 126
anomie 193
anthropocentrism 167, 205, 216
anticipation 70-71, 73, 79-80, 93, 99-101, 120, 133, 140, 142
Anwesen 16, 105, 184, 203, 205
Anwesenheit 210
anxiety 56-57, 60, 160, 226
appetitio 212
apprehending 186-187
appropriation 123-124, 130, 132, 141, 155, 228, 230, 234, 236, 239-40, 243-245, 248, 255
arche 238
aristocrat 177
art 90-91, 157, 189, 215, 221, 276
Augenblick xxx, 122, 132-133, 135-136, 143-144, 148-150, 153, 155, 157-158, 160-169, 181, 255
Ausdauer 246

Auseinandersetzung 160, 178
authenticity xix,ff., 1, 3, 12, 17,
    19, 24, 40-46, 52, 54-55, 58,
    62-63, 67, 69, 71, 75, 77, 79,
    81-82, 84, 86, 89, 93-94, 96-
    100, 114, 120-125, 128-129,
    131, 133-135, 139-142, 144,
    146-150, 153, 155, 158, 160,
    161, 163-164, 166-169, 172-
    173, 176, 184, 185, 188-
    190, 196, 198-199, 228-275,
    284
autonomy 74, 129
averageness 46
awareness 109, 187, 234

becoming 156, 165-166, 203,
    215, 237
Befindlichkeit 53-54
begreifen 108
being xxvii, 84, 99, 102, 106-
    108, 111-113, 120, 122, 124,
    125, 130, 153-154, 155, 156,
    161-166, 181, 184, 186, 198,
    201-204, 208, 240, 247, 249,
    255, 251, 267, 270
Being xx, xxii, xxv, xxviii, 1-2,
    5, 8, 11-12, 16, 18, 20-21,
    24-25, 31-32
Being and Time xx-xxv, 1-2,
    11-12, 14, 16, 21, 26, 31-42,
    43-49, 52-53, 55-58, 62, 64-
    66, 69-70, 78, 86, 89, 93-
    94, 96, 98, 100-103, 113-
    119, 125, 130, 132-135, 138,
    142-143, 163, 199, 201-202,

    229, 231, 233, 239, 244-46,
    250
Being-in 53, 58, 62
Being-in-the-truth 66-67
Being-in-the-untruth 66-67
Being-in-the-world 30, 39, 47,
    102, 133
Being-towards-death 34, 40, 68-
    70, 84, 99, 119, 121, 139
beingness 23, 212, 215
Bestand 219
bestialitas 213
bestowing 166
Bible 26, 50
Bild 221
Brahman 257
brutalitas 213
Buddha-nature 258, 261, 263,
    265
Buddhism 88, 255-276
business 214

capital 224
capitalism 170, 177, 179, 182-
    183, 193
care 30, 44, 64-67, 71, 74,
    97, 100-101, 103, 111, 115,
    128, 130, 157, 246
categories 8, 10, 21, 101, 106,
    107, 109-111, 212
Catholicism 6, 98, 208-209
certainty 208-213
certitudo 210
challenging 219
character-structure 193
Ch'en 265

choice 89
chreon 204
Christianity 5, 14-15, 129, 197, 206-209, 211, 248, 271
Christendom 207-209, 214
circumspection 56
clearing xxix, 1, 16, 19, 22-23, 25, 37-38, 105, 111, 148, 161, 181, 202, 230, 245, 248, 250
cogito 28, 210
collective unconscious 86
commodity 147, 197-198, 220, 223
communism 91, 170, 177, 182-183
community 84-87, 126, 131-132, 148, 151, 172, 176, 190, 194, 199, 208
compassion 94-95
conatus 212
concealment 67, 96, 153-154, 164, 181, 185, 187, 191, 197, 201-205, 217, 230, 232-233, 238, 251
concipere 108
connectedness 102, 118-120
conscience xxiii, 13, 29, 55, 60, 73-76, 78, 98, 121, 129, 139, 149, 175, 199, 208, 214, 229, 254
consciousness 26, 136, 190, 224-25, 261
constitution 165
construction 35
contemplation 179

conversion 97-98
courage xxiii, 34, 78, 92-93, 129, 229, 233, 250, 253
cowardice 71, 78
creating 156, 162, 165-166, 184-185, 190, 192, 214
curiosity 53, 55-58, 66, 82, 225-226

Danken 247-248
Darwinism, social 178, 194
Dasein xxii, xxix, 1, 2, 9, 16, 18-19, 23, 25, 27-29, 31, 33, 35, 37-39, 41, 45, 47, 56, 58, 63, 64-65, 71, 79, 80, 86, 95-97, 102-106, 113-114, 116, 118-119, 121, 123-124, 130, 135, 139, 154, 163, 167-168, 180, 183, 188-189, 201, 229-232, 243, 248, 251, 254, 274
death 54, 59, 64, 72-73, 79-84, 87, 90-92, 101-102, 120, 123, 138-140, 142, 144-145, 157, 160, 207, 225, 250-251, 261, 270
death of God 188, 206, 235
decision 12, 19, 58, 60-61, 70-71, 78, 80, 89, 113, 118, 141, 146-147, 152, 168, 172-73, 175, 177-178, 180, 198-199, 219
deinon 188
deinotaton 188
delusion 89, 128, 160, 181, 258, 262-63, 273

democracy 91, 253
demonic, the 183
de-mythologizing xxv, 16, 61, 135, 137, 266
Denken 219, 247-248
desire 49, 175, 211, 225-226, 258
despair 79, 220, 273
destiny 11, 86, 130, 148, 162, 172-173, 177, 180, 185, 188, 192, 199, 200, 204, 252, 253
destiny of Being 96, 113, 123, 132, 166-167, 173, 180, 195, 199, 201, 228
destitution 220
destruction 35, 137
detachment 248, 255, 265, 270, 275
Dharma 274
Dhyana 265
dialogue 131, 256-257
Dichtung 178
dike 188
disclosedness 23, 40, 43-44, 52-53, 55-56, 65-67, 75, 100-101, 103, 113, 118, 124, 231
disclosure 233
discourse 53, 55, 56
divine comedy 88
domination 116, 141, 155, 164, 166, 186, 193, 195, 200, 211, 215, 219, 221, 224, 226-227, 258
dualism 25, 109, 202, 264
dwelling 249
dynamis 24, 123-124, 130, 273

earth 127-128, 131, 161, 170, 183-184, 189, 216, 219-221, 223, 226, 235, 246, 253-255, 268, 273-274
eclipse xxvii, 276
ecology 128, 223, 230, 295
economics, as world destiny 222-223
ecstases 105-107, 111-113, 120, 141, 202, 233
Edelmut 246
ego 17, 23-25, 27, 29, 35, 41-43, 49-50, 58, 64, 72, 74, 82, 84, 87-88, 97, 101, 103-104, 107-108, 111, 119-120, 139, 142, 144, 148, 151, 153, 160, 162, 167, 187, 194, 209, 211, 230, 246-47, 256, 258, 263-265, 270, 273, 276
egoism xxiii, xxvi, 43-44, 47, 50, 51-53, 57, 60, 63-64, 67, 73, 86-87, 94-95, 99, 128, 132, 135, 139-141, 144, 149-150, 152-153, 157, 162-168, 194, 197, 206-207, 211, 222, 224, 226, 245, 254, 258-259, 261-263, 268, 270, 276, 283
ego cogito 206, 209, 211, 216
eidos 16, 204-205
Eigenen 239
Eigenschaft 231
Eigensinn 247
Eigentlichkeit xxv, xxx, 135, 231, 242
Eignung 124

Einfache 274

ekaksana 261

ek-sistence 15, 231, 262

emptiness 49, 64, 153, 185, 201, 250, 255, 257-258, 260, 268

En 206

endurance 246

energeia 204-205

enframing 219

enlightenment 230, 251, 255, 258, 260-61, 264-265, 267

Enlightenment, the 168, 195

Entschlossenheit 76

Entselbstung 208

entziehen 270

epoch 145, 166, 199, 202-203

epoche 202, 264

Ereignis xxi, xxv–xxvii, 124-125, 132, 135, 157, 161, 167, 180, 191, 197, 228-229, 243, 254-55, 260, 266, 269, 274

Erleben 26

errancy 202-203

erschliessen 76

Erschlossenheit 23, 76

essentia 215

eternal return of the same xxiv, 92-93, 155-168, 215-216, 253

eternity 89, 123, 136-139, 141-144, 148, 150-151, 157, 160-161, 163, 165, 261

ethics 19

event of appropriation 135, 157, 191, 247

everydayness 39-40, 42-47, 51, 53, 64, 67, 72, 88, 90, 96, 100, 115, 119, 121, 145, 155, 223-228, 253-254, 260, 264, 268, 270-271

existence xx, 12, 14-16, 19-20, 22-23, 33, 38-40, 44-49, 59, 65, 72-73, 76-78, 84, 98, 105-106, 111, 113, 117, 120, 122, 125-126, 130, 132, 137, 139, 141, 144, 146, 150-151, 153-154, 163-164, 166, 185, 187-188, 232-233, 243, 245, 247, 274

Existenz 76, 143

existential xxix

existentialia xxix

existentialism 12, 32, 143, 150

existentiell xxix

experience 107-109, 112, 114, 119, 123, 137-138, 149, 162, 168, 212, 235, 239, 240-242, 250, 254, 263, 265-269, 272, 274, 276

facticity 15, 40, 44, 63, 65

faith 13-14, 17, 24, 81, 98, 121, 123, 138-142, 144-145, 206-207, 211

faithfulness xxii, 2, 13, 16

Fallen 48

falling 40, 43-44, 46, 48, 52-53, 58, 60, 62, 64-67, 105, 203, 225, 227

fascism 172, 196

fate xxiv, 19, 65, 120-122, 125, 130-131, 134, 137, 146-148, 152, 155, 157-158, 160-164, 166, 168, 172-173, 191, 193, 199, 208, 234

Fatum 166

fear 54, 64

finitude 15, 19, 56, 72-73, 78, 80, 87, 103, 121, 130, 133, 140-141, 144-145, 152-153, 157, 159, 212, 216, 225, 227, 262

Flying Dutchman 227

fourfold, the 235-236

framework 251

Fug 188

future xxiv, 14, 16, 60, 65-66, 71, 75, 100, 105, 115, 120-121, 123, 125, 132-133, 137, 140-141, 143-145, 148-151, 160-162, 164-166, 183, 192, 226, 253

gathering 185, 204-205, 233, 235, 241, 254

Gegend 245

Gegenstand 109, 209, 245

Gegnet 245

Geist 147, 150, 170, 177

Geisteswissenschaft 7, 10-11

Gelassenheit 180, 243, 275

Gelâzenheit 248

gelten 223

Geltung 7-8

genesthai 14

genius 181

Gerede 53, 55

Geschehen 11, 166

Geschehnis 187

Geschichte 11, 166

Geschick 11, 123, 166

Gestalt of the laborer 170

Gestapo 179

Gestell 219-220, 250

Gewalt 188

Gewesenheit 14, 122, 137, 153

Gewicht 223

gift 169, 198, 229, 241, 247-248, 275

givenness 22

golden gleam 251, 254, 259

God xxv, xxix, 11, 14-18, 29, 59-61, 73-74, 85, 88, 91, 97, 129, 136, 137-139, 141-142, 144, 150-154, 167, 191, 193, 198, 200, 202-203, 205-211, 214, 216-217, 224, 227-228, 237, 248, 255, 265, 268, 270, 273

gods 183, 187, 220, 225, 242

good 78, 151-152, 166, 175, 193

grace xxiii, 17, 64, 97-98, 129, 137-138, 144-145, 149, 197, 206-208, 248-249, 256, 263

great chain of being 209

Great Depression 270

greed 61, 89, 128, 224, 227, 258, 263

ground 23, 150-152, 154, 201, 205-206, 208-209, 211

Grund 150, 238, 249

Grundfrage 164-165

guilt 13, 18, 60, 75, 78-80, 92, 121, 137, 141, 226

Habilitationsschrift 1, 8, 278-279
haiku 267-269
handiness 36, 116
happening 186, 240
happiness 194, 214, 220, 227, 236
hate 89, 258, 263
heaven 91, 144, 152, 166, 194, 207, 257, 268, 273
Hebrews 227-228
Herausfordern 219
herd 91, 93, 157-159, 178
heritage 126, 130-131, 133, 155, 164, 172, 182, 184, 199
Herkunft 181, 246
hermeneutic circle xxi-xxii, 38, 100
hermeneutics 10-11, 37-38, 100
hermeneutical situation 39, 71, 100
hero xxvi, 69, 81-82, 84-89, 95, 121, 132, 135, 141, 150, 152-153, 164, 166-168, 180-181, 185, 188-192, 194, 199, 244, 249-250, 274
Herstellen 221
heteronomy 74, 168
historicality xxiv, 86, 119, 122
historicity 13, 81
history 9, 11, 113, 118, 121, 134, 148, 159, 166-167, 179-180, 183, 187, 193, 201-203, 213, 216, 220, 238, 241, 243, 271, 273
history of Being xxiv, 134, 179, 202, 216, 229, 243, 255
Holy, the 191, 208
Holy Grail 87
Holzwege 276
homecoming 247
hope 248
horizon 20-21, 23, 32-33, 40, 47, 101-107, 110-112, 115, 201, 216, 239, 245
house of Being 37, 255
hubris xxiv, 169-170, 174
humanism xxvi, 96, 113-114, 118, 125, 148, 183, 191, 197, 200, 208
hypokeimenon 209

I 109, 111, 130, 216, and *passim*
idea 203, 209
ideology 57
idle talk 53, 55-58, 62, 66, 72, 82, 225-226
idolatry 227
Ignatian Way 266
image 154
image, pure 110
imperialism, planetary 222
inauthenticity xx, xxii-xxiii, 1, 12, 17, 19, 41-47, 50, 52-54, 57, 62-64, 67, 94, 103-104, 120, 130, 138-139, 162, 172, 197-200, 220, 224, 228
In-der-welt-sein 39

individuation 72, 80, 85-86, 133, 158, 193
individual, world-historical 134, 164, 181, 199, 244, 249, 252
individualism 177
individuality 48, 50, 71, 97, 158
indulgences, sale of 207
industrialization 127, 147, 158, 170, 173, 178-179, 181-184, 194-195, 197, 218, 221, 227, 273
Instandigkeit 246
intentionality 25, 37
intentions, fulfilling 21-22
intentions, meaning 21-22
interpretation 35-36, 38
intuition, categorial 21-22
intuition, pure 109
inzuruckgehen 124
irrationalism 172
iustitia 208

Jansenism 98
Jemeinigkeit 33
Jesuits 98
Jews 194
joy 81, 88-89, 91, 93, 138, 145, 160, 260, 270
judgment 8, 22, 107-110, 263
jug, the 235-236
justice 298, 210, 222
justification 207, 222

kairos xxiv, 101, 123, 135, 137-138, 144-149, 167, 207, 261

Kampf 77, 184, 274
Kehre xx-xxi, 231
kensho 258
koan 264, 266
koto ba 256

labor 115, 127
language xxviii, 23, 37, 55, 154, 169, 179-180, 185, 200, 203, 231, 241-242, 254-255, 260, 267-268, 270-272, 274-276
Lebensphilosophie 26, 116, 195
Lebensraum 221
legein 180, 185-186, 204, 234, 241, 243
Leitfrage 164-165
letting be 157, 165, 181, 189, 250, 259
liberalism 158
Lichtung 37, 148, 202
life 91-96, 114-116, 120, 125, 137, 140-141, 144-145, 148, 157-158, 159-160, 162, 168, 174, 208, 213, 220, 226-227, 246, 255, 261, 263, 274
light of Being 202-203, 257, 259
lightning flash 250-251, 254, 260, 270
logic 7
logic of domination 219
Logos xxv-xxvi, xxviii, xxx, 23, 55, 146, 185-186, 204-206, 233-235, 238-244, 254, 256,

260, 268, 270-271, 273-274, 276
loneliness 158
love 49, 60, 85, 95, 128, 142, 150, 153, 157-158, 161, 165-166, 228, 248-249, 265
loyalty 125

Macht 183
man 113-114, 116-118, 130, 134, 136, 146, 151-152, 154, 159, 161, 166, 173, 182-184, 187-189, 199, 202-203, 208, 211, 215, 217-220, 223-228, 230, 237-238, 240-241, 244, 249, 252, 271, 274
Man 44, 48
manifestness 25, 84, 116, 136, 153-154, 164, 185, 198, 201, 203-204, 230, 233, 255, 258-260, 272
Marxism 115, 159, 183
mass culture 51-52, 127, 179, 182, 218, 220, 291-282
meditation 255, 264-266
me kalon 188
metaphysics 23, 25, 32, 117, 143, 155, 162, 169, 174, 205-206, 211-213, 218, 231-232, 271-273
mindfulness 258
mineness 33, 47
Mitteilen 166
moira 204
moment of vision xxiv, 122, 140, 142-143, 147, 251, 254
monads 211-212, 236-237

moods 54, 66, 160
mortality xxiii, 41-42, 48-49, 52, 54, 64, 67, 72, 74-76, 80, 82-84, 88, 96, 120, 128, 139, 157, 160, 207, 225, 251
mortals 235, 253, 274
myth of the cave 87-88
myth of the hero 69, 81-82, 84-89
myth of the sun 106
mythology 184
mysterium tremendum 206
mystery 240, 251, 256, 263
mysticism 217. 248-49, 265-266, 270

Nähe 190
Nahheit 239
nationalism 158, 172, 174
National Socialism xxiv, xxvii, 4, 62, 127, 158-159, 168, 169-197, 289-290
Nationalsozialistische Deutsche Arbeiterpartei (NSDAP) 171
Nature 3, 10, 116, 146-147, 184, 193, 200, 211, 213, 216, 218, 227, 230-231
Naturwissenschaft 7, 11
nearness 239
necessity xxiv, 19, 120-121, 131, 152, 158, 160, 162, 173, 241, 247, 270
Neugier 53
New Testament 13-17, 61, 98, 101, 135-137, 140, 148, 167, 206, 243, 268

Nichts 118, 201
Nihilism 96, 115, 158-159, 199, 201, 205, 214, 216, 291
noble-mindedness 246-247
noein 186
no-mind 258
no-self 258
not-doing 246-147
nothingness 23, 50, 54, 64, 88, 118, 125, 144, 153-154, 185-186, 201, 205, 230, 243, 251
nunc stans 138, 150

obiacere 209
object 25-27, 78, 107-110, 112, 114-116, 147, 164, 182, 200, 202-203, 209, 212, 216, 218, 235, 245, 247-248, 259, 264, 268
objectification 115, 221
objectivity 116, 175, 205, 212, 252, 263
Old Testament 227-228, 243, 294
one-dimensional society 253
ontical xxix
ontological xxix
ontological difference 106
ontology 11-12, 17, 32, 78, 153, 197, 245
openness xxii, 23, 28, 43, 47, 49-50, 54, 64, 75-76, 96, 99-100, 102, 105, 109, 119, 129-130, 142, 144, 154-155, 165, 198, 203, 226, 229, 232-233, 236, 238, 246, 248, 253, 257, 259

order, overpowering 188
origin 181
original sin 50, 52, 58
ought 8
ousia 23-24, 105, 123, 204
overcoming 92
Overman xxiii, 69, 89-96, 147, 155, 159-161, 192, 215-216, 253
owning 242

pantheism 150
parousia 14, 136, 138
past xxiv, 14, 16, 60, 65-66, 72, 75, 100, 115, 120-121, 132-133, 137, 140, 143-144, 148, 150, 150-151, 157, 160-162, 164-165
pathwat 3, 274-276
patience 264
peasantry 126-127
person 26
personality 9, 87
perspectivism 90, 96, 116, 118
phenomenology 12, 17, 19-22, 36
phenomenalism 263
phenomenon 36-37, 110, 124, 137, 168
philosopher king 179
philosophy 9, 15, 18-20, 24-25, 62, 70, 77, 79, 124, 135, 144, 167, 169, 180, 182, 184, 196, 206, 216, 221, 245, 257, 260, 266, 269-270, 276
philosophy of life 26, 116

phronesis 175-178, 261
physis 184-186, 203, 239
pity 91, 94-95
plants 124, 126, 131, 185-186
Platonism 205, 207
play xxv, 91, 158-159, 167-
168, 188, 191, 199, 201,
203, 217, 230, 233, 236,
238, 240, 250-251, 253-256,
260, 270-271, 275-276
poet 37, 87, 135, 155, 161,
166, 190, 230, 268
poetry 178, 202, 268-269
politics 132, 169-197, 221-223
positivism 183
possibility 19, 75, 80, 87, 92-93,
96, 101, 105, 118, 120-
122, 125-126, 128, 130-133,
140, 146, 148-149, 157, 160-
162, 166, 172, 175, 185,
199, 206, 237, 251, 254,
262
potentiality-for-being 71, 103,
122
potentiality-to-be 60, 144
power 156, 183-184, 188-189,
193-194, 205-206, 213-214,
221-222, 225-226, 231, 241
Präsenz 210
praxis 218, 252
predestination 208
presence 101, 105, 127, 136-
137, 140-141, 143-144, 154,
156, 185, 203, 205, 207,
209-210, 215, 233, 235, 237,
239-241, 245, 258, 261, 263,
267-270, 272

present 16, 65, 73, 100, 105,
120-121, 123, 132-133, 137,
140, 143-144, 161, 164, 192,
205, 207
present-at-hand 208
principle of sufficient reason
211-213, 237-238, 263
productivity 220
profit 224
project 160
projection 66, 106
Protestantism 6, 146, 193, 208-
209
prudence 175
psychologism 2, 7, 116

racism 178, 182, 191
rationality, instrumental 196
raw material 147, 156, 218-
219, 221-222, 246
reality 8, 112, 140, 144, 153,
159, 198, 205-207, 209, 237,
240, 257, 268, 273
reason 201, 211-214, 219, 225,
238, 247, 260, 262
rectorship 171-174, 179, 192
Rede 54-54
redemption 13-14, 17, 61, 98,
129, 138-141, 144-145, 207,
248, 259, 267
reduction 35, 137
reflection 29-30, 79, 81
Reformation, the 98, 207
region 245-246
Reich, Thousand Year 189
releasement xxiv, 166, 196, 198,
228, 230, 243-275

repetition 86, 119, 122-124, 133, 140-141
representation 108, 209, 218-219, 221-222
representational thinking 244-246, 251
res cogitans 25
res extensa 25
resentment 159
resignation 141
responsibility 92, 94, 132, 146, 242
resurrection 190
retrieving 141, 156
revelation 129, 134-135, 148, 161, 164, 179, 184-185, 187, 191, 197-198, 203, 205, 208, 217, 219, 230, 232-233, 238, 242, 244, 250-253, 258, 272
revenge 91, 226
revolution 169, 178, 195
Rinzai Zen 263-265
romanticism 172
rootedness 3, 127, 130, 147, 278

Sache 156, 239
sacrifice 192, 194, 250, 276
Sagen 241-243
salvation 123, 138-139, 150, 206, 298, 249, 259
samurai 262
satori 255, 258-259, 264-267, 270-271
Satz vom Grund 237-238
Saying 241-243, 256
schematism 101, 110-112

Schicksal 123
Schuld 75
science 77, 218, 221
Scripture 5, 8, 10, 55, 266
Second Coming 136
security 50, 57, 60, 63-64, 78, 97, 137, 193, 207-210, 215, 225, 227, 238, 258-259, 273
seer 234
Seiendheit 23
Sein xxviii-xxix
Seinsfrage 32
Seinkönnen 69, 71
self 9-10, 15, 19-24, 27, 29, 31, 35, 43, 45, 49-50, 59, 63, 79, 87, 89-90, 97, 102-103, 105, 110-113, 117-118, 125, 130, 132, 140-141, 148, 151-152, 160, 166, 197, 221, 225, 229, 239, 247, 258-259, 262, 273, 276
self as substance xxii 2, 24-25, 47, 64, 103-104, 112, 119
self-abnegation 208
self-acceptance 155
self-actualizing 212, 243, 253
self-affection 108-109
self-analysis 33
self-assertion 152, 162, 168, 211, 223
self-centered 203
self-certainty 81, 200, 209-211, 224-225, 227, 238
self-concealment 96, 139, 150-151, 153, 198-199, 201-203, 217, 230, 237, 243, 268

self-consciousness xxii, 2, 24, 28, 30, 81, 109, 134, 174, 215, 247
self-constancy 103
self-creating 200
self-deception 58, 91, 271
self-deification 211-213,   227, 237
self-development 120, 223
self-disclosure 114, 167
self-discovery 87
self-grounding 146, 200, 212
self-hatred 91, 128, 140, 166
self-ignorance 140, 168
self-integration 140
self-justification 242
self-knowledge 82, 213
self-manifestation 150-153, 213
self-objectification xxiii, 41, 43, 47, 51-52, 67, 225, 254
self-pity 63, 91-93, 132
self-possessedness xxx, 125
self-preservation 199
self-renunciation 250
self-responsibility 163
self-revelation 243
self-understanding 71,   81-82, 144, 168, 184, 224, 258, 262, 272-273
self-will 59-60, 134, 141-142, 151, 169, 197, 200, 206, 222, 225, 230, 243-245, 247-248, 250-251, 265, 275
selfhood xxii, xxvii-xxviii, 2, 23-24, 26, 28-29, 48, 70, 100-102, 107-108, 116-118, 124, 187

selfishness 14, 47, 52, 61, 67, 137, 151, 194, 222, 228
selflessness 49
sheltering 185, 204
shepherd of Being 232
Simple 274
sin 18, 59, 74, 137, 141, 145, 152
sinfulness xxii, 2, 17, 43, 58, 144
skiing 4
sky 235, 254-255
socialism 91, 158-159, 214
society of the spectacle 51
Soto Zen 263-265
soul 83-84, 90, 104-105, 111, 141, 178, 200, 207, 225, 248
space 108-109, 148, 212
speculum vitale 237
spirit 183
Spirit, Absolute 11, 29, 84, 134, 150, 212-213
spirit, living 2, 8-9, 140
spontaneity 261-262, 265, 275
Sprache 256
standing reserve 219
state-of-mind 44, 53, 55, 66, 75
statesman 161
stellen 219
stiften 166
structuralism 298
struggle 77, 81, 84, 131, 145-146, 152-153, 184, 188-189, 194, 196, 217, 244, 249, 263, 274-275

subject xxv, 1, 8-10, 14, 24-26, 59, 77-78, 87, 101-107, 112-114, 116, 119, 130, 146, 200, 203, 205, 209-219, 221, 224, 226-229, 231, 235, 247, 263-264, 268
subjectivism xxi, xxv, 41, 86, 96, 102, 113-114, 116, 125, 143, 148, 155, 179, 191, 196-197, 201, 205-206, 208, 218, 229-233, 243, 246, 276
subjectivity 27, 78-79, 101, 109, 112, 117, 245, 262
sub specie aeternaetatis 167
substance 24, 103, 108, 110
substantia 24, 103, 108, 110
suchness 258, 267
suffering 258-259, 263, 273, 276
sunyata 257, 260
superbia 54
superego 74
Supreme Being 201, 203
symbol 85, 185

Tao xxvi, xxx, 256-257, 260, 274
Taoism 271
tathata 258, 267
techne 175
Technik 182, 197, 200, 218, 226, 237-238, 249, 253-254, 276
technology 127, 169, 182-184, 196, 198, 216, 244, 292-293

temporality xxiii-xxiv, 1, 12-14, 16, 20, 22, 24, 32, 38, 40, 65, 72, 99, 101-133, 135-144, 147-150, 152-153, 157-158, 161, 163, 167, 201-202, 212, 224, 238, 254, 261
Ten Commandments 85
thanking 166, 247-248
thanksgiving 88, 140-141, 145, 166, 168, 247-248
thinking 106, 206, 247-248
theology 5, 16-19, 98, 135, 191
theoria 179
they 44-45, 48, 62-63, 72-73, 75, 93, 172
thing 235-236
thing-in-itself 107
thrownness 63, 172
time 15, 20, 104-105, 108-115, 120, 128, 136-138, 140, 142-144, 146-148, 162, 201, 212, 227, 239-240, 261
time-Being 202
time of destitution 220
time of fulfillment xxiv, 123, 135, 137, 146, 150
tool 36, 101, 114-116, 201
totalitarianism 195-196
total mobilization 198, 221, 226
tradition 12, 85-87, 104, 130-132, 136-137, 143, 161-162, 166, 170-171, 190, 208, 217, 255, 276
tragedy 157
transcendence 23, 25-26, 28, 35, 37, 96, 105-106, 108, 110,

112, 118, 203-204, 216, 221, 224-225
transcendental philosophy 23, 29, 100-114, 243-246, 254
Treaty of Versailles 172
truth 2, 19, 21-22, 33, 40, 52, 56, 82, 90-91, 96, 103, 118-119, 132, 144, 147, 149, 153, 198, 201, 208-211, 215, 224, 229, 231, 239, 246, 254, 263-264, 266, 273
truth of Being 148, 156, 167, 232
turning 249
two-fold 204

Umsicht 56
un-being 188
unconcealment 2, 19, 22, 118, 133, 154, 164, 201, 203-204, 229, 239, 241, 246, 257
understanding 44, 53, 55, 58, 66-67, 75, 101, 105-106, 114, 123-124, 131, 140, 148, 166, 202, 226, 233, 242, 244, 263
unhiddenness 232
untruth 97, 201

validity 7-8
value 7-9, 10, 90-93, 96, 130, 158, 182-183, 198, 198, 200, 205, 213-216, 221, 223, 225
Verbindung 194
vereignen 191, 228, 230-231, 232, 242

Verfassung 165
vernehmen 186
verstehen 10, 35, 53
via negativa 217
violence 161, 180, 188-190, 212, 249
virtue 176
Void 233, 249, 257, 259-260
Volk 96, 170-172, 180, 195
voluntarism xxiv, xxvi, 41, 54, 76, 90, 96, 98, 125, 129, 134, 169, 172, 197, 199, 232, 244, 254
Vorhandenheit 116
vorstellen 210, 219, 221

Wagnerians 192, 214
wanting-to-have-a-conscience 76, 78
Way 3, 272-276
Wegmarken 276
Weimar Republic 173, 177
Wesen 203, 219, 223, 228, 241, 245
wiederholen 124, 141
will xxiii, xxv-xxvi, 19, 23, 59, 74, 76-78, 89-90, 92, 96, 98, 129, 134, 149, 151-152, 155, 161-162, 165, 167, 169, 173, 180-181, 198, 200, 212-215, 224-225, 229, 244-253, 264, 274
Will to Power xxiv, 23, 90, 96, 156-157, 164-165, 179, 196-198, 212, 214-216, 218-219, 221-223, 244, 253
will to survival 90

will to will 215
Wirklichkeit 7, 212
withdrawl of Being 200
Wo 232
works, good 63, 206-208
Wu-hsin 258

zazen 264-265
Zeitlichkeit 125

Zeitenfülle 146
Zen Buddhism xxvi, 230-231,
    255-276, 296-298
Zuhandenheit 36, 116
Zuspiel 239
Zweideutigkeit 53

Index of Names

Abe Masao 261
Abraham 140
Adam 50
Anaximander 12, 204
Aristotle 6, 17, 21, 39, 49, 89, 98, 104-105, 122-124, 129, 136, 167, 174, 202, 204, 212, 217, 237
Augustine, St. 6, 15, 98, 117, 129, 142, 243

Barth, Karl 17
Basho 267
Braig, Carl 5
Brentano, Franz 5, 9
Buddha 258, 265, 267
Bultmann, Rudolf xxiii, 6, 6-17, 58-62, 117, 144-145, 261

Caesar 253
Calvin, John 98
Capra, Fritjof 257
Caputo, John D. 228, 242, 248, 295
Cassirer, Ernst 86

Cebes 83-84
Char, Rene 247
Christ 13-14, 17, 85, 87, 97, 139-141, 158, 206, 253, 266-267

Demske, James M. 121
Descartes, Rene 24, 34, 179, 209-210, 212, 215
Dilthey, Wilhelm xxii, 6, 10-13, 26, 41, 136, 243, 271
Dogen 261
Dostoevsky, Fyodor 6, 117
Dunne, John S. 287

Eckhart, Meister 248-249, 274
Erikson, Erik 85-86, 88
Eve 50

Feuerbach, Ludwig 200
Fichte, Johann Gottlieb 28-29, 174
Fink, Eugen 184
Freud, Sigmund 20, 74, 136, 224

Fromm, Erich 50, 193-194
Fu, Charles Wei-hsun 271

Gadamer, Hans Georg 62, 70, 81, 174
Gandhi, Mahatma 88, 132
Gitlin, Todd 51
Gold, Herbert 176
Goldstein, Leon 290
Gröbner, Konrad 5

Habermas, Jürgen 32
Hartmann, Nicolai 4, 31
Hegel, Georg Wilhelm Friedrich xxvi, 11, 29, 31-32, 34, 84, 134, 143, 154, 167, 207, 212, 217, 243, 251, 271
Heidegger, Martin, *passim*
Heraclitus xxv, 156, 164-165, 186-187, 204, 232, 238-241
Hitler, Adolf xxvii, 169-170, 173-178, 182, 191, 193-195
Hölderlin, Friedrich 86, 166, 174, 178, 189, 191, 241
Howey, Richard L. 95-96
Hühnerfeld, Paul 172, 174
Husserl, Edmund xxii, 2, 6, 8, 20-23, 25, 29, 81, 89, 136, 280

Jaspers, Karl xxiv, 4, 11, 20, 142, 144-145, 278
Jesus 13, 59-60, 140, 248
Job 140
John, St. 60
John of the Cross, St. 265
Jung, Carl Gustav 4, 20, 81-82, 85-86, 184-189, 278, 284

Junger, Ernst 170, 222

Kant, Immanuel xxiii, 11-12, 22, 29, 34-35, 41, 74, 89, 100-113, 124, 129, 136, 167, 205, 212
Kierkegaard, Søren xxii, xxiv, 6, 9, 11-13, 30-33, 39, 41-42, 51, 69, 77-79, 81, 89-90, 117, 120-123, 139-144, 146, 150, 164, 167-168, 199, 206, 220, 261
King, Martin Luther, Jr. 132
Kolbenheyer, E.G. 178
Kosik, Karl 115-116, 286
Kreeft, Peter 270

Lao Tzu 256-257
Lehmann, Karl 148-149
Leibniz, Gottfried Wilhelm 129, 210, 212, 236-237
Lovitt, Harriet and William
Luke, St. 61, 145
Luther, Martin 6, 14-15, 39, 98, 117, 129, 142, 207-208, 210

Marcuse, Herbert 195-196, 217, 242, 253
Marx, Karl 127, 200, 223-225, 252-253, 293-294
Merton, Thomas 259, 264, 267
Michelangelo 116
Moses 85

Natorp, Paul
Neumann, Erich 82, 85-86, 189-190, 284, 290

Nietzsche, Friedrich xxii-xxiv, xxvii, 6, 9, 11-12, 34, 39, 41, 69, 81, 89-96, 101, 116-117, 129, 132, 134, 136, 144, 147, 150, 155-168, 174, 179-180, 189, 192, 196-197, 200, 205-206, 212-217, 226

Parmenides 156, 164-165, 186, 204
Pascal, Blaise 63-64, 98, 117, 142
Paul, St. 13-15, 22, 59, 98, 117, 128-129, 136, 139-140, 145, 206, 267
Pericles 175
Pinder 6
Plato xxiii, 16, 34, 49, 69, 81-82, 84, 87, 106, 128, 153, 158-159, 174-175, 198-199, 200, 202, 204-205, 207, 214, 224-225, 232
Pöggeler, Otto 13-15, 178
Prather, Hugh 128

Richardson, William J. xxi, 297
Richmond, Lew 296
Rickert, Heinrich xxii, 7-9
Ricoeur, Paul 294
Rilke, Rainer Maria 6-7
Rosales, Alberto 45
Rosenberg, Alfred 178, 192

Scheler, Max 26
Schelling, Wilhelm Joseph von xxiv, 6, 28, 101, 134, 147, 149-154
Schlageter, Leo 171-172

Schopenhauer, Arthur 90
Schrag, Calvin O. 11-12, 30, 89, 120
Schürmann, Reiner 248, 295
Scotus, Duns 8
Sessions, George 292
Sheehan, Thomas J. 13-14, 32, 123-124, 286
Sherover, Charles M. 112-113
Silesius, Angelius 237
Socrates xxiii, 69, 82-83, 88, 176
Sophocles 188
Spengler, Oswald 178
Spinoza, Benedictus 167
Stack, George J. 12-13, 122
Suzuki, Daisetz T. 260, 262-264, 267-268, 272
Suzuki, Shunryu 260, 265, 272

Tawney, R.H. 193
Tezuka 256
Tillich, Paul xxiv, 145-147, 261
Trakl, Georg 6
Tucker, Robert 213
Tugendhat, Ernst 96-97

Vaihinger, Kurt 116
Van Gogh, Vincent 70, 189
von Herrmann, Wilhelm-Friedrich 66, 113-114

Weber, Max 193

Yasotuni 258
Yorck, Graf Paul 13

Zarathustra 157-160
Zeus 206